David Naffan:

Lambeth at Canterbury. 1978.

ANGLICANISM
AND THE
LAMBETH CONFERENCES

ANGLICANISM
AND THE
LAMBETH CONFERENCES

Alan M. G. Stephenson

Foreword by the Archbishop of Canterbury

LONDON

SPCK

First published 1978
SPCK
Holy Trinity Church
Marylebone Road
London NW1 4DU

The publishers gratefully record the assistance towards the publication of this book which has been provided by the Archbishop of Canterbury, through the Davidson Bequest Trust, and by the Archbishop of York.

Printed in Great Britain by
The Camelot Press Ltd, Southampton

ISBN 0 281 03580 6

To
David, Elizabeth, and Jonathan

THE TEN LAMBETH CONFERENCES
1867–1968

	Date	President	No. of Bishops
1	1867	Charles Thomas Longley	76
2	1878	Archibald Campbell Tait	100
3	1888	Edward White Benson	145
4	1897	Frederick Temple	194
5	1908	Randall Thomas Davidson	242
6	1920	Randall Thomas Davidson	252
7	1930	Cosmo Gordon Lang	307
8	1948	Geoffrey Francis Fisher	329
9	1958	Geoffrey Francis Fisher	310
10	1968	Arthur Michael Ramsey	462

CONTENTS

ACKNOWLEDGEMENTS

Thanks are due to the following for permission to quote from copyright sources:

Church Historical Society, Austin, Texas: *An Anglican Turning Point* by S. F. Bayne

Church Missions Publishing Company: *Pan Anglican*, Spring 1959 and Fall 1968

Church Times: Letter from Cyril Eastaugh, Bishop of Peterborough, 13 September 1968

The Literary Executor of the late Archbishop Fisher: Sermon by Archbishop Geoffrey Fisher, preached in Great St Mary's, Cambridge, 1946

Michael De-la-Noy: *A Day in the Life of God* by Michael De-la-Noy

Hodder & Stoughton Ltd: *Well Remembered* by C. M. Blagden; *Convictions* by Donald Coggan; and *Fisher of Lambeth* by W. Purcell

McGraw-Hill Book Company: *The Long Shadows of Lambeth X* by James B. Simpson and Edward M. Story. Copyright © 1969 by Simpson and Story. Used with permission of McGraw-Hill Book Co.

John Murray (Publishers) Ltd: *The Recollections of a Bishop* by G. F. Browne

Oxford University Press: *Randall Davidson, Archbishop of Canterbury* by G. K. A. Bell; *Retrospect of an Unimportant Life* by Herbert Hensley Henson; and *George Bell, Bishop of Chichester* by Ronald Jasper

SCM Press Ltd: *Nairobi Narrative* by Kenneth Slack; and *On Being the Church in the World* by John A. T. Robinson, © J. A. T. Robinson 1960 (published in the U.S.A. by The Westminster Press and used by permission)

The Society for Promoting Christian Knowledge: *Partners in Mission: Report of the second meeting of the Anglican Consultative Council, Dublin 1973*; *Anglican Congress 1963. Report of Proceedings*, edited by Eugene R. Fairweather (by permission also of the Anglican Book Centre, Toronto); *The Church of England 1815–1948* edited by R. P. Flindall; and *The Mission of the Anglican Communion* by E. R. Morgan and R. Lloyd (by permission also of The United Society for the Propagation of the Gospel)

The United Society for the Propagation of the Gospel: *Bishop Montgomery: A Memoir* by M. M. (Maud Montgomery).

ANNOTATED LIST OF ILLUSTRATIONS

1
facing page 48

The Alms Dish given by the American Church to the Archbishop of Canterbury (A. C. Tait) in St Paul's Cathedral in 1872 (see p. 48, also p. 22). In the centre of this silver dish is the hemisphere, showing the Atlantic ocean, the Old World in the East, and the New World in the West. A scroll on the ocean bears the inscription '*Orbi veteri novus, Occidens orienti, Filia matri*'. At the South Pole is the date 1871, the year when Selwyn visited America. In the upper part of the hemisphere is a circular chased medallion, covering nearly the whole of Great Britain and bearing a little ship leaving England for America. This ship represents the Church, having the cross as its prow and the monogram of the word 'Christ' (i.e. the labarum) on its sail and the Pastoral Staff of the Apostolic Episcopate as its mainmast, upheld by two ropes which represent the diaconate and the priesthood. S.S. on the vessel stands for Sacred Scriptures. Outside the hemisphere is a band an inch wide with the names of the Six Undisputed Councils in Greek uncials upon it. These are separated from each other by six spheres of lapis lazuli. From the outside of the band spring twelve oak leaves and between them twelve twigs, each bearing three acorns. The twelve symbolize the Apostles and the three the Trinity. From behind the oak leaves spring maple leaves and palmeto leaves, symbolizing the North and South of the U.S.A. respectively. The rim, which is broad and flat, has the inscription 'It is more blessed to give than to receive'. The Alms Dish, which is held by the Archbishop of Canterbury and reproduced with his permission, is at present kept at the U.S.P.G. Headquarters.

2 The bishops at the 1878 Conference, photographed outside Lambeth Palace. Archbishop Tait stands in the centre, with the Archbishop of York (W. Thomson) on his right and the Bishop of Winchester (E. H. Browne) on his left. The black Bishop Holly of Haiti is in the front row. (*Photograph at U.S.P.G.*)   49

The jacket photograph shows the bishops at the 1920 Lambeth
Conference outside Lambeth Palace. Archbishop Davidson is in
the centre (above the letters PC of SPCK) with Archbishop Lang
on his right.

Thanks are due to the owners, copyright holders, and photographers
cited above for permission to reproduce these illustrations.

FOREWORD

Ten years ago, Dr Stephenson gave us his book *The First Lambeth Conference, 1867*. It was a careful piece of historical research, a thorough and well-documented study of the first of the ten Conferences which were to take place up to and including that of 1968. In reviewing it, I said: 'I would like to think that this book might be compulsory reading for those who are to attend Lambeth 1968.'

Now Dr Stephenson has given us another book, of similar dimensions but dealing with a much larger subject. It is a worthy sequel to his first volume and shows the same marks of good scholarship, lightened with flashes of humour. I would say of it, as I said of its predecessor, that I would like all the bishops who are coming to the Conference to read it as part of their preparatory work.

But it deserves a much wider circle of readers than that. For not only does it tell, with some care, the story of all the Lambeth Conferences which have taken place, but it also gives a wonderful introduction to Anglicanism as a whole, its genius, its achievements, its failures, its perils. In its pages we catch glimpses of many famous names within Anglicanism and beyond – from Archbishop C. T. Longley who presided over the first Conference in 1867 to Archbishop Janani Luwum whose name is added to the list of 'the noble army of martyrs'.

To those of us who, like myself, have already attended more than one Lambeth Conference, a reading of this book conjures up pictures of a multitude of friends and elicits deep gratitude to God for the enrichment which comes to us from the privilege of knowing them and working with them.

I am deeply grateful to Dr Stephenson for his work and I know that many others, as they read this book, will share my gratitude.

DONALD CANTUAR:

PREFACE

The origin of this work is as follows. In January 1966 Dr V. H. H. Green, of Lincoln College, Oxford, acting for the S.P.C.K. in connection with some proposed Church Historical Society Booklets, wrote to me with a request for an 'essay on some aspects of 19th Century Church History, viz. biographical or Lambeth Conferences'. I took up his Lambeth Conference suggestion and agreed with the S.P.C.K. that I would write a history of all the Lambeth Conferences that had taken place, though I was already engaged on a full-scale study of English Modernism and its Apostle, H. D. A. Major, and had yet to complete my life of Archbishop Longley, works which I hope will soon be ready for publication.

The first draft of the present book was given as lectures in the Examination Schools at Oxford in Trinity Term 1971 and a later version was given at St Stephen's House. The size of the work grew and in the end had to be reduced. I now offer it to the public as a sequel to my *The First Lambeth Conference, 1867*, published by the S.P.C.K. in 1967 and now out of print. I am not unaware of its limitations, but I also feel sure that a full account of the Lambeth Conferences is a *desideratum* and that the present volume will quite supersede such attempts as have been made to produce a connected history, like the writings of Walter Hobhouse, Sidney Dark, Bernard Heywood, William R. Curtis, and Dewi Morgan, whose *The Bishops Come to Lambeth*, though full of minor errors of fact, has done yeoman service for many as an introduction to the subject of Anglicanism. Doubtless, the present work will, in turn, be superseded, once all the papers at Lambeth relevant to the subject have been catalogued and completely opened up to the public. Indeed, I should like myself to supersede it in ten years' time with additional material and an account of the 1978 Lambeth Conference. I would emphasize that the Bibliography, which is full, though not by any means exhaustive, is an important part of the book, inasmuch as it lists many articles and pamphlets which have had a bearing on the subject, but which have not always been alluded to, or commented upon, in the main text.

I am very grateful to the Trustees of the British Museum for permitting me to have Xerox copies made of Gregory T. Bedell's *The Canterbury Pilgrimage* (of which, I suspect, they have the only copy in this country), and of Bishop W. H. de Lancey's *The Mission to the Jubilee* (which I did not use in my *The First Lambeth Conference, 1867*, and which again, I think, is only available in the British Museum), and Bishop L. G. Mylne's *The Counsels and Principles of the Lambeth Conference of 1888*. My former pupil, Dr Winthrop Brainerd, kindly obtained for me a Xerox copy of Bishop W. Bacon Stevens's *The Lambeth Conference of 1878* from the Widener Library, Harvard, and almost by the same post came a second copy from St Mark's Library, The General Theological Seminary, New York, which I have passed on to Pusey House Library. I should also like to record my gratitude to John H. Evans, author of *Churchman Militant*, for sending me from New Zealand a Xerox copy of part of Bishop S. T. Nevill's Notebooks in the Hocken Library, University of Otago. I am indebted to several libraries for loans of books and particularly to St Stephen's House, Oxford (which has a number of valuable books once belonging to Dorchester Missionary College), Ripon College, Cuddesdon, the library of the U.S.P.G., and Sion College. Needless to say, the Bodleian Library and the Lambeth Palace Library have both been helpful.

I am grateful to the U.S.P.G. for allowing various photographs of past Lambeth Conferences to be copied as illustrations for the book and also for permission to have a photograph taken of the lovely silver alms dish presented by the American Church to the English Church in 1872. A previous photograph of it appeared in C. F. Sweet, *A Champion of the Cross* (New York, 1894) and in Georgiana M. Forde's *Missionary Adventures* (S.P.G. 1919); but few people have seen these and few, too, will have seen the original.

Dr Michael Ramsey, President of the Lambeth Conference 1968, took a great interest in my *The First Lambeth Conference, 1867* and wrote to me after Lambeth '68 to say, 'I find that many of those present at the Lambeth Conference have profited from your history of the First Lambeth Conference and I have been increasingly grateful to your account of the first in trying to tackle the problems of the tenth.' He has bestowed an equal interest on the writing of the sequel. Dr Donald Coggan, who will be President of Lambeth 1978, has been similarly interested and helpful in connection with the present volume and has kindly written the Foreword. I am grateful to both Archbishops for grants towards the publication.

Since my completion of the book a number of new works which touch upon the subject of Lambeth Conferences have appeared. Carolyn Scott has written a new life of Dick Sheppard and Bartha de Blank has produced a memoir of her brother, Joost de Blank. Alan Dunstan and John Peart-Binns have written a biography of Bishop Joseph Wellington Hunkin, and Bishop Colin Winter has written a book about Damaraland. The S.P.C.K. have also published *Anglican-Orthodox Dialogue: The Moscow Agreed Statement.* An important volume on the future of the papacy is *A Pope for All Christians?*, edited by Peter J. McCord (S.P.C.K.). Bishop Henry R. McAdoo has written on *Being an Anglican* (S.P.C.K.) and Eric Mascall has written a reply to *The Myth of God Incarnate* in *Theology and the Gospel of Christ* (S.P.C.K.), which is likely to be far less ephemeral than *The Truth of God Incarnate.*

I note the growing interest in Lambeth Conferences and their history on the Continent. Dr Max Keller-Huschemerger published his *Die Lehre der Kirche im Urteil der Lambeth Konferenzen* in 1977: I met the author when he was working at Pusey House, Oxford. Unfortunately Pusey Library did not then have W. R. Curtis's *The Lambeth Conferences* and he has not made any use of it. Since his visit the Library has acquired the late Frederic Hood's copy; the only other copy in England is in the University of London Library.

As my former work, *The First Lambeth Conference, 1867*, was dedicated to my wife, so *Anglicanism and the Lambeth Conferences* is dedicated to our three children.

Steventon Vicarage, Abingdon   ALAN M. G. STEPHENSON
All Saints Day, 1 November 1977

1

ANGLICANISM AND THE ANGLICAN COMMUNION

What is Anglicanism? In 1908 there took place in London, when Randall Davidson was Archbishop of Canterbury, the first of three Anglican congresses. The second of them was held in 1954 at Minneapolis, the year also of the Evanston Conference of the World Council of Churches, a year commonly referred to as 'the Year of Hope'. The third of them took place in 1963 at Toronto. The first Anglican congress, or rather pan-Anglican congress, to give it its correct title, produced the largest report of the three, no less than seven hard-backed volumes. Volume VII contains Section F on 'The Anglican Communion: Its place in Christendom'. Among the preliminary papers, produced for study by those many bishops, clergy, and laity attending the congress is one by Dean Armitage Robinson of Westminster, the uncle of Bishop John Robinson of *Honest to God* fame, and the first non-episcopal clergyman to preach to a Lambeth Conference of bishops. The title of Robinson's paper was 'The Anglican Communion. What it is'. In it he wrote as follows:

The Anglican Communion may in general terms be described as a portion of the Holy Catholic Church, independent of the Latin and Oriental branches of the Church, maintaining the Nicene faith and the historic order of ministry and sacraments, and offering its worship by means of an English liturgy, translated where occasion requires into other vernacular tongues. It has grown with the expansion of the Anglo-Saxon race, and is predominantly Anglo-Saxon in character. But it is not narrowed by limitation to the empire of Great Britain, and finds its home also in the great Anglo-Saxon nation of the West whose political destinies have become separated from those of the mother country. It thus witnesses to a unity which survives political separation: and to those who believe that the Anglo-Saxon race as a whole has a providential mission, the Anglican Communion may well appear destined to play an important part in the interpretation and fulfilment of that mission.

The ideal function of the Anglican Communion is to express and guide the spiritual aspirations and activities of the Anglo-Saxon race. It has a duty besides to those other races whom Providence has in various degrees of closeness linked with that race; but towards some of these its ultimate responsibility may prove to be that of offering a type of the Apostolic faith and order which they may hereafter appropriate and develop in independence.

Such seemed the character of the Anglican Communion in the age of Edward VII and Rudyard Kipling, with its talk of the British Empire and the glories of the Anglo-Saxon race. Today many may well read these words with a certain amount of embarrassment. Before, however, we dismiss too readily this Anglo-Saxon background to Anglicanism, it is as well to heed some words of an Indian, the Rev. E. Sambayya, a man brought up in Brahminism, converted to Methodism, and then to Anglicanism, and who was, when he wrote them, a lecturer at Bishop's College, Calcutta. They appear in an article 'The Genius of the Anglican Communion' in *The Mission of the Anglican Communion* (1948) edited by E. R. Morgan (then Bishop of Southampton) and Roger Lloyd, a Canon of Winchester. After becoming quite lyrical in expressing his love for the Book of Common Prayer, he goes on in this vein:

It is with a sense of tremendous joy that I realize that the Anglican Communion is of the universal Church, for she holds the faith of the universal Church in entirety, i.e. the truths of Christ contained in the *Holy Scripture*, stated in the two *Creeds*, expressed in the *Sacraments* of the Gospel, the rites of the primitive Church as set forth in the Book of Common Prayer, and safeguarded by the historic threefold order of the *Ministry*. With this fourfold doctrinal basis, the Anglican Communion can go into every part of the world, proclaim the Gospel, and discipline all manner of people unto holiness of life. The question may be raised whether the universal character claimed for the Anglican Communion does not suffer damage by its belonging to a particular tradition, i.e. the Western tradition, and by its reaching us as the Church of a particular people, the Anglo-Saxons. In answer to that difficulty it may be pointed out that the genius of Anglicanism lies in the fact that it represents the Reformed Catholicism of the West as expressed by the English people. It is, however, a puzzle to our minds why the Eastern Churches should have been so dangerously exposed to the onslaughts of the enemies of Christianity, why they should have been trodden underfoot, and allowed for centuries only a nominal existence in a state of paralysis, while the Western branch of Christendom should have been allowed to grow and become the receptacle of the living tradition of the Universal Church. As the Reformed Catholic Church, it comes to us with the twofold heritage of Catholicism and Protestantism. To a person like me, living in India, the Anglican Communion is most valuable because she puts me in the full heritage of Catholicism as well as of the Protestant tradition. I view the Church as a living organism which always reacts to its environment by incorporating elements from it which are beneficial for its well-being and healthy development, and by rejecting those which are unnecessary or harmful. The Anglican Communion is of the Universal Church which has come down through the ages with the precious heritage of the Fathers, rich experiences of the Middle Ages, benefits of the Reformation, and the healthy influences of the Evangelical and Tractarian movements. Through her sanctified common sense, and her sense of history, the Anglican Communion has maintained her Catholic character unimpaired through the ages; and she has never shut the door against the Holy Ghost, nor refused to be led into fresh avenues of truth. Thus her ability to look at her faults with sorrow and discontent, and her willingness to be made whole, constitute a precious trait of Anglicanism. She never claims to be perfect, but, on the other hand, is ever ready to repent and be taught of the Holy Ghost.[1]

Though in 1977 we may be tempted to play down and minimize the Anglo-Saxon or English element in our assessment of Anglicanism, we must resist this temptation. In the second half of the nineteenth century, when the Anglican Communion at last reached self-consciousness, its bishops had every desire to be reminded of their English background and heritage. Thus every Lambeth Conference, except the first of 1867, involved a journey to Canterbury Cathedral. In 1897, to celebrate the arrival of St Augustine in 597, the bishops made a visit to Ebbsfleet. In Canterbury their thoughts as well as turning to St Augustine have also turned to Anselm, Lanfranc, and Becket. Again the bishops have often visited York, with its memories of St Paulinus. They have often visited Durham, with its associations with St Cuthbert, John Cosin, and Joseph Butler; and in 1908 they went on pilgrimage to Lindisfarne, when several ladies accompanying them fell from their carriages into the water. While staying in that part of England they have not forgotten Bede of Jarrow and Wilfrid of Hexham. Often they have visited Lincoln, with its reminders of Robert Grosseteste and St Hugh of Lincoln. Bath and Wells they have visited – as, for example, in 1878 – and have recalled the saintly Bishop Thomas Ken. They have journeyed to Salisbury, once presided over by Bishop John Jewel of *Apology* fame, and from there have gone to Bemerton, sacred to the memory of George Herbert, just as, when at Canterbury, they have gone out to

[1] Op. cit., pp. 21f.

Bishopsbourne, once the parish of the judicious Richard Hooker. They have also visited Lichfield with its many reminders of St Chad. Apart from 1867, they have always held services at Westminster, place of consecration of many bishops, with its memories of Edward the Confessor and so many great figures of Church and State, and at St Paul's Cathedral, with its reminders of John Colet and John Donne. Often the bishops have been given honorary degrees at Cambridge, as, for example, in 1867, when the undergraduates clapped their hands and shouted, 'Hurrah for the red men of the prairies!'[2] There they have recalled the Puritan Divines and the Cambridge Platonists. Oxford also has conferred degrees on episcopal visitors to Lambeth Conferences, who have there been reminded of the English martyrs, Ridley, Latimer, and Cranmer, and the heroes of the Oxford Movement. While at Oxford they have usually made a visit to Cuddesdon. At times the bishops have been drawn back behind the century of St Augustine, as when in 1897 they went to Glastonbury and everyone thought that Frederick Temple, now getting on for eighty, would faint in the excessive heat. But Temple was made of very stern material.

That then is part of the background to nineteenth- and twentieth-century Anglicanism and we cannot neglect it. But obviously one has to go back beyond even the British Christianity of Glastonbury. Dean Stanley, when he lectured as Professor of Ecclesiastical History at Oxford, always started with Abraham. There is a sense in which the history of the Anglican Communion starts with Abraham. For that Communion has never had any desire to throw out the Old Testament, even though individual members of it, like Dean Inge, have sometimes contemplated it. In 1867 the assembled bishops said in their Pastoral or Encyclical Letter, 'We beseech you to hold fast, as the sure word of God, all the canonical Scriptures of the Old and New Testament' – a sentence which had as its background the speculations of Bishop Colenso and *Essays and Reviews*.

Besides this holding fast to the Old and New Testaments, nineteenth- and twentieth-century Anglicanism cannot be understood without being reminded about its constant looking back to the primitive Church. In 1867 the Lambeth Fathers said: '. . . we do here solemnly record our conviction that unity will be most effectually promoted by maintaining the Faith in its purity and integrity, as taught in the Holy Scriptures, held by the Primitive Church, summed up in the Creeds, and affirmed by the undisputed General Councils.' There had been great battles

[2] Hall Harrison, *Life of Bishop Kerfoot*, vol. ii, p. 462.

indeed at Lambeth over that last reference! To the second century the Anglican Communion looked back for its threefold ministry of bishops, priests, and deacons. Though the bishops in 1867 did not emphasize this threefold ministry in any statement they made, the bishops who assembled in 1878 did make a declaration about it:

> We proclaim the sufficiency and supremacy of the Holy Scriptures as the ultimate rule of faith, and commend to our people the diligent study of the same. We confess our faith in the words of the ancient Catholic Creeds. We retain the Apostolic order of Bishops, Priests and Deacons. We assert the just liberties of particular or national Churches. We provide our people, in their own tongue, with a Book of Common Prayer and Offices for the administration of the Sacraments, in accordance with the best and most ancient types of Christian faith and worship. These documents are before the world and can be known and read of all men. We gladly welcome every effort for reform upon the model of the Primitive Church. We do not demand a rigid uniformity; we deprecate needless divisions; but to those who are drawn to us in the endeavour to free themselves from the yoke of error and superstition we are ready to offer all help, and such privileges as may be acceptable to them and are consistent with the maintenance of our own principles as enunciated in our formularies.[3]

In 1888 the bishops, under the leadership of Archbishop E. W. Benson, reiterated this point about the threefold ministry in the famous 'Lambeth Quadrilateral' which should really be called the 'Chicago–Lambeth Quadrilateral' (as many Americans have pointed out), since it is almost the same as a document issued at the General Convention at Chicago in 1886. In this celebrated text nothing is said of Reformation or Book of Common Prayer. It does not so much express the opinion of the Conference on the whole ethos of Anglicanism, but rather gives expression to four things which are so essential to Anglicanism that reunion with other communions could not be contemplated unless they had all four. In Resolution 11, they said,

> That, in the opinion of this Conference, the following articles supply a basis on which approach may be by God's blessing made towards Home Reunion:

[3] The reference to those freeing 'themselves from the yoke of error and superstition' is to the Old Catholics and 'other persons on the Continent of Europe who have renounced their allegiance to the Church of Rome, and who are desirous of forming some connection with the Anglican Church, either English or American.' For the passage see R. Davidson, *Origin and History of the Lambeth Conferences of 1867 and 1878*, p. 136.

(A) The Holy Scriptures of the Old and New Testaments, as 'containing all things necessary to salvation', and as being the rule and ultimate standard of faith.

(B) The Apostles' Creed, as the Baptismal Symbol; and the Nicene Creed, as the sufficient statement of the Christian faith.

(C) The two Sacraments ordained by Christ Himself – Baptism and the Supper of the Lord – ministered with unfailing use of Christ's words of Institution, and of the elements ordained by Him.

(D) The Historic Episcopate, locally adapted in the methods of its administration to the varying needs of the nations and peoples called of God into the Unity of His Church.

There was another attempt to define Anglicanism at the Conference held in 1930. Its Report, which has a reference to the place of the Lambeth Conference within Anglicanism, has often been quoted and it is right that we should quote it here. In Resolution 49, the bishops, under the presidency of Cosmo Gordon Lang, made this statement:

The Conference approves the following statement of the nature and status of the Anglican Communion, as that term is used in its Resolutions:

The Anglican Communion is a fellowship, within the One Holy Catholic and Apostolic Church, of those duly constituted Dioceses, Provinces or Regional Churches in communion with the See of Canterbury, which have the following characteristics in common:

(*a*) they uphold and propagate the Catholic and Apostolic faith and order as they are generally set forth in the Book of Common Prayer as authorised in their several Churches;

(*b*) they are particular or national Churches, and, as such, promote within each of their territories a national expression of Christian faith, life and worship; and

(*c*) they are bound together not by a central legislative and executive authority, but by mutual loyalty sustained through the common counsel of the Bishops in conference.

The Conference makes this statement praying for and eagerly awaiting the time when the Churches of the present Anglican Communion will enter into communion with other parts of the Catholic Church not definable as Anglican in the above sense, as a step towards the ultimate reunion of all Christendom in one visibly united fellowship.

Such was the definition of Anglicanism and the Anglican Communion of the 1930 Lambeth Fathers. If one went back one hundred years to 1830, one would discover that the terms 'Anglicanism' and 'Anglican Communion' were not then in use. Indeed, the Encyclical letter issued by the Bishops in 1867 does not use the word 'Anglican Communion' but speaks of 'the Anglican branch of the Catholic Church'. However, the term 'Anglican Communion' does appear in Resolutions I, IV, and VI. The term 'Anglicanism' nowhere appears in 1867, nor does it appear in the Lambeth documents of 1878, though there are several appearances of 'Anglican Communion'. However, there are more frequent references to 'the Anglican church' or even 'Anglican Churches'. As we shall see later, this term 'Anglican Communion' had not made its first appearance until 1851. It is worth noting, that, though by 1878 the word 'Anglican' was becoming accepted, it had its opponents. Lord Plunket, Bishop of Meath, and later Archbishop of Dublin, who is well known for the interest he took in breakaway movements of Reform from the Roman Catholic Church in Spain and Italy, wrote in the *Guardian*, soon after the Second Lambeth Conference:

I should be glad . . . through the medium of your paper, to suggest to those who are more competent than myself for such a task, the desirability of finding, if possible, some more appropriate term than 'Anglican' whereby to describe the great communion from which the Conference at Lambeth has taken, hitherto, its name.

As an Irish Bishop I have a special reason for desiring some change. It is the habit of certain Roman Catholic controversialists in this land to try and enlist the patriotism of their fellow-countrymen against the claims of our communion by asserting that our church is the church of the Anglo-Saxon invaders. . . .

So far at least as the Irish Church is concerned, the term 'Anglican' does not seem an altogether accurate description. And may I be permitted, with all deference, to ask whether it be altogether wise or right that the English church should on her part entirely ignore those early centuries of British Christianity which preceded the mission of St Augustine? As regards the Episcopal Churches of Scotland and America, I may, I think, with confidence add that there are many in those churches who are not quite satisfied with the name by which the communion to which we all belong is at present described.

The opposition to the name, however, was not so strong as Bishop Lord Plunket imagined. It stuck and is not likely to be changed now.

The word 'Anglican' comes, of course, from the Latin *Anglicana*. In the Magna Carta the English part of the Catholic Church is defined as *Ecclesia Anglicana*. That Church had been firmly attached to the papacy from the Synod of Whitby in 661. At the Reformation, with the change from Latin services to English and from Latin Vulgate to

English versions of the Bible, the term 'Church of England' became the official title of the Reformed Church of England. Thus, the Prayer Book of 1662 is entitled, 'The Book of Common Prayer and Administration of the Sacraments and other Rites and Ceremonies . . . according to the Use of the Church of England'. The phrase 'Anglican Church' may sometimes have been used, but it was undoubtedly a rare thing. John Fell, Bishop of Oxford (1625–86), in his *Life of Henry Hammond* (1684), vol. i, p. 12, speaks of 'The sober principles and old establishment of the Anglican Church'. It would appear that then it did not simply mean belonging to the Church of England, but rather was used like 'Gallican', to denote opposition to Rome. It indicated High Church opinions, as distinct from Romish opinions. One can read books written in the twentieth century where the word 'Anglican' is used as a synonym for 'Anglo-Catholic', such as J. G. Edwards, *Progress in Religious Thought in the Eighteenth and Nineteenth Centuries* (1904). It was a term of which Evangelicals were slow to make use. It is in line with this hesitancy that we discover that the Evangelicals were suspicious of the First Lambeth Conference and some were still suspicious of the Second. The Church Missionary Society would have nothing at all to do with these two Conferences. In Australia the term Church of England still sticks, and if you want the parish church, you ask, 'Where is the Church of England?' That part of the Anglican Communion is still called 'The Church of England in Australia'.

When the Church in England broke off from the papacy and became the 'Church of England', there was no thought of a world-wide communion developing. But that is precisely what happened, and hence there developed such titles as 'the Church of England in Canada' and 'the Church of England in Australia'. There was certainly no suggestion of a world-wide communion in the Book of Common Prayer. The only reference to the Church of England overseas is in the Preface, where, speaking of Baptism of such as are of riper years, it says that this service 'though not so necessary when the former Book was compiled, yet by the growth of Anabaptism, through the licentiousness of the late times crept in amongst us, is now become necessary, and may be always useful at the baptizing of Natives in our Plantations, and others converted to the Faith.' That remained the only reference in the Prayer Book to the Church overseas in 1867 when the First Lambeth Conference was called.

Turning to the growth of the Church of England overseas, we must note that the most remarkable thing about its expansion was the failure of the portions of the Church of England overseas to be provided with episcopal government. For years they all came under the jurisdiction of the Bishop of London. A relict of that jurisdiction remained until recently in the control which the Bishop of Fulham (a suffragan of London) exercised over North and Central Europe.[4] Settlers going abroad to the Plantations (to use the Prayer Book phrase) took with them the Bible, the Book of Common Prayer, priests (and possibly deacons) but not bishops. If one thinks of America, we find that Virginia Dare, the first white person to be baptized on American soil, would have had to live to the ripe old age of 197 before she could be confirmed on American territory by an Anglican bishop, unless she had been able to contact the two non-juring bishops, Talbot and Welton, who penetrated American soil in 1724. Otherwise she would have had to make the perilous journey to Fulham Palace. In the same way, ordinands were obliged to make their way 'home' to London. It is not surprising that men lost their vocations after being captured by pirates or shipwrecked. Many were lost at sea or died of smallpox. There is no need to tell of the efforts of Archbishop Laud to send a bishop to America or to recall the relations with the American church of Bishops Compton, Gibson, and Sheldon of London and of Archbishops Tenison and Secker. No Bishop of London ever visited that distant part of his diocese. Arthur Foley Winnington-Ingram was the first Bishop of London to do so. In the seventeenth and eighteenth century the Bishops of London worked through Commissaries, of whom the most famous are James Blair and Thomas Bray. Bray is a very important figure in the history of Anglicanism, since he had so much to do with the foundation of the Society for Promoting Christian Knowledge in 1698 and the Society for the Propagation of the Gospel in 1701. Both these societies have played an enormous part in the evolution of the Anglican Communion and in that Communion's arrival at self-consciousness.

Failure to provide America with a bishop was due to a multiplicity of causes. The association of episcopacy with prelacy no doubt prejudiced the office in the eyes of many colonists of Puritan descent. Another difficulty lay in the hostility of colonial legislatures, who would refuse a clergyman elected bishop permission to depart for consecration to England. Again, in England there was hesitation to provide America with a bishop from a desire to appease the Dissenters; and, also, there was a reluctance to confer upon the colonies anything that might suggest adult status. In the end. America did not get a bishop until after

[4] The suffragan see of Fulham is now joined with the diocese of Gibraltar.

the War of Independence and the political break with England. 14 November 1784 is a very significant date in the history of Anglicanism, for it was then that Samuel Seabury was consecrated Bishop of Connecticut at Aberdeen in Scotland. It was a most humble beginning for the Anglican overseas episcopate. Seabury was consecrated by the despised Scottish episcopalians. The consecrating bishops were Robert Kilgour, Bishop of Aberdeen, who had recently become Primus, Arthur Petrie, Bishop of Ross and Moray, and John Skinner, Coadjutor Bishop of Aberdeen. The event took place in a chapel in the house of John Skinner, which was in a little frequented lane – the Longacre – where carriages never passed. Thus was forged a link between the Protestant Episcopal Church of Scotland and what was in due course to become the Protestant Episcopal Church of the United States of America (PECUSA), a link one can see in a comparison of their historic liturgies. Both churches have had coadjutor bishops with right of succession. Both churches have seen fit to dispense with the archiepiscopal and the archidiaconal office. Both churches have had a Presiding Bishop or Primus. It will be recalled that Martin Routh, the President of Magdalen College, Oxford, suggested that Seabury should go north to Scotland, when it was found impossible for Archbishop Moore to consecrate him. Routh's part in the event has sometimes been denied, but in the teeth of much evidence that points to it.[5] However, the part played by Dr Berkeley, son of the famous Bishop Berkeley, has been somewhat neglected. It is worth recalling that some had contemplated Seabury's consecration by the Eastern Orthodox Church, or by the Non-Jurors, or the Church in Denmark, or the Church in Sweden, or even, apparently, the Church of Rome. The first centenary of Seabury's consecration was celebrated with pomp and ceremony in 1884 both in Aberdeen and in London. After Seabury the next American bishops were consecrated in Lambeth Palace Chapel, an Act having been passed legalizing the consecration of a foreigner. On 4 February 1787 William White and Samuel Provoost were consecrated Bishops of Pennsylvania and New York respectively. Archbishop Moore of Canterbury was assisted by Archbishop Markham of York, Charles Moss, Bishop of Bath and Wells, and John Hinchcliffe, Bishop of Peterborough. The consecration of White and Provoost by these English bishops was perhaps the most important act in their episcopal careers. The fourth American bishop to be consecrated was James Madison, who was consecrated Bishop of Virginia on 19 September

[5] See R. D. Middleton, *Dr. Routh*, pp. 48–64.

1790 – again in Lambeth Palace Chapel – by Archbishop Moore, assisted this time by Beilby Porteus, Bishop of London, and John Thomas, Bishop of Rochester. There were no further consecrations of American bishops in the British Isles. In September 1792 the four American prelates consecrated Thomas John Claggett as Bishop of Maryland. This was the first Anglican consecration outside the British Isles.

So much for American episcopacy. What of the colonies? Archbishop Moore also had the task of consecrating the first colonial bishop, Dr Charles Inglis, who, before the War of Independence, had been rector of Trinity Church, New York. He was consecrated on 12 August 1787 at Lambeth Chapel by the Archbishop, assisted by Beilby Porteus and John Thomas. The diocese of Nova Scotia, over which Inglis presided, was a very large one. It consisted of New Brunswick, Prince Edward Island, Lower and Upper Canada, and after 1825 Bermuda. It can hardly be said that after the first colonial bishopric had been set up the foundation of others was rapid. In 1793 Jacob Mountain became Bishop of Quebec. Then no further bishop was consecrated until 1814, when the Bishop of London rejoiced to be relieved of his responsibility for India by the appointment of Thomas Fanshawe Middleton as first Bishop of Calcutta. In 1824 there were bishops for Barbados and Jamaica. 1835 saw Daniel Corrie going out to India as first Bishop of Madras. Australia was an archdeaconry in the diocese of Calcutta until 1836 when that outstanding figure in the history of the Anglican Communion, William Grant Broughton, was made Bishop of Australia. When other bishoprics were set up in Australia, Broughton became Bishop of Sydney. In 1837 a third diocese, Bombay, was established in India. 1839 saw a Bishop of Newfoundland and a Bishop of Toronto. Thus by 1840 there were but ten colonial bishoprics.

The year 1841 is another most significant date in the history of Anglicanism, since that year saw the inauguration of the Colonial Bishoprics Fund, which arose out of a sermon preached by that great administrator, Charles James Blomfield. He had copied the idea expounded in that sermon from one preached by Bishop Doane of New Jersey at the consecration of Jackson Kemper as missionary bishop in the west. Blomfield argued, like Doane, that the bishop should not go out after the church had been established, but that he should lead out the church and be in the vanguard. The outcome of Blomfield's sermon was the Colonial Bishoprics Fund, which did a very great deal for the expansion of the overseas episcopate. Hence, by 1867, the date of the

First Lambeth Conference, there were no less than 144 Anglican bishops. There were 10 dioceses in Canada, 6 in India, Burma, and China, 9 in Africa, 9 in Australia, 7 in New Zealand, and 6 in the West Indies. There was also a Bishop in Gibraltar, a Bishop in Jerusalem (this was the result of the controversial Jerusalem Bishopric Act) and a Bishop in Honolulu. There were 35 dioceses in the U.S.A. There were also several assistant and coadjutor bishops, making a total of 144.

We must now turn from episcopacy to the subject of synodical government. Here we discover first the influence of the U.S.A. upon the colonies and then the influence of both the U.S.A. and the colonies upon the Church of England at home. The Church of England's provincial synods, or Convocations, go back ultimately to Archbishop Theodore. Originally they consisted of bishops only, but in 1225 Archbishop Stephen Langton summoned proctors. They were constituted in 1283 to include bishops, abbots, deans, and archdeacons, together with two representatives from the clergy of the diocese and one from each chapter. From the fifteenth century there have been Upper and Lower Houses. In 1552 the Act of Henry VIII known as the Submission of the Clergy limited the powers of Convocation, and reference was made to this Act in the nineteenth century, when synodical government was started in the colonies and people wanted to object to it. The seventeenth century saw the great controversies between the Upper House of Whiggish bishops and the Lower House of Tory clergy. In 1717 the effective power of Convocation was lost as a result of the Bangorian Controversy, when the Lower House of Canterbury Convocation was on the point of condemning a sermon of that latitudinarian Bishop, Benjamin Hoadly of Bangor. From then till the middle of the nineteenth century Convocation was not allowed to conduct any effective business.

While synodical government slumbered in England, remarkable things were happening in America. Another key date in the history of Anglicanism is 27 September 1785, when there met at Philadelphia the first General Convention of what was to become the Protestant Episcopal Church of the United States of America (PECUSA). This assembly adopted a constitution which accepted synodical government and included lay representation. It also drew up rules for the election of bishops by clergy and laity in each diocese. Henceforth clergy and laity were given an equal right to ecclesiastical legislation. The second General Convention met at Philadelphia in two sessions in 1786, when twenty-two clergymen and sixteen laymen were present. They approved and adopted a Constitution and a set of Canons and a Prayer Book which remained in use, with but slight variations, for 113 years.

The movement for synodical government in the U.S.A. had repercussions in the British colonies, where synods came into existence before Canterbury Convocation was revived. In 1844 that great Bishop of New Zealand, George Augustus Selwyn (a friend of George Washington Doane of New Jersey), summoned a synod of clergy – two archdeacons, four priests, and two deacons. There were no laity present. This seemingly needful and harmless assembly was frowned upon by some in England. A second synod took place in 1847 when Selwyn produced a constitution for the New Zealand Church. On that occasion he definitely stated his desire to involve laymen in the government of the Church. In those days there was no thought of involving laywomen!

In 1850 Bishop Broughton called a famous meeting of the bishops of Australia, Tasmania, and New Zealand, so that date became a key date in the history of Anglican synodical government. There were present at Sydney, Broughton, Bishop of Sydney, F. R. Nixon, Bishop of Tasmania, Augustus Short, Bishop of Adelaide, Charles Perry, Bishop of Melbourne, William Tyrrell, Bishop of Newcastle, and G. A. Selwyn, Bishop of New Zealand. The meeting had been called for two reasons. The first was the need of the Church in that area to organize itself synodically in the face of the increasing disestablishment. The second was the recent Gorham Judgement, by which Henry Phillpotts, Bishop of Exeter, that High Church Nestor of the Church of England, was compelled to have George Cornelius Gorham as incumbent of Brampford Speke, though he had condemned him as unsound in the matter of baptismal regeneration. That Judgement caused Phillpotts himself to summon his own diocesan synod at Exeter, a year after Broughton's Sydney meeting. All the bishops at Sydney were High Churchmen, with one exception, the Evangelical Charles Perry of Melbourne, and all except Perry sympathized with Phillpotts.

In 1851 a similar gathering to the synod at Sydney took place in Canada, where the bishops met at Quebec, under the presidency of George Jehoshaphat Mountain, Bishop of Quebec, the son of Jacob Mountain already mentioned. Other bishops in attendance were Francis Fulford of Montreal, John Strachan of Toronto, John Medley of Fredericton, and Edward Field of Newfoundland. Bishop David Anderson of Rupertsland and Bishop Hibbert Binney of Nova Scotia could not be present, the latter having only just arrived in his diocese.

The basic purpose of the bishops' meeting was precisely that of the Sydney party. They saw the need for synodical government, with the laity participating.

The next logical step was contact between Sydney and Quebec. This came about in 1853 when Broughton and Mountain met in England. Their great wish was to get an Act passed by the imperial parliament which would remove any doubts about the legality of synodical government in the colonies. At this critical point, Broughton died in England. There followed a period when various attempts were made to legislate at home for the church overseas, which all ended in frustration and failure. In the end the colonial church was forced to go ahead without imperial legislative sanction. Then two courses were open to them. They could get their constitutions legalized in the colonial parliaments, or else they could proceed, without such legislation, on the basis of what became known as 'consensual compact'. The first synod proper in the colonies was that which Bishop Short of Adelaide called in 1856. Another met at Melbourne a little later and Tasmania followed in 1857, the year the same process commenced in New Zealand, when in May there took place the first meeting of bishops (two of them), clergy, and laity, which adopted a constitution involving a General Synod and diocesan synods. The first General Synod met in 1859. It was the first provincial synod in the colonies. Selwyn, as always, was very much a pioneer.

Similar things happened in Canada. In 1854 the Toronto synod met for the first time. In 1856 Bishop Binney of Nova Scotia organized his first diocesan synod. Bishops Mountain of Quebec and Fulford of Montreal followed suit in 1859, though both encountered opposition from Evangelicals. 1862 saw Bishop John Travers Lewis calling his first synod at Ontario, and Bishop Medley at Fredericton as well. In 1859 the Canadian bishops petitioned the Queen for a metropolitan bishop to be appointed. This office was bestowed upon Francis Fulford, though he was not given the title of Archbishop. Bishop Fulford called the first provincial synod in Canada in 1861. The House of Bishops then had a membership of five.

In South Africa, Bishop Robert Gray of Capetown called a synod with lay representatives in 1857. Walter Long, an Evangelical, refused to attend it and became a thorn in the flesh to his moderate High Church Bishop, who suspended him. Long appealed to the Privy Council and the result was the Long Judgement of 1865, with its famous words:

The Church of England, in places where there is no Church established by law, is in the same situation with any other religious body, in no better but in no worse position, and the members may adopt, as the members of any other Communion may adopt, rules for enforcing discipline within their body which will be binding on those who expressly or by implication have assented to them.[6]

That might seem to have played into Gray's hands. But there was a sting in the tail, for it was pointed out that, when Long originally swore canonical obedience to Gray, there was no thought that the Bishop had power to call a synod. In the end, Gray had to reinstate Long. Gray's synod of 1857 was followed by a diocesan synod in the diocese of Grahamstown, called by Bishop Cotterill in 1860. However, synodical government on the provincial level in South Africa was a post-Lambeth Conference development.

These, then, were the repercussions which the growth of synodical government involving the laity in the U.S.A. had upon the colonial church. It is a fascinating subject, which should be of interest to people in England, in view of the recent start of full synodical government on a similar pattern here.[7] The important thing to observe is the influence which the American and colonial churches had upon this country in the nineteenth century in respect to synodical government. Thanks to men who read about what was happening abroad, or who, in some cases, like that of Henry Caswall, witnessed what was happening there, Canterbury Convocation was revived in 1852.[8] Henry Hoare, the banker, commemorated in the present Church House, Westminster, and Samuel Wilberforce, who wrote the first history of the American church, played a large part in the revival of that Convocation.[9] York did not follow suit until Charles Thomas Longley was installed as Archbishop in 1862.[10] Longley, like others, could see the value of the participation of the laity in synodical government. However, it was not until 1885, when Benson was at Canterbury, that a House of Laymen

---

[6] See C. Gray, *Life of Robert Gray*, vol. ii, p. 586.

[7] Some of the details about it can be read in H. Lowther Clarke's book *Constitutional Church Government in the Dominions beyond the seas and in other parts of the Anglican Communion*.

[8] For Caswall, see H. G. G. Herklots, *The Church of England and the American Episcopal Church*, ch. 13, 'Henry Caswall the Interpreter'.

[9] See 'The Revival of an Active Convocation of Canterbury', *Journal of Ecclesiastical History*, 1959, pp. 188ff.

[10] See D. A. Jennings, *The Revival of the Convocation of York* (Borthwick Papers No. 47).

came into existence in each province. Yet, if the laity were not associated with the Convocations until 1885, the sixties at least saw the start of diocesan conferences, like that at Ely in 1864. The subject of diocesan synods was one frequently on the agenda of Convocation in the period immediately preceding the Lambeth Conference of 1867. Another factor to be kept in mind are the church congresses, which started at Cambridge in 1861. The following year saw the repetition of the experiment at Oxford, under the presidency of Samuel Wilberforce. In 1866 a congress took place at York and on that occasion Archbishop Longley of Canterbury gave his support and preached the sermon. Henceforth such congresses were less suspect. Bishops, clergy, and laity all participated, and often there was episcopal representation from America and the colonies. In fact, these congresses were an essential preliminary to the Lambeth Conference of 1867. Sidney Dark said that the 'Lambeth Conferences were episcopalized Church congresses'.[11] But the Lambeth Conferences were occasioned by a demand not for an episcopal synod of the Anglican Communion, but for a synod involving bishops, clergy, and laity. That did not come about and not until the Lambeth Conference of 1968 did clergy and laity play any significant part.

We have already alluded to the importance of the S.P.G. in the history of Anglicanism and we shall see how the Third Jubilee of that society brought about a definite self-consciousness in the Anglican Communion. It was at that time that the term 'Anglican Communion' came into operation. Shortly before the Third Jubilee of the S.P.G. there took place another event of far-reaching significance in the history of Anglicanism, the foundation in 1848, while John Bird Sumner was Archbishop of Canterbury, of St Augustine's College, Canterbury, by A. B. Beresford-Hope and Edward Coleridge. It was designed as a college to train missionaries for the overseas church. Later there were a number of such missionary colleges. St Augustine's, being a High Church creation, had close connections with the S.P.G. From 1948, under the primacy of Geoffrey Fisher, it was the Central College of the Anglican Communion.[12] It has played a significant part in Lambeth Conferences. From the second Conference onwards the bishops generally met in the college before or after their visit to Canterbury Cathedral. Indeed, for some of the overseas bishops it was the place

---

[11] See *The Lambeth Conferences. Their History and their Significance*, p. 10.

[12] The College is now closed and its buildings are used by the King's School, Canterbury.

where they had received their training. It became a place of pilgrimage, reminding the bishops of their connection with the see of Canterbury and its first bishop, St Augustine.

Yet the place which especially attracted the bishops was not at Canterbury, but in London – Lambeth Palace. There, in the chapel, the first American bishops were consecrated, and when American churchmen came to this country, they would make a solemn pilgrimage to that place. There, too, the first colonial bishops were consecrated, before Lambeth Parish Church, Westminster Abbey, and St Paul's Cathedral were used for that purpose. Lambeth, which, apparently, means 'Landing stage in the mud', has been the main residence of the Archbishops of Canterbury since Archbishop Baldwin acquired it from the Bishop of Rochester in the twelfth century, when it was called Lambeth House. It did not get the name Lambeth Palace until 1658, when the old palace at Canterbury had decayed. The chapel, heavily damaged in the war, but restored by Archbishop Fisher, is the oldest part of the Palace, going back to 1245 and Archbishop Boniface. The Great Hall, built by Archbishop Juxon in 1663, has been the scene of the majority of the Lambeth Conferences, until the 1968 Conference moved right out of Lambeth into the Church House. The Great Hall for many years had in it the large book-shelves housing the famous Lambeth Library, started by Archbishop Bancroft in 1610. In that Library are the documents of the Lambeth Conferences, carefully preserved and guarded, read by very few, and those who do read them are supposed not to reproduce their exact words. This embargo on publication was the result of the peculiar circumstances of the first Lambeth Conference.

2

TOWARDS A FIRST CONFERENCE

The Third Jubilee of the S.P.G., celebrated from the summer of 1851 till the summer of 1852, was a very important event in the development of Anglican self-consciousness. Not surprisingly, it was the party of the moderate High Churchmen who especially saw the significance of the occasion. This group were particularly interested in the Anglican Church in Scotland and in the United States of America. A typical example was Walter Farquhar Hook who, at the time of the S.P.G. Festival, was Vicar of Leeds. Anyone who reads the two-volume life of Hook by Dean Stephens will see clearly revealed the ethos and background of the party. As a young man, Hook had friends among the Clapton Sect or Hackney Phalanx, whose leading light was Joshua Watson. We see him as a young clergyman travelling to Scotland and preaching sermons for the despised Scottish episcopalians. We see him welcoming American High Churchmen, like that remarkable prelate John Henry Hobart of New York. One discovers from a reading of N. S. Wheaton's *A Journal of a Residence during several months in London in the years 1823 and 1824* that, when that author came to Christ Church, Oxford, Hook was the ecclesiastic who looked after his needs. Hook's party were keen on emphasizing that the Scottish episcopalians and the American episcopalians were all part of one Church. This group worked for the removal of the restrictions and embargoes which prevented Scottish and American episcopalians from officiating in English churches. Thus, at the consecration of the new Leeds Parish Church in 1841, both a Scottish and an American bishop participated with Bishop Longley of Ripon and the aged Archbishop Vernon Harcourt of York. Longley of Ripon belonged to the group, as also did Henry Phillpotts of Exeter and Samuel Wilberforce of Oxford. In the lower ranks one finds Henry Caswall, who had been ordained by Bishop Philander Chase in the U.S.A. and then came back to a living in Salisbury diocese. Ernest Hawkins, who for years worked for the S.P.G. and knew more about the overseas church than anyone else, and J. W. Burgon, Vicar of the University Church at Oxford for many years, and author of *Lives of Twelve Good Men* (a collection of moderate High Churchmen) also belonged to this group.

Let us now look into the Third Jubilee of the S.P.G. The Archbishop at this time was an Evangelical, John Bird Sumner. J. B. Sumner and his brother, C. R. Sumner, were the next Evangelicals to be appointed bishops after Ryder of Gloucester (later Lichfield) who is known as 'the first Evangelical bishop', and whose kneeling statue can be seen in Lichfield Cathedral. C. R. Sumner, who lived on some years after his brother and played a part in the First Lambeth Conference, was still in occupation of Farnham Castle when Samuel Wilberforce succeeded him as Bishop of Winchester. Although the Sumners were more orientated towards the C.M.S. than the S.P.G., they both joined in the proceedings of the S.P.G. Festival of 1851–2.[1] It was suggested at this time that J. B. Sumner, as Archbishop of Canterbury, should write to the Protestant Episcopal Church in America and bid that body have special services commemorating the Festival also, since they owed a great deal to the S.P.G. So Sumner wrote to each bishop and the letters which he received in reply were later published. The most significant reply was that from Bishop John Henry Hopkins of Vermont, who later was Presiding Bishop. 'It is always a grateful theme', he said, 'to an American Churchman when a prelate of our revered Mother Church speaks, as your Grace has been pleased to do, of the "close communion which binds the Churches of America and England". For my part, I would that it were closer than it is, and fervently hope that the time may come when we shall prove the reality of that communion in the primitive style, by meeting in the good old fashion of Synodical action. How natural and reasonable it seems to be, if "in a time of controversy and division" there should be a Council of all the Bishops in communion with your Grace!'[2] Hopkins, like Hobart, a member of the moderate High Church party, was a man devoted to the Fathers, and had written a book in which he envisaged a future great Council of the Church in which all communions should participate. Being thus greatly interested in the history of General Councils, his suggestion of a Council of the Church was far more appealing to him than to Archbishop Sumner of

---

[1] It has often been pointed out that the S.P.G., the preserve of High Churchmen and emphasizing the Church, should have been called the Church Missionary Society, and the C.M.S., with its keenness to preach the gospel to every creature, should have been called the Society for the Propagation of the Gospel.

[2] See *Letter of the Most Rev. Father in God the Archbishop of Canterbury to the Bishops of the Reformed Church in America on the Third Jubilee of the S.P.G. With the answers that have been received from the American Bishops*, pp. 21f.

Canterbury, who at this very time was hostile to efforts to revive the synodical action of Canterbury Convocation, much to the annoyance of Samuel Wilberforce. However, Henry Caswall did not allow Hopkins's suggestion to be forgotten. Towards the end of 1851 Caswall republished his *America and the American Church* and there quoted what the Bishop of Vermont had said and added:

> An Anglo-Saxon Synod, like that proposed above, might settle many important questions connected with the promotion of Christianity, and the definition of the doctrines of the Reformation. It could not, indeed, unsettle what General Councils have already lawfully determined; and however respectable in moral weight, it would be far from possessing the attribute of infallibility. But its members might pray earnestly for Divine assistance, and might consult with learned and grave deliberation.[3]

Though he did not take up the idea of a council, Sumner suggested that the American Church should send representatives to this country in order to attend the closing services of the Festival. In April 1852 the American Church chose S. A. McCoskry, Bishop of Michigan, and W. H. De Lancey, Bishop of New Jersey, to represent them. Dr Wainwright, the non-episcopal secretary of the House of Bishops accompanied them.[4] They were present in Westminster Abbey when Samuel Wilberforce preached. On the next day (16 June) Bishop McCoskry preached in St Paul's Cathedral. De Lancey in his report of the proceedings gives this account of the two events:

> On Tuesday, the 15th, we attended the Jubilee Services, in Westminster Abbey, in the morning. The Archbishop and the Bishop of Gloucester were at the altar, and sixteen other Bishops, including four Bishops from Scotland, two from the United States of America, one from the English Colonies, one from Jerusalem, and two who had been in the East Indies, were present. It was allotted to the Bishop of Michigan to read the Epistle for the day, and to myself to read the Second Lesson (the fifteenth chapter of the Gospel according to St Mark). The Sermon was preached by the Bishop of Oxford. We also aided in distributing the elements at the Holy Communion, in which duty, at one time, twelve of the Bishops were engaged, while about one thousand communicants partook of the Holy Supper. About two thousand persons attended the impressive services in the Venerable Abbey.
>
> I refrain from attempting to describe, I leave to your own minds and

---

[3] Op. cit., p. 395.
[4] See *The Mission to the Jubilee. Bishop De Lancey's Report to the Convention of the Diocese of Western New-York*. The only copy in this country seems to be that in the British Museum.

hearts to imagine, the feelings excited by the sight of Christian Bishops, Clergy and Laity from the four quarters of the Globe, attesting the reality of catholic unity among Protestants, by mingling their voices in worship, praise and prayer, reciting the Creeds of the earliest ages, kneeling together in love at the Holy Communion, and receiving from the able and eloquent lips of a Minister of God, a Bishop of the Church, whom many before had never seen, the soul-stirring truths of the blessed Gospel of the Son of God. Our hearts swelled with the joyful confession – 'Lord, it is good for us to be here.'

In the evening of that day, I preached the concluding sermon of the Jubilee Services to a large congregation, in St James' Church, Piccadilly, Westminster, and shared the hospitable attentions of the Rector, the Rev. John Jackson.

On Wednesday afternoon, the 16th of June, the services were held in St Paul's Cathedral, in commemoration of the two Societies, viz: the Society for the Propagation of the Gospel, and the Society for the Promotion of Christian Knowledge. The Archbishop and nineteen Bishops attended, with an immense congregation. The sermon was preached by the Bishop of Michigan, whose commanding figure, powerful voice and fearless enunciation of his views of truth and duty, filled the eyes, and ears, and hearts of multitudes with joy and admiration. The Lord Mayor was present on the occasion, and after the services, proceeded, as usual, with the Archbishop and Bishops, to the Mansion House, where more than two hundred and thirty ladies and gentlemen were hospitably entertained, and where, both the Bishop of Michigan and myself, responded in brief speeches, to the cordial expressions from his Lordship, of regard and welcome to us as Bishops of the Protestant Episcopal Church of the United States.[5]

Henry Caswall was present at the Westminster service and he too waxed eloquent about it:

What a procession! Such a procession as the Anglican Church has never before witnessed. Jerusalem and Michigan; Bombay and Sodor and Man; Madras and Western New York; Ripon and St Asaph; Edinburgh and Gloucester; Oxford and Argyll; Salisbury and Glasgow and Moray and Ross; his Grace of Canterbury closing the line of apostolic brotherhood. As they advance, the assembled thousands rise up in token of respect. . . . While that procession of Bishops advances towards the *sacrarium*, let us inwardly pray for them, and for the 108 Bishops of the Anglican Communion whom they may be considered to represent.[6]

[5] Op. cit., pp. 4–5.
[6] *The Jubilee, or What I saw and heard in London on the 15th and 16th of June, 1852*, p. 6.

He then went on to plead for a synod 'of the entire Anglican Church'. On 18 June the Americans were welcomed at the offices of the S.P.G. which were then in Pall Mall. Dr Wainwright on this occasion read a letter from William Rollinson Whittingham, Bishop of Maryland, who was himself just about to arrive in England, in which he pleaded the advantage of 'an assemblage of the whole Anglican episcopate, either absolutely or representatively, in council, for organization as one branch of the Church Catholic.'[7]

Two other interesting meetings took place. One was held at Exeter College, Oxford, where there was an assembly of High Churchmen, among them Henry Phillpotts, Bishop of Exeter, and Dr Pusey, the Regius Professor of Hebrew. This was very much a gathering to demonstrate approval of Henry Phillpotts's stand for baptismal regeneration, but the American bishops were much honoured. McCoskry, De Lancey, and Wainwright were presented with an alms dish by the Regius Professor of Divinity, William Jacobson (later Bishop of Chester, and in that capacity present at the First Lambeth Conference). This dish depicted the offering of the Magi, and bore the inscription:

Ecclesiae Americanae
Delectae in Christo
Oxonienses
1852[8]

Many years later, as we shall see, the American Church presented the Church of England with a similar, but much more elaborate, alms basin.

The other noteworthy occasion during the visit of the Americans was at Leeds, in the parish of Hook, and in the diocese of Ripon, presided over by Bishop Longley. On that occasion, De Lancey spoke of the new phenomenon of the coming together of the Anglican Churches. Roman Catholics, he maintained, could no longer speak of the disunity of the English Church. If the Anglican Church could but come together in council, then the unity of the Church would be yet more clearly demonstrated.[9] De Lancey was so impressed by his visit to England, on which he was accompanied by his wife, that, when he got home, he published his pamphlet, *The Mission to the Jubilee*, of no less than 98

---

[7] *The Mission to the Jubilee*, pp. 4–5.

[8] See *The Mission to the Jubilee*, pp. 7ff.

[9] See the *Guardian*, 8 September 1852, p. 596. Details of the speech are not given in *The Mission to the Jubilee*.

pages. Henry Caswall, besides the pamphlet that has been mentioned, wrote another about the visit of the delegation to St Augustine's College, Canterbury.[10]

In the year 1853 the American Church invited the English Church to send a return delegation to the U.S.A., which could be present at their General Convention. One might have expected a diocesan bishop to be sent from this country; but the episcopate appear to have been unwilling to dispatch one. George Augustus Selwyn, when Bishop of Lichfield, seems to have been the first English diocesan bishop to visit the American shore. The 1853 delegation consisted of a retired missionary bishop, Spencer of Madras, the leader, Ernest Hawkins of the S.P.G., John Sinclair, the Archdeacon of Middlesex, and Henry Caswall. Another gentleman present, though it seems in a private capacity was Edmund Hobhouse, then Vicar of St Peter in the East, Oxford, but later Bishop of Nelson, who took to the American Presiding Bishop a letter from the aged Martin Routh and a copy of his most famous literary production, *Reliquiae Sacrae*.[11] Caswall fortunately wrote a very full account of this important visit in his book *The Western World Revisited*. At the General Convention some measure of Anglo-American co-operation was achieved with respect to the work that the two Churches were doing in China and regarding the status of American clergy in England and English clergy in America. The Convention decided that copies of its minutes should be sent to every bishop in the Anglican Communion. One wonders whether this still goes on. Voices were heard at the Convention in favour of an Anglican Council, but there was no lack of Evangelicals willing to speak against the suggestion. Henry Caswall took to America, from the society formed in this country to agitate for the revival of full synodical powers for Canterbury Convocation, a memorandum signed by the society's chairman, Thomas Collins. This he submitted to the General Convention. It is worth quoting that part of the document which advocates an Anglican Council.

And although confined by the constitution of their Society, as a voluntary association for a temporary purpose, to the single object of procuring the revival, through the existing Convocations, of the Synodical functions of the English Church, the Council cannot refrain from looking forward, with humble prayer and in holy hope, to the time when the several reformed branches of the Church Catholic in England, in Ireland, in Scotland, and the

[10] See *A Pilgrimage to Canterbury in 1852*.
[11] R. D. Middleton, *Dr. Routh*, p. 57.

United States of America, in the Colonies of the British Empire, and elsewhere, may – themselves purified and strengthened – bear united testimony for 'the faith once delivered to the Saints' against the usurpations of the See of Rome, as well as against every form of schism, of heresy, and of infidelity; and when, by this and by other means, the long-lost privileges and blessings of intercommunion between orthodox Churches may be recovered, for the furtherance of the Gospel, for salvation of souls, and for the promotion of the Kingdom and glory of the great God and our Saviour Jesus Christ.[12]

In this same year, John Henry Hopkins, Junior, son of the Bishop of Vermont, a talented musician and artist, author of the carol, 'We three kings of Orient are', founded and edited the *Church Journal*. In this magazine he aired the subject of an Anglican Council, and published a long fulsome poem, depicting the Anglican bishops in procession at Canterbury.[13]

The next suggestion in favour of an Anglican Council was again voiced on American soil, but this time by a Canadian bishop. In 1854 Bishop Francis Fulford of Montreal preached at the consecration of Bishop Horatio Potter of New York. As with De Lancey's speech at Leeds, there was an anti-Roman aspect to his address. At this time Pope Pius IX was about to promulgate the dogma of the Immaculate Conception, and Fulford asked whether the Church of the Reformation could not come together and protest against this innovation:

Must it, however, always be the unfulfilled yearning of earnest spirits that the day may come when the whole body of the Reformed Church shall meet together in her corporate character, bearing witness for Catholic truths, and testifying, in some recognized and official manner, both for her own true Catholicity, and for the unity of her members in every quarter of the globe?[14]

It is to be noted that, though Fulford in this sermon uses the name 'Reformed Church' or 'Church of the Reformation', he clearly is referring to the Anglican Communion. John Hopkins, Junior, not surprisingly, was most sympathetic towards Fulford's suggestion and wrote, 'Let the Archbishop of Canterbury invite all the Bishops of the Reformed Church throughout the world to assemble at Canterbury,

[12] See H. Caswall, *The Western World Revisited*, pp. 320f.
[13] See C. F. Sweet, *A Champion of the Cross*, pp. 148f.
[14] See F. Fulford, *Sermons, Addresses and Statistics of the Diocese of Montreal*, pp. 42–3.

once more to protest, solemnly, against "the new blasphemous and dangerous deceit" of Rome . . ."[15]

Archbishop Sumner, unsympathetic towards synodical government, was not disposed to take up any of these suggestions. He was probably more interested in co-operation with the Nonconformists and Continental reformed bodies rather than in initiating a synod in which the whole Anglican Communion would be involved, a scheme which he thought might end in disaster. Moreover, he probably questioned the legality of any such step. Hence the voices uniting in favour of an Anglican Council during the period 1851–5 fell upon deaf ears as far as Canterbury was concerned. It would be different when Longley succeeded Sumner at Lambeth.

However, the Jubilee and its aftermath did a great deal of good. It brought England and America closer together. For example, we find American bishops coming to this country and assisting at episcopal consecrations. Perhaps even more important, it initiated a real upsurge of Anglican self-consciousness. The phrase 'Anglican Communion' now began to be used, though it is remarkable that Fulford never used it in his address of 1854 from which we have just been quoting. The American scholar, Dr Robert S. Bosher, made this important discovery of the coming into use of the phrase 'Anglican Communion' at the time of the S.P.G. Jubilee of 1851 and gives the evidence in his *The American Church and the Formation of the Anglican Communion, 1823–53* (1962). My own researches have borne out Bosher's contention.

Before passing on, it would be helpful at this juncture to analyse what the advocates of an Anglican Council saw as its purpose. The anti-Roman purpose has already been indicated. To this we may add five, more positive, purposes:

1 The formation of a new canon law for the whole communion.
2 The settling of doctrinal disputes.
3 The easing of inter-communion between the various branches of the Anglican Communion.
4 The voicing of the Church's conscience on social questions.
5 Co-operation in literary publication.

There were, as far as I know, no further requests for an Anglican council from America before the first Lambeth Conference. In 1861 the American Civil War broke out and the Church became divided and

[15] See C. F. Sweet, op. cit., p. 147, and W. R. Curtis, *The Lambeth Conferences*, p. 81.

concerned with its own internal problems. The story of its reunion, at the General Convention of 1865, is a remarkable one, but there is no space to recount it here.

From America we turn to the colonies, where we have already examined the growth of synodical government. We have seen how in the fifties and sixties of the last century diocesan synods had started in the colonial Church and, in some areas, provincial synods had commenced as well. Now it was natural that the Church in the colonies, hearing the demands made for an Anglican Council, at the time of the S.P.G. Third Jubilee, should themselves see the logic of 'capping the edifice' with a synod of the whole Anglican Communion. In this movement in the colonies for an Anglican Council, Bishop Robert Gray of Capetown was a leading light. Certainly from 1860 onwards he was pressing for what he called a national synod, embracing all the Anglican Churches apart from America. In that year, there came forth from Canterbury Convocation a report on missionary bishops, drafted by Bishop Wilberforce of Oxford, who put in a paragraph, for which Gray had been responsible, which ran as follows:

> . . . There seems to us to be a special need of combined counsels to maintain in unity the Church as it extends. That by a regular gradation of duly constituted Synods all questions affecting unity might be duly settled; Diocesan Synods determining all matters not ordered by the Synod of the province; Provincial Synods determining all matters not ordered by a National Synod; a National Synod ordering all matters not determined by a General Council.[16]

Elsewhere, Gray called the national synod a 'patriarchal' or 'imperial' synod, and, presumably, he intended it to contain presbyters as well as bishops. It must be noted that Gray's plea for such a synod came before his troubles with John William Colenso, Bishop of Natal, whom Gray brought out to Africa and then found necessary to depose, because of what he conceived were his heretical opinions. It is true that Gray had an additional reason for pressing for an Anglican Council, once he had deposed Colenso and wanted his sentence of deposition confirmed by the whole Anglican episcopate.

Moving from South Africa to Canada, we find that John Travers Lewis, Bishop of Ontario, who prided himself on being the primary author of the Lambeth Conferences, first made a plea for a 'national council of the English Church, with representatives from every

---

[16] See *Chronicle of Convocation*, 8 June 1860, pp. 292–3.

ecclesiastical province in the Empire' in his charge to his clergy in 1864. Clearly *Essays and Reviews* and the writings of Colenso provoked him to make this request. In the following year, at the Canadian Provincial Synod at Montreal, he persuaded his fellow bishops to send such a request to the Archbishop of Canterbury. What especially troubled him was the seeming abandonment of the Bible as the Word of God and the non-insistence on a belief in eternal punishment. It will be recalled that the Judicial Committee of the Privy Council seemed to countenance both these departures from what was considered traditional orthodoxy. At the same meeting of the Canadian Provincial Synod, the Lower House sent a letter, with a similar request, to the Convocations of Canterbury and York, both of which were functioning once again. The letter of the Lower House, however, had a somewhat different slant. It was less concerned with these two doctrinal aberrations than with the growing danger of separation of the colonial churches from the Mother Church and the possibility that they might end up with different canons. What must be carefully noted is that the Canadian Church wanted a synod of bishops, presbyters, and laymen. This is clear from the episcopal letter to Longley.

When Longley replied from Addington (the other residence of the Archbishops of Canterbury in the nineteenth century until Frederick Temple sold it), he did not, like Sumner, shelve the issue. 'The meeting', he said,

> of such a Synod as you propose is not by any means foreign to my own feelings, and I think that it might tend to prevent those inconveniences, the possibility of which you anticipate. I cannot, however, take any step in so grave a matter without consulting my episcopal brethren in both branches of the United Church of England and Ireland, as well as those of the different colonies and dependencies of the British Empire.

It is evident from Longley's words that, as yet, there was no suggestion of bringing in the United States; the requests of Hopkins and other American ecclesiastics were temporarily forgotten. On the receipt of the letter from Canada, York Convocation did nothing at all about it until October 1867. By that time the first Lambeth Conference had already met! Canterbury Convocation, however, acted very differently. This is not, perhaps, surprising, when we consider that one of its most active members was George Anthony Denison, Archdeacon of Taunton, a Tractarian High Churchman, who delighted in synodical action. Denison pressed the matter upon the attention of Canterbury

Convocation and was opposed in his enthusiasm for the Canadian request by Broad Churchmen like Dean Stanley of Westminster. There were few things on which Stanley and Denison agreed! Denison won to the extent of getting a committee to look into the matter. This reported in June 1866 and put forward all the advantages of a synod or council. The committee wished to widen it so that it would include not only the United Church of England and Ireland and the Church in the colonies, but also the Scottish and American parts of the Anglican Communion. They thus wished to revert to the original request of Bishop Hopkins at the time of the S.P.G. Third Jubilee, though they made no allusion to it, and were probably ignorant of it or had forgotten it. This report was printed and circulated but nothing more was done in Convocation in 1866. In October of that year, Bishop Thirlwall of St David's spoke quite disparagingly of the whole idea in a charge to his clergy. He was to remain hostile to the first Lambeth Conference.

In December, in Christ Church Cathedral, at Oxford, a big impetus was given to the Anglican synod idea by Bishop Fulford of Montreal, who was in this country and whom Wilberforce had asked to preach at his Advent ordination. He made use of the occasion to draw attention to the request that had come from the Canadian church. Towards the end of his sermon he spoke about efforts for reunion with English Nonconformists, the Eastern Orthodox Church, the Scandinavian Church, and the Church of Rome; he suggested that, before any schemes of reunion with such Churches could be realized, the Anglican Communion must first demonstrate its own unity by coming together in council. Once such a gathering had taken place, no one any longer could criticize the Church of England as 'isolated', for it would be demonstrated as a world-wide communion. Fulford afterwards published this sermon under the title *A Pan-Anglican Synod*, and added an appendix. This, I think, was the first use of the word 'pan-Anglican', a word against which J. W. Burgon raised the objection that it was 'a barbarous epithet, unlawfully compounded of Greek and Latin; distasteful to persons of education – not understood by the vulgar – unsanctioned by authority. Partly heathenish, partly ludicrous, the first half of the word will surely not find many defenders.'[17] However, the name caught on and was used officially of the first Anglican Congress of 1908, the famous Pan-Anglican Congress. The Congresses of Minneapolis (1954) and Toronto (1964) were called 'Anglican' rather than 'pan-Anglican' Congresses. However, the name is preserved today

[17] See *Guardian*, 16 October 1867, p. 1104.

in that occasional periodical for the whole Anglican Communion
known as the *Pan-Anglican*. If Fulford invented the word, and he
certainly seems to have been the first person to use it, it caught on
unofficially and we find all three Lambeth Conferences of 1867, 1878,
and 1888 being referred to as 'pan-Anglican synods', though they were
not, of course, so designated officially. W. S. Gilbert used the term 'Pan-
Anglican Synod' in the *Bab Ballads* in his 'The Bishop of Rum-ti-foo'
and 'The Bishop of Rum-ti-foo again'. Here we may quote some stanzas
from the second poem.

> I often wonder whether you
> Think sometimes of that Bishop, who
> From black but balmy Rum-ti-foo
>   Last summer twelvemonth came.

> Unto your mind I p'raps may bring
> Remembrance of the man I sing
> To-day, by simply mentioning
>   That PETER was his name.

> Remember how that holy man
> Came with the great Colonial clan
> To Synod, called Pan-Anglican
>   And kindly recollect

> How, having crossed the ocean wide
> To please his flock all means he tried
> Consistent with a proper pride
>   And manly self-respect.

In February 1867, Canterbury Convocation debated the matter
again, in the light of Fulford's sermon and its appendix, in which he had
made some concrete suggestions as to what such a pan-Anglican synod
should do. Again there was Broad Church opposition, but, in the end, a
motion got through asking the Archbishop of Canterbury to assemble
all the bishops in communion with the Church of England. While
Canterbury Convocation was deliberating these matters, there took
place at Lambeth Palace a private meeting of the episcopate, graced by
the presence of Bishop Fulford and Henry John Whitehouse, a voluble
American bishop who presided over the see of Illinois. On Friday, 8
February, they dealt with item 4 on the agenda which read, 'A Petition of
the Colonial Bishops for a General Synod'. A number of the
Evangelical bishops absented themselves from the discussion, since
they did not approve of the subject. The influential Bishop Tait of

London also was not there. Fulford spoke and outlined the arguments of his sermon and its appendix. Whitehouse also spoke effectively. Tait had written a letter asking for an assurance that the decisions of such a proposed assembly should not be binding on all the member Churches. Longley gave such an assurance. In the end, Wilberforce of Oxford proposed the resolution:

> We, the Archbishops and Bishops of English, Irish, Colonial, and American Sees, here assembled, pray your Grace, to invite a meeting of all the bishops of the various Churches holding full communion with the United Church of England and Ireland.[18]

Fulford seconded it and it was passed unanimously. At this meeting, the largest gathering so far held of bishops of the Anglican Communion, there were twenty-three bishops, eight colonials, ten English, four Irish, and one American. This meeting was held in February of 1867. In September the first Lambeth Conference met.

[18] G. H. Sumner, *Life of Charles Richard Sumner, D.D., Bishop of Winchester*, p. 451.

3

ARCHBISHOP LONGLEY AND THE CONFERENCE OF 1867

Though a representative gathering of Anglican bishops decided in February of 1867 that it was desirable that a meeting of the whole Anglican episcopate should be held, a number of Evangelical bishops had not attended this meeting (as later in the year they did not attend the Lambeth Conference) because they doubted the legality of such a step. This opposition came from the majority of the bishops in the York province, from one or two in Canterbury province, and several in the Irish part of the United Church. When he reported to Convocation what had come about at the bishops' meeting, Longley said:

> It should be distinctly understood that at this meeting no declaration of faith shall be made, and no decision come to that shall affect generally the interests of the Church, but that we shall meet together for brotherly counsel and encouragement. . . . I should refuse to convene any assembly which pretended to enact any canons, or affected to make any decisions binding on the Church. . . . I feel I undertake a great responsibility in assenting to this request, and certainly if I saw anything approaching to what is apprehended as likely to result from it, I should not be disposed to sanction it, but I can assure my brethren that I should enter on this meeting in the full confidence that nothing would pass but that which tended to brotherly love and union, and would bind the Colonial Church, which is certainly in a most unsatisfactory state, more closely to the Mother Church.[1]

Longley then got together a preliminary committee, which included Samuel Wilberforce, Bishop Browne of Ely (the writer of a famous book on the Thirty-nine Articles), and Bishop Ellicott of Gloucester (a great biblical commentator whose writings are now being reprinted). Ellicott in due course became the episcopal secretary for the Conference and played a similar part in the Conferences of 1878 and 1888, while in 1897 he was registrar.

On 22 February, Longley wrote a letter of invitation, which was copied and sent to the 151 Anglican bishops, a number which included

[1] *Chronicle of Convocation*, 15 February 1867, p. 807.

the retired bishops, who, on this first occasion, were all asked, with possibly one, or at most two, exceptions. In this letter, Longley wrote, 'I propose that, at our assembling, we should first solemnly seek the blessing of Almighty God on our gathering, by uniting together in the highest acts of the Church's worship. After this, brotherly consultations will follow. In these we may consider many practical questions, the settlement of which would tend to the advancement of the kingdom of our Lord and Master Jesus Christ, and to the maintenance of greater union in our missionary work, and to increased intercommunion among ourselves.' In these words he, in fact, summed up what were to be the main concerns of the first Lambeth Conference, very much domestic concerns of the Anglican Communion. The meeting, modelled on a church congress, was to begin on 24 September, a Tuesday, and finish on Friday, 27 September. The date was not far in the future, and the time allotted to the Conference was not of long duration.

All the invitatory letters went out in February or March, with the exception of those for the York province. Longley wanted to get permission from Archbishop Thomson of York before sending them and he hoped in the process to persuade his fellow-primate to come. Longley had preached the sermon at the church congress held at York in 1866 and he thought that Thomson would be the most fitting preacher at the 'Episcopal Church Congress' of 1867. But Thomson was not to be moved and most of the northern bishops kept away with him. In the end Longley thought in terms of an American prelate as preacher.

Almost all the replies of the Anglican bishops were fortunately preserved with care by Archbishop Longley and they can be read by anyone at Lambeth Library. There were many who excused themselves, some from old age, some from the expense of the journey, some from the fact that they had but recently settled in their dioceses, or were pressed down with work. A legal difficulty prevented an Indian bishop from moving out of his diocese; he could only get leave at certain stated intervals. Some of the bishops in the U.S.A. were still recovering from the devastation of the Civil War.

Longley asked for suggestions for business to be transacted by the Conference and the following suggested subjects came up in letters:

1 The Reunion of Christendom.
2 Putting down the Ritualists.
3 Putting down the Rationalists.

4 The Revision of the Prayer Book.
5 Co-operation in Missionary work.
6 Intercommunion within the Anglican Communion.
7 The Revision of the Authorized Version of the Bible.
8 The Relationship of the Colonial Church to the Church of England.
9 The Colenso Scandal in Natal.
10 The Role of the Laity in Church Life.
11 The Social Application of the Gospel.

The last subject was suggested only by Bishop Whipple of Minnesota, who was unable himself to come. Not until 1888 did this subject get on to the agenda of a Lambeth Conference. There were other less significant subjects suggested, like that of how far the colonial Church had to obey the English canons on marriage law; one bishop wanted a discussion on burial. Other matters alluded to were the use of lay readers and the method of getting better incomes for the clergy. Of all these subjects, those which occupied the attention of the first Lambeth Conference were intercommunion within the Anglican Communion, the relationship of the Church overseas to the Church of England, and co-operation in missionary work. Reunion and rationalism both managed to get in at some point. The other suggestions were dropped.

On 20 July, Longley issued a tentative programme for the Conference. The first day, Tuesday, 24 September, was to deal with 'Intercommunion between the Churches of the Anglican Communion' and had as its main item a declaration stating the position of the bishops and their ultimate objectives. This was based upon a suggested declaration in the appendix of Bishop Fulford's published sermon *A Pan-Anglican Synod.* These are the words of the declaration in the suggested programme:

We, the Bishops of Christ's Holy Catholic Church, professing the faith of the primitive and undivided Church, as based on Scripture, and defined by the first four General Councils, now assembled by the good providence of God at the Archiepiscopal Palace of Lambeth under the presidency of the Primate of all England, desire first to give hearty thanks to Almighty God for having thus brought us together for common counsels: Secondly, we desire to express the deep sorrow with which we view the divided condition of the flock of Christ throughout the world; and, Lastly, we do here solemnly declare our belief that the best hope of future reunion will be found in drawing each of us for ourselves closer to our common Lord, in giving ourselves to much prayer and intercession, and in the cultivation of a spirit of charity.

The second day, Wednesday, 25 September, was to be devoted to the colonial Church. The third day, Thursday, 26 September, was to be devoted to co-operation in missionary action. Presumably, the fourth day, Friday, 27 September, was to be given up to 'left-overs'. A revealing discovery which I made in 1964 was that this programme was based upon a tentative programme drawn up by Bishop Gray of Capetown in South Africa and submitted by him to Samuel Wilberforce. Looking at Gray's programme, which still exists in South Africa, one notes with interest two things not taken up. One was a suggestion that the Anglican Communion should make contact with the Swedish Church. The other was a suggested declaration supporting the Thirty-nine Articles. It must be noted that the moderate High Churchmen, to which party Gray belonged, were much more sympathetic to the Thirty-nine Articles than Pusey and his ilk.

Once the programme had been published, two wavering bishops decided to come, Thirlwall of St David's and Pelham of Norwich. Thirlwall, the most learned of the bishops, relieved that the Colenso business was not on the programme, felt that he could come. Evangelical bishops, however, were not a little alarmed at the Declaration and its reference to the first four General Councils and what they considered its inadequate attitude to the Bible, the Reformation, and the Thirty-nine Articles. Thomson of York reaffirmed his decision not to participate.

The revised programme came out on 23 August. It took into account criticisms by the American Evangelical, Charles Pettit McIlvaine of Ohio, a frequent visitor to this country, a friend of Bishop Sumner of Winchester and the proud possessor of Charles Simeon's cassock.[2] The Declaration, as now revised, ended with a sentence, which spoke about a return 'to the Faith and Discipline of the undivided Church which was the principle of the English Reformation'. Now it was the turn of the Tractarians to be angry. Pusey deplored this reference to the Reformation. It did not, however, unduly worry Gray, who was disturbed by the failure to have any reference to the Colenso affair. He decided to work upon the colonial bishops now arriving in England so that they could get the programme altered and the Natal scandal included. He succeeded in getting together a quite unofficial committee of twelve colonial bishops who together prepared a revised programme for the second day.

[2] See W. Carus, *Memorials of the Right Reverend Charles Pettit McIlvaine, D.D., D.C.L., late Bishop of Ohio.*

On 17 September there was a preliminary meeting of those bishops who were to attend the Conference. Here it was agreed that the press should be excluded – a decision which has affected every Lambeth Conference except the last one in 1968. There would be two stenographers to make a secret copy of the proceedings. It was agreed that there should be a conversazione at St James's Hall on the Friday. This was a feature of the church congresses. It was also hoped that there would be a service on the Saturday at Westminster Abbey or some London church. Gray who could not keep quiet about Colenso, denounced him as the greatest heresiarch of all time. Longley felt that it would be best if Colenso were left out of it, but Gray was supported by Wilberforce. Tait, on the other hand, was greatly opposed to any discussion of Colenso. Bishop Benjamin Cronyn, the Evangelical Bishop of Huron, wanted ritualism discussed and found himself supported by Tait. In the end, ritualism did not come into the discussions of the First Lambeth Conference. Tait was unwilling to keep it out, when he was President of the Second Conference.

On 19 September, the caucus of colonial bishops met at the house of Christopher Wordsworth, Archdeacon of Westminster, in Little Cloister. They prepared their revised programme for the Wednesday of the Conference. Included in it was a proposition for the appointment of a committee to discuss the Natal affair. On Sunday, 22 September, the bishops were out and about, preaching in various churches. Selwyn, not at all satisfied with the arrangements for the Conference, preached on Acts 19.32, 'Some therefore cried one thing, and some another: for the assembly was confused; and the more part knew not wherefore they were come together.' On the next day, the Monday, the day before the opening of the Conference, Gray's caucus met yet once more. They agreed on a resolution to put to the Lambeth Conference, to the effect that 'the whole Anglican Communion is deeply injured by the present condition of the Church in Natal'. Gray had drawn up a formula with which he wanted the Conference to endorse his condemnation of Colenso. There was also an American bishop hot upon Colenso's tail, but, being an American, he felt unable to join in the deliberations of the colonial bishops. This was John Henry Hopkins, Bishop of Vermont and Presiding Bishop of the American Episcopal Church. He was also very much in favour of the general councils and in the Declaration would have preferred a reference to six rather than four.

Next day, Tuesday, 24 September, the first of this historic series of ten Conferences began. It was the shortest and most leisurely of them all. Some of the bishops stayed with Longley, a widower, at Addington Park, and enjoyed croquet with the Archbishop's two daughters. Others resided at Fulham with Tait and his daughters, one of whom, Edith, was, years later, to be the wife of Archbishop Davidson.[3] Others were entertained by the Bishop of Winchester at his London residence. Some spent the time in hotels. They began with a quiet service of Holy Communion in Lambeth Palace Chapel at 11 a.m., the usual hour for Lambeth private meetings of bishops. The sermon was preached by Bishop Whitehouse of Illinois, who, presumably, had not been home since March. He was verbose and his sermon came in for heavy criticism. The seventy-six bishops present were a remarkable gathering of men. In his pamphlet about the 1958 Lambeth Conference Professor Eric Mascall wrote that few of the bishops present that year had much theological learning.[4] That, certainly, could not be said of those seventy-six bishops in 1867. Some of them had been professors at Oxford and Cambridge. There were notable theologians, church historians and classicists, men with legal knowledge and men with medical knowledge. They were all white men. The Anglican Communion boasted but one black bishop, Samuel Adjai Crowther, but he could not come to Lambeth in 1867. He did not come until 1888. The public were not admitted to the opening service. There was obviously no room for them. In 1878 there was a non-episcopal presence in Tait's wife and daughters assisting with the singing from the gallery. But in 1867 there was no note of music and Longley's daughters were, doubtless, at Addington, superintending the making of the episcopal beds. The communion bread was made with corn from Bethlehem. The wine came from Jerusalem. Who supplied these items history does not record. Lunch followed the service, after which the bishops got down to business in the Guard Room.

The metropolitans sat with Archbishop Longley, who introduced the proceedings with an address, in which he reiterated that the gathering was not a synod but a conference. He said that not all the suggested topics had been taken up in the resolutions, for it seemed best to avoid attempting too much at their first gathering. Then various memorials were received. These have been a constant feature of Lambeth Conferences. The first Conference received them and then did nothing about them. This has been the practice for the most part ever since. There were five memorials (including one from St Augustine's,

[3] See M.C.S.M. [i.e. Mary Mills], *Edith Davidson of Lambeth*.
[4] Eric L. Mascall, *Lambeth and Church Unity*.

Canterbury) asking for Colenso to be dealt with. There was a memorial on reunion with the Eastern Orthodox Church and with Rome. There was one from some London curates asking for the betterment of their lot, and another in favour of the reserved sacrament. Some clergy (Charles Kingsley among them) wanted full communion with the Swedish Church. There was also a memorial from some of the American bishops regarding the Italian reformed churches. Next, when the question of the final service came up, it was revealed that Dean Stanley did not want the bishops at the Abbey, if they came officially as the Lambeth Conference. This was because of his sympathy with Colenso, whom he thought the bishops were about to condemn. It was agreed that the Conference should go to Lambeth Parish Church instead. Later Lambeth Conferences never again went to Lambeth Church for an opening or closing service, but we do find the bishops there for quiet days.

Now they got down to the discussion of the Declaration. Sparks were set flying in the debate on the general councils. Hopkins (like Pusey) wanted six mentioned. Others, generally of the Evangelical party, wanted them excluded; after all, the one thing that the Thirty-nine Articles said about the general councils was that they could err. Bishop McIlvaine fought powerfully for their exclusion. On this first day, Hopkins was defeated and went home miserable. The general councils were excluded. The opening of the Declaration now read:

> We, Bishops of Christ's Holy Catholic Church, in visible communion with the United Church of England and Ireland, professing the faith delivered to us in Holy Scripture [this instead of 'based on Scripture'] maintained by the primitive Church and reaffirmed by the Fathers of the English Reformation.

With the introduction of the Reformation, McIlvaine and Sumner had triumphed. However, when the bishops met again on the Wednesday, they appointed a committee to deal with the remaining section of the Declaration and this committee brought the general councils back in at the conclusion! It would seem that, before the bishops went home on the Tuesday, they were presented with a suggested revised programme for the next day – the programme drawn up by the caucus of colonial bishops and printed in exactly the same format as that used for the official one. Obviously it had archiepiscopal support. When the bishops met on the Wednesday, Longley came down in favour of the new programme, but there was strong opposition to it from Tait and Thirlwall. One of the items on the new agenda was a suggested graduated system of synods – diocesan, provincial, and some higher synod of the Anglican Communion. The idea of a pan-Anglican synod met with opposition. Some said that, as far as the Church of England was concerned, such a synod would be illegal. The American Hopkins supported the idea and among the colonial bishops who advocated it were Selwyn, Gray, Fulford, Cotterill of Grahamstown. Of the English bishops it was supported by the Tractarian, Hamilton of Salisbury, who was anxious for the Archbishop of Canterbury to be created a patriarch. After much battle, Selwyn persuaded the conference to accept the following resolution:

> That in the opinion of this conference unity of faith and discipline will be best maintained among the several branches of the Anglican Communion by due and canonical subordination of the synods of the several branches to the higher authority of a synod or synods above them.

This involved a definite endorsement of the synodical system; and clearly the assembly seemed in favour of diocesan and provincial synods. Also it was possible for those who wished it, to find a reference in this ambiguous formula to a pan-Anglican synod. Hence the second day of the Conference was of great importance. The bishops had shown some endorsement of the synodical system. As G. W. O. Addleshaw says in *The Mission of the Anglican Communion*, 'The Conference encouraged them [i.e. the colonial bishops] to base their authority on diocesan and provincial synods, and for this reason it is an important landmark in the constitutional development of Anglicanism overseas'.[5]

On Thursday the Colenso question came up. As we have seen, the Natal situation had been put on the revised programme for Wednesday but so completely had the bishops occupied their time with synodical government that they did not arrive at the Colenso issue. On Thursday, the Bishop of Vermont made the speech of a lifetime requesting the bishops to endorse the Bishop of Natal's deposition and excommunication. Bishop Charles Wordsworth of St Andrews (the brother of Archdeacon Christopher Wordsworth of Westminster) pleaded in similar terms and suggested a formula of condemnation much shorter than the exceedingly lengthy one put forward by Hopkins. Bishop Gray of Capetown offered a yet shorter proposition – 'That the Conference, while pronouncing no opinion upon any question as to legal rights, acknowledges and accepts the spiritual sentence pronounced by the Metropolitan of South Africa upon the Right Rev.

[5] Op. cit., p. 75.

J. W. Colenso, D.D., Bishop of Natal.' John Travers Lewis, the Bishop of Ontario, and Bishop Hamilton of Salisbury strongly advocated action against Colenso. Needless to say, all this intensely annoyed Thirlwall, who had agreed to come to the Conference only after he had seen Longley's programme and had been satisfied that the Natal question found no place in it. Longley, the President of the Conference, allowed the bishops to let off steam and then himself spoke. He said that, though the words 'Colenso' and 'Natal' did not appear on the programme he had sent out, yet trials of bishops by their metropolitans did find a place in it, so that it could hardly be said that he was doing wrong in allowing the discussion. In the end, he permitted a committee to be appointed to consider the Natal question. Even this annoyed Thirlwall and Tait and their supporters. Many bishops were by no means content with this and during the lunch interval an extraordinary thing happened. Samuel Wilberforce and two other bishops drew up this resolution: 'We the undersigned Bishops declare our acceptance of the sentence pronounced upon Dr Colenso by the Metropolitan of South Africa and his Suffragans, as being spiritually a valid sentence.' Of the seventy-six bishops present at the Conference no less than fifty-six of them signed this document. Gray, Cotterill of Grahamstown, and Edward Twells of Orange Free State could obviously not sign, since they were the bishops concerned. Hence one can say that fifty-six out of seventy-three signed. Among those who refused to sign was Bishop Alexander Ewing of Argyll and the Isles, a Scottish Broad Churchman. He was the only bishop with any sympathy for Colenso's theology. Bishops like Tait and Thirlwall did not share Colenso's theology but felt that Gray's trial had been illegal.

After lunch the assembly dealt with the question of appeals and particularly the possibility of an appeal from disciplinary tribunals in the colonies to a spiritual tribunal in England. (Obviously this was a question which was part and parcel of the Colenso troubles.) Bishop Selwyn wanted a supreme spiritual court to decide on questions of heterodoxy, either for the whole Anglican Communion or, at least, for the home and colonial Church. Bishop Cotterill thought it would be possible to have such a court for all but the American and Scottish Anglicans. The opposition naturally came from Tait of London. In the end, a committee was appointed to go into the matter. There had been yet another committee appointed to compose a pastoral or encyclical letter. This committee had evidently met and done its work. Wilberforce, who had written most of the letter, now read it out. It exhorted its readers to hold fast to all the canonical scriptures and issued a warning against papal pretensions and mariolatry. We must remind ourselves that it was the year 1867 and preparations were already in hand for the Vatican Council of 1870, when the doctrine of papal infallibility was to be promulgated. Indeed, a leader of *The Times* at the time of the Second Lambeth Conference of 1878 suggested that the 1867 Lambeth Conference had been called with the very purpose of voicing opposition to the forthcoming plans of Rome.[6] The encyclical had a reference to Christ dying 'to reconcile the Father to us', which was in accordance with the second article of the Thirty-nine Articles, but not in accordance with Pauline theology. Bishop Ewing of Argyll nearly refused to sign the encyclical because of this. At this same session the full Declaration was read and also approved.

On the next day, Friday, the last day of this hurried Conference, Bishop Wordsworth of St Andrews again tried to get through his proposition about Colenso. However, Longley quietened him. Then the encyclical was formally signed. I believe that this was the only Conference at which the encyclical was signed in this way by all the bishops present. Others not present were allowed also to sign it later. It was then realized that there were some items from the Archbishop's programme for Tuesday which had been omitted – regarding the setting up of new bishoprics and the question of letters commendatory for Anglicans passing from one province to another – and so resolutions on this were passed in a revised form. Bishop Jackson of Lincoln (who was later to succeed Tait as Bishop of London) now pointed out that the whole of Longley's programme for Thursday had not been touched. This subject and that of conflicting episcopal jurisdictions were thereupon handed over to yet another committee.

Then the question of whether the proceedings of the Conference should be published was discussed. Hopkins of Vermont wanted full publication. In the end it was decided not to publish, a decision which has affected every Lambeth Conference since, with the exception of the last in 1968. Bishop Gray of Capetown was still fuming over Colenso. While the bishops were preparing to leave, he unexpectedly brought up another resolution. This called upon the bishops to agree with a resolution made by Canterbury Convocation concerning the steps to be taken, *if* a new bishop were to be consecrated for Natal in place of Colenso. After a great row, this got through by 43 votes to 3. The three

[6] See *The Times*, 3 July 1878, p. 9, 'It was in anticipatory rivalry to the Vatican Council for which the invitations had already gone forth.'

against it were Thirlwall, Tait, and Sumner. The action of Gray made Tait boil with rage for the rest of the day. The Archbishop of Armagh (M. G. Beresford) as the senior bishop present after Canterbury (York being absent), moved a vote of thanks for the meeting. Selwyn, in seconding this, upbraided the Conference in a lengthy speech for not officially condemning the heretic Colenso and not organizing a general synod for the Anglican Communion. They were, he felt, altogether too Erastian. Yet, even so, he thought the Conference had been worth while and expressed a hope that Longley would live to summon another Conference. Bishop McIlvaine thought that the Conference should have said something about ritualism. The meeting concluded with the Nicene Creed and the Gloria in Excelsis, led by Bishop Talbot of Indiana, to a tune familiar in America but not so well known in this country. There followed the photograph, after which the bishops had to attend the conversazione at St James's Hall. They did not get there until five o'clock, although people had been awaiting them since three.

The closing service was held the next day at Lambeth Parish Church (the scene of Colenso's consecration). Bishop Fulford of Montreal preached, though the full text of his sermon has not survived. Ironically, Psalm 133 was sung, 'Behold, how joyful a thing it is: brethren, to dwell together in unity.'

The encyclical was soon published and many incumbents read it publicly in their churches. There followed the publication of the resolutions. The encyclical was sent to the Eastern Orthodox Church (the first official contact since the primacy of William Howley) and other communions. After this the various committees got to work. This meant some hard work for Bishop Ellicott of Gloucester, the secretary of the Conference, and Bishop Cotterill of Grahamstown, secretary of several committees. Gray, Selwyn, Fulford, and Tait of London all played a leading part in the committee work. The committee on the Final Court of Appeal was enlarged to include an American, Bishop Whitehouse of Illinois. This committee produced an elaborate scheme for such a tribunal, but nothing came of it. The committee on synodical government realizing that it was impossible yet to hold a pan-Anglican synod, reported as follows:

Under present circumstances, indeed, no Assembly that might be convened would be competent to enact canons of binding ecclesiastical authority on these different bodies [i.e. the provincial synods] or to frame definitions of faith which it would be obligatory on the Churches of the

Anglican Communion to accept. It would be necessary, therefore, in the judgement of your Committee, to avoid all terms respecting the Assembly that might imply authority of this nature, and to call it a Congress, if even the term Council should be considered open to objection. Its decisions could only possess the authority which might be derived from the moral weight of such united counsels and judgments, and from the voluntary acceptance of its conclusions by any of the Churches there represented. Your Committee consider that his Grace the Archbishop of Canterbury, as occupying the See from which the Colonial and American Churches derive their succession, should be the convener of such an Assembly. That it should differ from the present Conference in being attended by both Clerical and Lay representatives of the several Churches, as consultees and advisers, each Diocese being allowed to send, besides its Bishops, a presbyter and a lay member of the Church, if they should desire to be represented; and further, in the proceedings being more formal, and in part at least, public.

What was here advocated was a church congress for the whole Anglican Communion and not a Conference confined to the episcopate. In the event, the Lambeth Episcopal Conference has been repeated nine times. There have been but three Anglican congresses.

On 10 December the bishops, or such of them as had stayed behind, met again at Lambeth to receive the reports. These were received, directed to be published, and given to the careful consideration of the bishops of the Anglican Communion. The committee report on Natal was dealt with by a somewhat different formula. That report alluded to the fact that unofficially at the Conference fifty-six bishops had signed a document agreeing with Colenso's deposition.

So the First Lambeth Conference came to an end. What had happened? A meeting of the representatives from a large part of the Anglican Communion had met, but only episcopal representatives. The meeting had not been a pan-Anglican synod, even though it was referred to by that title in the newspapers – as, indeed, were those Conferences which followed in the nineteenth century. It had met in great secrecy and its proceedings had not been made public. There had been published an encyclical, resolutions, and committee reports. Thus was set the pattern for future Conferences. Every Conference except that of 1968 has issued an encyclical letter. There have always been plenary sessions, followed by committee sessions, then further plenary sessions. Committees, not envisaged when Longley drew up his programme, evolved at the first Conference, in the way we have seen and this pattern has been followed ever since.

It is important to note the atmosphere of hostility from the press in which the first Conference took place. *The Times* and *Punch* were especially antagonistic. This hostility of the press towards the Conference tended to be shared by Bishop Tait of London. When he left the 1867 Conference, it hardly seemed likely that he would wish to repeat the experiment. What, then, caused him to send out invitations to a second? To this subject we must now turn.

4

BETWEEN THE FIRST
AND SECOND CONFERENCES

Archbishop Charles Thomas Longley died in the year after his courageous call of the First Lambeth Conference, worn out by the deliberations of the Ritual Commission in the Jerusalem Chamber. Edward Carpenter writes in *Cantuar. The Archbishops in their Office*: 'His archiepiscopate is an interesting example of what can be achieved by an honest man without distinguished talents, who yet acts with courage and determination when a critical decision is imposed upon him.'[1] Samuel Wilberforce did not follow Longley to Canterbury.[2] Instead, in 1869, he was moved by Gladstone to Winchester, in succession to C. R. Sumner. However, he died in 1873 after falling from his horse; so, he, like Longley, vanishes from this story. Walter Kerr Hamilton, the one Tractarian bishop of the 1867 Conference, died in 1869, to be succeeded by the moderate High Churchman, George Moberly.[3] Robert Gray of Capetown died in 1874 and was succeeded by W. W. Jones.[4] So he, too, passes out of the story in which so far he has played a pretty considerable part. Francis Fulford of Montreal died in 1869, to be succeeded by Ashton Oxenden.[5] Bishop Alexander Ewing and Bishop Connop Thirlwall both died in 1874. Of the American bishops, John Henry Hopkins died in January 1868 and thus survived the Conference by a few months, Bishop C. P. M. McIlvaine of Ohio, the leader of the Evangelicals, died in 1873, and Henry John Whitehouse of Illinois in 1874.

One can see that half of the leading lights in the 1867 Lambeth Conference died before the next was summoned. Who remained? There was Tait, who in 1869 succeeded Longley at Canterbury, George

---

[1] Op. cit., p. 333.

[2] On this, see the recent life by Standish Meacham *Lord Bishop: The Life of Samuel Wilberforce 1805–72*.

[3] See *Dulce Domum, George Moberly, His Family and Friends* by C. A. E. Moberly.

[4] See M. H. M. Jones, *A Father in God William West Jones*.

[5] See A. Oxenden, *The History of My Life*.

Augustus Selwyn, who left New Zealand to be Bishop of Lichfield (in succession to John Lonsdale, who died immediately after the 1867 Conference), Charles Wordsworth, the Bishop of St Andrews (who lived to see two more Conferences), John Travers Lewis, Bishop of Ontario (who was to see three more Conferences), Edward Harold Browne, Bishop of Ely, who succeeded Wilberforce at Winchester in 1874, Charles James Ellicott, Bishop of Gloucester and Bristol, and Henry Cotterill, who left Grahamstown in 1872 to become Bishop of Edinburgh until 1886. John Jackson of Lincoln went to London in 1869 when Tait was translated to Canterbury. His successor at Lincoln was Christopher Wordsworth, who had played an important part in the background at the 1867 Conference. William Connor Magee, the Dean of Cork, succeeded the Evangelical Jerseyman, Francis Jeune, at Peterborough in 1869.[6]

Besides this change of personnel there were three notable events which made their impact in the years between the first and second Conferences. First, the Anglican Church in Ireland became disestablished. Disestablishment had been looming in the background as the First Conference took place, and in 1868 Longley had presided at a great meeting of protest against it. For the Roman Catholic Church the first Vatican Council took place in 1870. At this the Ultramontanes like Manning were in favour of the heightening of papal authority, while the more liberal leaders, Newman, Döllinger, and Dupanloup, were against it. The decree of papal infallibility was eventually passed. Those who refused to submit, like Döllinger, were excommunicated. The result was a growth of Old Catholics, with whom the Anglican bishops began to negotiate terms of union.[7] The third event of importance was the passing in Tait's primacy of the Public Worship Regulation Act of 1874. The seventies were a decade of ritualist controversy and it became assured that the subject of ritualism would come up at the next Lambeth Conference.

George Augustus Selwyn played the greatest part in bringing about the Second Lambeth Conference, but had the misfortune to die just before it assembled. Two other men who made a significant contribution towards its preparation were John Barrett Kerfoot, Bishop of Pittsburgh, who was present at the 1867 Conference and left an interesting account of it — although, as he himself played an insignificant part in it, his name has not yet been mentioned — and John Henry

[6] See J. C. Macdonnell, *Life and Correspondence of William Connor Magee.*
[7] On the Old Catholics, see C. B. Moss, *The Old Catholic Movement.*

Hopkins, Junior, who had accompanied his father to England in 1867 and written an account of the Conference in *The Church Journal*. In 1873 Hopkins wrote a full-length study of his father's life, in which a whole chapter treated the First Lambeth Conference and his father's complaints about it (which became his own) were given full play.[8] These complaints were mainly twofold – that the Conference was not a synod, and that it had been so secretive. This book, reviewed by William Benham in the *Guardian*, drew people's attention to the Conference anew and encouraged them to hope for another. A. J. Ross's *Memoir of Alexander Ewing* (1877) and Charles Gray's *Life of Robert Gray* (1876) both dealt with the First Lambeth Conference and played their part in preparing the way for a second Conference.

Undoubtedly the most important figure in the movement for a second Conference was Selwyn, Bishop of Lichfield, who was to have the task of convincing the Anglican Communion that the experiment was worth repeating. Tait, upon whom a great deal would hinge, was quite unlikely to take up the idea of his own accord, for he had never been enthusiastic about the Conference, and was especially annoyed by the actions of Bishop Gray and the anti-Erastian effusions of Bishop Selwyn. Would Selwyn succeed in swaying Tait? Selwyn had at the adjourned meeting of the First Lambeth Conference in December 1867 been appointed Corresponding Secretary of the whole Anglican Communion.[9] When, in 1871, he was invited to visit America and attend the General Convention of the Episcopal Church at Baltimore, he accepted with alacrity and thus became the first English diocesan bishop to visit American soil. Dean Howson of Chester, Prebendary E. J. Edwards of Trentham, in the diocese of Lichfield, and three other Lichfield clergymen went with him. The American bishops, who had returned home thankful that the First Lambeth Conference had taken place and that they had sat as equals with their British and colonial brothers, now gladly welcomed one of the stars of the Conference. Dr Venables, Bishop of Nassau, was also present at the Baltimore Convention. Selwyn had the honour of preaching at the consecration of William Bell White Howe as Assistant-Bishop of South Carolina. Part of the

---

[8] *Life of the late Right Reverend John Henry Hopkins, First Bishop of Vermont, and Seventh Presiding Bishop.*

[9] There is a two-volume life of Selwyn by H. W. Tucker. The life by G. H. Curteis is helpful on Selwyn's voyages to America and Canada. More recently there has appeared John H. Evans's *Churchman Militant. George Augustus Selwyn, Bishop of New Zealand and Lichfield.*

General Covention's proceedings were the jubilee celebrations of the Missionary Society of the American Church. On this occasion, Selwyn was introduced to the assembly by William Bacon Stevens, Bishop of Pennsylvania, who was, in due course, to attend the Second Lambeth Conference and write an account of it. On this occasion Selwyn gave a masterly address on missions.[10] But it was in his sermon before the General Convention that Selwyn directed attention to the subject of pan-Anglican organization, especially in relation to the dangers from ritualism. In the course of his Convention sermon he said:

> Every particular branch of the church hath authority to ordain and change ceremonies and rites of the church ordained only by man's authority, so that all things be done to edifying. It is the duty of all loving members of the Church of England to submit their own private opinion, in matters indifferent, to the judgment of their brethren; for truth of doctrine and fervency of devotion are best promoted when Christian men are seen to be of one heart and soul. There need be no servile uniformity, if there be but recognised authority which all are willing to obey. The whole of our church is interested in obtaining this happy combination of elastic freedom with efficient control. May we not hope that some central authority, elected and obeyed by every member of every branch of the whole Anglican Communion, may be appointed to exercise this power of controlling inordinate self-will, and zeal not tempered with discretion: saying to the too hasty minds, who claim as lawful, things which are not expedient, 'Thus far shalt thou go, and no further'.[11]

After preaching this sermon, Selwyn went into Canada for two days. But his idea of a central authority to control ritualistic activities made an impression upon Benjamin Bosworth Smith (a bishop not present at Lambeth in 1867), who had succeeded Hopkins as presiding bishop. Before Selwyn left New York, Bosworth Smith wrote to him a letter suggesting an Anglican 'Patriarchal Council' to which all branches of the Anglican Communion should send representatives – bishops, clergy, and laity. Smith said it should be held at Canterbury or Lambeth. At a farewell breakfast at New York Selwyn, quoting this letter, said, 'I hope the suggestion will be carried out in 1877, under the presidency of the Archbishop of Canterbury, who should be recognized by all the bishops of the Anglican Communion as virtually, if not

[10] See H. W. Tucker, *Life of Bishop Selwyn*, vol. ii, pp. 291–302.
[11] See *Sermon delivered before a General Convention of the Protestant Episcopal Church in the United States, Baltimore, October 4–26*, pp. 8–9, quoted by W. R. Curtis, *The Lambeth Conferences*, p. 202.

actually, patriarch.' He added that he always thought that the 1867 Conference had been the greatest event since the Reformation.[12]

The American church decided to mark Selwyn's visit by the presentation to the English church of an alms-dish. The English church had given such a dish to the American at Exeter College, Oxford, in 1852. The American gift was designed by John Henry Hopkins, Junior. It shows the Old World and the New and has the words 'The New World to the Old, the West to the East, the Daughter to the Mother'. Around it there is a band with the names of the six general councils. The amusing thing is that the alms-dish was presented to Archbishop Tait in St Paul's Cathedral on 3 July 1872, at the anniversary service of the S.P.G. by Bishop Selwyn and Bishop McIlvaine, the Evangelical Bishop of Ohio, who had fought so vigorously for the exclusion of the six general councils from the First Lambeth Conference Declaration! William Carus in his life of McIlvaine, quotes the bishop's description of the event:

> Yesterday I went to St Paul's – the Anniversary of the Society for the Propagation of the Gospel – when the beautiful Alms basin from our Church was to be presented. I had no expectation of being called to do anything, and so was there in common dress. Indeed, I did not bring my robes from home. But I might have borrowed a set. So I was sitting in the choir with the Bishops of Edinburgh [H. Cotterill] and Rupert's Land [R. Machray], when the Secretary of the Society for the Propagation of the Gospel [W. T. Bullock] came, and asked me to follow him to where the Bishops were. I found them all (i.e. of the Convocation) in scarlet robes. I was asked to take part with the Bishop of Lichfield in the presentation, and my plea of no robes did not avail to excuse me. It was done after the Ante-Communion, and just before the Offertory. The scene was striking, and the whole thing was well managed. I must confess, I felt it awkward to stand at the steps of the table in my common coat, amidst so many in scarlet. The Archbishop made a very happy address in reference to the presentation. You will see my name among the guests at the Lord Mayor's dinner; but I declined going – fatigued enough in the morning. The Archbishop said some kind things about me in his speech.[13]

[12] G. H. Curteis, *The Life of George Augustus Selwyn*, p. 306, in mentioning this incident, gets the name of the presiding bishop wrong. It was not Horatio Potter but Benjamin Bosworth Smith, for whom see *Dictionary of American Biography* and Henry Codman Potter, *Reminiscences of Bishops and Archbishops*. Smith had already suggested this graduated scheme of synods in his letter to Archbishop Longley before the First Lambeth Conference: see *Longley Letters*, vol. vi, p. 267.

[13] See W. Carus, *Memorials of Bishop McIlvaine*, pp. 324–5. See also W. Benham, *Catharine and Craufurd Tait*, p. 604, for this presentation.

1. The Alms Dish given by the American Church to the Archbishop of Canterbury (A. C. Tait) in St Paul's Cathedral in 1872

2. The bishops at the 1878 Conference, outside Lambeth Palace

At this time Christopher Wordsworth wrote a Latin poem thanking the American church for their gift. His poem and a translation are given in *A Champion of the Cross*, where there is a photograph of the dish, which is now in the safe keeping of the U.S.P.G.[14]

In the following year, 1872, Archbishop Tait spoke some favourable words about the 1867 Lambeth Conference in a charge to his clergy. That he should so have spoken after his criticism of the Conference was an encouraging sign, though he did not at this time give anyone to understand that he wished to repeat the experiment.

As the Canadian church took the first steps to summon the First Lambeth Conference, so it was with the Second. On 13 December 1872 the five Canadian bishops, A. Oxenden of Montreal, J. T. Lewis of Ontario, J. W. Williams of Quebec, A. N. Bethune of Toronto,[15] and J. Helmuth of Huron signed a document directed to the Archbishop of Canterbury, as President of the Canterbury Convocation, which read:

> We, the Bishops of the Ecclesiastical Province of Canada, availing ourselves of the opportunity afforded by the meeting of a Special Provincial Synod, desire that the following address touching the Lambeth Conference be forwarded by the Metropolitan to his Grace the President and to the Prolocutor of the Lower House of Convocation of the Province of Canterbury.
>
> We, the Bishops aforesaid, encouraged by the successful results of the address presented to his Grace the late Archbishop of Canterbury by the Provincial Synod of Canada, whereby the Lambeth Conference was convened, humbly and earnestly petition that the Convocation of Canterbury will take such action as may seem most expedient to unite with us in requesting the Archbishop of Canterbury to summon a second meeting of the Conference. We are persuaded that such meeting will be most efficacious in uniting the scattered branches of the Anglican communion, and in promoting an extension of the Kingdom of God throughout the world; and we, therefore, pray that it may be again convened at the earliest day that may suit the convenience of the Archbishop of Canterbury.
>
> A. Montreal (Metropolitan)   A. H. [*sic*] Toronto
> J. T. Ontario   J. Huron
> J. W. Quebec
> Montreal, December 13, 1872.[16]

The Canadians sent this petition to the Bishop of Lichfield, as a

---

[14] Wordsworth's poem without the translation is also given in H. W. Tucker, *Life of Bishop Selwyn*, vol. ii, p. 305.

[15] Lewis, Williams, and Bethune had all been at the First Lambeth Conference.

[16] See *Chronicle of Convocation*, 1873, p. 168.

sympathizer towards them and their views. Selwyn presented the petition in Convocation on 12 February 1873 but nothing further happened that day. On the next, however, he was able to speak about the matter at length and requested a joint committee to consider these four propositions:

(1) That the various branches of the Anglican communion throughout the world be invited to concur with the Convocation of the Province of Canterbury in requesting his Grace the Lord Archbishop of Canterbury to undertake an office, by whatever name it be called, equivalent to that of patriarch in the ancient Church.

(2) That in accordance with the petition of the Bishops of the ecclesiastical provinces (sic) of Canada, his Grace the Lord Archbishop of Canterbury be requested to convene a general conference of the Bishops of the Anglican communion, to carry on the work begun by the Lambeth Conference in 1867.

(3) That it seems to be expedient that the proposed general conference should be held in the year 1875, because the General Convention of the Episcopal Church of the United States, and the Synod of the Ecclesiastical Province of Canada, and the General Synod of the Anglican Church in New Zealand all hold their meetings in the year 1874.

(4) That the reports of Committees presented at the adjourned session of the Lambeth Conference, but not adopted or even discussed, be taken into consideration by the proposed general conference of the Anglican communion.[17]

Selwyn in a long speech supporting these proposals, pointed out the precarious situation of the Church in the colonies, which, by Privy Council judgements, was shown to be in no better or worse position than any other religious denomination. When letters patent were issued to colonial bishops, an oath of allegiance had been taken to the Archbishop of Canterbury. Now those letters patent were abolished. No law in the British Empire could compel a bishop to obey the Archbishop of Canterbury. Hence it was necessary to set up the Archbishop of Canterbury as officially head of this 'great Christian confederation'. He said:

We are sitting here comparatively at ease. We have laws, however imperfect; but the Colonial Churches look to us to supply them, not with a complete system, for in some respects their system is as complete as our own, but with a system that would prevent them from diverging so widely from the mother Church that we can scarcely recognise them as our own children. This is what the Colonial Church and the American Church desire.

[17] Idem.

He then went on to speak of his trip to America and the wish of Bishop Benjamin B. Smith for a decennial council of the Anglican episcopate. He also mentioned a visit to England in 1872 by Bishop Barker of Sydney to get the Privy Council to set up a final court of appeal 'for the express purpose of restraining the Church in his own province from those deviations from the English standard of doctrine, which he believed would certainly precipitate the separation of the two branches of the Anglican Church.'

The resolution was seconded by Bishop Wilberforce of Winchester, who made the additional suggestion that the Archbishop of Canterbury should first consult the Archbishop of York. The Church of Ireland, now disestablished, would also be interested in the subject, though they were passing through difficulties owing to the 'storm to which they had been subjected'. Selwyn agreed to this postponement of the question. At the same time Prebendary Edwards of Lichfield brought the subject of the document from Canada before the Lower House. But after this, nothing further was done until the following year.

On 29 April Selwyn brought forward the Canadian petition once again and announced that he had also received this petition from the bishops in the West Indies:

> The West Indian Bishops join in the request lately made to the Archbishop of Canterbury by the Bishops of the Canadian and Australian provinces, that he would summon another meeting of the Bishops of the Anglican communion throughout the world at as early a date as may seem to his Grace practicable and expedient.[18]

This West Indian request, signed by the bishops when assembled at Georgetown, Demerara (British Guiana), in 1873, indicates that the Australian bishops had also been memorializing the Archbishop of Canterbury. Selwyn said that he had not yet seen the Australian document, but he had received a communication again from Bishop Benjamin Smith in the U.S.A., asking what progress had been made towards calling another Lambeth Conference in 1875. Selwyn felt it imperative that a move be made. Now instead of his four resolutions of 1874 he submitted three, having altered the wording at the suggestion of Tait.

> 1 That the various branches of the Anglican communion throughout the world be invited to concur with the Convocation of Canterbury in considering what is the exact position that it is desirable the Archbishop

18 *Chronicle of Convocation*, 29 April 1874, pp. 73–4.

of Canterbury should hold in reference to the various branches of the Anglican communion scattered throughout the world.

2 That in accordance with the memorial of the Bishops of the Ecclesiastical Province of Canada, and the resolution of the Bishops of the West Indian dioceses, his Grace the Lord Archbishop of Canterbury be requested to convene a general conference of the Bishops of the Anglican Communion, to carry on the work begun by the Lambeth Conference in 1867.

3 That the reports of the Committees presented at the adjourned Session of the Lambeth Conference in 1867, but not adopted, or even discussed, be taken into consideration at the second conference proposed to be convened in the year   .[19]

Tait had got rid of the title 'patriarch' and had left the suggested date for the Conference blank. The suggested title of 'patriarch', however, was pressed for in Selwyn's speech. He also spoke at length on the need for a tribunal for the colonies to deal with doctrinal disputes. He also treated the question of the Lambeth Conference as a body which could state terms of union with such bodies as the Greek Church and the Old Catholics. The Old Catholic Congress at Cologne in 1872 had been attended by Bishop Browne of Winchester, Bishop Christopher Wordsworth of Lincoln, and Bishop William R. Whittingham of Maryland.[20] He also spoke about the Book of Common Prayer and indicated how the Lambeth Conference could control its revision and concluded, 'I am convinced that the time has come when the Anglican Communion must have a recognized head – a federal bond of union – and above all, a living voice to speak with authority for the Church. We know in whom the authority should reside, whatever the character and title of the head should be.'

Bishop Browne of Winchester seconded Selwyn's motion and supported his plea for a second Conference. He added:

Whether we should desire the Archbishop of Canterbury to become again an *alterius orbis Papa* may be a question; but I think there is no question that the whole Anglican communion is ready to acknowledge the Primacy of the Archbishop of Canterbury, his position as presiding Bishop of all the branches of that Church. I believe that even the Bishops of the American Church look to him as the Primate of the whole Anglican communion. Whether there will be any means by which all the different Metropolitans should distinctly hold themselves as subject to the Archbishop of Canterbury in the same manner that we do I cannot say. I do not think they

[19] *Chronicle of Convocation*, 29 April 1874, p. 74.
[20] See G. W. Kitchin, *Edward Harold Browne*, p. 409.

could. It is scarcely possible that we could expect all the Metropolitans and Bishops of all branches of the Anglican communion to acknowledge that obedience to the Archbishop of Canterbury which in former times was given to a Patriarch. But that is not necessary. An acknowledgement of readiness to act in a Synod presided over by the Archbishop should be quite enough.

Bishop Ellicott of Gloucester and Bristol then argued that the proposed Conference should not deal with matters of faith and quoted words of Archbishop Longley on the subject before the first Conference. Then Tait pointed out how two separate questions were being dealt with – the first was the question of another gathering of bishops at Lambeth; the second was that of the position of the Archbishop of Canterbury in relation to the various branches of the Anglican Communion. He pointed out that, though they had received requests from Canada and the West Indies for a repetition of the Lambeth Conference, those requests only came from the bishops. Whether, if the matter had been submitted to the full synod, and all the three orders had been consulted, they would have agreed with the request, he did not know, though he thought it likely that they would. He then referred to the first Conference and how Archbishop Longley had been careful to make clear the limited amount of authority which it possessed. The distinct rights of individual churches had to be kept in mind, and 'while a friendly council and gathering of all the Bishops of the Anglican communion may be productive of the greatest good, they must be very careful not to claim any power or authority beyond that which is willingly conceded to them by the several voluntary bodies whom they may represent.' In the end the proposition of Bishop Selwyn was agreed to. Then, on the motion of the Bishop of Gloucester and Bristol, seconded by the Bishop of London, it was agreed that some communication should take place with the Convocation of York and their opinion asked on the three propositions contained in the resolution.

In July 1874 a committee of Convocation was appointed to consider the matter of a pan-Anglican gathering. From the Lower House, Edward Bickersteth, the Prolocutor, Bishop M'Dougall, who had been present at the First Lambeth Conference as Bishop of Borneo and was now Archdeacon of the Isle of Wight, Dean Payne Smith of Canterbury, Bishop Mackenzie, Archdeacon and Bishop of Nottingham, Dr James Fraser (later Bishop of Manchester), Dr Gee, Dr Jebb, Mr Campion, Prebendary J. E. Edwards (who had gone with Selwyn to America), and Canon Perry, were all members. The episcopal members were Bishop Christopher Wordsworth of Lincoln (substituted for Jackson of London), Bishop Browne of Winchester, Bishop Ellicott of Gloucester, Bishop Selwyn of Lichfield, and Bishop Magee of Peterborough. This body met at the Bounty Office on 8 July. Two days later their report was ready. They expressed their opinion that 'the relation of the Archbishop of Canterbury to the other bishops of the Anglican Communion should be that of primate among archbishops, primates and bishops.' They recommended that the Archbishop of Canterbury should be respectfully requested to convene a 'general conference of the Bishops of the Anglican communion to carry on the work begun by the Lambeth Conference in 1867' and that this should be in 1876. They also requested that the 'reports of Committees presented at the adjourned Session of the Lambeth Conference in 1867, but not adopted or even discussed, be taken into consideration at the second conference.' In the discussion of the report, Bishop Christopher Wordsworth referred to the idea of giving the Archbishop of Canterbury the title of 'patriarch' and said that it had been objected to because it might seem to be setting up the Archbishop as a rival to the pope. Hence it had been dropped. The title of 'primate' seemed to be more generally acceptable. After this brief discussion, the Upper House of Canterbury Convocation communicated the report to the Lower House. However, 10 July was the last day of the session and the report was never discussed by the Lower House. The report was also communicated to the Convocation of York.

We must now pass from England to America again. For in September of this same year, 1874, Selwyn again went to America for the General Convention held at New York from 7 October to 3 November. Prior to this he went to Canada and paid a longer visit there than had been possible in 1871. Landing with his party at St John's, Newfoundland, from there he went to Halifax and then to Montreal, where he attended the Canadian Provincial Synod. This synod made suggestions to the Bishop of Lichfield about the proposed Second Lambeth Conference.

1 The year should be 1876.

2 There should be a session of a month. Four days in each week should be days of session, i.e. there should be two weeks of full sessions.

3 The Reports of 1867 should be considered.

4 Suggestions of subjects for discussion should be invited from the bishops.

5 The topics accepted for discussion should be made known in the invitatory letter.

After visiting Fredericton, Selwyn went on to New York for the General Convention. From Canada came the Bishops of Montreal and Quebec. The Bishop of Kingston, Jamaica (Reginald Courtenay), was also there. The English clergy present with Selwyn were Bishop Tozer (lately Bishop of Zanzibar), two clergymen from the diocese of Rochester, and Mr Hodson, the legal secretary to the Bishop of Lichfield. Selwyn and the two Canadian bishops brought up the subject of the Lambeth Conference in their addresses. It became clear in the House of Deputies that there was some strong feeling against a second Conference. When Dr Schenck, the clerical deputy for Long Island, suggested a resolution, 'That the House of Deputies respectfully submit for the consideration of the House of Bishops its cordial approbation in any measures that may be proposed by the Church of England for the reassembling of the Lambeth Conference in a second session', the Rev. Dr Paret of Central Pennsylvania wanted it amended to, 'That this House having received with deep interest the intimation given by the Lord Bishop of Lichfield of a probable call to a renewed Lambeth Conference, will, for action, wait definite information from the House of Bishops on the subject.' The Rev. Dr Rudder, of Pennsylvania, then moved that the whole matter be laid on the table. This motion, however, was severely defeated, so the discussion went on. Now the Rev. Dr Adam of Wisconsin offered another resolution:

> That we do hereby express our desire for the reassembling of the Lambeth Conference, and we hope that our Bishops, personally, may attend, according to the best of their judgments, and, while expressing their opinion, we hereby most solemnly and emphatically declare that the Church in the United States is not, in any sense, a member or a branch of the Anglican Communion; but is a sister Church, which, in one faith and belief, will be, in the future, the Church of the whole people of this great land, and we request the Bishops of our Church, to attend upon the Lambeth Conference, to take their stand distinctly upon this ground.

This resolution did not satisfy. Then a Texas clergyman, Benjamin A. Rogers, offered the following:

> That all exchange of friendly greetings; all evidence of the existence of the unity of the spirit in the bond of peace between the Church of England and the Protestant Episcopal Church in America, whether by Bishops in conference, or otherwise, are especially welcome to the Church.

This got through by 108 votes to 96.[21]

The bishops took action in the form of a resolution drawn up by Bishop Kerfoot of Pittsburgh and Bishop Horatio Potter of New York and signed by forty-two bishops, including the Presiding Bishop, Bosworth Smith. They said that they 'do most cordially express in their individual capacity their interest in the subject [of the Lambeth Conference] and their hope that his Grace the Archbishop of Canterbury will find it is consistent with his views of duty to take steps towards the assembling of such a conference.'[22] This resolution cannot be found in the printed minutes of the 1874 General Convention, and it seems clear that the bishops took this action in their private capacity. This was, doubtless, because of the trouble caused by the subject in the House of Deputies. Bishop Kerfoot, who had been to Europe in 1874 for the Bonn conference, explained in a letter to Archbishop Tait, written on 3 November (the last day of the Convention) that the *Life of Bishop Hopkins* had done harm.[23]

In addition to the *Life of Bishop Hopkins*, John Henry Hopkins, Jun., had also recently written an article on 'The Next Lambeth Conference' in the *American Quarterly Church Review* for July 1874. There he reiterated his criticisms of the Lambeth Conference of 1867. He criticized the shortness of the Conference, whose duration the Archbishop had limited in advance. Objecting to Longley's programme of business, he said, 'The programme was utterly swamped in the inconceivable imbecility of the original supposition that such an amount of such business could be transacted by such a body of men in four days.' He argued that the only thing they could do to save themselves was to produce the encyclical which had not been originally planned. He also upbraided the dead Longley for having made (as he thought) a compact with Thirlwall to keep the Colenso business out of the First Lambeth Conference. There followed an attack on the secrecy of the Conference and the non-publication of the minutes. Then he put forward certain propositions for the American church to accept — presumably at the then forthcoming General Convention.

That the proposed convening of another Lambeth Conference by the Archbishop of Canterbury is regarded as most desirable by the Church of

[21] See *Journal of the Proceedings of the Bishops, Clergy, and Laity of the Protestant Episcopal Church in the United States of America, assembled in a General Convention held in the city of New York, From Oct. 7th to Nov. 3rd, 1874*, pp. 45–9.

[22] See R. T. Davidson, *Lambeth Conferences of 1867 and 1878*, p. 106.

[23] See H. Harrison, *Life of Bishop Kerfoot*, vol. ii, pp. 584–5.

America; and that, in our opinion, the action of that august body will reach its highest conditions of usefulness to the Church at large, if it should please his Grace to include in the Letter of Invitation, among other points, the following:

1 That the clergy and laity of each organised diocese are requested to elect one clerical and one lay representative to take part in the Conference.

2 That when called for, the vote on any question should be taken by orders, nothing to stand as the act of the Conference unless carried by a majority of each of the three orders there present.

3 That no limits should be fixed in advance, with which the sessions should close; but that the Conference should be free to decide by their own vote the time of the adjournment.

4 That the full liberty of changing any programme of business by addition, alteration or omission as decided on in the meeting of 1867, should not be impeded or embarrassed by any 'private understanding' with only a portion of those invited; but that the subjects to be discussed and the decisions to be made thereon, should at all times be with free control of the Conference itself.

5 That all the sittings and debates of the Conference, from first to last, should be open to the public.

6 That a stenographic Report of the entire proceedings and debates should be made, and should be published as speedily as is consistent with accuracy.

7 That the published *Record* should be preceded in the same printed volume by the stenographic *Report* of the Conference of 1867, now in manuscript in the Library at Lambeth.

8 That no act of the Conference, at any meeting, should be binding upon any National or Colonial Church of the Anglican Communion, unless and until it be freely and expressly 'received', as such, in accordance with the forms of legislation provided by its own Constitution.

Though Hopkins's article had helped to stir up questioning about the advisability of a Second Lambeth Conference, these detailed suggestions of his were not taken up at the New York General Convention.

In February 1875 Archbishop Tait received support for the calling of a second Conference from the York Convocation. Archbishop Thomson, who had held aloof from the 1867 Conference, indicated that all the bishops had discussed the matter and that there had been an earnest desire to consult the feelings of all parties. He advised the Convocation to say that 'we shall have no objection, or indeed that we shall be glad, to see another Lambeth Conference in 1876. They should, however, say nothing on the subject of the jurisdiction of the

Archbishop of Canterbury and what title should be conferred upon him.' This was done.

In April 1875 we find Tait writing to Kerfoot. He had quite taken up the suggestion for a second Conference, but it could not be held in 1876, since that was the year of his visitation of Canterbury diocese. He suggested therefore 1877. Matters of doctrine and discipline already settled by our formularies should not be reopened, but be left to each separate church. On 7 June Tait wrote to the bishops as a whole in America in reply to the letter that had been signed by forty-two of them. He wrote this official letter, in the light of consultation with his brother bishops. He suggested that the Conference should be held in the summer of 1877. He realized that 1877 was the year of the next General Convention, but felt that if the Conference were held in July, the American bishops would be enabled to return in time for it. Then he spelt out what he had said to Kerfoot about matters of doctrine and discipline.[24]

Tait does not seem to have considered that it would have been rather burdensome for the American bishops to have both a Lambeth Conference and a General Convention in the same year. The Americans certainly did not want the year 1877 and it was decided to postpone it until 1878. On 28 March 1876 Archbishop Tait sent out a circular letter of inquiry to all bishops of the Anglican Communion. He wrote:

> Before I decide upon the important step of inviting the Bishops of our Communion throughout the world to assemble at Lambeth, I have thought it right, after consultation with the Bishops of England, to give all our brethren an opportunity of expressing their opinion upon the expediency of convening such a Conference at this time, and upon the choice of the subjects which ought to engage its attention, if it be convened.
>
> I therefore beg leave to intimate to you our readiness to hold a Conference at Lambeth in or about the month of July, 1878, if it shall seem expedient, after the opinions of all our brethren have been ascertained, and I need scarcely assure you that your advice is earnestly desired, and will be respectfully considered.[25]

This letter, in which Tait's hesitation is still exhibited, was sent to all bishops, through their metropolitans. Before the close of the year 1876 Tait had received ninety replies. These showed a preponderance of opinion in favour of the Conference, though, it must be noted, there

---

[24] See H. H. Harrison, *Life of Bishop Kerfoot*, vol. ii, p. 587.

[25] R. T. Davidson, *Lambeth Conferences of 1867 and 1878*, pp. 113f.

were objectors. In England, for instance, Bishop Baring of Durham, an Evangelical, was no more in favour of the 1878 Conference than of the 1867 one.

The bishops who replied indicated their desire for a longer period of Conference than the four days of 1867. Tait now took counsel with an episcopal committee and especially with Bishop Selwyn as to what subjects that had been suggested should in fact be discussed. On 10 July Tait sent out his official invitations. The Conference was to begin on 2 July 1878 and to last for four weeks. The subjects selected for discussion were six:

1 The best mode of maintaining union among the various Churches of the Anglican Communion.

2 Voluntary Boards of Arbitration for Churches in which such an arrangement may be applicable.

3 The relations to each other of Missionary Bishops and of Missionaries in various branches of the Anglican Communion acting in the same country.

4 The position of Anglican Chaplains and Chaplaincies on the Continent of Europe and elsewhere.

5 Modern forms of infidelity, and the best means of dealing with them.

6 The condition, progress, and needs of the various Churches of the Anglican Communion.[26]

Apart from subject 5 we have here the same ground as was covered in the 1867 Conference. It will be noted that there is no allusion to reunion or ritualism. This invitatory letter was again sent out via presiding bishops and metropolitans.

Now came two tragedies. On 17 July 1876, Craufurd Tait, the only son of the Archbishop, went to America with the invitations to the Conference for the bishops of the Episcopal Church. He was received with great friendliness by the American church and was present at the General Convention held at Boston in October. He returned to become incumbent of St John's, Notting Hill. Then sickness attacked him. He spent some time of his illness at Addington Park and then was moved to the Archbishop's private residence at Stonehouse. There he died towards the end of May 1878. It was a terrible blow to his father, for Craufurd was the apple of his eye.[27]

The other tragedy was the death of George Augustus Selwyn. He had, without question, been the main architect of the Second Lambeth

[26] See R. T. Davidson, *Lambeth Conferences of 1867 and 1878*, p. 116.
[27] See W. Benham, *Catharine and Craufurd Tait.*

Conference, but he died on 11 April 1878. Thus a gloom was cast over the Second Lambeth Conference. Then into the gloom came a scandal. William Benham, the friend of the late Archbishop Longley and now the friend of Archbishop Tait, had managed to borrow from Lambeth the records of the proceedings of the First Lambeth Conference and having copied them out very extensively proceeded to publish them without asking Tait's permission. History does not record what the reaction of Tait was and the whole business of the publication remains a great mystery. That Tait could not have been unduly annoyed with Benham is indicated by the fact that the Archbishop chose Benham to edit *Catharine and Craufurd Tait*. W. R. Curtis in *The Lambeth Conferences* says Benham's 'action was so mysterious that it was actually unexplainable because there is no way by which it can be explained.' He adds:

> The behavior of the *Guardian* in printing this account of the conference and Benham's letter to the Archbishop [which was published with it] is equally unexplainable. It made the affair all the more mysterious because the *Guardian* was the semi-official organ of the Church of England. Small wonder, then, that the decision that the proceedings should be private was decided upon for the Conference of 1878, as well as for all succeeding conferences![28]

[28] Op. cit., p. 220. The public were admitted for the first time in 1968.

5

ARCHBISHOP TAIT AND THE CONFERENCE OF 1878

In 1877 the Anglican episcopate numbered 173 bishops, of whom 108 accepted invitations to the Second Lambeth Conference. In the end it seems that 100 came, though, according to a transcript of the Conference at Lambeth, in one speech Tait referred to the number as 98. At this Conference only Tait signed the encyclical, so that one has no list of episcopal signatures to count.

There were three preliminary gatherings of the bishops before the Conference proper. One was at St Paul's Cathedral on 24 June for the consecration of W. D. Maclagan as Bishop of Lichfield, F. A. R. Cramer-Roberts as Bishop of Nassau, and G. H. Stanton as Bishop of North Queensland. On 27 June there took place in St Paul's the 177th Anniversary of the S.P.G. The third preliminary gathering was on Saturday, 29 June, and Sunday, 30 June, at Canterbury. The bishops were welcomed on St Peter's Day to St Augustine's, Canterbury, when the Bishop of Western New York (Cleveland Coxe) preached the sermon. In the afternoon Tait welcomed the bishops – between thirty and forty of them – in Canterbury Cathedral. On this occasion Tait spoke from the chair of St Augustine. In his address he made a touching allusion to the welcome given by the American church to his son Craufurd. The next day, Sunday, there were further sermons at Canterbury, from Bishop Oxenden of Montreal and Bishop William Bacon Stevens of Pennsylvania, who later wrote an account of the Conference.[1] Then on Tuesday, 2 July, the opening service of the Conference commenced in Lambeth Palace Chapel at 11 o'clock. As in 1867, there was a service of Holy Communion but in 1878 the Archbishop of York, who had held aloof in 1867, preached a sermon which Bishop Kerfoot described as a 'strong, solid, fit sermon'[2] on the

---

[1] See *The Lambeth Conference of 1878*. A Lecture delivered in the Church of the Holy Trinity, Philadelphia, 9 December 1878, by the Rt Rev. William Bacon Stevens (1879).

[2] H. Harrison, *Life of Bishop Kerfoot*, vol. ii, p. 590.

text Galatians 2.11, 'But when Peter was come to Antioch, I withstood him to the face because he was to be blamed.'[3] Kerfoot continued, 'When the one hundred bishops turned eastward and all said with one voice the Nicene Creed – the faith, the whole faith and naught else – it was very significant. Then we were all photographed in the quadrangle, though the painting from our photograph of 1867, in the hall, is not encouraging. . . . Archbishop Tait made some fun of several of us about our pictures.'[4]

At the 1867 Conference no black bishop was present. In 1878 one was there. This was Bishop Holly of Haiti from the American Episcopal Church, who was entertained at Westminster Deanery by Dean Stanley. We find Bishop James Fraser of Manchester, the very popular successor of the unpopular Prince Lee, writing to a friend:

> Stanley wished me to stay at the Deanery, to meet the 'Black Bishop' who (by the way) is a very bright-looking, intelligent, man, realizing (as Stanley said) the description of the Song of Solomon, 'I am black but comely'. But I said I could not consent to turn his house into an hotel; and he himself upon reflection, asked, 'Well, perhaps, it would be best if you are going to say anything at the Conference that it should not be known that you come from here!'[5]

Stanley was not asked to have anything to do with the Second Lambeth Conference and the final service was held at St Paul's, where Richard Church had succeeded Milman as Dean.

After lunch, the Conference began – not in the Guard Room as in 1867, but in the Old Library. Bishop Perry of Iowa, who wrote what Tait considered the best account of the Second Lambeth Conference, thus described the scene:

> The Primate's seat was placed at the end of the library hall, while on either side were the Archbishops of York, Armagh and Dublin. In front were the Primates of Scotland, the Metropolitans of Canada, Sydney, Christ Church (New Zealand), Capetown and Rupertsland, and the Senior Bishop of our own Church, who was first the Bishop of New York, Dr Potter and later the Bishop of Delaware, Dr Lee. At the Secretaries' table were the Bishop of Gloucester and Bristol, the learned Dr Ellicott, whose exegetical works are so well known throughout the Church, and the Bishop of Edinburgh, Dr Cotterill, also favourably known as an author, while the Lay Secretary, Dr

[3] The sermon is printed in R. T. Davidson, *The Lambeth Conferences of 1867, 1878, and 1888*, pp. 154–62.
[4] The painting made from the 1867 photograph perished in the Second World War.
[5] See J. W. Diggle, *The Lancashire Life of Bishop Fraser*, pp. 181–2.

Isambard Brunel, the Chancellor of the Diocese of Ely, with the short-hand reporters, occupied positions in the nearest alcove at the left. In front of the officers and occupying two-thirds of the length of the library, which is between ninety and a hundred feet in extent, with books of reference all around them, and tables for writing within easy access, sat the assembled Bishops, in all numbering thirty-five from England, nine from Ireland, seven from Scotland, nineteen of our own Church, including our colored brother of Haiti, ten from the British possessions at the north of us, three from India, four from the West Indies, three from Australia, two from New Zealand, five from South Africa, two from South America, and one from the shores of the Mediterranean.[6]

Of the English bishops only the two Evangelicals, Baring of Durham and Philpott of Worcester, stayed away, believing that even the calling of the Second Lambeth Conference was unwise. This opposition to the Second Lambeth Conference has been completely forgotten. It is worth noting that there was criticism of Tait for not inviting all the retired colonial bishops as Longley did in 1867. Only such bishops who were still acting as assistant bishops to English diocesans were invited. The office of suffragan bishop was not reconstituted until after the Second Lambeth Conference.[7]

After the Archbishop's opening address[8] the first item discussed was the question of privacy and publication. Bishop Lewis of Ontario brought this up on the Tuesday and the Bishop of Saskatchewan on the Wednesday. Tait said that they would follow the example of 1867. Archbishop Thomson of York moved that the shorthand reports be never published. This was carried. Bishop Browne of Winchester deplored the publication by Canon Benham of the account of the 1867 Conference in the *Guardian*.

Then, on this first day, the bishops got down to the discussion of 'The best mode of maintaining union among the various churches of the Anglican Communion'. The Bishop of Winchester opened the discussion and Bishop Perry of Iowa followed. The question of a Patriarchate of Canterbury was still very much in some people's minds – Bishop Browne of Winchester among them. Indeed, the *Guardian* for

[6] See William Stevens Perry, *The Second Lambeth Conference, A Personal Narrative*, pp. 25ff.

[7] John Walter Lea criticized Tait in the *Guardian*, 5 June 1878, p. 794.

[8] For this see R. T. Davidson and W. Benham, *Life of Archbishop Tait*, vol. ii, pp. 371–5. Bishop Bacon Stevens remarks, 'It was carefully prepared and thoughtful, touching upon the marked features of the Church and its needs, and was delivered with a gravity and unction which gave it power.'

19 June had contained a long letter on this subject from the Archdeacon of George, Cape of Good Hope. However, Bishop Nevill of Dunedin had come to the Conference with a determination to scotch the idea.[9] In the end the subject of 'Intercommunion' was handed over to a committee to deal with.

On Wednesday, the bishops discussed the question of voluntary boards of arbitration. The chief speakers were Bishop Barker of Sydney, Bishop Cotterill of Edinburgh, and the Bishop of Christ Church, New Zealand. Apart from Bishop Lee of Delaware, the Americans took no part in the debate, because they felt that under no circumstance would their church consent to having their decisions revised by any foreign ecclesiastical court. However, they appreciated that the colonial bishops needed some court of arbitration. In the end, the subject was delegated to a committee of colonial and English bishops. In the afternoon, the bishops dealt with 'The relations to each other of missionary bishops and of missionaries in the various branches of the Anglican Communion acting in the same country'. Bishop Bedell of Ohio and Bishop Schereschewsky of Shanghai spoke on the subject. The territories concerned were Japan, China, and West Africa, where English and American missionaries were both at work. The Bishop of Colombo, Ceylon (Copleston), also spoke. He was having trouble with C.M.S. missionaries in Ceylon, who were proving not very amenable to episcopal jurisdiction. In the end this matter was referred to another committee.

On Thursday morning, the bishops turned to the subject, 'The position of Anglican Chaplaincies on the Continent of Europe', which was introduced by Bishop Jackson of London, who had jurisdiction over all English chaplaincies on the Continent, except those in the diocese of Gibraltar. Bishop Littlejohn of Long Island, the American bishop in charge of U.S.A. chaplaincies, spoke, as also did the Assistant Bishop of North Carolina (Lyman). Again the matter was handed over to a committee. On Thursday afternoon came the most interesting debate of all, on 'Modern Forms of Infidelity and the best means of dealing with them'. Archbishop Thomson had been expected to open this debate, but now declined, and so Bishop Bedell of Ohio introduced the subject. No other American took part in the discussion, but among the other speakers were Magee of Peterborough, Wordsworth of Lincoln, Mackarness of Oxford, Ellicott of Gloucester, and Browne of

[9] This is apparent from his diary. I have seen a Xerox copy of the part which deals with the 1878 Conference, but his memories are confused.

Winchester. The Archbishop of York made a contribution towards the end. Bishop Kerfoot of Pittsburgh was much impressed by the afternoon's doings. 'The Conference today – chiefly this afternoon – was the grandest time of debate any of us ever knew. The topic was "The Modern Forms of Unbelief and How to meet them". Grand, strong addresses came from the bishops of Ohio, Killaloe, Peterborough, Lincoln, Oxford, Montreal, Gloucester, Winchester, Llandaff, and the Archbishop of York. Such brains and heart! This one afternoon was well worth the voyage. Archbishop Tait adopts my suggestion to have the speeches put in print from the shorthand writer's report. The papers would be worthy of the Conference.'[10] Nothing, however, came of this suggestion. Again a committee was appointed to continue the discussion and it had the most difficult task of all.

On Friday, 7 July, both morning and evening saw a discussion on 'The Condition, Progress and Needs of the various Churches of the Anglican Communion'. This subject was introduced by the Bishop of Delaware. A large number of bishops took part in the discussion.[11] An influential committee, comprising the Bishops of Lincoln, Manchester, Barbados, and others, was appointed, under the chairmanship of Archbishop Tait, 'to receive questions submitted in writing by bishops desiring the advice of the conference on difficulties or problems they have met with in their several dioceses'.

Now the committees got down to work. They met at Lambeth, Fulham, Farnham, and elsewhere. The committee last appointed met daily at Lambeth under Tait and dealt with the question of the Old Catholics and other churchmen on the Continent of Europe, who had renounced their allegiance to the pope. This was a question in which Bishop Christopher Wordsworth of Lincoln was greatly interested and it was doubtless he, as a member of the committee, who brought up the subject. They also treated the question of applications for inter-communion with the Anglican Communion from persons connected with the Armenian Church and other Christian communities in the East; the position of Moravian ministers within the territorial limits of the Anglican Communion; the West Indian dioceses; the Church of

[10] H. Harrison, *Life of Bishop Kerfoot*, vol. ii, pp. 591f.

[11] The *Guardian*, 10 July 1878, p. 964, mentions the Archbishops of Canterbury, York, Armagh, the Metropolitans of Sydney, Cape Town, and Rupertsland, and the Bishops of Moray and Ross, London, Lincoln, Winchester, Gloucester and Bristol, Ripon, Salisbury, Chichester, Oxford, Down, Meath, Brechin, Kingston, Niagara, Saskatchewan, Fredericton, Adelaide, Barbados, Nova Scotia, Iowa, Pittsburgh, Ohio, Central Pennsylvania, and Albany.

Haiti; local peculiarities regarding the law of marriage; a board of reference for matters relating to foreign missions; and difficulties arising in the Church of England over ritual and confession.

While the Committees were meeting there were also various social engagements. The Lord Mayor of London held a banquet for the bishops in the Egyptian Hall of the Mansion House. There were garden parties at Fulham, Kensington Palace, and Westminster. There were conversaziones at Westminster Palace Hotel and King's College. On Sundays the bishops preached in various churches.[12]

The bishops assembled again on Monday, 22 July – not, as originally intended on Tuesday, 23 July. That Monday was devoted to the colonial bishops, who were given an opportunity to represent, in detail, the conditions, peculiarities, and needs of their dioceses. Then from Tuesday until Friday the Conference dealt with the committee reports. A great deal of discussion took place on the possibility of an encyclical. Christopher Wordsworth spoke of the great value of the 1867 encyclical. Magee of Peterborough and Thomson of York opposed the idea. At one point Thomson said emphatically that he would not sign any encyclical. As it turned out, he was not called upon to do so, as the encyclical was signed only by Tait and the reports of the committees were embodied in it. Let us look at the main points in these reports.

The committee on the best mode of maintaining union among the various churches of the Anglican Communion gave a definition of the Anglican Communion which was of value. On the question of an Anglican synod it spoke thus:

[12] Details of these events are given in the *Guardian*, in George Thurston Bedell's *The Canterbury Pilgrimage*, and in Perry's *The Second Lambeth Conference*. Perry has a neat summary of this entertainment: 'The interim before the re-assembling of the Conference for its final session, which extended from the 22nd to the 26th July, inclusive, together with the unused hours of the days of meeting themselves, were largely given to social entertainments, in which the unbounded hospitality of our English hosts knew no stint. Breakfasts at Lord Cranbrooke's, to meet the Duke of Richmond and Gordon, Earl Beauchamp, and others; at the Rt Hon. J. E. Hubbard's, to meet the Archbishops and Bishops; at Mr Beresford Hope's, a brother-in-law of Lord Salisbury, to meet several of the nobility and Bishops; dinners at the Archbishops of Canterbury and Armagh, at the Bishops of London, Ely, and others, at the Lord Mayor's, in the celebrated Egyptian Hall of the Mansion House, at the "Charterhouse", where we were most kindly entertained throughout the Conference by its learned master, Dr. Currey; garden parties at Fulham and Kensington Palaces, at Mr John Murray's, the celebrated publisher, at the Dean of Westminster, Dr. Stanley's; evenings at the Baroness Burdett Coutts', the Bishop of Gloucester and Bristol, Dr. Ellicott's, and others; conversaziones at the Westminster Palace Hotel and King's College, were among those I especially recall.' (pp. 28f.)

The assembling, however, of a true General Council, such as the Church of England has always declared her readiness to resort to, is, in the present condition of Christendom, unhappily but obviously impossible. The difficulties attending the assembling of a Synod of all the Anglican Churches, though different in character and less serious in nature, seem to us nevertheless too great to allow of our recommending it for present adoption.

However, the Committee favoured the continuation of the Lambeth Conference:

The experiment now tried twice, of a Conference of Bishops called together by the Archbishop of Canterbury, and meeting under his presidency, offers at least the hope that the problem, hitherto unsolved, of combining together for consultation representatives of Churches so differently situated and administered, may find, in the providential course of events, its own solution.[13]

The Report suggested that such conferences 'might with advantage be invested in future with somewhat larger liberty as to initiation and selection of subjects for discussion'.

The report on voluntary boards of arbitration was dealt with next. This did not recommend any central tribunal, but held that any province which desired to provide for an appeal should itself determine the conditions of reference, and only in the case of isolated dioceses should there be an appeal to Canterbury, when the case should be heard by five metropolitans or chief bishops, of whom the Archbishop of Canterbury should be one. The committee on missionary jurisdiction dealt, among other things, with the problem in Ceylon and reported that every missionary, whether appointed by a Society or not, should be obliged to obtain a licence from the bishop, but that, if a bishop refused a licence, he should state his reasons to the metropolitan.

There was a report on Anglican chaplains and chaplaincies incorporated in the encyclical, but there was no report on 'Modern Forms of Infidelity'. It is clear from the documents at Lambeth that there had been some failure on the part of the committee to agree on a final report. Archbishop Benson, who was present in 1878 as Bishop of Truro, declared as Archbishop of Canterbury in his opening address at the 1888 Conference that the discussion on infidelity was the most fruitful and stimulating of all the debates in 1878, and this is borne out by the already quoted remarks of Kerfoot. In view of the disagreement over the report it was decided 'that the main object had been served by

[13] R. T. Davidson, *The Lambeth Conferences of 1867 and 1878*, p. 120.

the interchange of opinion and that the time was inadequate and the subject too wide for the acceptance of a formal report'.

Archbishop Tait's committee in their report had something to say about the Church of Rome, and the Vatican Council of 1870. 'The fact that a solemn protest is raised in so many Churches and Christian communities throughout the world against the usurpations of the See of Rome and against the novel doctrines promulgated by its authority, is a subject of thankfulness to Almighty God.' The reference was of course to the decree of papal infallibility. 'It is therefore our duty to warn the faithful that the act done by the Bishop of Rome, in the Vatican Council, in the year 1870 — whereby he asserted a supremacy over all men in matters of faith and morals, on the ground of assumed infallibility — was an invasion of the attributes of the Lord Jesus Christ.'[14] The committee recommended certain steps for the organization of the Church in the West Indies into a province. The report also welcomed the formation of part of the Anglican Communion in Haiti. The report did not say anything specifically about the Old Catholics and Moravians but recommended that the Archbishops of England and Ireland, the Primus of Scotland, the Presiding Bishop of the American Church, the American bishop responsible for the citizens of the U.S.A. in Europe, and the Bishop of Gibraltar, should act and give advice on definite cases. The committee on chaplains in Europe noted the existence of 'the Spanish and Portuguese Episcopal Church', which had come into being in 1871 and whose birth was largely due to the Anglo-Continental Society. A similar movement of reform had taken place in Mexico. The Committee now therefore referred to a request from the Spanish and Portuguese church for the consecration of a bishop and they expressed their hearty sympathy with them in the difficulties of their position. They suggested that as the American church was about to extend the episcopate to the church in Mexico, perhaps the bishop consecrated for Mexico might be able to visit Spain and Portugal. This approval of the suggestion of a bishop in Mexico was followed by the consecration of Dr H. C. Riley as Bishop of the Mexican Church.[15]

On the Thursday and Friday of the Conference the question of ritual, which had been brought before Tait's committee, was discussed. The two English Archbishops, who wanted something said upon the subject,

[14] Randall Davidson, *Origin and History of the Lambeth Conferences 1867 and 1878*, pp. 135–6.

[15] See W. R. Curtis, *The Lambeth Conferences*, pp. 272–3.

had managed to get it into the report. It is pretty clear that the debate on the subject was acrimonious. Bishop James Fraser alluded to it in a letter to his wife:

> Last night the discussion being on the question of Ritual and Confession the clouds were dark indeed, and there was a very threatening appearance of a storm; but it seemed as though God had breathed a calm spirit upon us all this morning, and, partly, by moderate demands on one side and prudent concessions on the other, we at last agreed unanimously – or rather I should say with only two dissentients – to a conclusion quite strong on both these questions for the purpose of bringing back by any influences, the extravagances of our younger men within the sober limits of the Church of England.[16]

The two dissentients seem to have been the Bishop of Bombay (L. G. Mylne) and the Bishop of Colombo (R. S. Copleston).[17] The Bishop of Peterborough, Magee, though a Protestant, also disliked the first draft of the report and opposed it keenly. He also wrote an account of these last two days of the Conference which is very vivid.

ATHENAEUM, July 26, 1878.

While the impression is fresh in my mind, let me tell you of the closing scenes of the Pan-Anglican – 'nothing in its life became it like leaving it.' It was very happy and very solemn. We broke up last night 'in most admired disorder'. A certain Report on Ritualism and Confession, on which Cantuar had set his heart, as I told you, had been very unfavourably received. American, Scotch, and Irish Bishops rose one after the other to repudiate it. The Archbishops of York and Cantuar advocated it strongly, almost angrily. Everything portended a stormy close to our session today. I went down with a heavy heart, hating to oppose the Archbishop in his sorrow, and yet angry with him for introducing a subject which he certainly had no right to introduce, and resolved to oppose him. His opening speech was powerful, but not conciliatory. All looked black as night. But when the report, amended after last night's discussion, was read, the scene changed as by magic. Much, if not all, that was objected to had vanished, and the whole report bore tokens of an anxious desire to meet the objections of the Conference. One by one the recalcitrants showed signs of giving way; and at last I, who had led them, rose and gave way in my adhesion, subject to one or two verbal alterations. Soon all was peace, or nearly so; and at last a very

---

[16] See J. W. Diggle, *The Lancashire Life of Bishop Fraser*, p. 183.

[17] W. Bacon Stevens remarks in *The Lambeth Conference of 1878*, p. 40, about the two 'negative votes', but does not say who voted in the negative. The *Guardian*, 31 July, p. 1071, indicates that it was Bombay and Colombo. See also J. C. Macdonnell, *Life of Archbishop Magee*, vol. ii, p. 96.

plain and strong condemnation of ultra-Ritualism and the Confessional was carried, with but *two* dissentients, out of more than eighty bishops! After that all went well, and there was really a marked spirit of self-surrender and love that quite impressed us all as seeming to overmaster us, and that led us to all but unanimous resolve. I do not think it presumptuous to say, I certainly felt, that we were being overruled for good.[18]

What then were the resolutions which were passed and which brought such calm? On ritual the bishops said that 'no alteration from long-accustomed ritual should be made contrary to the admonition of the Bishop of the Diocese'. On Confession they said that:

no minister of the Church is authorised to require from those who may resort to him to open their grief a particular or detailed enumeration of all their sins, or to enjoin or even encourage the practice of habitual confession to a Priest, or to teach that such a practice of habitual confession, or being subject to what has been termed the direction of a Priest, is a condition of attaining to the highest spiritual life. At the same time your Committee are not to be understood as desiring to limit in any way the provision made in the Book of Common Prayer for the relief of troubled consciences.[19]

Dr Pusey was very disturbed when in due course he read this resolution and immediately set to work to write his pamphlet, *Habitual Confession not discouraged by the Resolution accepted by the Lambeth Conference.*[20]

The conclusion of the business part of the Conference is again well described by Magee. 'The session' he said

lasted until seven in the evening, marred a little towards the end by those crude and unreasonable proposals which always break out at the close of every session of public bodies, when crochets are led out in a kind of half despair by those who feel that it is now or never with them. Lincoln, as usual, was inopportune and mischievous in the most saintly way.[21] But it was soon

---

[18] J. C. Macdonnell, *Life of Archbishop Magee*, vol. ii, pp. 94–5.

[19] See R. T. Davidson, *Lambeth Conferences of 1867 and 1878*, p. 140.

[20] See H. P. Liddon, *Life of Edward Bouverie Pusey*, vol. iv, pp. 312ff. which gives Pusey's discussions with Tait over the resolution.

[21] Wordsworth had (as is clear from the Lambeth records) planned an encyclical and penned it. Magee refers to this (see p. 96): 'By yielding too, I secured from the two Archbishops their refusal to join in a preposterous "Encyclical" which old Lincoln was pressing upon us as the panacea for all troubles. A heap of sweetly solemn platitudes, such as he alone can indite, and such as he alone believes can be of the slightest use to man, woman or child. Thank God, my declaration that nothing would induce me to sign an Encyclic backed up as it was by other English bishops, secured us this: and now, on the whole, as I have said, we have come well out of the whole matter.'

over with him, and then came the end. The Archbishops of York and Armagh, the Primus of Scotland, and the senior American bishops rose in succession to propose thanks to the Archbishop. Nothing could have been in better taste, or more really touching and dignified, than their speeches. The Archbishop was too much moved to reply by more than one simple sentence of thanks. Then came the 'Gloria in Excelsis', sung by the bishops, and then the Benediction; and so we parted, not all of us, certainly, to meet again in this world, and all of us feeling that this was so, and yet happy that we had met.

And so ended the Pan-Anglican.

Tomorrow's service will be its apotheosis. Tonight was its peaceful departure.[22]

On Saturday 27 July, the Conference ended officially with a great service in St Paul's Cathedral when the sermon was preached by Bishop W. Bacon Stevens, who had, according to Kerfoot, been chosen out of their number by the Americans.[23] Bishop Fraser was a little critical of it:

The sermon, by the Bishop of Pennsylvania, was very unequal; parts of it were in the true American 'spread-eagle' style; parts were very eloquent, simple and pathetic. There was a considerable sprinkling of such phrases as 'blood bought earnestness' which to me are always offensive and nearly meaningless; and what were meant to be, perhaps, the finest parts of the sermon were to my mind the weakest. Still, on the whole, the effect was good; and the manner was less strained than the manner of American preachers is apt to be.[24]

The English bishops seemed to have been impressed by the Americans. Fraser remarked, 'The Bishops who were present were very good specimens of the American episcopacy, and have left a very good impression behind them. I think also they will carry pleasant impressions back with them, for they have received a good deal of attention, which they appeared warmly to appreciate.'[25] Magee said, 'My opinion of these Americans is greatly raised by the conference. They are, for the most part, shrewd, able, ready and right-minded men. The Colonials, on the other hand, were not nearly up to this mark. The difference was marked and instructive.'[26] It was evident that the colonial bishops who had made the greatest impression were Bishop Oxenden

22 J. C. Macdonnell, *Archbishop Magee*, vol. ii, p. 95.
23 H. Harrison, *Life of Bishop Kerfoot*, vol. ii, p. 600.
24 See J. W. Diggle, *The Lancashire Life of Bishop Fraser*, p. 185.
25 J. W. Diggle, *The Lancashire Life of Bishop Fraser*.
26 J. C. Macdonnell, *Archbishop Magee*, vol. ii, p. 96.

of Montreal,[27] Bishop Harper of Christ Church, New Zealand,[28] Bishop Barker of Sydney,[29] and Bishop William West Jones, the successor of Gray at Capetown.[30]

There can be little doubt that Tait's reputation was enhanced by his handling of the Conference. Bishop Perry said that:

> the Archbishop's presidency was above praise. While avoiding all appearance of dictation, his presence and position were always felt; and the harmony and unanimity of the Conference were largely due to his uniform affability and good temper and his masterly leadership. One was proud to recognise in the foremost man of the Anglican Episcopate a Bishop who felt that the dignity of his lawn was by no means compromised by preaching in the open air to the crowds in Covent Garden market, or to the cabmen in a stable yard at Islington, or to the weavers of Bethnal Green.[31]

For a concluding estimate of the Conference we may turn once again to a passage of Archbishop Magee:

> Altogether, I feel that I have learned much from this Pan-Anglican, and I see too, that it is really an institution which will root itself and grow, and will, in all human probability, exercise a powerful influence in the future of the Anglican Communion. This is a good deal to say on the part of one who greatly disliked and dreaded the whole affair at the first.[32]

The Conference had been marred for Tait by the death of his son Craufurd. Before the year was out Catharine Tait, who had looked after her guests so well, was herself dead. The impression that Catharine had made upon the Americans is evident in Benham's *Catharine and Craufurd Tait*:

> The Bishop of Louisiana, Dr Wilmer, of whose sweet aged face many of us retain so happy a recollection, was staying at Lambeth, and was impressed in these last days of her life, as other friends had been in the days of her youth, with Mrs Tait's unfailing desire to make religion the very essence of her daily life. 'I delight,' he said to a Church dignitary, from whom I received it, 'in my stay with these people. From the early service in the morning to the late prayers at night, life seems always in God's presence.' Another American prelate, as he watched her unflagging courtesy, as she ministered – pale

[27] See Ashton Oxenden, *The History of My Life*.
[28] See H. T. Purchas, *Bishop Harper and the Canterbury Settlement*.
[29] See W. M. Cowper, *The Episcopate of the Rt. Rev. Frederick Barker, Bishop of Sydney and Metropolitan of Australia*.
[30] See M. H. M. Wood, *A Father in God The Episcopate of William West Jones*.
[31] *The Second Lambeth Conference*, pp. 31–2.
[32] J. C. Macdonnell, *Archbishop Magee*, vol. ii, pp. 96–7.

and sorrow-stricken – to the multitude of guests, remarked that he could scarcely believe that such fortitude and self-constraint were possible. They were only so by an effort too great for heart and brain. Her mind was steadfastly set upon the world unseen from which her thoughts now never wandered. Yet on the evening before he left Lambeth Bishop Wilmer sat beside Mrs Tait at dinner. He spoke of the deep pleasure he had received by his visit, and of the improbability of his ever seeing England again. 'I hope it may be otherwise,' said Mrs Tait, 'and that we may, if it please God, meet in ten years at this table,' 'No', said the Bishop, 'possibly my brother here,' turning to the Bishop of Nebraska, 'but not I'.[33] And so they parted. And on the selfsame day, she in Edinburgh, he in America, passed away, to meet again in the sanctuary and presence above.[34]

Mrs Tait died at the age of 59 on 3 December, but at least she lived to see her daughter Edith married to the Archbishop's chaplain, Randall Thomas Davidson.

[33] The Bishop of Nebraska was Robert Harper Clarkson, for whom and for Bishop Joseph Pere Bell Wilmer, see Henry Codman Potter, *Reminiscences of Bishops and Archbishops*.

[34] W. Benham, *Catharine and Craufurd Tait*, pp. 600–1.

6

ARCHBISHOP BENSON AND
THE CONFERENCE OF 1888

Archbishop Campbell Tait died on 3 December 1882, three weeks before his seventy-first birthday. A number of names were mentioned as possible successors, Harold Browne of Winchester (72), J. B. Lightfoot of Durham (54), E. W. Benson of Truro (53), and Dean Church of St Paul's (67). In the end, thanks to Randall Davidson, Edward White Benson was selected. He was a High Churchman, keenly interested in synodical government and the see of Canterbury, and hence naturally bent on calling a Third Lambeth Conference. He had already, as a fresh recruit to the episcopal benches, participated in the Second of 1878.

In the Third Lambeth Conference requests to the Archbishop of Canterbury for an episcopal meeting from the colonies or the U.S.A. played no part at all. Instead, in July 1886, Archbishop Benson gave notice of his intention of holding another Lambeth Conference in July 1888, exactly ten years after the Second. Bishop C. J. Ellicott was to be episcopal secretary and Randall Davidson his assistant. Davidson, who was to be connected with five Lambeth Conferences, had been selected as Dean of Windsor in May 1883, having before that continued acting as chaplain to Benson in the way he had done to Tait. The two men worked well together.

In November 1887, Benson sent out his invitations to the Conference:

> In accordance with the precedent of 1878, it has been arranged that the Conference shall assemble on Tuesday, July 3rd, 1888. After four days' session there will be an adjournment, in order that the various Committees appointed by the Conference may have opportunity of deliberation. The Conference will re-assemble on Monday, July 23rd, or Tuesday, July 24th, and will conclude its session on Friday, July 27th.[1]

He said that the various suggestions for topics of discussion had been

---

[1] *The Lambeth Conferences of 1867, 1878, and 1888*, pp. 36–7.

weighed by himself and other bishops in the preparatory committee. He then submitted the programme of subjects for discussion.

1 The Church's practical work in relation to (A) Intemperance, (B) Purity, (C) Care of emigrants, (D) Socialism.

2 Definite teaching of the faith to various classes, and the means thereto.

3 The Anglican Communion in relation to the Eastern Churches, to the Scandinavian and other Reformed Churches, to the Old Catholics, and others.

4 Polygamy of heathen converts. Divorce.

5 Authoritative standards of doctrine and worship.

6 Mutual relations of dioceses and branches of the Anglican Communion.[2]

It will be seen how the agenda had been considerably broadened compared with the two previous Conferences. Social and practical questions were much to the fore.

Benson sent out no less than 211 invitations – 38 more than were sent out by Tait. There were 147 acceptances, though the final number of those who attended was 145, which was 45 more than came in 1878. The losses in the episcopate between the Second and Third Conferences were not so great as those between the First and the Second, but are worth noting. Bishop Christopher Wordsworth of Lincoln had been succeeded by the saintly Edward King. Bishop James Fraser of Manchester had been succeeded by James Moorhouse, who had previously been Bishop of Melbourne.[3] The industrious Bishop Cotterill, who had done so much in the First and Second Lambeth Conferences had passed on, as also had Bishop Kerfoot of Pittsburgh, whose biography contains such fascinating accounts of his visits to England for the first two Conferences. Some great names had made their appearance on the episcopal bench. Joseph Barber Lightfoot had succeeded Baring at Durham in 1879.[4] William Stubbs had succeeded William Jacobson at Chester in 1884.[5] John Wordsworth, the very erudite son of that very erudite father, Christopher Wordsworth, had succeeded George Moberly at Salisbury in 1885.[6] Frederick Temple

---

[2] R. T. Davidson, *The Lambeth Conferences of 1867, 1878, and 1888*, p. 37

[3] See Edith Rickards, *Bishop Moorhouse.*

[4] See G. R. Eden and F. C. Macdonald, *Lightfoot of Durham.*

[5] See W. H. Hutton, *Life of William Stubbs, Bishop of Oxford.* Stubbs succeeded Mackarness at Oxford in 1889, the year after the Lambeth Conference.

[6] See E. W. Watson, *Life of Bishop John Wordsworth.*

had moved from Exeter to London in 1885, in succession to John Jackson.[7] William Dalrymple Maclagan, who in 1878 had been present as the newly consecrated Bishop of Lichfield, was still bishop there and Thomson was still Archbishop of York and Magee Bishop of Peterborough.[8] At the 1888 Conference Samuel Adjai Crowther, the first black bishop of the Anglican Communion was present. He had been invited to the first and the second but prevented from attending.

Part of the background of the Conference was the threatened prosecution of Edward King for ritualistic practices by the Church Association. The famous Lincoln Judgement, for which Benson received so much praise, came about two years after Lambeth. But the trouble was already beginning.

Proceedings began on Saturday, 30 June, at Canterbury, but many of the bishops were present at the St Peter's day celebrations at St Augustine's College, on the previous day, when the original dedication of the College on St Peter's day, 1848, was commemorated. An elaborate account of the proceedings was written again by Bishop Perry of Iowa.[9] St Augustine's College welcomed the bishops who were able to be present, including Bishop Medley of Fredericton, who had been present in 1848. It was he who preached the sermon. Perry describes the scene on the following day:

A special train brought the Bishops from the Victoria Station, London, and on the way there were many most pleasant meetings of long-separated friends. At noon the end of the pilgrimage was reached, and in a few moments we found ourselves, with Mrs and Miss Benson, driving through the narrow streets of Canterbury to the great gate of the old Abbey of St Augustine, through which were passing Bishops, Deans, and ecclesiastical dignitaries, with other noted guests assembled from all quarters of the world.

Among the visiting prelates, the Oriental Bishop, Mar Gregorius, Bishop of Homs, the ancient Edessa, and representing the Patriarch of Antioch, was conspicuous in his quaint head-gear and long, flowing robes.[10]

Lunch took place in the Hall of St Augustine's College, then the assembly proceeded to the Cathedral for the opening service. The Archbishop himself left in his diary an account of the impressive service.

---

[7] See E. G. Sandford (ed.), *Memoirs of Archbishop Temple by Seven Friends.*
[8] For Maclagan, see F. D. How, *Archbishop Maclagan.*
[9] William Stevens Perry, *The Third Lambeth Conference 1888.*
[10] *The Third Lambeth Conference 1888*, pp. 17–18.

The arrangements in the Cathedral were beautiful – and Lord Northbourne, a very sharp and experienced old critic of such things, said, 'It is simply the most impressive thing I have ever beheld.' First I was taken by Dean and Chapter to West Doors inside Nave. Doors were opened, and 100 Bishops entered in double file, dividing to right and left as we greeted each other, and passing up the Nave and the great steps of the Screen, and so into the Choir, the Minor Canons and singing-men and choir-boys standing in three lines – two wings and one central line on the steps, and singing all the time the procession was going up – we turned and followed and went up the lower flight of the sanctuary steps, and there was placed the great grey 'Chair of Augustine'; when I reached it we knelt in silence and then stood and sang Te Deum gloriously, the whole Choir and Aisles full of people, as well as the Aisles of the Nave, and the Bishops standing choir-wise on the steps – the Chapter about the Altar – and my ten chaplains round and behind the Chair with the beautiful primatial Cross. Then I sate down and gave them a short address exhorting all to obey the Church and not themselves, if they wished any loyalty to be left in the Church.[11]

Davidson, hearing this address, contrasted it with that given by Tait in 1878. 'The Archbishop's address,' he wrote,

from St Augustine's Chair was wise and generous if somewhat obscure. Seldom to my mind has the contrast been more remarkable than between the big simplicity of the words *spoken* from the Chair in 1878 and the somewhat eager, apologetic, and involved utterance *read* from the same chair in 1888. But it was thoroughly *good* all the same – and no-one is more effective *looking* in a function of this sort, or more genial and kindly as the centre of such a gathering.[12]

These were the opening words of the Archbishop's allocution:

Brethren most dear, and to me most reverend, few privileges of my office can surpass that which, though unworthy, I exercise to-day.

It is to bid you welcome in the name of the Lord. Happy should my soul be if it were given me to take in all that such welcome means.

Welcome from all continents and seas, and shores where the English tongue is spoken.

Welcome, bearers of the great commission to be His witnesses unto the ends of the earth.

Welcome, disciples of the great determination to 'refuse fables' and seek the inspiration of the Church at the fountain-head of inspired reason.

Welcome to the chair, which, when filled least worthily, most takes up its own parable, and speaks of unbroken lines of government and law and faith,

[11] A. C. Benson, *The Life of Edward White Benson*, vol. ii, p. 213.
[12] G. K. A. Bell, *Randall Davidson*, vol. i, p. 120.

and forgets not the yet earlier Christianity of the land whose own lines soon flowed into and blended with the Roman and Gallic and the Saxon strains.

From this quotation one can see the point of Davidson's remark. The anthem at this service was from Mendelssohn's 'The Sorrows of Death', which would have been more appropriate in 1878!

In his account Perry says:

No better proof of the catholicity of England's Church could have been afforded by the very grouping of the assembled Bishops, representing as they did, the farthest corners of the earth. As the long array was marshalled in order, we could not fail to note, walking side by side with the courtly and elegant Bishop of Western New York, Dr Cleveland Coxe – poet, author, scholar, preacher, publicist, as well as prelate – the black Bishop of the Niger, Dr Crowther, who, in his youth had been sold as a slave for a puncheon of rum and later exchanged for a hogshead of tobacco.[13]

On Monday evening, 3 July, the Conference had another opening service in Westminster Abbey at which Benson again preached, and took as his text, Ephesians 4.16, 'The whole body, joined and knit together by every joint with which it is supplied.' Bishop Cleveland Coxe's hymn, 'Saviour, sprinkle many nations', was sung. Benson again left his impressions of this second service, which was the first Conference service to take place in Westminster Abbey, where Dean Bradley had succeeded Dean Stanley.

In Westminster Abbey a service in some ways more impressive than that at Canterbury itself. The Chapter and the Bishops occupied every part of the Choir and the Chaplains the square beneath the Tower. Metropolitans the Sanctuary. I preached for three quarters of an hour – but such was the interest of the event that it kept people awake and *still* in the most marvellous way and gave me an opportunity – which I wish I had been worthy worthily to take – I continued to press the Church to keep its Diocesan centres very strong, not comminuting their resources, not reducing the size of the Dioceses so that the strong influence of each ceases to radiate through all. Then I pressed extension of organisation, – new religious orders free from the snares of the past, in intimate connexion with dioceses – and thirdly to hold no work true which is not absolutely *spiritual* work.[14]

Before the Conference commenced work on the Tuesday, there was

[13] Bishop Cleveland Coxe had been to England for the 1878 Conference, and also before that: see his delightful book, *Impressions of England*.

[14] A. C. Benson, *The Life of Edward White Benson*, vol. ii, pp. 213–14.

yet another service in Lambeth Palace Chapel. This time the preacher
was Bishop Henry B. Whipple of Minnesota, who was on his first visit
to England for a Lambeth Conference. Then the bishops moved to the
library for the opening session. 'In the open space between the alcoves,'
writes Bishop Perry, 'on a semicircular dais, the Archbishop of
Canterbury in the centre and the Archbishop of Armagh on his left, sat
the Archbishops and Metropolitans of Dublin,[15] of Calcutta, Rupert's
Land, Sydney, Cape Town, the Primus of Scotland, and here would
have sat our own Primate, the beloved Bishop Williams of Connecticut,
had he been present.[16] Arranged in front of the Archbishops and
Metropolitans were the seats of the Secretaries, the Lord Bishop of
Gloucester and Bristol, who had been Secretary of the preceding
Conferences, being the chief, assisted by the Very Reverend the Dean of
Windsor, Dr Davidson, and Archdeacon Smith.' This was B. F. Smith,
the Archdeacon of Maidstone, who had been added as assistant
secretary a few weeks before the Conference began, owing to the
unexpected pressure of correspondence.[17]

In his diary Benson wrote what he said at the opening of the
Conference. 'I opened the Conference by pointing out that the
Conference was in no sense a Synod and not adapted, or competent, or
within its powers, if it should attempt to make binding decisions on
doctrines or discipline – the unsuitableness to the constitution of our
Church – and to its relation to America – the fact that they had been
foreseen and settled by Abps Longley and Tait in their addresses, etc.'[18]
Then they got down to discussing subject (2) on the agenda, definite
teaching of the faith. The subject was opened by Frederick Temple,
Bishop of London, followed by Bishop Neely of Maine and then Harvey
Goodwin, the Bishop of Carlisle. When the time for adjournment came
at a quarter to five, the Conference appointed Bishop Temple as
chairman of the committee which was to continue the discussion. On
that committee two of the most effective members were Bishop Webber
of Brisbane and the eloquent Bishop Boyd Carpenter of Ripon.[19]

On Wednesday, 4 July, after the Litany had been sung in Lambeth

[15] Archbishop Trench had died in 1885, and was buried in Westminster Abbey,
where he had been Dean. His successor was Lord Plunket.
[16] Bishop Williams of Connecticut had been present in 1867 but not in 1878 or 1888.
See H. C. Potter, *Reminiscences of Bishops and Archbishops*, pp. 25–55.
[17] See R. T. Davidson, *The Lambeth Conferences of 1867, 1878, and 1888*, p. 43.
[18] A. C. Benson, *Life of Edward White Benson*, vol. ii, p. 214.
[19] See Perry, *The Third Lambeth Conference*, p. 48.

Chapel by Bishop Wordsworth of Salisbury, and certain memorials had been received, the bishops directed their attention to the third subject on the agenda, 'The Anglican Communion in relation to the Eastern Churches, to the Scandinavian and other Reformed Churches, to the Old Catholics and others.' The subject was opened up by Archbishop Lord Plunket of Dublin, who was followed by Harold Browne of Winchester, Bishop Sandford of Gibraltar, Bishop Maclagan of Lichfield, Bishop Nuttall of Jamaica, and Bishop Blyth of Jerusalem. Bishop Browne dealt with the Swedish Church, Bishop Sandford spoke on the Eastern Church, Bishop Maclagan on the Old Catholics, Bishop Nuttall on the Moravians, and Bishop Blyth on the Eastern Church. Lord Plunket's suggestion of consecrating a bishop for the Reformed Church in Spain and Portugal received some attention.[20] Out of these discussions grew two committees. The first dealt with the Anglican Communion and the Eastern Orthodox Church and had as its chairman Bishop Browne of Winchester. The second, of which Browne was also chairman, though the membership was different, dealt with (a) the Scandinavian and other Reformed Churches and (b) the Old Catholics and other reforming bodies.

After lunch, the bishops reassembled to discuss the fourth subject on the agenda, 'Polygamy and Heathen Converts' and 'Divorce'. The debate was prefaced by two learned addresses from Bishop Lightfoot of Durham and Bishop Stubbs of Chester. Bishop Douglas Mackenzie of Zululand and Bishop Crowther of the Niger both spoke. Perry remarks that Dr Crowther 'gave a most interesting recital of experiences, together with the results of wide observation bearing on the subject under discussion. The quaintness of manner and the intense earnestness of the aged Bishop; his color, the marvellous vicissitudes of his life, and the position he holds, gave to his words a singular force and quite enchained his auditory.'[21] Bishop Crowther was among the several colonial bishops who was put on the committee to deal with this subject, which was chaired by Bishop Lightfoot of Durham. Another committee, under the chairmanship of Bishop Stubbs of Chester, was assigned the subject of 'Divorce, and whether it may be practicable for the Conference to offer any advice or suggestions which may help the Bishops and Clergy towards agreement in their actions concerning it'.

In addition to the committees already mentioned, there was also a committee on 'Home Relations' appointed 'to consider what steps (if

[20] See Perry, *The Third Lambeth Conference*, pp. 49–50.
[21] Idem, p. 52.

3. The bishops at the 1888 Conference, outside Lambeth Palace

4. The bishops at the 1897 Conference, outside Lambeth Palace

any) can rightly be taken on behalf of the Anglican Communion towards the reunion of the various bodies into which the Christianity of the English-speaking races is divided'. This committee had been appointed at the request of the Bishop of Sydney, Dr Barry, who produced a memorial from the synod of the Australasian province. Bishop Atlay of Hereford was chairman. As a great deal of controversy resulted from their report it would be as well to name all those upon it. They were Bishop Machray of Ruperts Land, Bishop Potter of New York, Bishop Nuttall of Jamaica, Bishop Jermyn of Brechin, Bishop Boyd Carpenter of Ripon, Bishop Moorhouse of Manchester, Bishop Charles Wordsworth of St Andrews, Bishop Dowden of Edinburgh, Bishop Suter of Nelson, Bishop Kennion of Adelaide, Bishop Whipple of Minnesota, Bishop Branch, Coadjutor of Antigua, Bishop Thorold of Rochester, Bishop Maclagan of Lichfield, and Bishop Walsham How of Wakefield.[22]

On this day the discussions broke up a little before the appointed time, as Benson called attention to the request made by the Americans that, as it was 4 July, they might pay their respects to the American Minister. In the evening the Lord Mayor of London gave a banquet for the archbishops and bishops in the Egyptian Hall of the Mansion House. Bishop Harris of Michigan, struck down with illness after this banquet, died quickly afterwards.[23]

On Thursday, 5 July, after the Litany had again been read by Bishop Wordsworth, the bishops discussed the fifth item on the agenda, 'Authoritative Standards of Doctrine and Worship'. The discussion was opened by Bishop Barry of Sydney, 'in a speech of great fluency'. Other speakers were Bishops Douglas of Aberdeen, Cleveland Coxe of Western New York, Wordsworth of Salisbury, and Doane of Albany. The chairman of the committee appointed to take the subject further was Lord Alwyne Compton, Bishop of Ely. A committee on the observance of Sunday owed its appointment to some remarks of Archbishop Thomson. 'In connection with the appointment of this Committee,' wrote Perry, 'few who were present could easily forget the earnest, impassioned plea for the sanctity of the Lord's Day, and the necessity of some action looking towards the repression of its all too-common desecration, which fell from the lips of His Grace, the

[22] See Perry, *The Third Lambeth Conference*, pp. 52–3.
[23] The *Guardian*, 1878, p. 992, refers to the American Bishop of New Mexico and Arizona as dying just before the Conference began.

Archbishop of York.'[24] Bishop Edward Bickersteth of Exeter became the chairman of this committee.

On Thursday afternoon they came to the subject of 'Mutual Relations of the Dioceses and Branches of the Anglican Communion'. Bishop W. W. Jones of Capetown opened the debate and was followed by Bishop Jermyn of Scotland (the Primus) and Bishop Alexander of Derry.[25] The committee appointed had Harvey Goodwin, Bishop of Carlisle, as its chairman.

On Friday, 6 July, again after the Litany had been sung by the Bishop of Salisbury, the Conference got down to the first subject on the agenda, 'The Church's Practical Work in Relation to (a) Intemperance, (b) Purity, (c) Care of Emigrants, (d) Socialism'. Bishop Temple of London introduced the subject of intemperance. Bishop Lightfoot of Durham led the way on purity. Bishop Ryle of Liverpool dealt with emigrants. Bishop James Moorhouse spoke on socialism. Bishop Perry of Iowa remarks that Moorhouse's speech was 'the most eloquent and effective speech of the session' and that it 'commanded the attention and absorbed the interest of each one present'. Bishop Thorold of Rochester was also impressed:

> The electrifying and overwhelming speech of the day, almost of the session was the Bishop of Manchester's on Socialism. It combined so much exhaustive study of the subject and of the writers upon it, analysis of the good and bad in it differentiated as secular and Christian, trenchant assertion of the subject as the subject of the day; and it was practical as indicating that co-operation is the true solution of the difficulty. Perhaps Oldham was in his mind. It was eminently, reverently, even passionately Christian, delivered with tremendous emphasis, and power, and seizing all of us, including Peterborough and Durham, with its verve and logic.[26]

The Bishop of London was appointed as chairman of the committee on intemperance, Bishop Walsham How on purity, Bishop Lewis of Llandaff on emigrants and the Bishop of Manchester (naturally) on socialism. There was one final committee appointed which had the task of dealing with any questions submitted to it in writing by members of the Conference.

Now the bishops moved off to their committees. 'Convened by their respective Chairmen, generally at the Palace of the Bishop named first on the list, these very committee meetings, proved the occasions of most

[24] Perry, *The Third Lambeth Conference*, pp. 56–7.
[25] For Bishop Alexander, see Eleanor Alexander, *Primate Alexander*.
[26] C. H. Simpkinson, *The Life and Work of Bishop Thorold*, pp. 290–1.

agreeable gatherings and added fresh experiences of graceful and abundant hospitality to those which had already been so abundant and agreeable.'[27] When the bishops reassembled on Monday, 23 July, the reports of the committees had been printed and circulated for discussion.

As in 1878 one report was never issued by the Conference – the report on infidelity – so a similar thing happened in 1888, when the report on the definite teaching of the faith was never published. Bishop Perry of Iowa explains the matter in his account of the Conference.

> It cannot escape notice that the published reports of the committees are deficient in not containing any paper from the important committee to which was assigned the subject, 'On Definite Teaching of the Faith to Various Classes and the Means Thereto.' The committee having charge of this matter was not derelict in duty in failing to consider the important theme committed to its consideration. A report was presented, in some respects the most able and masterly of all the reports offered; but after a discussion, the earnestness and solemnity of which could not fail to impress each member of this body, the report was recommitted by an overwhelming vote, in consequence of a few expressions which seemed to convey the impression, or at least to take the position for the sake of argument with the unbeliever, that the Church felt well assured only of the *substantial* truth of the New Testament; and, further, conceding, or seeming to concede, that the opening portions of the Word of God, like its close, were a vision or an allegory. The conclusions seemingly to be deduced from the few phrases we have indicated of this report, were denied by the members of the Committee, but the sense of the reverence due to the Word of God was such that no explanations were deemed sufficient to prevent the recommitment of the whole report, with a view to the elimination of its objectionable features. On its reappearance, with modifications in its language and expressions, at a later day, objection was still made to what were deemed unwise and unnecessary admissions, and finally, the report, able and excellent in all but a few words, as it certainly was, was refused a place among the printed proceedings of the Conference.[28]

As one can readily see, the battle was all part of the geology and Genesis controversy.

As the report on definite teaching caused controversy, so also did that produced by the committee on home reunion. However, this report was in the end published though with a major excision. We are fortunate in having Perry's account of the treatment of this report and there

[27] Perry, *The Third Lambeth Conference*, p. 64.
[28] Idem, pp. 74ff.

exists in Appendix VI of the *Episcopate of Charles Wordsworth* by John Wordsworth a document, written by the chairman of this home reunion committee, Bishop Barry of Sydney. It was in this report that there was printed for the first time in England the famous Lambeth Quadrilateral. This Quadrilateral had appeared in a report of the committee on Christian unity at the General Convention of the American Episcopal Church at Chicago in 1886. Having established two principles: (1) concession in matters of human ordering, and (2) steadfastness in matters of divine origin, the committee developed this sacred principle in these words:

> As inherent parts of that sacred deposit, and therefore as essential to the restoration of unity among the divided branches of Christendom, we account the following, to wit:
>
> 1 The Holy Scriptures of the Old and New Testament as the revealed Word of God.
>
> 2 The Nicene Creed as the sufficient statement of the Christian Faith.
>
> 3 The two Sacraments – Baptism and the Supper of the Lord – ministered with unfailing use of Christ's words of institution and of the elements ordained by Him.
>
> 4 The Historic Episcopate, locally adapted in the methods of its administration to the varying needs of the nations and peoples called of God into the unity of His Church.

The document was accepted by the House of Bishops in 1886. The House of Deputies did not concur in the report until the General Convention of 1892. Now this formula was not original to the compilers of the report. It went back to a great Evangelical leader, William Reed Huntington, who suggested the formula in his book, *The Church Idea* (1870).[29] Barry's committee drew attention to the Chicago Quadrilateral and they now produced it with some rephrasing:

> That, in the opinion of the Conference, the following Articles supply a basis on which approach may be, by God's blessing, made towards Home Reunion:
>
> (a) The Holy Scriptures of the Old and New Testaments, as 'containing all things necessary to salvation', and as being the rule and ultimate standard of faith.
>
> (b) The Apostles' Creed as the Baptismal Symbol; and the Nicene Creed, as the sufficient statement of the Christian Faith.

[29] See H. G. G. Herklots, 'The Origins of the Lambeth Quadrilateral' in *Church Quarterly Review*, Jan. to March, 1968; see also Louis A. Haselmayer, *Lambeth and Unity*.

(c) The two sacraments ordained by Christ himself – Baptism and the Supper of the Lord – ministered with unfailing use of Christ's words of Institution, and of the elements ordained by Him.

(d) The Historic Episcopate, locally adapted in the methods of its administration to the varying needs of the nations and peoples called of God into the Unity of His Church.

The committee unanimously accepted this Quadrilateral. But Bishop Barry in his valuable account of what happened in committee says that some members, led by Bishop Charles Wordsworth of St Andrews, felt that the suggestion of conferences with separated brethren would be

> fruitless, unless we were prepared to suggest some means of bridging over the transitional period in any process of Reunion in regard to the crucial question of the Ministry of Non-Episcopal Communions. That we held it to be irregular, and contrary to primitive Church Order, was indicated by our previous determination to accept the historic Episcopate as one of the permanent bases of Reunion. But were we to require that the members and ministers of these communions should acknowledge it to be absolutely invalid? Or, considering 'the present distress', could we go into Conference with some acknowledgement on our part of a spiritual reality in it – as evidenced by spiritual fruits of its ministration – sufficient to prepare, if not for Corporate Reunion, at least for such relations as might lead to it in the hereafter? . . . Certainly we had the Presbyterians, and perhaps also the great Wesleyan Body, especially in mind. . . . It must be remembered that they desired to see steps taken 'either towards corporate reunion or towards such relation as may prepare for fuller organic unity hereafter.' I imagine that the latter of these alternatives was chiefly before their minds, as more likely to be practicable, and that they had the idea of a kind of Federation of Congregations of the Non-Episcopal Bodies – if any proposal for Reunion was accepted – retaining their own present Ministers under Episcopal recognition, with the understanding that in the hereafter there should be Episcopal Ordination for their successors. Probably also some consecration to the Episcopate *per saltum* was contemplated in the case of leading Ministers of any of these Communions. But these ideas were not, and could not be, embodied in the Resolution. . . . Bishop Wordsworth attended the final meeting of the Committee and signified his cordial adhesion to the Resolution. . . . I do not think he took any part in the discussion in the Conference itself.[30]

We must now set out the paragraphs which the Conference refused to receive and which are conveniently quoted *in toto* by Bishop Perry of Iowa.

[30] John Wordsworth, op. cit., pp. 363ff.

As, however, it is well known that the one crucial difficulty in the way of all such action is the question of the recognition by the Anglican Communion, of the existing Ministries of non-Episcopal Communions, the committee, although they are well aware of the grave difficulty and responsibility of any utterance on the subject, cannot refuse to submit to the Conference some suggestions upon it.

It will be seen that, as one of the elements of the proposed basis of Reunion, they here, in accordance with the principles of the Church of England – as declared in the Preface to her Ordinal – included 'the historic Episcopate', with such adaptations as may be in different portions of the Church required by present circumstances and conditions. But they observe, that, while the Church in her XXXIII Article lays down the necessity of the Ministry as a sacred Order, commissioned by those 'who have public authority given unto them in the Congregation', and while for herself she had defined the latter term by insisting in her own Communion on Episcopal Ordination, she has nowhere declared that all other constituted Ministry is null and void. They also note that in the troubled period following the Reformation (up to the year 1662), Ministers not Episcopally ordained were, in certain cases, recognized as fit to hold office in the Church of England, and that some chief authorities, even of the High Church school, defended and acted upon this recognition in England, Scotland and Ireland.

The question which, therefore, presents itself to them is this: 'Whether the present circumstances of Christianity among us are not such as to constitute a sufficient reason for such exceptional action now?' To this question – looking to the infinite blessings which must result from any right approach towards Reunion, both in England and still more in the American and Colonial Communities – looking still more to the unquestioned fact, that upon some concession upon this matter depends, humanly speaking, the only hope of such an approach – they cannot but conceive that our present condition, perhaps in a higher degree than at any former time justifies an affirmative answer. They therefore humbly submit the following Resolution to the wisdom of the Conference:

'That, in the opinion of this committee, Conferences are likely to be fruitful, under God's blessing, of a practical result, only if undertaken with willingness on behalf of the Anglican Communion – while holding firmly the threefold order of the Ministry as the normal rule of the Church, to be observed in the future – to recognize, in spite of what we must conceive as irregularity, the Ministerial character of those ordained in non-Episcopal Communions, through whom, as Ministers, it has pleased God visibly to work for the salvation of souls and the advancement of His Kingdom; and to provide, in such way as may be agreed upon, for the acceptance of such Ministers as fellow-workers with us in the service of our Lord Jesus Christ.'[31]

[31] Perry, *The Third Lambeth Conference*, pp. 77ff.

These paragraphs, which came between what are now paragraphs III and IV of the Report, raised a great deal of debate. In fact Perry remarks, 'The most brilliant debate of the session was thus begun.' He went on to recount the part played by Bishop Lightfoot in that debate.

It was in connection with this discussion and during the most exciting moments of the debate that the Bishop of Durham, Dr Lightfoot, showing even then by his voice and manner that the hand of death was already upon him, took occasion in his singularly clear and strong expression of unqualified opposition to this scheme, to 'disclaim wholly the interpretation the Bishop of St Andrews' had 'put upon his words' in his essay in *The Christian Ministry*,[32] as well as the interpretation given them by Presbyterian controversialists. The Bishop then proceeded to say, – and no one who was present could ever forget the impressiveness of his words – 'It is sometimes convenient to extract one sentence from a long essay, all of which is meant to hinge together, and to use that sentence for a purpose.' It was a testimony to the Historic Episcopate and the threefold Ministry then and there solemnly pronounced, which this profound scholar a few days later reiterated in his address at the re-opening of the historic St Peter's Chapel, at Auckland Castle.[33]

Perry clearly had a vivid memory of Lightfoot's words, though Barry says that he thought that Lightfoot did not speak.[34] It would seem that the great opponents of the paragraphs were Bishop Doane of Albany[35] and Bishop Jermyn of Scotland. The American bishops, with one exception, were against the idea. Perry contends that, had it been passed, the Church would have been disrupted and a large number of bishops would have decamped from the Conference. Perhaps one of the most moving speakers was the young Bishop Bickersteth of Japan.[36] This episode over home reunion is undoubtedly the most fascinating part of the Conference, yet Dewi Morgan in his *The Bishops Come to Lambeth* omits any reference to it.

The Report on Intemperance said that 'If it cannot be considered the most sinful of sins, it is difficult to deny it is the most mischievous.' The Report on Purity made a number of emphatic statements:

We declare that a life of chastity for the unmarried is not only possible, but is

---

[32] This essay is in Lightfoot's famous Commentary on Philippians.

[33] Perry, op. cit., pp. 80–1.

[34] J. Wordsworth, *The Episcopate of Charles Wordsworth*, p. 365.

[35] Perry, *The Third Lambeth Conference*, p. 81; cf. the reference to 'a leading Bishop of the American church' in Barry's account in *The Episcopate of Charles Wordsworth*, p. 365.

[36] Perry, *The Third Lambeth Conference*, p. 82.

commanded by God. We declare that there is no difference between man and woman in the sinfulness of sins of unchastity. We declare that on the man, in his God-given strength of manhood, rests the main responsibility. We declare that no one known to be living an immoral life ought to be received in Christian society. We solemnly protest against all lowering of the sanctity of marriage.

This quotation leads naturally to what the committee on divorce, under William Stubbs, said, which was far less stringent than the attitude taken later.

They recognise the fact that there always has been a difference of opinion in the Church on the question whether our Lord meant to forbid marriage to the innocent party in a Divorce for adultery: and they recommend that the Clergy should not be instructed to refuse the Sacraments or other privileges of the Church to those who, under civil sanction, are thus married.

But whereas doubt has been entertained whether our Lord meant to permit such marriage to the innocent party, the Committee are unwilling to suggest any precise instructions in this matter, and recommend that, where the laws of the land will permit, the determination should be left to the judgement of the Bishop of the Diocese, whether the Clergy would be justified in refraining from pronouncing the blessing of the Church on such unions.

It must be remembered that at this date St Matthew's Gospel was regarded as prior to St Mark's and it was customary to accept the Matthaean exception.

The question of polygamy was thrashed out in committee. L. G. Mylne, Bishop of Bombay, in his account of the Conference, says:

Not a word, I think, was said in favour of compulsory Divorce; not a voice raised in favour of injustice; of throwing helpless women on the world, or of granting them maintenance alone without a husband's care, unless they elected for that alternative. And in the end, by about a four to one majority, it was decided that in the opinion of the Conference polygamists could not be baptised retaining more wives than one, but that they must wait under Christian instruction until in the Providence of God they were in a position to live by Christ's law.[37]

The Conference felt that the wives of polygamists could in some circumstances be admitted to baptism, but it would be for local church authorities to decide under what circumstances.

[37] See L. G. Mylne, *The Counsels and Principles of the Lambeth Conference of 1888*, p. 11.

The committee on Sunday observance said nothing new. That on socialism said:

> The Clergy may enter into friendly relations with Socialists, attending, when possible, their club meetings, and trying to understand their aims and methods. At the same time it will contribute no little to draw together the various classes of society if the Clergy endeavour, in sermons and lectures, to set forth the true principles of Society, showing how property is a trust to be administered for the good of humanity, and how much of what is good and true in Socialism is to be found in the precepts of Christ.[38]

The Report suggested that candidates for orders should have some knowledge of economic science.[39] In connection with the debate on socialism, Bishop H. C. Potter of New York tells an amusing story, which shows the good sense of the chairman. 'At the Lambeth Conference', he writes,

> one of the topics was 'Socialism'; and one of the speakers enlarged upon the vices of modern Society with a good deal of heat; dwelling, I remember, with especial bitterness upon what he called the 'irritating indulgence of display, by the rich, as illustrated particularly by their "liveried menials".' The phrase seemed to me, as I caught it, somewhat infelicitous; and I found myself recalling the archbishop's servants in their sober liveries, and thinking, in view of their courteous guidance, and our frequent appeals to them for that guidance – which we should hardly have ventured to make if we had not been enabled, by their dress, to identify them – I found myself thinking, I say, that the philippic concerning 'liveried menials' might wisely have been omitted, or that, at any rate, such acrid criticism of a usage followed by our gracious host might wisely have been postponed.
>
> It was while my mind was occupied with these reflections that the paper was concluded, and the speaker sat down. The essay had been able, and the subject was profoundly interesting. But the pause that followed its conclusion was considerable, and the situation was awkward. In a moment, however, the silence was broken by the voice of the archbishop, as he drew his watch from his pocket, and having consulted it, turned towards us a most genial face: 'It is now twenty minutes after one' he said, 'and luncheon is to be served in ten minutes. No adequate discussion of the admirable paper to which we have just listened could be had in ten minutes; and it will be well to postpone it until after the mid-day recess. I will, therefore, declare the conference adjourned for that purpose; and now, brethren,' added the archbishop with that charming twinkle in his eye, 'the "liveried menials" will show you the way to the dining-room.' There went up, straightway, a shout

[38] *The Lambeth Conferences of 1867, 1878, and 1888*, p. 309.
[39] Idem, p. 308.

of laughter from the Conference, and, in parliamentary phrase, 'the incident
was closed.'[40]

The Care of Emigrants Report was pretty thorough but nothing
merits precise quotation. The committee on mutual relations dealt
among other things with the question of the title of archbishop for
overseas metropolitans. It spoke as follows:

> The Committee have been asked to express an opinion as to the desira-
> bility of assigning the title of Archbishop to the Primate of Australia and
> Tasmania. The Committee feel that there is great difficulty in coming to
> a clear judgment upon a question which must, of necessity, to some extent
> depend for its answer upon local circumstances; but taking the question
> upon broad grounds, and looking to the general interests of the whole
> Church, the Committee have no hesitation in expressing their opinion that
> there are cases of important Provinces in which distinct advantages would
> result from adopting the ancient and honoured title of Archbishop.[41]

Soon there was an Archbishop of Ontario and an Archbishop of
Ruperts Land. The Bishops of Sydney, Cape Town, and the West Indies
received the title of 'Archbishop' from their synods but did not use it
until the question had been discussed again at Lambeth in 1897, when a
more definite approval was given. It seems that Benson was not
especially pleased at the idea of the multiplication of colonial
archbishops.[42]

The committee dealing with the Scandinavian Church and Old
Catholics and other reforming bodies welcomed any approaches that
could be made to the Church in Sweden, 'as its standards of doctrine are
to a great extent in accord with our own', it said much about the history
of the Old Catholics and dealt very briefly with reforming bodies in
Italy, France, Spain, and Portugal. On the Moravians they said they
would welcome 'any clearer illustration of their history and actual
status'. The committee on the Eastern Church referred to the visit of
Archbishop Lycurgus of Syra and Tenos in 1870 and felt pleased that
they were not separated from the Eastern Church by the doctrines of
the immaculate conception or papal infallibility. They commented on
the recent discovery of the Didache 'which throws unexpected light
upon the early development of ecclesiastical organisation'. They said
something on the difficulty over icons, and the *filioque* clause. It was felt

---

[40] H. C. Potter, *Reminiscences of Bishops and Archbishops*, pp. 216–17.
[41] *The Lambeth Conferences of 1867, 1878, and 1888*, p. 323.
[42] See H. J. T. Johnson, *Anglicanism in Transition*, p. 197.

that the Anglican Communion had some obligations to the Coptic, Abyssinian, Syrian, and Chaldean churches and referred to the Assyrian mission started by Tait and continued by Benson.[43] The committee on authoritative standards spoke about the first General Councils and remarked, 'our Communion has always recognised the decisions of the first four Councils on matters of faith, nor is there any point of dogma in which it disagrees with the teaching of the fifth and sixth.' It recognized that the seventh Council was a disputed one and 'it is our duty to assert that Our Church has never accepted the teaching of that Council in reference to the veneration of sacred pictures.'[44] On the Thirty-nine Articles they said, '. . . we feel that the Articles are not all of equal value, that they are not, and do not profess to be, a complete statement of Christian doctrine, and that, from the temporary and local circumstances, they do not always meet the requirements of Churches founded under wholly different conditions.'[45] Finally, they said, 'We are unable, after careful consideration of the subject, to recommend that any new declaration of doctrine should, at the present time, be put forth by authority. We are, however, of opinion that the time has come when an effort should be made to compose a manual for teachers which should contain a summary of the doctrine of the Church, as generally received among us.'[46] In the published documents of the Conference the final part was a statement about the Cummins schism. Bishop Cummins, Assistant Bishop of Kentucky, who had been present at the First Lambeth Conference, had seceded from the Church in 1873.[47]

During the Conference Benson had been asked to draft an encyclical letter, with such assistants as he should choose. It is indicated in the Life of Bishop Durnford of Chichester that Durnford, Lightfoot, and Stubbs did this drafting.[48] Davidson later recalled sitting up almost the whole night with Stubbs and Lightfoot while the process of revision was going on.[49] When this encyclical was published, Bishop Ryle of Liverpool disowned it and vented his wrath in the newspapers, noticing its failure

---

[43] See A. C. Benson, *The Life of Edward White Benson*, for various passages on the Assyrian mission.

[44] *The Lambeth Conferences of 1867, 1878 and 1888*, p. 355.

[45] Idem, p. 357.

[46] Idem, p. 358.

[47] On Bishop Cummins and the Reformed Episcopal Church, see E. Clowes Chorley, *Men and Movements in the American Episcopal Church*.

[48] See W. R. W. Stephens, *A Memoir of Richard Durnford*, p. 264.

[49] G. K. A. Bell, *Randall Davidson*, vol. i, p. 121.

to say anything about divisions in the Church over Holy Communion.[50] The Protestant Lord Grimthorpe also delivered a salvo against it.

On Friday, 27 July, after the encyclical had been accepted without a dissentient voice – Ryle no doubt being absent – a Loyal Address to the Queen was made, and the Doxology sung and the benediction given. Bishop John Wordsworth did what his father had done in 1867 and 1878 and translated the encyclical and resolutions of the Conference into Greek and Latin.

On the Saturday, the final service took place in St Paul's Cathedral. An innovation was the presence of the Canterbury House of Convocation and the House of Laymen and the York House of Convocation. The *Church Times* bewailed the fact that the bishops were in black chimeres rather than red. It also criticized some bishops for receiving the sacrament in their fingers instead of the palm of their hand. It drew attention to the fact that the *Daily News* had stated that 'a tall Crucifer was borne before the Archbishop in the procession' – 'a sight surely that would have warmed the hearts of any Church Associationist.'[51] The sermon was preached by Archbishop Thomson of York on Romans 8.19, 'The earnest expectation of the creature waiteth for the manifestation of the sons of God.' It was his second and last Conference sermon.

Though the Conference received a memorial from certain High Churchmen objecting to union with the Old Catholics, some very favourable comments upon the Conference came from this body. Archbishop Benson won golden opinions for his conducting of the Conference. The American bishops attending the Conference presented him with an altar-cross.[52]

Benson wrote to Queen Victoria giving her an account of the meeting. She replied from Osborne on 18 August, 'The Queen thanks the Archbishop of Canterbury very much for his kind letter giving an account of the large Meeting of Bishops at Lambeth. It must have been most satisfactory to see how harmonious it was. The Archbishop will have had the opportunity of making many interesting acquaintances.'[53]

The Report of the Conference was produced by Davidson in record time. He also won golden opinions for his work at the Conference.

[50] *Guardian*, 1888, 22 August, p. 1252.
[51] *Church Times*, 1888, 3 August, p. 670.
[52] See A. C. Benson, *Edward White Benson*, vol. i, p. 583.
[53] Idem, vol. ii, p. 216.

Bishop Ellicott wrote to him, 'We all owe you a great debt of gratitude, and I say this most deliberately, that the great success of the Conference is to a very large degree due to your unflagging energy and rapidity of successful labour.'[54]

[54] G. K. A. Bell, *Randall Davidson*, vol. i, p. 121.

7

FREDERICK TEMPLE AND
THE CONFERENCE OF 1897

We noticed that before the Lambeth Conference of 1888 began there were already indications of coming troubles between the saintly Edward King, Bishop of Lincoln, and the Church Association, bent on putting down ritual. Two years after the Third Lambeth Conference, 1890, Archbishop Benson gave his famous Lincoln Judgement, which Dean Church characterized as 'the most courageous thing that has come from Lambeth for the last 200 years'.[1] By the time of the 1897 Conference the Judgement had receded into the background and ritualism did not appear on the programme.

The years before the Conference of 1897 were marked by attempts at reunion with Rome made by Lord Halifax with the Abbé Portal. The question of Anglican orders came very much to the fore, and Pope Leo XIII appointed a Commission to examine Anglican orders, which finished sitting in June 1896. In September there came the publication of the Bull *Apostolicae Curae*, which declared English orders entirely null and void, partly on the ground of previous Roman decisions, partly on the ground of defects of 'form' up to 1662, and also on the ground of defective intention on the part of the framers of the Prayer Book. Obviously the Bull was an enormous obstacle to thoughts of reunion. Benson decided that some reply must be made to it and in his task received great assistance from Bishop John Wordsworth of Salisbury. The day on which Benson died in October 1896 at Hawarden, where he was a guest of Mr W. E. Gladstone, he had received, but left unopened, a draft reply by John Wordsworth. Eventually, on this basis a reply was made to the Pope by Archbishop Frederick Temple, in March 1897.

When Benson died, he had already sent out letters of invitation to the Fourth Lambeth Conference, which he was calling in July 1897. The year 1897 had been chosen rather than 1898 since it was the anniversary of the landing of St Augustine at Ebbsfleet in 597. It was

[1] A. C. Benson, *The Life of Edward White Benson*, vol. ii, p. 367; Mary C. Church, *Life and Letters of Dean Church*, p. 349.

also the year of Queen Victoria's Diamond Jubilee. Two hundred and forty invitations went out in August 1896 and 194 bishops in due course attended the Conference, presided over by Benson's successor, Frederick Temple.

Randall Davidson was now Bishop of Winchester, over which diocese he presided from Farnham Castle.[2] He was not such a power behind the scenes at Lambeth under Temple as he had been under Benson. Nearly twenty years of close knowledge of the doings at Lambeth came to an end. It seems that Temple felt that Davidson was chagrined at not getting the primacy. This was untrue. Davidson wished Temple to succeed Benson and felt that no one else would fit the bill. Temple continued suspicious of him. However, Davidson became episcopal secretary of the 1897 Lambeth Conference, though Temple hardly consulted him.

I had been appointed the Episcopal Secretary [wrote Davidson] and was conversant with everything, yet he hardly consulted me about anything, leaving me a perfectly free hand about things that were in any sense within my province and saying absolutely nothing to me, unless under pressure, about the policy, or the plans, or the order of proceedings, for which he would have to be when the time came technically responsible, but in which I was necessarily closely concerned. The whole thing was done by him like other things in his life, vigorously, brusquely, and effectively but with no attempt to touch any vein of sentiment or to recognise the work of Archbishop Benson in the programme laid down or the matters selected for discussion.[3]

There was a suggestion that the 1897 Conference be held not at Lambeth Palace but in Church House, Westminster, which had been erected since the 1888 Conference. In 1888 some had found the Lambeth library an unsatisfactory conference room.[4] Bishop H. C. Potter of New York records a meeting at Church House to discuss arrangements for the Conference. Temple had hardly taken his seat

before the Bishop of Durham (Dr Westcott) rose in his place, and with a face flushed with emotion, read from a paper that he held in his shaking hand, some outlines of the arrangements, prepared by the Archbishop of Canterbury himself. These arrangements contemplated that the Conference should hold some of its sessions in the Church House rather than in the library of Lambeth Palace. . . . It was upon this proposal that the Bishop of

[2] Davidson had been Bishop of Rochester, 1891–5.

[3] G. K. A. Bell, *Randall Davidson*, vol. i, p. 303.

[4] See, for example, L. G. Mylne, *The Counsels and Principles of the Lambeth Conference of 1888*, p. 56.

Durham fastened, with what seemed to me, needlessly vehement emotion. He described the plan of holding some of the sessions elsewhere than at Lambeth as sure to cause many of the bishops unmixed grief. He described it as the menace of changes still more radical, yet to come; and concluded by saying, 'Most Reverend Sir, at this rate, I should not be surprised to hear it proposed, before we adjourn, that the next Lambeth Conference shall be held in *New York!*' The Bishop of Durham sat down, and the Bishop of Manchester (Morehouse) [*sic*] controlled his mirth sufficiently to say, 'The Bishop of New York is present; and I am sure he will assure the Bishop of Durham of the great pleasure that it would give our American friends to welcome the Lambeth Conference.' The Bishop of Durham, who, until that moment, had been quite unaware of my presence, turned to me with a most rueful countenance, and made his apologies. . . . But what, most of all, impressed me in this somewhat amusing as well as awkward scene, was the absolute silence of the archbishop. He bent his head and covered his face with his hands while his brother of Durham denounced the archiepiscopal proposals; but he said nothing to stay the storm of disapproval with which his plans had been visited, save that, when the committee adjourned, and we scattered, he turned to me and said, 'Come over to Lambeth to dinner!' I did so; and though for some hours he made no further allusion to the subject, he turned to me at the dinner-table and said, 'How would this room do for the conference?' We were dining in the noble 'state dining-room', an apartment quite vast enough for the meetings of the conference, but not easily surrendered, for two or three weeks, to any such use, without the probability of grave inconvenience to the archbishop's household. I ventured to say so; whereupon the archbishop promptly replied, 'Oh, they can't have it, if Mrs Temple disapproves!' Mrs Temple did disapprove, and we didn't have it.[5]

In the end it was decided to have the meetings in the Guard Room, which was the place of conference in 1867. It has not been used since.[6]

Frederick Temple was 75 years old when appointed archbishop, but he was made of stern stuff. Edward Carpenter in *Cantuar* calls him 'A Man of Stature'. He was indeed brusque, but some liked him. Bishop Montgomery, father of Field-Marshal Montgomery, remarked

Archbishop Temple acted characteristically as Chairman, wholly honest and humble and very strong. He did not pay much attention to smaller rules of procedure, but guided us in a commonsense way. He could not stand 'gas'

[5] Op. cit., pp. 220ff.

[6] I am not so sure that Bishop Potter has not made a mistake and the 'dining room' was used for the Conference, since the Guard Room was the 'dining room' at any rate in summer. See *Bishop Montgomery. A Memoir*, p. 72, 'The Conference of 1897 met in the Guard Room (Dining-room) . . .' and A. C. Benson, *Edward White Benson*, vol. i, p. 582 '. . . the Guard-room as it is called – always used as a dining-room in summer . . .'

and would put down anyone, and in the manner of a Schoolmaster. The American Bishops were nettled at first, but they soon saw the big nature of the man and his utter freedom from pretence or desire for power. . . . He was a big man. I got to love him in after days as the kindest and wisest of men . . .[7]

The Diamond Jubilee celebrations were in June just before the Conference began. On Sunday, 21 June, a great Service of Thanksgiving was held at St Paul's. With the Archbishop was the Archbishop of Finland, deputed by the Holy Synod of Russia to represent the Orthodox Church at the celebration of Queen Victoria's sixty years' reign. Bishop Creighton of London preached the sermon.[8] On the following Tuesday, 23 June, Temple and the bishops received the Queen at the west front of St Paul's. The *Te Deum* was sung, Dean Gregory led the Lord's Prayer and Bishop Creighton read a prayer written by Temple. The Archbishop then gave the blessing, and then everyone sang, 'All people that on earth do dwell'.

> Then came a silence. There was a delay somewhere. The Queen's carriage did not move. The explanation was evident to those who occupied posts of vantage. The carriages (seventeen) which contained the Princesses had to move off before the Queen's carriage could move. There would be an appreciable time during which no one would know what to do. But the Primate knew. 'Three cheers for the Queen!' he cried. Needless to say, it was taken up, and carried on, and the threatened hiatus was filled in a way that brought the tears coursing down the cheeks of the dearly loved and venerable Queen.[9]

The proceedings of the Conference began with a Quiet Day for the bishops on 30 June, conducted by the saintly Bishop King of Lincoln. The account of the 1888 Conference had some reference to a retreat for bishops at Whitelands College,[10] but this seems to have been the first year that proceedings began with an official retreat.[11] On Thursday, 1 July, the bishops attended Evensong at Westminster Abbey,

[7] See *Bishop Montgomery. A Memoir*, pp. 72–3. Bishop Montgomery, who was interested in the smoking habits of bishops, went on to remark, 'I need not say that those were days when *smoking* was not even mentioned. I suppose Bishops smoked in the garden. American Bishops were sorely put to it. I don't think English Bishops ever smoked, or if they did, they did not acknowledge the fact.'

[8] See *Memoirs of Archbishop Temple by Seven Friends*, vol. ii, p. 267, and L. Creighton, *Life and Letters of Mandell Creighton*, vol. ii, pp. 237–8.

[9] See *Memoirs of Archbishop Temple*, vol. ii, p. 268.

[10] See *Guardian*, 1888, p. 630.

[11] For King's sermon, see *Guardian*, 7 July 1897, pp. 1083–4.

when the Archbishop of York, W. D. Maclagan, preached. On the following day (Friday, 2 July) a large number of bishops were brought by train from Charing Cross to Ebbsfleet and then to Richborough Castle. This remembrance of St Augustine had been planned by Archbishop Benson. Mrs Benson and Miss Tait (Mrs Davidson's sister) were both present at Richborough. On Saturday, the bishops were welcomed at Canterbury in St Martin's Church and then in the cathedral. The *Guardian* said of the cathedral service,

> It was even more imposing as a spectacle than the service at Westminster Abbey. On no former occasion has there been such a large number of members of the Episcopate assembled in the cathedral. Vested in their scarlet robes and wearing doctors' hoods, and occupying a position elevated so much above the level of the congregation, the scene at the east end was an exceptionally brilliant one, whilst the civic and military representatives gave variety of colour in other parts of the service.[12]

Temple spoke his address from the Chair of St Augustine 'with great emotion' but without any allusion to Benson. 'In his opening address at Canterbury,' wrote Davidson,

> everyone had supposed that his main theme would be the absence of the master mind to whom the Conference in its details was due. He made a speech about duty and did not allude in the remotest way to Archbishop Benson's existence. Everyone spoke of this, and I made bold on the morning of the day when the Conference was to meet for discussion to say something as to our hopes that he would allude to Benson in his opening address. I did it gingerly not knowing what answer I might receive. I simply asked him whether it would be his wish that the American Bishops should make such allusion as was appropriate to Archbishop Benson or whether he would do it himself. He replied that he thought nothing of the sort was necessary. I said that I knew some of the Bishops would wish for it and he answered, 'Then I will do it' and spoke some admirable and telling sentences.[13]

After the service there was the customary luncheon at St Augustine's College, while the Home Reunion Society entertained the Nonconformists at the County Hotel.

On Monday, 5 July, proceedings commenced with a celebration of the Holy Communion at 9 o'clock in Westminster Abbey – not as in 1867, 1878, and 1888, in Lambeth Palace Chapel. Then the bishops assembled in the Guard Room at Lambeth.

[12] *Guardian*, 7 July 1897, p. 1085.
[13] G. K. A. Bell, *Randall Davidson*, vol. i, p. 303.

It was found that great care had been taken for the convenience and comfort of the members. Each bishop had his own arm-chair, with useful adjuncts for making notes; the chairs were arranged in deep rows, facing one another on either side of a central space down the middle of the Guard Room. This arrangement worked excellently well in practice, and it can scarcely be improved upon. The provision of lockers for all the bishops in another part of the palace, places marked with their names for coats, etc., long lines of tables for luncheon in broad passages, and many other arrangements to which the best thought of a practical mind had been given, had the effect of making the whole machinery of the sessions of the Conference work to the end in a most orderly, convenient, and comfortable manner. These arrangements, to which the Archbishop himself had given much attention, were made under the skilful superintendence of Mr W. D. Caröe, the architect of the Ecclesiastical Commission. All of the metropolitans, and all of the bishops from the United States of America, were invited in turn to stay for some days at Lambeth. The house-party numbered as a rule about twenty-two, from Mondays to Wednesdays, and from Wednesdays to Saturdays. The Archbishop kept the Sundays as days of rest.[14]

A word about the bishops present. Archbishop Thomson had died and been succeeded by Magee, who died shortly afterwards, and was succeeded by Maclagan of Lichfield. Bishop Lightfoot of Durham, who had been present in 1888, was dead, and his successor, B. F. Westcott, prevented by illness from participation in the debates. Harold Browne of Winchester, who had been present for three Conferences, had died and been succeeded by Randall Davidson. Davidson and Bishop Kennion of Wells (late of Adelaide) were the joint episcopal secretaries. They were assisted by Dr F. W. Pennefather as lay secretary. Bishop Harvey Goodwin of Carlisle, Charles Wordsworth of St Andrews, Cleveland Coxe of Western New York, and Medley of Fredericton had all died. The see of London was occupied by Mandell Creighton but his wife's biography indicates that he took little part in the Conference. That other great historian, William Stubbs, was still Bishop of Oxford. C. J. Ellicott was still Bishop of Gloucester and acted as registrar at what was his last Conference. There were two black bishops present, I. Oluwole and Charles Phillips, both Assistant Bishops in Western Equatorial Africa.

The programme facing the bishops, which had been prepared by E. W. Benson, was as follows:

[14] E. G. Sandford (ed.), *Memoirs of Archbishop Temple*, vol. ii, pp. 270–1.

1 The organization of the Anglican Communion.
2 Religious communities.
3 The critical study of holy Scripture.
4 Foreign missions.
5 Reformation movements on the Continent of Europe and elsewhere.
6 Church unity in its relation:
   (a) To the Churches of the East.
   (b) To the Latin Communion.
   (c) To other Christian bodies.
7 International arbitration.
8 Industrial problems.
9 The Book of Common Prayer.
   (a) Additional services.
   (b) Local adaptation.
10 The duties of the Church to the colonies.
11 Degrees in divinity.
12 To consider questions of difficulty which may be submitted to it by bishops attending the Conference.

It will be noticed that the six subjects of the 1888 Conference have expanded into twelve. An innovation is the placing of 'religious communities' on the agenda. Here was one of the definite fruits of the Oxford Movement upon which the bishops needed to pronounce. It is interesting, too, to find 'the critical study of the Bible'. It will be recalled that Frederick Temple had written in *Essays and Reviews* and since 1888 the volume of essays called *Lux Mundi* had come out (1889), proving that the High Church party had taken biblical criticism and evolution into its system. Perhaps the most controversial subject was the first, that on the Anglican Communion, since the agenda had suggested the possibility of both a central consultative body of the Anglican Communion and a court of reference, topics which had appeared before. Moreover, in 1895, a committee of bishops had been appointed to consider the organization of the Anglican Communion. This body drew up a report, in which Bishop John Wordsworth figured prominently, but the report, though presented to the bishops in 1896, was never published. Two such bodies had been mooted in this report. The Americans feared both possibilities. Bishop Doane of Albany wrote to Davidson before the meeting in February 1897 expressing his fears.

I have myself the very deepest convictions that in the light of all historical experience, and in the existing conditions of the Church today, it is most unwise to attempt and would be absolutely impossible to create anything like a Canterbury Patriarchate, to which National Churches would be willing either to refer, or with which they would be willing to consult, or to which they would be willing to establish any relation. I am sure that we have shewn here in America, and I am sure that you know how strongly my own feeling runs in this way, the strongest reverence and regard for the old See and for the Church of England. I am very clear in my own mind that the suggestion of this subject for discussion has been injurious to the best interests of the Conference; that its discussion would be inevitably painful; and that if it could, now that the change has come, (alas, alas,) in the personality of the Archbishopric, be dropped from the list of subjects; . . . I think it would give a much better impression at the beginning, and secure a very much better feeling throughout the Conference and conduce to far better results in its deliberations.[15]

To this Davidson replied on 6 April:

Your very important letter of (I fear) many weeks ago respecting the Lambeth Conference programme has been constantly in my thoughts and I have often wondered whether I ought to speak to the Archbishop of Canterbury confidentially about it. But on the whole I have considered that I should do more harm than good by so speaking. *Ere your letter reached me* the formal programme of the Conference (including the names of suggested speakers specified *by you* on behalf of the Presiding Bishop) had been posted to every Bishop of our Church entitled to attend, and it was clearly too late to change the programme even if it had been desirable. And, notwithstanding all your weighty and most kindly words, the importance of which I cordially appreciate, I do still doubt whether such a change would be desirable. That anything of the nature of a Canterbury *Patriarchate* will receive the support of the Conference I do not for a moment believe. Some would wish for it, but they will be few. On the other hand the idea of some central tribunal of reference, for disputes on doctrinal or even disciplinary questions, has got a firm hold on the minds of very many, perhaps I ought to say of *most* of the Colonial and Missionary Bishops. I did not realise that it was wholly unpopular even in the United States, though of course it is suggested for the help of our South African, Australian, and Missionary Bishops rather than with any direct thought of *your* branch of our Church, a branch eminently capable of taking care of itself! I believe the S. African and Antipodean Bishops regard the question as quite the most important of any that are to come up for discussion, and, considering the immense weight of authority with which the subject was *suggested*, I don't see how dear Archbishop Benson could do otherwise than place it on our agenda. I suppose it would be perfectly in order for the American Bishops, should they

15 G. K. A. Bell, *Randall Davidson*, vol. i, pp. 300–1.

so desire, to say that they preferred to be left out of consideration in that matter and to take no part in forming any such tribunal of reference or consultative body.[16]

What became of the desire for a tribunal and consultative council we shall see in a moment.

The plenary sessions ended on 10 July and then the twelve committees met until the Conference reassembled on Thursday, 22 July. In this period of committee work some interesting social events took place. On 13 July the bishops visited Windsor and attended a service at St George's Chapel. 'The Bishops', reported the *Guardian*,

> then proceeded to the East Terrace, where they assembled on either side of the carriage-drive to await the Queen. Her Majesty's carriage was preceded by an outrider and was drawn by a pair of grays. On the Queen's left sat Princess Beatrice, and facing her Majesty were the Grand Duke and Grand Duchess of Hesse. The Queen, who looked remarkably well, was dressed in black, with a black and white bonnet, and carried a black sunshade bordered with white. As the Queen's carriage, which proceeded at a walking pace, advanced, the Bishops stood bareheaded, and bowed low to her Majesty who graciously acknowledged their salutations. On arriving at the place where the Archbishop of Canterbury and the Bishop of Winchester were standing, the carriage stopped, and the Queen engaged in conversation with the Primate and the Bishop of Winchester, who presented a number of their colleagues.[17]

The two black bishops were among those presented.[18] On Monday, 19 July a Garden Party was held at Lambeth Palace.[19]

The next plenary sessions were held from 22 July until 31 July. They resulted in the passing of sixty-three resolutions and approval of eleven committee reports. The most important report from the point of view of Anglicanism was that on 'The Organization of the Anglican Communion', produced by a committee over which Bishop John Wordsworth had presided. The report recommended that Lambeth Conferences should be held every ten years. It also proposed the setting up of a 'tribunal of reference'. These were the resolutions concerning this tribunal which the committee wished to put to the Conference:

> That it is advisable that a tribunal of reference be appointed, to which may

---

[16] Idem, p. 301.
[17] *Guardian*, 1897, 14 July, p. 1096.
[18] Idem, p. 1154.
[19] Idem, p. 1154.

be referred any questions submitted by the Bishops of the Church of England, or by Colonial and Missionary Churches.

That it is expedient that the Archbishop of Canterbury should preside over the tribunal, and that it should further consist of the Archbishop of York, the Bishops of London, Durham, and Winchester, and representatives of each province not in the British Isles which may determine to accept the decisions of the tribunal; the Bishops of each such province having the right to elect and appoint any one Bishop of the Anglican Communion for every ten or fraction of ten Dioceses of which it may consist: and that the tribunal have power to request the advice of experts on any matters which may be submitted to them.[20]

These resolutions, however, were not adopted by the full Conference. The idea of a 'consultative body' was taken up at the plenary sessions. Resolution 5 of the Conference reads:

That it is advisable that a consultative body should be formed to which resort may be had, if desired, by the National Churches, Provinces, and extra-Provincial Dioceses of the Anglican Communion either for information or for advice, and that the Archbishop of Canterbury be requested to take such steps as he may think most desirable for the creation of this consultative body.

This consultative committee was, indeed, set up by Frederick Temple. Walter Hobhouse, writing just before the 1908 Conference, said, 'We understand that such a Body was formed by Archbishop Temple, and that it has held more than one important meeting; but none of its proceedings have been made public, although more no doubt will be heard of it at the coming Conference.'[21]

There is no doubt that John Wordsworth was somewhat disappointed that only the consultative body and not the tribunal of reference was taken up. In a letter to the *Guardian* he distinguished between the two bodies in this way:

The consultative body is intended to give information or advice to any part of the communion such as a province or non-provincial diocese that chooses to ask. The questions submitted to it will, I presume, be questions of policy and such like.

The 'tribunal of reference', whenever it comes into being, will be of the nature of a court of arbitration on judicial matters. The scope of the Committee's resolution was limited to Colonial Churches and to English

[20] *Conference of Bishops of the Anglican Communion, holden at Lambeth Palace in July, 1897*, p. 56.

[21] Op. cit., p. 55.

dioceses. Such a tribunal may be created at any time by the colonies especially interested, some of which feel that their judicial strength is at present too small to decide serious cases – e.g. of heresy within their own limits.[22]

The American bishops who objected strongly to anything in the nature of a tribunal of reference for the Anglican Communion, were very suspicious of the consultative committee and were opposed to any suggestion of a Canterbury patriarchate. Here we may quote some words of Bishop Mitchinson, suffragan Bishop in the diocese of Peterborough, which were printed in the *Peterborough Diocesan Magazine*.

But the nett result is somewhat disappointing. Nothing is settled; no perplexing problem solved, no burning question bravely grappled with. And so apparently it will always be, if the Lambeth Conference continues on its present basis – viz. a friendly gathering of Bishops, invited to talk over matters of general interest, not to settle disputed questions by a formal pronouncement. This the Americans – and not only the Americans – are determined it shall continue to be. They passionately resist any proposal which seems to clothe the conference with even the semblance of authority. We have indeed got our Central Consultative Body, but its action is so jealously guarded that it will most likely expire of inanition.[23]

John Wordsworth's disappointment at the failure of the Conference to set up the tribunal of reference is revealed in his words at the Nottingham Church Congress at the end of September, when he spoke about the two resolutions which the plenary Conference had failed to take up:

All I need say on these resolutions is that the procedure advocated in them is, in my opinion, certainly desirable wherever a local branch of our Church consists of only one provincial or primatial jurisdiction, with a small number of bishops, as is the case in South Africa, the West Indies, Australia and New Zealand, and I may add in Scotland, though that is a peculiar and more difficult case.[24]

Another interesting resolution on this question of the organization of the Anglican Communion was Resolution 7:

Recognising the almost universal custom in the Western Church of

[22] *Guardian*, 18 August 1897, p. 1279.
[23] See *Guardian*, 1 September 1897, p. 1360.
[24] *Report of the Church Congress, Nottingham*, 1897, p. 51.

attaching the title of Archbishop to the rank of Metropolitan, we are of opinion that the revival and extension of this custom among ourselves is justifiable and desirable. It is advisable that the proposed adoption of such title should be formally announced to the Bishops of the various Churches and Provinces of the Communion with a view to its general recognition.

Two colonial metropolitans, the Bishop of Ruperts Land and the Bishop of Ontario, had assumed the title of archbishop before the 1897 Conference. As a result of Resolution 7 of the 1897 Conference the Bishops of Sydney, Capetown, and Jamaica assumed the title of archbishop.[25]

We turn now to the other committees. The committee dealing with religious communities was chaired by the Bishop of Oxford, William Stubbs, who was Bishop of a diocese where several communities were established. They observed with thankfulness the great revival of religious communities in the Anglican Communion. They said that every priest ministering to a religious community should be licensed by the diocesan bishop. They also hailed 'with thankfulness the revival of the ancient office of Deaconess,' and noted 'the increasing recognition of its value to the Church.' It was urged that the term 'deaconess' should be reserved for those who had been set apart by an episcopal act. The committee contemplated a further report on the question of a uniform approach on setting apart and licensing deaconesses. 'Upon this point also we hope to speak more fully hereafter.' A later report on this question did materialize and went out with the agenda for the 1908 Conference.[26]

The committee on the 'critical study of holy Scripture', chaired by C. J. Ellicott, the Bishop of Gloucester, need not detain us. They were in favour of the 'reverent and reasonable use of criticism in investigating the structure and composition of the different books' of the Bible, and affirmed that 'the Bible in historic, moral, and spiritual coherence, presents a Revelation of God, progressively given, and adapted to various ages, until it finds its completion in the Person and teaching of the Lord Jesus Christ.' They added, 'We have been bidden to study the Bible like any other book, but such study has shown us how absolutely the Bible differs from any other book.' In their last paragraph they

---

[25] See H. Lowther Clarke, *Constitutional Church Government*, p. 29.
[26] See Walter Hobhouse, *A Short Sketch of the First Four Lambeth Conferences*, p. 57. For the report see R. Davidson, *The Six Lambeth Conferences 1867–1920*, pp. 442–4. The report is dated 28 November 1898 and signed by Stubbs.

expressed their 'conviction with regard to the New Testament that the results of critical study have confirmed the Christian faith.'

There was a lengthy report on foreign missions, produced under the chairmanship of Edgar Jacob, Bishop of Newcastle. The report on reformation movements on the Continent and elsewhere surveyed the state of the Old Catholics in Germany and in Switzerland and dealt with the Reformed movements in Spain, Portugal, Italy, and France, Austria, Mexico, and Brazil. The resolution of sympathy did not add anything to that of 1888. In the case of Germany and Switzerland there was a repetition of the offer of admission to Holy Communion. The report on church unity, in dealing with the Churches of the East, spoke of the cordial welcome given to Bishop Mandell Creighton when he attended the coronation of the Czar in 1896 and the visit to Russia of Archbishop Maclagan.[27] In a section on the Church of Rome allusion was made to the bull *Apostolicae Curae* of Pope Leo XIII and the reply from the English Archbishops, and the resolution of 1888 was repeated 'that, under present conditions, it is useless to consider the question of Reunion with our brethren of the Roman Church.' Regarding other Christian bodies, English Nonconformists, Scottish Presbyterians, Moravians, and the Swedish Church, the committee quoted the Lambeth Quadrilateral.

The committee on international arbitration, chaired by Bishop Boyd Carpenter of Ripon, caused a resolution to be passed by the whole Conference that international arbitration was consistent with the religion of Christ (Resolution 41). In its report, the committee said this on the subject of war:

> But under any circumstances before the decision of war is invoked, it appears to them to be the solemn duty of the people to make sure that it is a great principle and not a prejudice or object of pride which is at stake, and to reflect that great principles may often be more effectively maintained by reasoning, fair dealing, and patience, than by war.

'War', they said, 'strikes at the heart of the highest interests of mankind.' The committee on industrial problems, under the chairmanship of Bishop Percival of Hereford, emphasized the four great principles of brotherhood, labour, justice, and public responsibility.

The committee on the Prayer Book, chaired by Lord Alwyne Compton, Bishop of Ely, considered the questions of additional services

---

[27] See L. Creighton, *Life and Letters of Mandell Creighton*, vol. i, ch. 5, and F. D. How, *William Dalrymple Maclagan*, ch. 34.

and local adaptation. They recognized the inherent right of the episcopate to exercise the *ius liturgicum* by adapting services to special circumstances, and by sanctioning additional prayers under due limitations, and in the report are mentioned some additional services and adaptations which seemed to be necessary. They also suggested that the Archbishop of Canterbury should be required to take such steps as might be necessary for a new translation of the Athanasian Creed. This resolution was accepted but nothing done about it until 1909.

The committee on the duties of the church to the colonies did not feel that the infamous Colonial Clergy Act of 1874 should be repealed, but administered by the English episcopate in a generous spirit.

There was a most interesting report from the committee on degrees in divinity, chaired by the Bishop of Goulburn (W. Chalmers). It felt that it would be a good idea to have some scheme of theological examinations for the whole Anglican Communion. It also spoke about the possibility of a Lambeth B.A. in Theology, followed by a Lambeth B.D. Nothing came of this.

The encyclical, which prefaced the resolutions, was drawn up by Temple himself without his consulting anyone else.[28] It was adopted with but slight alterations. Into it came three new subjects, temperance (a topic which Temple had much at heart), purity, and the sanctity of marriage. On temperance, he wrote, 'It is important to lay stress on the essential condition of permanent success in this work, namely, that it should be taken up in a religious spirit as part of Christian devotion to the Lord.' On purity, 'The sin of impurity is a degradation of those who fall into it, whether men or women, and purity is within reach of every Christian who, trusting in the grace of God, fights the battle of his baptismal vow.' On marriage, he said, 'The maintenance of the dignity and sanctity of marriage lies at the root of social purity, and therefore of the safety and sacredness of the family and home. The foundation of its holy security and the honour is the precept of our Lord. "What therefore God hath joined together let not man put asunder."' So keenly did Temple feel on the subject of purity that he caused the 1888 Report on Purity to be published again at the end of the 1897 Conference Report. George Forrest Browne in *Frederick Temple* relates one episode about the Archbishop's encyclical. Temple

had used very strong language about the negligence of the Church of

---

[28] E. G. Sandford, *Memoirs of Archbishop Temple*, vol. ii, p. 273.

England in the matter of missionary work among the heathen and in foreign parts. More than one bishop begged that the severe phrases of censure might be seriously moderated, to bring them within cover of what those who spoke believed to be the real facts. The Archbishop declined to change the phrases. The objectors persisted, going so far as to declare that the expressions used were unjust, and would greatly grieve the keen supporters of missions without having any useful effect upon such as were negligent. Still the Archbishop declined to change, and after a time the session came to its appointed end. The next morning the Archbishop commenced the proceedings by announcing that he proposed to modify the phrases objected to, although for his own part he thought them not too strong. He then read the passage in the form in which it appeared in the published encyclical letter. A leading American bishop sprang up and began to thank the Archbishop warmly for acceding to the wishes expressed the evening before. The Bishop's words were interrupted by a stern pronouncement from the President's chair – 'Bishop of ———, you may thank me as much as you like; but you must thank me in silence.'[29]

There were certain words in the encyclical about persecution by Jews of Jewish converts to Christianity. 'The conversion of the Jews is also much hindered by the severe persecutions to which Jewish converts are often exposed from their own people, and it is sometimes necessary to see to their protection if they are persuaded to join us.' Grave objection to these words was made by the Jew Sir Oswald John Simon.[30]

The final service of the Conference took place in St Paul's Cathedral on Monday, 1 August, at 10 a.m., following a service held there on the Sunday in connection with the Boards of Missions of Canterbury and York. At both these services Temple preached. At the Monday service his text was on John 15.4, 'Abide in me and I in you.'[31] The report in the *Guardian* said

The Archbishop of Canterbury and all the home Episcopate, as well as most of the colonial and American Bishops wore their scarlet robes, but a few appeared in black chimeres and two or three in violet. There was also a large number of chaplains in attendance, some wearing the broad black scarf, and others stoles of red, white or green.

[29] *Memoirs of Archbishop Temple by Seven Friends*, vol. i, pp. 277–8.
[30] See *Guardian*, 11 August 1897, p. 1258.
[31] The Monday was August Bank Holiday Monday – a recent innovation. A correspondent in the *Guardian* suggested before the service that, as the public buildings nearby St Paul's would not be in use because of the public holiday, they could be used for the robing of the bishops. He added that in 1888 bishops were seen robing in the aisles. See *Guardian*, 28 July, p. 1187.

Bishop Herzog of the Old Catholics was in the congregation.[32] On Tuesday, 3 August, Temple and more than a hundred of the bishops proceeded to Glastonbury by special train for a ceremony organized by Bishop Kennion of Bath and Wells. It had been suggested that in the 1300th year since the coming of St Augustine of Canterbury, the whole Anglican Communion should make special pilgrimage to a site connected intimately with the much earlier Christianity of the British race. There was a vast procession to the Abbey ruins. 'When the Archbishop emerged at the end of the procession into the full light of the sun, he was urged to place some covering on his head, as almost everyone else was forced of necessity to do, "No," he said, with characteristic energy of utterance, "No; my skull is thicker than yours!"'[33] A full account of the proceedings at Glastonbury was published by the Church Historical Society.[34] Some of the bishops also visited York and others Norwich.

In the end Temple had emerged as a remarkable chairman and leader in the 1897 Conference. Bishop Mitchinson wrote:

The president of 1897 won his way, almost in spite of himself, to the esteem and – yes – enthusiastic loyalty of all (excepting, perhaps, those few whom he mercilessly snubbed) by his firmness, his'prompt deference to the obvious feeling or expressed wishes of the conference, his fairness, his chivalrous generosity and his unsparing sacrifice of time and brains. If to the *fortiter in re* there could have been added the *suaviter in modo*, he would have been simply ideal.[35]

The Bishop of Colombo (R. S. Copleston) said of him:

We had a noble example in our chairman. His unwearied attention to business and ability in the conduct of it, were the wonder of all. A genuine considerateness and a frequent gaiety and lightness of touch for which many were not prepared, were varied by an occasional growl of that humorous brusqueness, which is, perhaps, popularly thought more characteristic, and which has certainly in him a characteristic charm. Such little instances of a rough touch were always received with delighted laughter, in which no one joined so heartily as the Archbishop.[36]

[32] See *Guardian*, 4 August, p. 1219. On Herzog, see C. B. Moss, *The Old Catholic Movement.*

[33] *Memoirs of Archbishop Temple by Seven Friends*, vol. ii, pp. 279–80. Cf. M. M., *Bishop Montgomery. A Memoir*, p. 74, who says that Temple replied, 'My head can stand more than that sun, thank you.'

[34] See No. XXX, *Glastonbury.*

[35] See *Guardian*, 1 September, p. 1360.

[36] *Guardian*, 3 November 1897, p. 1731.

Evidently the American bishops were in the end so satisfied with the Archbishop that they wished to present him with a mitre. Bishop Doane of Albany (who was so worried about the Conference beforehand) consulted Davidson about this. He put them off the idea of giving a mitre. What was sent across the Atlantic were 'vessels for private Communion, of gold, exquisitely designed and richly jewelled. To add to the interest of the gift, the execution of the work had been entrusted to one who had been a pupil of Dr Temple at Rugby.' The gift was accompanied by this inscription

F. CANTUAR
Archbishop Primate Metropolitan
presiding over the
Lambeth Conference of 1897
in the spirit of power and of love and of a sound mind
from his brothers in the American Episcopate
an affectionate recognition of his wise leadership
his justice his generosity his gracious hospitality.

The gift was brought to England by Bishop E. S. Talbot of Rochester and was received by Temple with genuine and effusive thanks.[37]

[37] See E. G. Sandford, *Memoirs of Archbishop Temple by Seven Friends*, vol. ii, pp. 272–3.

8

RANDALL DAVIDSON
THE CONGRESS AND CONFERENCE
OF 1908

Frederick Temple lived on after the 1897 Conference until 23 December 1902. The latter part of his archiepiscopate was marked by the death of Queen Victoria on 22 January 1901 and the coronation of King Edward VII. Mandell Creighton, the Bishop of London, an historian with a European reputation and a possible successor to Frederick Temple, died a week before the Queen. Randall Davidson, Bishop of Winchester, who had been involved in three Lambeth Conferences, now seemed the natural successor to Temple. On 31 December the Prime Minister, Arthur J. Balfour, wrote to Davidson to tell him he was submitting his name to the King for the Primacy of All England. On 12 February 1903 Davidson was enthroned at Canterbury.

The next Lambeth Conference would be held in five years' time. Before that event Davidson became the first Archbishop of Canterbury to visit North America. On 20 May 1903 the Bishop of Rhode Island, Thomas March Clark, who had been present at the First Lambeth Conference of 1867, invited the Archbishop to attend the General Convention in 1904. Bishop Clark wrote, 'It would be a great gratification to us all if you would come over to that Convention. We have gladly received from time to time English Bishops, especially Bishop Selwyn. The coming of the Archbishop, however, would do much towards bringing into closer and more sympathetic relations the two branches of the Anglican Communion.'[1]

In a speech delivered by Davidson in the Faneuil Hall at Boston (the city where the General Convention was held), he spoke of the old rumour that Archbishop Laud was once going to be punished by transportation to New England. He ended:

[1] See G. K. A. Bell, *Randall Davidson*, vol. i, p. 442. Bishop Clark makes the astonishing error of imagining that the Archbishop who summoned him to the First Lambeth Conference was J. B. Sumner!

To-day we have, I am thankful to say, a constant stream of visitors from this side of the Atlantic who come to see the historic home in which it is my privilege to dwell, and as they stand in Lambeth Palace Chapel, the place which is identified with the last of the struggles, the pathetic struggles of the old man Laud before he was led forth to his death, I think I may say that no visitors look upon those historical associations, those mementoes of a day that is gone, with more tenderness and sympathy, with a truer understanding of what the relation is of this present to the old past, than do the descendants of the very men whom the rigid autocratic rule of Laud and his friends and colleagues had caused in the first instance to cross the sea.

Randall Davidson and his wife were presented with a piece of silver, which the House of Bishops ventured to hope would 'find place on the table of most catholic hospitality in the Guard Room of Lambeth Palace with the request that it may be counted as a personal gift to your Grace and Mrs Davidson'.[2]

The year 1908 saw two great Anglican gatherings – the pan-Anglican Congress and the Fifth Lambeth Conference – so it was a veritable *annus mirabilis* for Anglicanism. The pan-Anglican Congress was the brain child of Bishop Montgomery of the S.P.G. When he preached the annual S.P.G. sermon in St Paul's Cathedral in 1903, he suggested a world-wide Anglican congress of churchmen and women. There followed five years of preparation. The Central Board of Missions was approached and asked to accept responsibility for the event, but it seemed terribly difficult at first to conjure up any enthusiasm. 'They were all frankly bored', we read in the life of Bishop Montgomery. 'One prelate actually got up and said that if this project materialized it would be the ruin of the Church of England.'[3]

However, after some months, the Board was induced to appoint a committee which would take all responsibility for the congress, financially and otherwise. Bishop Montgomery and Dr Eugene Stock of the C.M.S. were appointed secretaries. Vast preparations went ahead. Three questions were sent out to each Bishop of an Anglican diocese:

1 What are the questions of supreme importance for the Church of God in your own region?

2 What, in your opinion, are the greatest problems outside your own region?

3 What is the chief corporate duty of the whole Anglican Communion at this time?

[2] See G. K. A. Bell, *Randall Davidson*, vol. i, pp. 449–51.
[3] Op. cit., p. 58.

To the third question no confident answers were forthcoming. Suggestions for discussion were tabulated and selected in consultation with the church overseas. It was E. J. Palmer (later Bishop of Bombay) who finally arranged the subjects. Then preliminary papers were published on all of them. Most of these can be found in the later published reports. At last enthusiasm increased and money began flowing in. As the time drew near the actual organization of the congress was placed in the hands of the Rev. A. B. Mynors of Langley Burrell, who was put into two tiny Westminster offices which had to be extended to eight.

The seven subjects selected for discussion were these:

(A) The Church and human society.
(B) Christian truth and other intellectual forces.
(C) The Church's ministry.
(D) Mission in non-Christian lands.
(E) Missions in Christendom.
(F) The Anglican Communion.
(G) The Church's work among the young.

Section F on 'The Anglican Communion' is of immense interest. It was divided into these sub-sections:

The Anglican Communion. Its place in Christendom.
Things essential and non-essential.
Historic episcopate.
Possibilities of intercommunion and reunion.
Local churches.
Equipment and organization.
Native episcopate.
Relation of organized churches to the whole Communion.
Question of a central authority.

The last sub-section is of particular interest in view of the debates and discussions which had gone on in 1897. E. J. Palmer, then Fellow of Balliol, wrote a preliminary paper on 'The Constitution of the Anglican Communion, with special reference to its central organization'. He asked:

Ought there not to be a General Synod of the Anglican Communion? With so much independent action there must arise questions such as these: What have Diocesan or Provincial Synods no power to alter? What is essential in faith? What is essential in practice? Is this novel doctrine compatible with the faith once delivered? Is that ancient practice to be retained in all circumstances? Real unity in the Anglican Communion means identity in some things, but what are these? A General Council of the Anglican Communion alone could determine.

He also elaborated on the need of an Executive Council. 'At the present moment there is no man, and no body of men, whose duty it is to survey the field of the operations of the Anglican Communion, and who, at the same time, has authority to direct the endeavours of the Churches composing it in particular points.' He also spoke of the need of a Supreme Ecclesiastical Court of Appeal. 'It is inevitable that causes of litigation should arise between the individual and the corporation, or the corporation and its officers, or between officers of different grades. For all questions in all bodies there must be some decision which is final, one court beyond which there is no appeal.' Palmer went on to make three suggestions:

(1) 'The practical question about a General Council or Synod of the Anglican Communion is "Does the Lambeth Conference satisfy the demand?" At its first inception the enactment of canons and the making of decisions binding on the Church were excluded from its scope by Archbishop Longley's speech in Convocation. Again, Archbishop Tait's letter of invitation, 1875, excluded the discussion of change of doctrine or authoritative explanation of doctrine, as also matters of discipline which he desired left to the independent Churches. But the fact remains that at the Lambeth Conference there meet the persons who might reasonably be summoned to form a regular General Council of the Anglican Communion. The Oecumenical Councils of the first ages no doubt dealt with all the matters which Archbishops Longley and Tait excluded from the purview of the Lambeth Conference of 1867 and 1878. Would it not be better that Lambeth should become a General Council of the Anglican world and make decisions on doctrine and discipline which should be binding on the whole Communion?'

(2) Palmer suggested an Executive Council of 'patriarchs' in the Anglican Communion. There would be 'patriarchs' for those regions of the Communion which contain nations actual or in the making. 'To these might be added a few to represent the portions of the Anglican Communion which fall outside such units.'

(3) If 'we can get the Patriarchs started as an Executive Council, and that Council becomes respected for its efficiency, men might in the future find in it, strengthened for the purpose by legal assessors, their wished-for common Supreme Ecclesiastical Court of Appeal.'

These viewpoints of Palmer were discussed on 22 June and very noteworthy is the summing up of the discussion by Bishop Collins of Gibraltar. Collins thought the Executive Council of Patriarchs would create a privileged oligarchy 'and I doubt whether any one would claim that an oligarchy has been in the long run conducive either to the preservation of liberty or the fostering of ordered life.' He said that what was needed was not so much closer union with Canterbury but closer union with each other.[4]

The inaugural service of the Congress took place at Westminster Abbey on Monday, 15 June. 'A vast congregation filled every part of the Abbey. There was no long-drawn-out procession of vested ministers; nave, choir and transepts were filled with worshippers kneeling silently. The Archbishop of Canterbury alone was in robes besides the Chapter.'[5]

During the eight days of the Congress, it was calculated that each day 17,000 people attended the different meetings in the various assembly halls, the Albert Hall, Kensington Town Hall, Holborn Town Hall, Caxton Hall, Caxton Council Chambers, Church House (in the Hoare Memorial Hall and in the Great Hall), and Sion College. A large thank-offering was raised and spent on the church overseas. It was all an immense achievement. Among the speakers were the youthful William Temple. On the Women's General Committee were Mrs Creighton (the President), Mrs Montgomery (the Hon. Secretary), Mrs Davidson, Mrs Benson, and Mrs Frederick Temple. Archbishop Davidson presided at some of the meetings and welcomed the representatives at Lambeth Palace, but the strain was great and he felt clear that never again would it be right to hold an Anglican Congress and a Lambeth Conference in the same year.

The concluding service was held in St Paul's Cathedral. Here is the description of it written at the time by Bishop Montgomery:

Five thousand people were accommodated in the cathedral. The small galleries were all filled; a special gallery was erected for a large orchestra. The Bishops robed in the crypt, and made a circuit of the cathedral outside in procession. They were grouped in Provinces, and each continent was headed by a macebearer, the city churches having kindly lent us maces. The Stewards were under the control of the Rev. G. E. Farran. Once more the weather was perfect, and crowds were assembled outside the cathedral, and were controlled by a large body of police, who managed the proceedings as

[4] *The Pan-Anglican Congress. Section F. Official Report*, p. 221.
[5] Bishop Montgomery's account of the Congress in the first volume of the *Official Report*, p. 12.

only English police can. The Service consisted of the Litany, sung by four
Minor Canons in unison and by the Choir; the Archbishop of Canterbury
addressed the vast congregation; the Bishops, in Provinces, came up to the
altar, advanced up the steps two by two, placed their offerings in two
almsdishes on the altar, humbly bowing the while; they then fell back
waiting till the other Bishops of the province or continent had made their
offerings; then in a body this group of Bishops was conducted back to its
place by the macebearer. The presentation was made by the Archbishop of
Canterbury, in words from the prayer of King Solomon; and the service
concluded with the *Te Deum*, the Metropolitans and Presiding Bishops
having first been ranged before the altar. The total sum actually presented
upon the occasion was £335,000 in round figures. By August 1 this sum was
increased to about £346,000.[6]

There is a long account of this final service in the *Guardian* for 1 July.
'The English Bishops' it reports,

> wore their scarlet Convocation robes, which added colour and contributed
> to the imposing character of the scene, but most of the American prelates
> were vested in the black chimere. The sombreness of this attire was relieved
> in some cases by festal stoles, and one prelate wore a purple chimere. There
> were two coloured Bishops in the procession – Bishops James Johnson and
> Oluwole, of Western Equatorial Africa.[7]

It adds, 'A striking figure was the Dean of Westminster [J. Armitage
Robinson], who occupied a stall next to Canon Scott Holland.' But
Dean Gregory could not be present, but watched the procession of
bishops from one of the Deanery windows. 'Prominent among the
congregation were Earl Roberts and Mr William Temple, whilst among
visitors, sundry and numerous, who applied to the stewards for a seat
was a Russian priest, whose sacred office was indicated by his jewelled
cross and chain.'[8]

The Fifth Lambeth Conference followed immediately after the Pan-
Anglican Congress. Archbishop Davidson had sent out his invitations
to this Conference in July 1907. In the end 242 bishops came to it. Let
us, therefore, first look at the episcopate. W. D. Maclagan was still at
York. Winnington-Ingram had succeeded Creighton at London, and his
suffragan bishopric of Stepney had been filled by Cosmo Gordon Lang.

---

[6] *Pan-Anglican Congress. General Report*, pp. 12–13.

[7] *Guardian*, 1 July, p. 1131.

[8] Idem. On the Pan-Anglican Congress see also Robert S. Bosher, 'The Pan-Anglican
Congress of 1908' in *Historical Magazine of the Protestant Episcopal Church*, June
1955, pp. 126–42, and H. Scott Holland, *A Bundle of Memories*, pp. 231–40,
'Romance in Gaiters'.

Bishop Ryle had been transferred from Exeter to Winchester, in succession to Davidson. Francis Paget had succeeded Stubbs at Oxford, and Handley Moule had succeeded Westcott at Durham. F. H. Chase, the Cambridge biblical scholar, had succeeded Lord Compton at Ely; Archibald Robertson, the author of *Regnum Dei*, was at Exeter, and F. J. Chavasse was at Liverpool. E. A. Knox, a strong Evangelical, father of Ronald and Wilfred, was Bishop of Manchester. E. S. Talbot had moved from Rochester to be first bishop of the new diocese of Southwark. The Archbishop of Armagh was William Alexander, who had attended the Conferences of 1878, 1888, and 1897, having been made Bishop of Derry in 1867. He was treated with the greatest respect. His daughter recorded, 'It is well remembered that, at the last Pan-Anglican Conference, they all, with one accord, rose to their feet when the old man was wheeled into the hall of assembly.' He was known in America for his visit there in 1891.[9] The Presiding Bishop of the American church was D. S. Tuttle of Missouri; he had been a bishop in 1867, but, like Alexander, was not present at the Lambeth Conference of that year. Bishop Percival was still at Hereford and William Boyd Carpenter at Ripon. These two liberals had a companion in Bishop J. W. Diggle of Carlisle, the biographer of James Fraser. An American liberal was Bishop Lawrence of Massachusetts.[10]

Davidson was determined that Bishop Montgomery of the S.P.G., the father of the Pan-Anglican Congress, should also participate in the Fifth Lambeth Conference, and so in 1907, as he was preparing for the Congress, the Archbishop appointed him one of the secretaries of the Conference. The other secretary was G. R. Eden, Bishop of Wakefield (a protégé of Bishop Lightfoot). Bishop Kennion of Bath and Wells was treasurer. Archbishop Jones of Capetown, who had been present in 1878, 1888, and 1897, took no part in the Congress or Conference, as he had died in Cornwall on 21 May.[11]

The official proceedings of the Conference began, as usual, at Canterbury. On Saturday, 4 July, there was a luncheon in the Coleridge Museum of St Augustine's College. Then at 3 o'clock the reception service was held in the Cathedral. Four thousand people filled the building. Nearly 200 bishops were present. Winnington-Ingram could not make it owing to a sprain while playing tennis!

[9] See Eleanor Alexander, *Primate Alexander, Archbishop of Armagh*, p. 246.
[10] See William Lawrence, *Fifty Years*.
[11] See *Guardian*, 27 May 1908, p. 896. Also M. H. M. Wood, *A Father in God. The Episcopate of William West Jones, D.D., Archbishop of Capetown.*

The processional hymn was Archbishop Benson's translation of *Urbs Beata*, sung unaccompanied to Smart's tune. The choir was augmented by men and boys from the choirs of Dover Parish Church and Holy Trinity, Folkestone. It would have been well if the organ could have assisted in the last few verses. Some of the Bishops tried to join in, but it was difficult to keep in touch with the choir so far away. . . . The recessional hymn was 'For all the Saints', sung to Barnby's tune. Again the absence of organ accompaniment somewhat marred the effect. A large number of people, as well as some of the Bishops joined in, with the result that groups in different parts of the Cathedral broke away from the choir, producing a very unedifying effect.[12]

The Archbishop spoke from St Augustine's chair on the altar steps, and made allusions to the association of Canterbury Cathedral with various junctures of English church life – the Magna Carta, the Becket shrine, the Black Prince, Matthew Parker, and Queen Elizabeth. He reminded them that it was the fourth of July, a date of great significance to all Americans.

There followed the customary garden party in the Deanery garden, by invitation of Dean Wace, joint author with William Smith of the famous *Dictionary of Christian Biography*. The bands of the Seventh Dragoon Guards 'played a good selection of music'. Then the bishops returned to London, since on the Sunday, at 11 a.m., there was another opening service at Westminster. The archbishops and bishops were marshalled for this service by Jocelyn Perkins, the sacrist. Dean Armitage Robinson preached the sermon. He had the honour of being the first non-episcopal ecclesiastic to preach at a Lambeth Conference.[13] Between 170 and 180 bishops took part.

On the following day, Monday 6 July, the Conference opened in the Old Library, the room of their meeting in 1878 and 1888. They met daily until Saturday, 11 July, and during the week eleven committees were appointed to deal with the subjects on the agenda:

1 The Faith and Modern Thought. Bishop E. S. Talbot of Southwark became the chairman of this committee.

2 The Supply and Training of the Clergy. This was the first time that the subject had been touched upon in a Conference. Bishop Winnington-Ingram acted as chairman.

3 Religious Education. The chairman was Bishop Knox of Manchester, a man devoted to the cause of church schools.

[12] *Guardian*, 8 July 1908, pp. 1148–9.
[13] For his sermon see *Guardian*, 8 July 1908, p. 1167.

4 Foreign Missions. Here the chairman was Bishop Edgar Jacob of St Albans. He had been chairman of this committee in 1897, when Bishop of Newcastle.

5 The Book of Common Prayer. Chairman, Bishop Jayne of Chester.·

6 The Administration of the Holy Communion. The chairman was Bishop Francis Paget of Oxford, who had written on 'The Sacraments' in *Lux Mundi.*

7 Ministries of Healing. Here again was a subject which had not been tackled before at a Conference. Herbert Ryle, Bishop of Winchester, was chairman.

8 Marriage Problems. George Forrest Browne, Bishop of Bristol, was chairman.

9 The Moral Witness of the Church. Augustus Legge, Bishop of Lichfield, acted as chairman.

10 Organization within the Anglican Communion. Archibald Robertson, Bishop of Exeter, was chairman.

11 Reunion and Intercommunion. This was a subject in which John Wordsworth had played a considerable part and he was not unnaturally chosen as chairman. It was his last Lambeth Conference, as he died in 1911. It will be noted that all the chairmen of committees were English diocesan bishops.

During the fortnight of 13–25 July the various committees held their sessions, some in the Church House, Westminster, some at Lambeth, others elsewhere. Again there were various social events while the committees were meeting. On Monday, 20 July, King Edward received the bishops at Buckingham Palace and, after they had been severally presented, he was given an Address signed by the Archbishop of Canterbury on behalf of the Conference.[14] On Thursday, 23 July, there was a Quiet Day at Fulham Parish Church, taken by R. S. Copleston, Bishop of Calcutta and Metropolitan of India. He had been Bishop of Colombo in 1897.

The Conference reassembled for its second series of plenary sessions on Monday, 27 July, and sat until Wednesday, 5 August, discussing the Reports and an encyclical on the theme of 'Service' prepared by the Archbishop, with the assistance of Bishops Paget of Oxford, Wordsworth of Salisbury, Palmer of Bombay, and Collins of Gibraltar.[15] The Report on 'The Faith and Modern Thought', slightly

[14] See *Guardian*, 22 July 1908, pp. 1227–8. The address is given on p. 1228 and the reply of the King on the same page.

[15] See G. K. A. Bell, *Randall Davidson*, vol. i, p. 570. E. J. Palmer of Balliol was consecrated Bishop of Bombay on 28 May 1908. For Collins see A. J. Mason, *Life of William Edward Collins, Bishop of Gibraltar*, p. 135.·

obscure in style, clearly showing signs of Talbot's penmanship, had some useful sentences on the criticism of the Gospels.

> We are well aware that in many minds there has been created an uneasy impression that the critical study of the Gospel narratives has reduced the history of our Lord's life upon earth to an uncertainty upon which we cannot build. But we wish to express our assurance that the fierce fire of modern criticism has only made it plainer that we have in the Gospels a definite and convincing picture of a unique personality. The record amply suffices to introduce to men and women the living Friend whom they learn to know better in the light of nearer and nearer personal communion.

There was also a valuable footnote on miracles:

> In using the word *miracles* in a report dealing with scientific thought we must guard ourselves against the often repeated misapprehension that the Church by that word means breaches or suspensions of the laws of Nature. To this end, instead of using any modern words, we prefer to quote the noble words of St Augustine, so often quoted by theologians (e.g. Trench, on 'The Miracles', p. 15, ed. 1866): 'Contra naturam non incongrue dicimus aliquid Deum facere, quod facit contra id quod novimus in naturâ. . . .'

The report on 'The Supply and Training of Clergy' noted the existence of a report the previous year on this subject, drawn up by a committee appointed by the Archbishop of Canterbury.[16] The Lambeth Conference committee said much on the deficiency in the number of clergy. On the question of training, they said that 'all candidates for Holy Orders should be graduates of some recognised University, as the increased facilities for obtaining degrees from the newer Universities, with or without residence, bring a degree within the reach of those who are being mainly trained at Theological Colleges.'[17] They added, under 'Special Training', 'In the case of graduates, all candidates should be required to receive *at least* one year of special training at a Theological College, or under some recognized supervision.' They continued,

> In addition to the usual curriculum of study generally followed in Theological Colleges, it is desirable that instruction should be imparted in social and economic questions; general business principles; applied moral theology and Church law. It is clear that, if these suggestions are to be carried out, a longer residence than is at present usual would be requisite at Theological Colleges, and that candidates should come there better

---

[16] *The Supply and Training of Candidates for Holy Orders.*
[17] Randall Davidson, *The Six Lambeth Conferences*, p. 353.

prepared. Affiliation of every non-graduate Theological College to some University is also desirable.

On the question of Latin they said, 'We are also of opinion that in exceptional cases a Bishop should be free to exercise a dispensing power as to a candidate being "learned in the Latin tongue".'[18]

Passing over the Reports on Religious Education and Foreign Missions we come to that on Prayer-Book Adaptation. Among the things they recommended was a revision of the Exhortation in the Marriage Service, the supply of additional suffrages in the Litany, the use of our Lord's Summary of the Law as an alternative to the Ten Commandments in the Communion service. Though unwilling to recommend that the Revised Version of the Bible be substituted for the Authorized, in the Book of Common Prayer, they regarded the subject 'as worthy of consideration'.[19] Passing over the Report on Holy Communion we arrive at that on 'Ministries of Healing'. Here the committee were not prepared to recommend the restoration of the unction of the sick, but did not wish to go so far as to advise the prohibition of its use, if it was earnestly desired by the sick person.

On the question of Marriage Problems, the committee concerned dealt first with divorce. In their last paragraph in this section, they said, 'It is well known that there is a difference of opinion on the question whether the really (or technically) innocent person should be allowed to marry in church with the Church's Service. It appears to a majority of the Committee that the objection to saying the solemn words over a person whose wedlock has been sundered, 'Those whom God hath joined together let not man put asunder', is very great. It is a grievous misfortune that in so many cases the really innocent party does not exist. The suggestion that the guilty person might be allowed to marry in church, the Committee unanimously condemn.'[20] In its resolutions the Conference as a whole repeated in Resolution 39 the resolutions passed in the 1888 Conference.[21] To these resolutions of 1888 the Conference as a whole added another on the question of divorce. '40. When an innocent person has, by means of a court of law, divorced a spouse for adultery, and desires to enter into another contract of marriage, it is undesirable that such a contract should receive the blessing of the Church.' This resolution, however, was carried by a slender majority –

[18] Op. cit., pp. 354–5.
[19] Op. cit., p. 387.
[20] Op. cit., p. 397.
[21] See pp. 87f.

87 votes to 84.[22] The committee was adamant in its opposition to any form of birth control. They asked that legislation should be promoted to secure – '(a) The prohibition of so-called Neo-Malthusian appliances, and of patent drugs, and corrupting advertisements. (b) The prosecution of all who publicly and professionally assist preventive methods.'[23] This resulted in Resolution 41 of the full Conference, 'The Conference regards with alarm the growing practice of the artificial restriction of the family, and earnestly calls upon all Christian people to discountenance the use of all artificial means of restriction as demoralising in character and hostile to national welfare.' There was also a resolution (42) on abortion: 'The Conference affirms that deliberate tampering with nascent life is repugnant to Christian morality.'

The committee on the Moral Witness of the Church in their Report said much on democracy and the brotherhood of man. In Resolution 52 the Conference urged 'upon all Christian people the duty of allaying race-prejudice'.

Committee Number 10 on 'Organisation within the Anglican Communion' dealt with the question of the Consultative Committee which had been set up as a result of a resolution of 1897. Archbishop Frederick Temple had instituted this body and had arranged its membership. It was to consist of the Archbishops of Canterbury and York, the Bishops of Durham, London, and Winchester, the Archbishop of Armagh, and the Primus of Scotland. One Bishop should also be appointed by these sections of the Anglican Communion:

1 India and Ceylon
2 Cape Colony
3 West Indies
4 Canada
5 Australia and New Zealand
6 China and Japan
7 the independent dioceses

The Episcopal Church in the United States was to appoint two bishops. The Committee was to meet every year after the second Sunday in July. It met for the first time in July 1901 and according to the Committee 'has already proved its utility by considering and advising on important

[22] On Lambeth Conferences and divorce see *Marriage, Divorce and the Church*. The Report of the Commission on the Christian Doctrine of Marriage.

[23] Randall Davidson, *The Six Lambeth Conferences*, p. 402.

questions.'[24] The 1908 Committee revised the basis of representation on the Committee. The Archbishop of Canterbury would be a member *ex officio*. The rest of the representatives were to be as follows.

2 from Canterbury province
1 from York province
1 from the Church of Ireland
1 from the Episcopal Church of Scotland
4 from the Protestant Episcopal Church in the U.S.A.
1 from the Canadian Church
1 from Australia and Tasmania
1 from New Zealand
1 from the West Indies
1 from South Africa
1 from India and Ceylon
1 from China, Korea, and Japan
1 from the extra-provincial or Independent dioceses

This would make a body of 18 in all which would meet yearly.

The Committee, as in 1897, examined the idea of a Tribunal of Reference. They did not advise the setting up of a Tribunal of Reference, but neither did they wish to set an obstacle in the way of any province or churches which might wish to find outside themselves a court for the final decision of disputes. It is evident that the American church showed some measure of hostility to even the Consultative Committee. *The Churchman* of New York had emphasized the necessity of avoiding any sort of organization which might lead to the formation of an Anglican *curia*.

The Reunion Committee followed the principles enunciated in 1888 and 1897. They dealt with the Roman Church, breakaway churches from Rome, the Moravians, and the Scandinavian Churches. The Archbishop of Uppsala (Dr Johan August Ekman) had sent the Bishop of Kalmar (Dr Henry William Tottie) to confer with the Lambeth Conference on the establishment of some alliance between the Swedish and Anglican Churches. The Archbishop was asked to appoint a commission to continue negotiations. This was done. The commission reported in 1911.[25] The Report contained a long section on 'Presbyterian and other Non-Episcopal Churches'. Here they remarked

[24] Op. cit., p. 417.
[25] See *The Church of England and the Church of Sweden*. Report of the Commission appointed by the Archbishop of Canterbury in pursuance of Resolution 74 of the Lambeth Conference of 1908.

that the Presbyterians fulfilled the first three parts of the Lambeth Quadrilateral. As regards the fourth, though they had not retained the historic episcopate, yet it belonged to their principles to insist upon definite ordination as necessary for admission into the ministry. They went on:

> Your committee fully recognise that a condition precedent to any project of reunion would be the attainment of a general agreement in doctrine and practice which would violate no essential principle of the Churches of our Communion. They admit that they are not satisfied that, except possibly in Australia, there is as yet evidence of a strong desire on the part of any of the Presbyterian Churches for a closer union with the Anglican Churches. The question of the recognition of Presbyterian orders seems to these Churches to present an insuperable obstacle.[26]

When the Reports were in due course published, there was added to them a Report on the Relation of Religious Communities within the Church to the Episcopate, the work of a committee appointed by the 1897 Conference and chaired by Bishop Stubbs of Oxford, which had been drawn up in 1898. The encyclical of 1908 was written by Archbishop Davidson with the help of several bishops. The central theme behind it was that of 'service'. In this encyclical there was a reaffirmation of the importance of the Creeds.

> We reaffirm the essential place of the historic facts stated by the Creeds in the structure of our faith. Many in our days have rashly denied the importance of these facts, but the ideas which these facts have in part generated and have always expressed cannot be dissociated from them. Without the historic Creeds the ideas would evaporate into unsubstantial vagueness, and Christianity would be in danger of degenerating into nerveless altruism.

This statement was in line with a resolution passed in the Upper House of Convocation at Canterbury in May 1905 reaffirming the faith presented in the Apostles' and Nicene Creeds. That resolution had been provoked by some Anglican liberal theology of the first years of the century, notably that of Dean W. H. Fremantle and the Rev. C. E. Beeby.[27] With respect to the Holy Communion the encyclical said, 'We hold that the Church cannot sanction the use of any other elements than the bread and wine which the Lord commanded to be received.'[28]

[26] *The Six Lambeth Conferences 1867–1920*, p. 432.
[27] See G. K. A. Bell, *Randall Davidson*, vol. ii, p. 1134, and vol. i, pp. 395–8.
[28] *The Six Lambeth Conferences*, p. 308.

The final service of the Conference – a solemn celebration of the Holy Communion – took place at 10 a.m. in St Paul's Cathedral on Thursday, 6 August. The *Guardian* in its report, said:

Most of the Bishops wore their scarlet Convocation robes. A striking effect was produced by the accessories – the cross at the head of the procession, the swaying banner of the Cathedral, and the cross of Canterbury; and the Archbishop of Canterbury, with his scarlet train, upheld by a surpliced chorister, was a dignified and stately representative of the great Communion over which he presides.

The sermon was preached by Bishop D. S. Tuttle, of Missouri, the Presiding Bishop of the American Episcopal Church, on Luke 19.13, 'Occupy till I come'.[29]

It was universally agreed that Archbishop Davidson had been a masterly chairman. Bishop Montgomery wrote,

Archbishop Davidson was so trusted for fairness and impartiality that he won through miraculously. He used to get up and say, 'We could spend a day over this one resolution. We have six others which must be passed to-day. Will you trust me? As soon as we rise I will guarantee that I and three or four others (naming them) will do the best we can and report tomorrow morning.' Next morning his verdict was always accepted.[30]

Appreciation had been shown to Archbishop and Mrs Davidson at the last session of the Conference (Wednesday). On that day the American bishops presented them with a piece of plate and the English bishops did the same, adding a bracelet for Mrs Davidson.

As had become customary the Conference was followed by a pilgrimage. This time it was to Lindisfarne in Northumberland. Bishop George Forrest Browne played a part in this and gives an account of it in his *The Recollections of a Bishop.*

The rebuilt nave of the Abbey Church at Hexham was to be opened, with an address by the Bishop of Bristol, and a pilgrimage was to be paid to Holy Isle. The date had been long arranged to suit the tide, so that such of the pilgrims as walked could get across to Lindisfarne fairly dry-shod. But the wise men had blundered. When the thousand pilgrims reached the taking-off place on the shore of the mainland, there was a wide expanse of sea to be crossed, and the great array of ramshackle vehicles could accommodate at most only eight hundred. Some three hundred faced the sea on foot, and plodged – as the graphic local name for ploughing through the water on its

[29] *Guardian*, 12 August 1908, pp. 1341–2.
[30] *Bishop Montgomery. A Memoir* by M.M., p. 77.

soft sand bottom has it. More than one of the breaks had accidents on the journey and deposited their loads in some two or three feet of water. Ladies, whether intentionally plodging or dismissed from breaks, were up to their waist, with petticoats floating in a circle round them. Our break was overloaded with chance passengers and we had to sit anyhow. When the driver unpacked my part of his load he sat a plump young woman on the shore and said to her 'You never forget, my lass, as you've rode on a bishop's knee.' The return journey was much the same. The present writer and another bishop gallantly plunged into the water to lighten their break when it stuck in the sand and push it on. Their effort succeeded. The driver got his horses into a splashing canter, and knowing his only chance was to keep going at full speed, left the two bishops to plodge it the rest of the way. The Lord of the Manor gave us an excellent luncheon. He and his men had been sitting on the tent pegs for hours during the night, to prevent the great marquee being blown away by a storm of wind which had happily abated before the plodging began. We had an excellent address from the Archbishop of Melbourne, Dr Lowther Clarke. Each of the Colonial bishops received two pieces of silk, printed from blocks reproducing the ornamentation of the robes found on the body of St Cuthbert, which had been made for me by Sir Thomas Wardle of Leek . . .[31]

There can be little doubt that 1908 was a remarkable year for Anglicanism. Davidson writing in the *Canterbury Diocesan Gazette* said that the numbers attending the Pan-Anglican Congress were 'without parallel in European history'. One who was captured by the pan-Anglicanism of 1908 was Canon Scott Holland of St Paul's, in a paper entitled 'Romance in Gaiters'.

Romance! We [clergy] don't look like it. It is, no doubt, our coyness that hinders us from displaying this character of ours with better effect. We hush it all up in gaiters and buttons. We creep about in obscure and ugly disguises. . . .

And that is why the Pan-Anglican business was so significant. Suddenly, we all rubbed our eyes, to find that something was up of quite another order. Strange things were all about us. Strange beings from strange places swarmed round every corner. Their titles stretched our spelling powers to breaking point. We had long ceased to remember whether these Dioceses, with their outlandish names, are in Australia or California. Is 'Oluwole' a name or a place? Who can say? Anyhow, there is not one island in the far seas that one or all these men had not touched at: there is not a river that they have not forded: there is not a veldt so wide and desolate that they had failed to cross it: there is no ocean that they had not sailed: there is no

[31] G. F. Browne, *The Recollections of a Bishop*, pp. 405–6.

people, black, brown, yellow or green, that they had not intimately greeted. They murmured weird sounds from unknown languages: they clicked: they snorted: they dropped liquid vocables, like rain. They carried about, in their names and in their talk, the fragrance of historic memories that had been to us fabulous, but which they had taken possession of. India, Persia, China, and all the wonders of Pacific Islands, were to them familiar ground. They had been rocked in the bullock carts: wrecked at sea: half-drowned in floods and fords: all but eaten alive by men and beasts. And here they were: and they were ours: and they made themselves quite at home. There was a Canadian Bishop who relieved the tedium of a Lambeth Conference by dropping in, during lunch-time, at a rifle-range to indulge his favourite tastes, by shooting at tin bears down a tube: and hitting at every shot. Probably at certain hours in the day, all those gentlemen who were in the habit of taking sliding headers down the shoots in the Westminster baths were members of the Episcopal Bench.[32]

Before we pass on to Archbishop Davidson's last Conference, let us get a glimpse from Bishop Montgomery of some of the 1908 arrangements, and the subsequent clearing-up process.

For the first time now a smoking and writing room was provided for the bishops in the palace. The crypt had been newly excavated and arranged for the purpose. Just outside the crypt lockers were erected, every bishop having one with his name inscribed. These became receptacles for the pamphlets, letters, appeals which poured upon the bishops from societies, cranks, etc. It was the duty of the secretaries to acknowledge these communications and to place them in the lockers. At the end of the conference these lockers were all cleared out and a bonfire made of the contents. Most of the petitions and pamphlets were unopened!

As in the conference of 1897 the speeches were all taken down by one shorthand reporter. One copy was made. Each bishop was asked to revise his speech. Then this copy, absolutely private, was placed in the Lambeth Palace Library together with the minute-books of the conference and the committees. They were all bound alike and labelled, and it was Bishop Montgomery's duty to see to this and consign them to the library in the end.[33]

[32] Henry Scott Holland, *A Bundle of Memories*, pp. 231–4.
[33] *Bishop Montgomery. A Memoir*, pp. 75–6.

9

1920
THE LAMBETH APPEAL

I think we can say, without fear of contradiction, that the Lambeth Conference of 1920 has been the most famous and best-known of all the Conferences. We are fortunate in having quite a wealth of material about it in the lives of the leading participants, Randall Davidson, Hensley Henson, Frank Weston, Theodore Woods, Henry Montgomery, and G. K. A. Bell. Let us therefore, first, look at the background of the Conference and see some of the things that had happened since that of 1908.

First of all, there was the horrible fact of the First World War. The indelible impression this had made upon the bishops of 1920 is seen in the encyclical, in which the bishops offered as the keynote to the Conference the word 'Fellowship'.

> Men never prized the universal fellowship of mankind as they did when the Great War had for the time destroyed it. For four terrible years the loss of international fellowship emphasized its value. But the war which broke one fellowship created others. Nations became associated in alliances, which they cemented with their blood. In every national army, comradeship, novel and intense, united men of different classes and most varied traditions. Thousands gained quite a new impression of what human nature might be, when they experienced the fellowship of man with man in danger and death. Comradeship ennobled war. To-day, men are asking, Can it not ennoble peace.[1]

A second part of the background to the 1920 Conference was the modernist controversy. The Churchmen's Union for the Advancement of Liberal Religious Thought had started in 1898, the year after the Fourth Lambeth Conference, but a new force had come into it with the accession to its ranks of Henry D. A. Major, Vice-Principal of Ripon Clergy College and, after 1918, when the Yorkshire theological institution moved to Oxford, Principal of Ripon Hall, Oxford. Major had started the *Modern Churchman* in 1911 and had been, with

[1] *The Lambeth Conference, 1920*, pp. 9–10.

5. The bishops in procession at Glastonbury, Somerset, after the Conference of 1897. (Photograph of a painting)

6. Some of the 'leading lights' of the 1908 Pan-Anglican Synod

7. The bishops at the 1908 Conference, outside Lambeth Palace

8. The bishops at the Conference of 1920

Foakes-Jackson and Kirsopp Lake, responsible for the first Conference of Modern Churchmen in 1914. Greater men than Major were in the modernist camp, like Hastings Rashdall, Dean of New College, Oxford, William Sanday, Lady Margaret Professor of Divinity at Oxford, J. M. Thompson, Dean of Magdalen College, Oxford, and B. H. Streeter, of Queen's College, Oxford. J. M. Thompson had written a book on miracles which caused a scandal and B. H. Streeter had dropped a bombshell into the theological world through his essay 'The Historic Christ' in *Foundations* (1912). M. G. Glazebrook, a Canon of Ely, had written a little book, now seemingly unobjectionable, entitled *The Faith of a Modern Churchman*, which brought upon him the wrath of the Bishop of Ely, F. H. Chase, who even wrote a book against it, *Belief and the Creed*, to which Glazebrook made reply in his *The Letter and the Spirit*. Another bishop who became an ardent searcher out of heresy was Frank Weston, Bishop of Zanzibar, a great missionary bishop. He attacked B. H. Streeter and also Hensley Henson, Bishop of Hereford from 1917, and from 1920 Bishop of Durham. Henson, who would be put in a separate camp from Major, Glazebrook, and Rashdall, had, early in the century, flirted with the Churchmen's Union, but never became a member of it. On his appointment as Bishop of Hereford a great outcry arose and Frank Weston attacked *The Creed and the Pulpit* (1912) which Henson had written when Canon of Westminster. Weston's book *The Christ and His Critics* (1919) was written very much with the forthcoming Lambeth Conference in view, as can be seen especially in Appendix V 'The Lambeth Conference and Liberalism'. The subject of modernism had come up in Convocation a year or two before the 'Hereford Scandal' in 1914 when the bishops made a statement on the subject recalling an earlier episcopal statement of 1904 and the judgement of the bishops at the Lambeth Conference of 1908. Clearly, it was very likely to be brought forward at the Lambeth Conference of 1920. Just before the Conference, in May, the Bishops of Gloucester (E. C. S. Gibson, author of a book on the Thirty-nine Articles), Ely (F. H. Chase), and Chichester (W. O. Burrows), who all had rooms in the Lollards' Tower sent a letter to Davidson, suggesting that some resolution on the subject be passed at the Conference. Davidson, however, was set on avoiding this controversial matter. In the event it was kept out of the way – perhaps an indication of the remarkable hold that the Archbishop had upon the bishops.[2]

The other inevitable subject was that of reunion. Since 1908 two

[2] See G. K. A. Bell, *Randall Davidson*, vol. ii, pp. 1005ff.

events had taken place which were of some importance in the history of reunion. One was the World Missionary Conference held at Edinburgh in 1910 which was being planned at the time of the 1908 Lambeth Conference, and which resulted in the setting up of the International Missionary Council. The second was the Kikuyu episode of 1913. In that year there met at Kikuyu a conference of Protestant missionaries inspired with the idea of uniting into one native Protestant church. Two leading Evangelical Anglican bishops were present – J. J. Willis of Uganda and W. G. Peel of Mombasa. Frank Weston, the neighbouring High Church Bishop of Zanzibar, did not approve of the Conference, which had ended with a communion service in which all the denominations had participated. Three months later Bishop Weston wrote a letter to the Archbishop of Canterbury denouncing the Bishops of Uganda and Mombasa for the part they had taken in the Kikuyu conference, and formally charged them 'with propagating and committing schism'. Weston's biographer defends his action, but admits that the charge was not, strictly speaking, true.

> Frank had been misinformed. Only proposals had been agreed to, and no federation had taken place. The two Bishops were not inspired by a schismatic temper; they were, on the other hand, trying to heal schisms of the past. They had no heretical intention, for they only accepted the proposals on condition that they were allowed and ratified by the Archbishop of Canterbury.[3]

However, when Frank Weston came home to England in February 1914, he found the whole ecclesiastical world in an uproar over his Open Letter to the Archbishop of Canterbury. All sorts of pamphlets were being produced against or in favour of what had happened at Kikuyu. The Church of England was split in two over the issue. Weston, be it noted, was not simply negative in his approach, for in March 1914 he published his *Proposals for a Central Missionary Council of Episcopal and Non-Episcopal Churches in East Africa*. The issue was brought before the Lambeth Conference Consultative Committee, but that body did not pronounce upon the subject until Easter 1915. The committee was sympathetic towards the Bishops of Uganda and Mombasa but disapproved of the proposed federation. The statement of the consultative committee went out with a letter from the Archbishop of Canterbury. Of this Maynard Smith says:

> His style is stately and dignified, his tone is impartial. He minimises as far as

---

[3] See H. Maynard Smith, *Frank, Bishop of Zanzibar*, p. 149.

possible the nature of the Kikuyu proposals and is anxious not to condemn anyone. As the very wise ruler of the Church, he is more concerned with composing differences than in formulating principles; he wishes to keep doors open for reunion in the future, while he cautiously recommends that it would be better for the present not to go through them. He looks forward to the next Lambeth Conference as the time for discussion.[4]

The next Lambeth Conference was due to take place in 1918. In August 1915 preliminary notices about the forthcoming Conference were sent out, but the continuation of the Great War made it less and less likely that it could take place then. When the statement on Kikuyu was issued it fell decidedly flat, as men's minds were occupied with more pressing things. However, when the Armistice came, Archbishop Davidson immediately took up the matter and wrote to all the metropolitans to ask them whether they would prefer to meet in 1920 or 1921. They unanimously requested 1920.

In February 1919, preliminary notices went out to all the diocesan and suffragan bishops. Among the recipients was Bishop D. S. Tuttle, of Missouri, the Presiding Bishop of the American Episcopal Church, who had received invitations to all six of the Lambeth Conferences and had preached at the final service in St Paul's in 1908. However, in 1920, he was unable to come because of ill health and Dr T. F. Gailor, Bishop of Tennessee, acted as Presiding Bishop at the Conference. In July 1919, definite invitations were sent out and notification was given of the subjects for the agenda, which had been worked out by the consultative committee, after they had seen the replies and suggestions of the bishops. Invitations were not sent out to assistant bishops until early in 1920, as there seemed some uncertainty as to their position. It is worth noting here that at the opening session of the Conference a resolution was passed inviting the presence of six retired bishops. Of these only three subsequently accepted – George F. Browne, previously Bishop of Bristol, R. S. Copleston, formerly Bishop of Calcutta, and G. L. King, formerly Bishop in Madagascar.

Before the Conference began there were pilgrimages to Salisbury Cathedral on 24 June, to commemorate its 700th Anniversary, and to Peterborough Cathedral to commemorate its 800th Anniversary. A

---

[4] See *Frank, Bishop of Zanzibar*, p. 162. Regarding the reply of the Lambeth Consultative Committee on the joint communion service, it was wittily said at the time, 'The Commission comes to the conclusion that the Service at Kikuyu was eminently pleasing to God, but must on no account be repeated.' (See G. K. A. Bell, *Randall Davidson*, vol. i, p. 708.)

noteworthy event, unconnected with the Conference, but not without significance for it, was the first Anglo-Catholic Congress, participated in by Frank Weston, Bishop of Zanzibar.[5] The enthusiasm of the audiences at the Albert Hall meetings inspired Weston to believe that he had an immense backing of clergy and laity.

Another important event was the publication by A. C. Headlam, not yet a bishop, of a notable set of Bampton Lectures, *The Doctrine of the Church and Christian Reunion*. They came out on 7 June, the day after the delivery of the final lecture and one month before the opening of the Conference. Headlam took the Lambeth Quadrilateral as a sufficient basis for reunion, no further agreement being needed. This was contrary to the original intention in 1888, but the influence of Headlam's view on Lambeth 1920 will be soon apparent.

Let us now look at some of the changes in the episcopal bench. Bertram Pollock was at Norwich, H. M. Burge, a liberal, was at Oxford, in place of Charles Gore, and Theodore Woods was at Peterborough. Woods and Bishop Montgomery of the S.P.G. acted as episcopal secretaries. G. K. A. Bell, Davidson's chaplain at Lambeth, acted as assistant secretary. M. B. Furse was at St Alban's, having returned from Pretoria, where he had been succeeded by Neville Talbot, one of the writers in *Foundations*. Neville Talbot's father, E. S. Talbot, was still Bishop of Winchester. Hence, for the first time there was a father and son at a Conference. C. F. Garbett was Bishop of Southwark and Sir Edwyn Hoskyns, the father of the great New Testament scholar, was at Southwell. Hensley Henson had recently been made Bishop of Durham, but was not yet enthroned. Luke Paget, brother of Francis, was at Chester, and E. A. Knox at Manchester. G. R. Eden, one of the episcopal secretaries in 1908, was still at Wakefield. A son of B. F. Westcott, F. Westcott, was Bishop of Calcutta. E. J. Palmer, who had played a significant part in the Pan-Anglican Congress, was Bishop of Bombay. There was a native Indian bishop in the famous V. S. Azariah, Bishop of Dornakal. W. M. Carter was Archbishop of Capetown. E. A. Parry was Archbishop of the West Indies. H. Lowther Clarke was still Archbishop of Melbourne. St Clair G. A. Donaldson was Archbishop of Brisbane. M. N. Trollope was Bishop of Korea. Bishop Oluwole came to his third Lambeth Conference as Assistant Bishop of Lagos. Willis of Kikuyu fame was still Bishop of Uganda, but Peel at Mombasa had been succeeded by R. S. Heywood. Among the American bishops,

---

[5] It was not at this Congress but at that of 1923 that the famous telegram was sent to the Pope. See *Frank, Bishop of Zanzibar*, pp. 303–4.

besides T. F. Gailor of Tennessee, there were Bishop Lawrence of Massachusetts, Bishop P. M. Rhinelander of Pennsylvania, and Bishop Brent of New York.

The Conference began with a Quiet Day on 2 July in Fulham Parish Church conducted by Charles Gore, who had recently retired from being Bishop of Oxford. Though invited to participate in the Conference, he felt unable to do so. Then on Saturday, 3 July, the formal proceedings began, as was customary, at Canterbury. There were the two usual functions, a lunch in the library of St Augustine's College and a service in Canterbury Cathedral. Archbishop Davidson welcomed the bishops from St Augustine's chair, placed for the occasion before the high altar. In his address, Davidson had a reference to the validity of the Creed (doubtless to placate the anti-modernists):

> An Anselm, a Langton, a Cranmer, a Secker, a Benson, had each of them a revelation to understand and to assimilate, a message to carry to his contemporaries, an interpretation to offer. So have we. But for us, as for them, it is the old Creed which stands. Round it, and with its use, the Christian Society had found ever new meaning and new strength in discipleship, brotherhood, ministry, sacraments: all of them for the good of men.[6]

The service in the cathedral was followed by a garden party – as, again, was the custom – given in the Green Court by the Dean and Chapter of Canterbury, after which the majority of the bishops returned to London by special train.[7]

Bishop Henson writing about the Canterbury service in his diary made some interesting observations on the subject of reunion:

> I, as the Elect of Durham, walked with the Bishop of London [Winnington-Ingram]. I had some conversation with the Archbishop of Rupertsland [S. P. Matheson] on the prospect of 'Reunion' in the Conference. He said that he was not hopeful: he found a change for the worse in the feeling of the bishops. He agreed that *either* we must go forward by frankly recognizing the validity of Presbyterian orders, *or* we must drop the subject altogether. He said that the Archbishop of Melbourne (Dr Lowther Clarke) was as depressed at the prospect as himself. I had a few words with D'Arcy, now Archbishop of Armagh, and he also seemed rather disheartened. On all of them I pressed the importance of keeping a stiff back, and insisting on taking

---

[6] *The Six Lambeth Conferences, 1867–1920*, p. 46e.

[7] *The Six Lambeth Conferences, 1867–1920*, p. 46g. Before the service Canon A. J. Mason delivered a short lecture on the shrine of St Thomas Becket in the Trinity Chapel, as 7 July was the 700th anniversary of the translation of his body to the shrine.

some forward step. Clearly there has been a considerable 'Catholic' reaction, and the bishops are, for the most part, timorous creatures.[8]

On Sunday, 4 July, the customary opening service took place at Westminster Abbey. The sermon was preached by Bishop Ryle, now no longer Bishop of Winchester, but Dean of Westminster. Henson remarked upon it: 'Ryle's sermon started well, but ended rather in bathos. He made a long and earnest appeal to the Bishops to restore the word "holy" to the Nicene Creed, from which it had been inadvertently dropped out at the Reformation! I thought that at least he would advocate the omission of the *"Filioque"*!'[9] The Bishop's text was Ephesians 4.3. The collection at this communion service was given to the fund for aiding candidates for holy orders in the navy or army.

We are fortunate in having an account of the internal workings and arrangements from Bishop Montgomery:

> The Conference of 1920 was notable for the fact that at length an Archbishop of Canterbury had been able to preside over two Lambeth Conferences. Before Davidson's reign it had come to be believed that this could never happen. Of course it simplified matters very much, for there was no detail with which Davidson was not familiar. Moreover, his character for fairness and his obvious distaste of being looked upon as a quasi-Patriarch made all the Bishops come to Lambeth without misgivings. . . .
>
> The number of Bishops had grown so much that it became a question whether even the Lambeth Library would be big enough for the Conference. It was; but the shape of the chairs had to be altered in order to save room. Special chairs had been made for each Conference which I attended, and were offered for sale afterwards to the Bishops. These chairs cost 7s 6d. in 1897 and 15s in 1920.[10]
>
> An office for the Conference was opened in Morton's Tower, just below the rooms of Mr Bell, the Archbishop's Chaplain, afterwards Bishop of

[8] H. H. Henson, *Retrospect of an Unimportant Life*, vol. ii, p. 3.
[9] Loc. cit.
[10] Note the words of Bishop Bernard Heywood in his *About the Lambeth Conferences* (1930), p. 26, where speaking of the likelihood of Lambeth Palace being too small for the Conferences (as it proved and in 1968 the Conference took place at Church House, Westminster) wrote: 'The nature of the loss may be difficult to define; but if the Conference met, for example, in the Church House, it might not be easy to maintain the privacy of Lambeth, nor to secure that atmosphere which was manifest during the discussions on Reunion in 1920. The Conference at present is unique, and there can be no doubt that its character is due in some degree to the surroundings and circumstances in which it is held. . . . "The indirect results which accrue from such gatherings are probably at least as great as those of an official kind." It will probably be agreed, at least by some of those who were present at the Conference of 1920, that the

Chichester. Here I was installed, and it is needless to say that Bell was a very strong helper and adviser in everything. Mrs Bell, too, presided most efficiently over the 'Book Room', now opened for the first time.[11]

In my office Honor Thomas was installed as my Secretary. She showed such marvellous aptitude and ability, she was so accurate and had such a memory, that gradually I left almost everything to her, and this fact soon came to be recognized by all the Bishops.[12]

In this Conference, too, the work of the Hospitality Committee developed greatly. Not only was hospitality found for all the Bishops and their families, but for the first time a most successful attempt was made to entertain the wives of the Bishops while their husbands were in session. For six weeks, three days a week, entertainments were arranged or expeditions planned to places of interest in or near London. Historical houses, ancient Churches, city factories, Hampton Court, Richmond Park — all these and many other places were visited and tea provided for. A fleet of omnibuses stood ready on the appointed days outside the National Gallery. Evening receptions were given by famous London hostesses, and everything was done to make the Lambeth Conference of 1920 a time of pleasure as well as profit for the visitors from overseas. Several of the Bishops had brought children with them. For these, visits to the Zoo, to the King's stables at Buckingham Palace, and a large children's party at Bishopsbourne, Chiswick, were organized. So splendidly was all this work done that it added enormously to the success of the Conference.

Another development from former Conferences was the smoking! A large room on the third floor of Morton's Tower was made into a writing and smoking room. Right well was it utilized! The growth of smoking filled me with astonishment. I remember one wet, cold morning, as I was going to my

---

report on Reunion would not have now so large a measure of agreement, as in fact it did, had it not been for the opportunity of informal talks during intervals between the sessions, which was afforded by the gardens of Lambeth.'

[11] See also *The Six Lambeth Conferences, 1867–1920*, p. 46i, 'The Library was arranged more or less as it had been in 1908, some of the bookcases being removed to accommodate the chairs, but an extra door was opened into the Library from the house, and an additional room added, in which a bookstall was arranged during the five weeks of the meetings. Here could be bought the books recommended for the different subjects on the agenda paper, as well as note-books and other stationery, while facilities were given for postage and telegraphy. A special telephone was installed for the use of the Bishops, and sets of large pigeon-holes, one for each Bishop, labelled with his individual number, were put up near the Library. Into these were sorted each day the vast amount of correspondence received by every member of the Conference, this being no light task, as the number of Societies and individuals who circularised every Bishop was immense.'

[12] I assume that Miss Honor Thomas wrote the account of the 1920 Lambeth Conference in *The Lambeth Conferences 1867–1920*.

office, I met coming down the stairs a solid, impenetrable mass of smoke! Moreover, one could hear above a roar of voices. It seemed as though there must have been a hundred Bishops all smoking and all talking together at the same time. Then, too, whenever the Conference adjourned, it was not uncommon to see 150 Bishops strolling about, nearly all smoking pipes. And I noticed that some of the most Evangelical Bishops were the greatest smokers. I used to wonder what the next development would be in 1930. Surely they will not smoke in the Conference itself!

The photographic department was also extended. Russell & Sons, as in 1908, had the sole right of photography inside Lambeth Palace, and they were permanently stationed at the big entrance to the Library. Photographs were being taken all day long, and for the first time snapshots were taken of Bishops strolling about, sometimes of pairs walking together, who were poles asunder in their views. A collection of these would be of great interest. Of course, Russell paid for this privilege and they must have made a fortune. They gave me a photograph of myself in colour, worth 9 guineas.

We must now leave this survey of the Conference from a back room and examine the official proceedings of the gathering. The programme which the bishops had to deal with was as follows:

A Relation to and Reunion with other Churches.
　 1 Episcopal Churches.
　 2 Non-episcopal Churches, with questions as to:
　　 a Recognition of Ministers;
　　 b 'Validity' of Sacraments;
　　 c Suggested transitional steps.

Archbishop Lang was in due course appointed to chair the committee dealing with this subject.

B Missionary Problems.
　 1 Missions and Government.
　 2 Missions and Growing Churches.
　 3 Liturgical Variations permissible to a Province or Diocese.
　 4 Marriage Questions and other practical problems.

Bishop Westcott of Calcutta became the chairman of the committee dealing with this topic.

C The Christian Faith in relation to:
　 1 Spiritualism.
　 2 Christian Science.
　 3 Theosophy.

Bishop Burge of Oxford was in this case appointed chairman of the committee.

D Problems of Marriage and Sexual Morality.

Bishop Winnington-Ingram of London was chairman.

E Position of Women in the Councils and Ministrations of the Church.

Bishop Chase of Ely was chairman.

F Christianity and International Relations, especially the League of Nations.

The Archbishop of Brisbane (St Clair Donaldson) was chairman.

G The Opportunity and Duty of the Church in regard to Industrial and Social Problems.

The chairman of the committee set up was Bishop Kempthorne of Lichfield.

H Development of Provinces in the Anglican Communion.

Archbishop Carter of Capetown acted as chairman.

On Monday, 5 July (a wet day, as Henson recalled), proceedings began with a discussion of the League of Nations in the morning and spiritualism, Christian science, and theosophy in the afternoon. Though Henson found it dull 'and not very serviceable', Bishop Montgomery thought Bishop Burge's presentation of the problem of spiritualism 'magnificent'.

Tuesday, 6 July, saw the debate on reunion, the morning being devoted to episcopal churches and the afternoon to the crucial question of relations with the non-episcopal churches. Archbishop Lang was praised by Bishop Montgomery. 'I think the finest and most moving speech of the whole Conference', he wrote, 'was by the Archbishop of York (Cosmo Lang) in laying before the Conference in the first week the whole problem of Reunion.'[13] Of the afternoon's discussion, Henson said in his diary:

> Burrows of Chichester made a disappointing speech, bad in form and substance. I followed him. My speech was closely listened to, and applauded at the close. At least I spoke with lucidity and decision. My demand was that we should acknowledge frankly the validity of Presbyterian Orders and

13 *Bishop Montgomery. A Memoir*, p. 83.

Sacraments. I said some things which needed saying, and which went home. A good many bishops came to thank me afterwards.[14]

On Wednesday, 7 July, foreign mission problems were discussed. Among the speakers were Bishop Westcott of Calcutta, Bishop Azariah of Dornakal, Bishop Roots of Hankow, and Bishop Weston of Zanzibar. On Weston, Hensley Henson remarked:

> The speeches of the Bishop of Zanzibar (Weston) are somewhat perplexing. He speaks contemptuously of the Conference and all its ways, tells the Bishops to live among the poor in the slums and ask them to dinner, describes the episcopal character very grotesquely, and is generally treated as a 'chartered libertine'. He is elaborately polite to me. I doubt whether he is taken quite seriously by anybody, though he is universally popular.[15]

If we turn to Maynard Smith's *Frank, Bishop of Zanzibar* we see another account of the Bishop's speech. According to him, Weston said:

> Why had the Episcopate failed in England and elsewhere! Because it had failed to represent the Fatherhood of God. He declared that he would like to scrap the agenda of the Conference, in order that they all might devote the time in learning from God how to reconcile the Episcopate with real paternal government. Each diocese should be a family, a real unit, and all dioceses should constitute a real unity.[16]

So spoke the greatly loved bishop, looking like Apollo in episcopal garb; yet he himself was rather an autocrat, albeit a benevolent one.

On Thursday, 8 July, another controversial subject was discussed – 'The place of women in the ministrations of the Church.' Henson remarked:

> At first it seemed likely that the subject would 'peter out' in the morning, but after lunch interest revived. I made a speech criticizing the assumptions and pleas of the feminists, and this had the effect of continuing the discussion till the end of the day. I find myself in rather an odd position. The Bishops who are ready to stand with me on Reunion are almost all feminists and Christian Socialists, and they cannot understand how I can oppose both. In that opposition, moreover, I find myself in the same camp with ancient obscurantists and 'Catholic' bigots![17]

---

[14] H. H. Henson, *Retrospect of an Unimportant Life*, vol. ii, p. 5.
[15] *Retrospect of an Unimportant Life*, vol. ii, p. 6.
[16] *Frank, Bishop of Zanzibar*, p. 228.
[17] *Retrospect of an Unimportant Life*, vol. ii, p. 6.

On Friday, 9 July, the Conference discussed 'The Church and industrial problems'. Henson found the session too 'socialistic'. 'Of the four appointed speakers,' wrote Henson,

> I noted that three were celibates, viz. London, Vermont [A. C. A. Hall] and an Australian Bishop and that these were all very rigorous. The Bishop of Birmingham [Wakefield] was comparatively tolerant. Bishop Gwynne gave us an account of venereal disease in the army, and the Bishop of Sacramento in California dilated on the extravagances of American divorce. In Nevada the proportion of divorces to marriages is 1 to 1·7. The discussion in the afternoon bored me stark. It dealt with the multiplication of provinces in the Anglican Communion. I deserted and went to the Athenaeum.[18]

Now the committees got to work. The large committee of seventy bishops on reunion met at Lambeth Palace under the chairmanship of Archbishop Lang. The other committees met at Church House, Westminster, with the exception of one at S.P.G. House. During the committee work there were various social events, among them a garden party at Buckingham Palace, on which Henson remarked, 'There was a great crowd, among whom the Bishops were scattered like rooks in a cornfield.' Two days later King George V received the bishops (as his father had done in 1908) and was presented with an address by the Archbishop of Canterbury on behalf of the bishops. There were various other gatherings, including the usual Mansion House dinner and receptions by the S.P.G., the C.M.S., and other societies.

We are fortunate in having several accounts of the work of the committee on reunion, undoubtedly the most important one, which started on Monday, 12 July. The next day a battle developed between the Bishop of Gloucester (Gibson) and Henson as to whether the English Church had recognized Presbyterian orders. The Bishop of Madras (Whitehead) spoke enthusiastically on the developing situation in South India. He said, 'he would consider his position as an Anglican Bishop if he were required by the Conference to refuse recognition of their ministry to the non-episcopal ministers concerned in the scheme for a South Indian church.' The South Indian scheme of reunion had been born in May 1919 at a conference at Tranquebar when thirty-three men participated – thirty-one Indians, one American, and one Englishman. Though so recent a scheme allusions were inevitably made to it in the the 1920 Conference.

On Wednesday, 14 July, various theologians came before the reunion

18 *Retrospect of an Unimportant Life*, vol. ii, p. 7.

committee – Charles Gore, Dean Ryle, Dean Armitage Robinson, and Professor C. H. Turner from Oxford. Of these only Ryle showed friendliness towards the Presbyterians. Robinson had grown stiffer since his sermon on 'Unity' in Westminster Abbey at the 1908 Conference.

On Thursday, 15 July, Dr Shakespeare, the Baptist leader, came before the committee and deprecated any separate treatment of the Presbyterians as likely to create a split among non-episcopalians. He pleaded for interchange of pulpits and the allowing Nonconformists to partake of Holy Communion when their churches were inaccessible. Bishops Furse of St Albans and Weston of Zanzibar were hostile to this. Bishop Palmer of Bombay was plainly hostile to any approach to non-episcopalians. When the South Indian scheme was introduced by Bishop Azariah, Palmer's dislike of the scheme was very evident.[19] Henson noted on this Thursday that there was 'a bad spirit among many members of the Conference'. However, on Saturday, 17 July, Henson noted, 'The outlook in the Committee seems to be improving'. On that day, Tissington Tatlow of the S.C.M., William Temple, Oliver Quick, and T. A. Lacey gave evidence. During these few days Henson found his main supporters in the Archbishop of Armagh (D'Arcy) and the Bishop of Chelmsford (the Evangelical Watts-Ditchfield). The Scottish bishops were bitterly opposed to him as also were most of the Americans. One can compare Henson's advocacy of recognition of the Presbyterians with the similar position of Bishop Charles Wordsworth in 1888.

At this point the idea of an 'Appeal to all Christian People' was suggested by Archbishop Lang. G. K. A. Bell speaks of this in his *Randall Davidson*.

> For many days the Committee sat in perplexity, and no progress was made. Then the Chairman, the Archbishop of York, conceived the plan of a Letter to Christian People, which might be warmer and more persuasive than any mere restatement of conditions of union. This plan seemed to fit in with an idea, which had been sketched in the opening week by the Bishop of Zanzibar, of a Great Church in which the denominations of non-episcopal origin might be groups: it had been taken up by one or two others, like Bishop Brent; and, with the Archbishop of Canterbury's connivance, a group of kindred souls met by themselves in Lollard's Tower to see whether anything might come from that. A new and hopeful 'statement on reunion'

[19] Later Palmer became an important architect in the South Indian Scheme. See B. Till, *The Churches Search for Unity*, pp. 295ff.

was prepared, with some of the younger Bishops such as the Bishop of Bombay (Dr Palmer), Pretoria (Dr Neville Talbot), and Pennsylvania (Dr Rhinelander) as its draftsmen.[20]

Evidently, the change came on the Sunday between the two weeks of sessions of the committee. Archbishop Davidson noted that on that Sunday afternoon (18 July),

> a little group sat all the afternoon under the tree on the lawn. It consisted of the two Archbishops, Bishop Rhinelander of Pennsylvania, Bishop Brent, the Bishop of Peterborough ... We went through the various drafts, Resolutions etc. which had been suggested, but on the whole decided to transpose it into an Appeal of a consecutive sort.[21]

To Bell's words in *Randall Davidson* we can now add the evidence of Ronald Jasper's *George Bell, Bishop of Chichester*. 'His Journal', he writes,

> reveals that the 'Appeal to all Christian People' owed something to his initiative. Archbishop Lang, the chairman of the Committee on Reunion, had conceived the idea of expressing the ideal of Christian unity in a letter addressed to Christian people rather than to Churches: and it was Bell who suggested to Dr Davidson that a small informal group of younger bishops, including Brent, Weston of Zanzibar, Neville Talbot of Pretoria, Azariah of Dornakal, and Edwin James Palmer of Bombay should be allowed to try and produce such a statement. He acted as their secretary; and his wife wrote later, 'I remember coming upon the group *very* late one evening in Lollard's Tower – Jimmy Bombay sitting cross-legged on the floor like an Indian Buddha, Neville Talbot draped along the mantelpiece, cups of tea everywhere, and George, pen and notebook in hand, correlating all the words of wisdom.'[22]

On Monday, 19 July, the second week of committee sessions opened. Henson noted on that day, 'All agreed that unless recognition of non-episcopal ministries were conceded, all hope of negotiations with the non-episcopal churches must be given up.'[23] Most of the afternoon was spent in discussing the draft 'Appeal'.

On Tuesday, 20 July, some progress was made with draft resolutions. We find Weston producing a draft and then Henson recasting it. Lang was evidently pleased that some progress was being

[20] G. K. A. Bell, *Randall Davidson*, vol. ii, pp. 1011–12.
[21] Idem, p. 1012.
[22] Ronald C. D. Jasper, *George Bell, Bishop of Chichester*, pp. 56–7.
[23] *Retrospect of an Unimportant Life*, vol. ii, p. 11.

made. However, the next day, Wednesday, 21 July, things slowed down. Henson noted 'signs that the truce between the two factions is breaking down. However, we managed to get through the day without an open breach.' Henson was regarded as the leader of the Protestant cause. His main supporters were the Archbishops of Armagh, Melbourne, Sydney, and Ruperts Land. The Anglo-Catholic zealots on the other side were Weston of Zanzibar, Ridgeway of Salisbury, Shedden of Nassau, and Furse of St Albans. The Evangelical leaders, Watts-Ditchfield of Chelmsford and Knox of Manchester, seemed to have played an insignificant part in these discussions.

On Thursday, 22 July, the draft of the Appeal was circulated. Henson carried several amendments. On Friday it was possible for the whole day to be spent on the work of the reunion committee. Henson confided in his diary, 'Things went badly on the whole. The return of the episcopal churches section of the Committee strengthened greatly the "Catholic" faction.'[24] On Saturday, 24 July, the last day of the committee's work, Henson, after a battle, got a paragraph added to the Report, noting that there was considerable difference of opinion among members of the committee 'with regard to the precise phrasing and practical effect of some of the resolutions'.

The final set of plenary sessions began on Monday, 26 July, and continued until Saturday, 7 August. Monday saw the Report on Industrial Relations discussed. Certain alterations took place. In particular, Henson, who was hostile to it as strongly 'Labourist', got what he thought a too flattering reference to American prohibition toned down. He joked about the consumption of wine by the American bishops at the Lord Mayor's Banquet. 'This made the assembly laugh heartily, but the Transatlantics didn't like it.'[25]

On Wednesday, 28 July, the morning was spent on the development of provinces. The committee in their Report had sought to strengthen the Consultative Body of the Lambeth Conference. It noted that 31 dioceses were not yet established in provinces. In the afternoon Lang introduced the Report on Reunion and was loudly applauded. The American bishops then had to depart for the unveiling of the statue of Abraham Lincoln. The bishops still left considered the Report on Women's Work, which had in it some noteworthy items. Here are one or two quotations:

[24] *Retrospect of an Unimportant Life*, vol. ii, p. 13.
[25] Ibid., p. 14.

In our judgment there is nothing to prevent our believing that the Apostolic commission recorded in St John XX, 19–23 was delivered to women as well as men.[26]

When we survey at any rate the recent history of some, if not all, parts of the Anglican Communion, we are obliged to confess that the Church has failed to treat women workers with generosity or even justice.[27]

On deaconesses, they said:

We are persuaded that . . . the time has arrived when in the interest of the Church at large and, in particular, of the Ministry of Women, the Diaconate (the revival of which ancient office was hailed with thankfulness by the Lambeth Conference of 1897) should be canonically and formally recognized in the several Provinces. . . . In our judgment the ordination of a Deaconess confers on her Holy Orders.[28]

Finally, they said, 'We submit that in every Diocese there ought to exist a Board of Women's Work, including among its members men as well as women.'[29] Henson noted on the question of the status of deaconesses, 'the proposal frankly to transfer women from the laity to the clergy startles and displeases the High Churchmen. Zanzibar gave expression to this feeling. The "Talbot set", however, are vehemently feminist, and the Archbishop himself is clearly in that camp.'[30] Discussion of this Report continued on Thursday.

On Friday, 30 July, the Reunion Report went through 'with little difficulty' and 'almost without alteration', according to Henson who continued:

Lang was in charge of the resolutions, and, on the whole, did his part well. There were two dangerous moments. First, when the Bishop of Vermont (Hall), denounced the whole report as inherently inconsistent with Catholic principles, and, next, when the Bishops of Ely (Chase) and Gloucester (Gibson) made an attempt to alter the resolution. The Conference, however, was in no mood for controversy, and had plainly set its heart on getting something done. The Bishops of Western New York (Brent) and Pennsylvania (Rhinelander) refused to follow the lead of the Bishop of Vermont (Hall), who could only carry three bishops with him when the vote on the address was taken. Somebody suggested the singing of the Doxology, when the Address was adopted, and this was done with much fervour. The

---

[26] *Lambeth Conference, 1920.* Report, p. 96:
[27] Ibid., p. 99.
[28] Ibid., p. 102. This acceptance of deaconesses as 'in orders' is noteworthy.
[29] Ibid., p. 106.
[30] *Retrospect of an Unimportant Life,* vol. ii, p. 15.

Bishop of Zanzibar was greatly applauded when he refused to follow the Catholic minority.

Let us look at the famous Appeal – an Appeal to all Christian people – not churches. The bishops acknowledged 'all those who believe in our Lord Jesus Christ, and have been baptized into the name of the Holy Trinity, as sharing with us membership in the universal Church of Christ which is His Body'. It recognized the grounds of disunity, the relationship of Anglican Churches to both the ancient episcopal communions of East and West, and the non-episcopal. 'We acknowledge this condition of broken fellowship to be contrary to God's will, and we desire frankly to confess our share in the guilt of thus crippling the Body of Christ and hindering the activity of His Spirit.' The Appeal called for a new vision of a united Catholic Church, within which 'Christian communions now separated from one another would retain much that has long been distinctive in their methods of worship and service'. In the sixth paragraph the bishops brought in the Lambeth Quadrilateral, somewhat altered. Instead of being in four sections, it was in three, Scripture and Creeds being lumped together.

> We believe that the visible unity of the Church will be found to involve the whole-hearted acceptance of:
>> The Holy Scriptures, as the record of God's revelation of Himself to man, and as being the rule and ultimate standard of faith; and the Creed commonly called Nicene, as the sufficient statement of the Christian faith, and either it or the Apostles' Creed as the Baptismal confession of belief:
>> The divinely instituted sacraments of Baptism and the Holy Communion, as expressing for all the corporate life of the whole fellowship in and with Christ:
>> A ministry acknowledged by every part of the Church as possessing not only the inward call of the Spirit, but also the commission of Christ and the authority of the whole body.

One sees at once that in this altered form there is no reference to the episcopate. However, the Appeal goes on;

> May we not reasonably claim that the Episcopate is the one means of providing such a ministry? It is not that we call in question for a moment the spiritual reality of the ministries of those Communions which do not possess the Episcopate. On the contrary we thankfully acknowledge that these ministries have been manifestly blessed and owned by the Holy Spirit as effective means of grace. But we submit that considerations alike of history and of present experience justify the claim which we make on behalf of the Episcopate. Moreover, we would urge that it is now and will prove to be in

the future the best instrument for maintaining the unity and continuity of the Church. But we greatly desire that the office of a Bishop should be everywhere exercised in a representative and constitutional manner and more truly express all that ought to be involved for the life of the Christian Family, in the title of Father-in-God. Nay more, we eagerly look forward to the day when through its acceptance in a united Church we may all share in that grace which is pledged to the members of the whole body in the apostolic rite of the laying-on-of-hands, and in the joy and fellowship of a Eucharist in which as one Family we may together, without any doubtfulness of mind, offer to the one Lord our worship and service.

One might describe the viewpoint represented here as that of the *plene esse* attitude towards episcopacy, exhibited years later in the book, *The Historic Episcopate in the Fullness of the Church* (1954) edited by K. M. Carey. As that book was criticized, so the wording of the Lambeth Quadrilateral in the Appeal has been criticized.[31] Here we may quote Louis A. Haselmayer, *Lambeth and Unity* (1948), who is heavy in criticism.

The articles themselves have been perilously rephrased and reworded so that in many instances they mean nothing, or at best admit of such diversity of interpretation as to amount to nothing. The grouping of the Holy Scriptures and the Creeds in one statement minimizes the scope of the doctrinal content of Christianity. The description of the sacraments omits any reference to the form and matter which had been previously given, and the statement 'as expressing for all the corporate life of the whole fellowship in and with Christ' is so extremely vague that it could encompass within itself almost any degree of sacramental theology. Even Zwinglianism could find a happy home in this description. The final article on the ministry leaves out entirely any specific reference to the Episcopate. The phrase 'Historic Episcopate' in the 1886 and 1888 Quadrilateral was open to certain objection and interpretation of meaning. But now *the complete removal* of the phrase opens the door to the possible abandonment of any traditional, historic, and apostolic ministry. It makes possible tempting and speculative suggestions for ways of equating episcopal and non-episcopal ministries into something novel, but certainly not apostolic.[32]

This lengthy quotation is an indication of how in later years High Churchmen have criticized the Appeal. It serves to bring out the

[31] For criticism of *The Historic Episcopate*, see, e.g., K. N. Ross, *The Necessity of Episcopacy*. 'The Historic Episcopate' considered.

[32] *Lambeth and Unity* by Louis A. Haselmayer for the American Church Union, pp. 21–2.

alteration made in the Lambeth Quadrilateral. We shall notice further alterations in a subsequent Conference.

There then followed in the Appeal a paragraph on the mutual recognition of ministries, a paragraph which has had considerable repercussions and which is very relevant as part of the background to the recent discussions on Anglican–Methodist proposals for union.

> We believe that for all the truly equitable approach to union is by the way of mutual deference to one another's consciences. To this end, we who send forth this appeal would say that if the authorities of other Communions should so desire, we are persuaded that, terms of union having been otherwise satisfactorily adjusted, Bishops and clergy of our Communion would willingly accept from these authorities a form of commission or recognition which would commend our ministry to their congregations, as having its place in the one family life. It is not in our power to know how far this suggestion may be acceptable to those to whom we offer it. We can only say that we offer it in all sincerity as a token of our longing that all ministries of grace, theirs and ours, shall be available for the service of our Lord in a united Church.
>
> It is our hope that the same motive would lead ministers who have not received it to accept a commission through episcopal ordination, as obtaining for them a ministry throughout the whole fellowship.
>
> In so acting no one of us could possibly be taken to repudiate his past ministry. God forbid that any man should repudiate a past experience rich in spiritual blessings for himself and others.[33]

The Appeal ended with the words:

> We do not ask that any one Communion should consent to be absorbed in another. We do ask that all should unite in a new and great endeavour to recover and to manifest to the world the unity of the Body of Christ for which He prayed.[34]

One clearly sees here, as we have already noted, the *plene esse* position. Episcopacy should be the system of a united Church. Those who do not have it should take it into their systems – to use a phrase taken up by Archbishop Fisher in 1946.[35]

Besides the famous Appeal, there were a number of resolutions passed as a result of the work of the Committee on Reunion. Of these the most important were:

---

[33] *Lambeth Conference, 1920*. Report, p. 135.
[34] Idem, p. 136.
[35] See William Purcell, *Fisher of Lambeth*, ch. 7, 'A Sermon at Cambridge'.

12

A In view of prospects and projects of reunion –

i A Bishop is justified in giving occasional authorization to ministers, not episcopally ordained, who in his judgement are working towards an ideal of union such as is described in our Appeal, to preach in churches within his Diocese, and to clergy of the Diocese to preach in churches of such ministers:

ii The Bishops of the Anglican Communion will not question the action of any Bishop who, in the few years between the initiation and the completion of a definite scheme of union, shall countenance the irregularity of admitting to Communion the baptized but unconfirmed Communicants of the non-episcopal congregations concerned in the scheme. . . .

B Believing, however, that certain lines of action might imperil both the attainment of its ideal and the unity of its own Communion, the Conference declares that –

i It cannot approve of general schemes of intercommunion or exchange of pulpits:

ii In accordance with the principle of Church order set forth in the Preface to the Ordinal attached to the Book of Common Prayer, it cannot approve the celebration in Anglican churches of the Holy Communion for members of the Anglican Church by ministers who have not been episcopally ordained; and that it should be regarded as the general rule of the Church that Anglican communicants should receive Holy Communion only at the hands of ministers of their own Church, or of Churches in communion therewith.

C In view of doubts and varieties of practice which have caused difficulties in the past, the Conference declares that –

i Nothing in these Resolutions is intended to indicate that the rule of Confirmation as conditioning admission to the Holy Communion must necessarily apply to the case of baptized persons who seek Communion under conditions which in the Bishop's judgement justify their admission thereto.

ii In cases in which it is impossible for the Bishop's judgement to be obtained beforehand the priest should remember that he has no canonical authority to refuse Communion to any baptized person kneeling before the Lord's Table (unless he be excommunicate by name or, in the canonical sense of the term, a cause of scandal to the faithful); and that, if a question may properly be raised as to the future admission of any such person to Holy Communion, either because he has not been confirmed or for other reasons, the priest should refer the matter to the Bishop for counsel or direction.[36]

There seemed to be a victory against the extreme High Churchmen.

[36] *Lambeth Conference, 1920*. Report, pp. 30–1.

Frank Weston of Zanzibar was praised for not going with them. Henson remarked:

> It is almost amusing to notice the compliments which are poured out on this odd prelate who only a few months since was hurling anathemas against all the bishops for their refusal to excommunicate me as a heretic! The Evangelical bishops appeared to be greatly pleased with the day's work, and, perhaps, the painful efforts at self-justification which the Catholics made, may be taken as some evidence that they feel themselves beaten.[37]

Bishop Knox of Manchester in his *Reminiscences of an Octogenarian* remarked:

> Popular anticipation had figured Frank Weston, the Bishop of Zanzibar, on one side, and Bishop Hensley Henson on the other, as the two irreconcilables. Had the public been admitted to our sessions, they would, again and again, have seen these two protagonists literally putting their heads together in search of some formula of agreement. The generous spirit of Christian charity, which characterized the report as a whole, won for it, and still wins for it, wide approval.[38]

On Saturday, 31 July, the Conference dealt with the subject of the Eastern Churches and the Swedish Church. The committee concerned with the Eastern Church had had the advantage of conferring with the Metropolitan of Demotica. The Report on the Swedish Church which had come out after the 1908 Lambeth Conference was received and its conclusions agreed to.[39] Swedish Christians were to be received at Holy Communion. Following upon the Conference, Bishop Henson and Bishop Theodore Woods went to Uppsala to join in the consecration of a Swedish bishop. Full communion was thus established – a big step forward. In treating the question of the Old Catholics the Conference dealt with the Rev. A. H. Mathew, who had been consecrated as an Orthodox bishop in England in 1908. Evidently the Old Catholics had refused communion with Mathew, who was something of an impostor. The Conference was also unable to agree to reunion with the Reformed

---

[37] *Retrospect of an Unimportant Life*, vol. ii, p. 16.

[38] E. A. Knox, *Reminiscences of an Octogenarian* (1934), pp. 319–20. See also Theodore Woods in *Lambeth and Reunion* (1921), pp. 52–3, for an account of Friday, 30 July.

[39] See *The Church of England and the Church of Sweden*. Report of the Commission appointed by the Archbishop of Canterbury in pursuance of Resolution 74 of the Lambeth Conference.

Evangelical Church, the result of the Cummins schism in the U.S.A.[40]

On Monday, 2 August, the bishops were still dealing with reunion. Bishop Pollock of Norwich wanted some statement made on the unanimity of the Conference, but Henson successfully protested against this. Then they moved on to the Report on Marriage Problems, which condemned contraception.

> Resolution 68. The Conference, while declining to lay down rules which will meet the needs of every abnormal case, regards with grave concern the spread in modern society of theories and practices hostile to the family. We utter an emphatic warning against the use of unnatural means for the avoidance of conception, together with the grave dangers – physical, moral and religious – thereby incurred, and against the evils with which the extension of such use threatens the race. In opposition to the teaching which, under the name of science and religion, encourages married people in the deliberate cultivation of sexual union as an end in itself, we steadfastly uphold what must always be regarded as the governing considerations of Christian marriage. One is the primary purpose for which marriage exists, namely the continuation of the race through the gift and heritage of children; the other is the paramount importance in married life of deliberate and thoughtful self-control.[41]

Resolution 70 is also to be noted:

> The Conference urges the importance of enlisting help of all high-principled men and women, whatever be their religious beliefs, in co-operation with or, if necessary, in bringing pressure to bear upon, authorities both national and local, for removing such incentives to vice as indecent literature, suggestive plays and films, the open or secret sale of contraceptives, and the continued existence of brothels.[42]

Henson was opposed to the wholesale condemnation of contraceptives. The Bishop of Dornakal, when asked how he liked the Conference, replied that he had enjoyed it until they arrived at the subject of contraceptives of which he had not known the existence.[43] On the question of divorce, the Conference said that marriage was a 'life-long and indissoluble union'. Henson wanted 'indissoluble' removed but without avail.[44]

[40] On the Cummins episode, see E. Clowes Chorley, *Men and Movements in the American Episcopal Church*, pp. 410ff.

[41] *Lambeth Conference, 1920*. Report, p. 44.

[42] Ibid., p. 45.

[43] *Retrospect of an Unimportant Life*, vol. ii, p. 19.

[44] Ibid., p. 18.

On Wednesday, 4 August, discussion continued on the question of marriage problems. Weston proved obstructive and the discussion went on until 8 p.m.

On Thursday, 5 August, Bishop Burge introduced the Report on Spiritualism, Christian Science, and Theosophy and greatly impressed the Conference.

On Friday, 6 August, in the morning, a further discussion of the question of contraception took place. The resolution we have quoted was passed but Henson disliked it intensely, 'The resolution', he said,

> showed that the Conference refused to face the real problem. Nobody was in doubt as to the legitimacy of using contraceptives in 'abnormal' cases; the question was raised with respect to their use in normal cases. I could not be a party to what branded as 'unnatural' the methods which modern science provided, and, considering the associations of the word, I thought its use offensive.[45]

They proceeded to consider the encyclical on the theme of fellowship, drafted by Bishop Palmer, which was amended in various ways. Discussion of it continued on the Saturday, after which the Archbishop of York put forward this resolution, 'that the President do now leave the chair and that Mrs Davidson, suitably attended, be invited to attend the Conference and become a member of it for the time being'. Mrs Davidson and some of her staff then entered the room. Lang made a speech of thanks to the Davidsons and Bishop Gailor of Tennessee presented to the Archbishop a primatial cross of silver and ebony and to Mrs Davidson a cheque. The Archbishop of Canterbury replied with much feeling, and Mrs Davidson said a few words of thanks. Then the Benediction was given and they went to lunch.

The final service for the Lambeth Conference took place in St Paul's Cathedral on Sunday, 8 August, at 10.30 a.m. The sermon was preached by Bishop Gailor of Tennessee. Henson said that 'it began well but tailed off badly. It was rather too long for its quality.'[46] Before announcing the Blessing, the Archbishop of Canterbury said a few words of farewell to the assembled bishops. It was to be his last Lambeth Conference. By 1930 he had both retired and died.

A press conference was held by the Archbishop on 11 August and the idea and motive behind the Appeal to all Christian people explained. The Appeal was later translated into Latin, Greek, French, German,

[45] *Retrospect of an Unimportant Life*, vol. ii, p. 20.
[46] *Retrospect of an Unimportant Life*, vol. ii, p. 21.

Italian, Russian, Chinese, and Esperanto. The Archbishop also sent out a 'Message to Men and Women of Goodwill', based on a first draft made by Bishop Theodore Woods. 'It can hardly be questioned', wrote Miss Honor Thomas,

> that far greater enthusiasm was shown by the Press for the Conference of 1920 than for any of its predecessors. That this increased keenness was shared by the general public was indicated not only by the very rapid sale of the Report, but also by the personal interest shown in the movements of the Bishops. The Hospitality Committee had no difficulty in getting offers to entertain the Overseas Bishops, and indeed some disappointment was caused by the fact that there were not enough Bishops to go round among the houses thrown open to them. Many leading Clubs offered honorary membership to the members of the Conference, proprietors of illustrated and other papers sent free copies of their periodicals for the Bishops' reading-room, while the demand by people all over England to buy the chairs used in the Library during the Conference was surprising. These chairs, each with its small leather case for papers hung on the back, had been specially made for the purpose, and each bore on it the name of the Bishop who used it. It would be invidious to mention whose chairs were most eagerly sought after, but those used by certain prelates could have been sold over and over again, and there were at least a hundred applicants who could not be supplied at all. As on previous occasions, many of the Bishops took their own chairs away with them, and the picture of a particular Archbishop who left Lambeth carrying two chairs, one under each arm, and refusing all offers of assistance, will not easily be forgotten by those who saw it.[47]

No one could buy the Bishop of Durham's chair. He bought it himself (£1).[48] Davidson won universal praise for his fairness at the Conference, but undoubtedly Lang came out of the Conference with a great reputation, especially for his work for reunion.[49] Burge had come away with credit for clarity and judicious statement. The surprise of the Conference was Frank Weston. 'He and Henson' wrote Davidson,

> became personal friends, and Uganda and Mombasa were constantly by his side, and he and they desired that I should be photographed with them as a group. This was done. Whether his strange temperament will show itself by some outbreak of another kind now that the Conference is over, I cannot tell. I feel a little uneasy sometimes. I hope this is not faithless.[50]

[47] *The Six Lambeth Conferences, 1867–1920*, p. 46n.
[48] *Retrospect of an Unimportant Life*, vol. ii, p. 20.
[49] See J. G. Lockhart, *Cosmo Gordon Lang*, p. 273.
[50] G. K. A. Bell, *Randall Davidson*, vol. ii, p. 1012.

Theodore Woods also gained renown as the episcopal secretary.[51] He lived on for the Conference of 1930, but did not act as secretary again. Instead, George Bell, then Bishop of Chichester, took on this task. There were doubtless some who saw Woods as a future primate. From Peterborough he moved in 1924 to Winchester. He died, however, in the year after the 1930 Lambeth Conference.

What was the public reaction to the Appeal? Lord Halifax wrote to Lang after the Conference and said that 'few things in his life have given him more pleasure'. The Methodist Scott Lidgett said that it was 'the most remarkable document since the Reformation'. Dr J. H. Shakespeare, Secretary of the Baptist Union, said it was 'the finger of God'. R. F. Horton, the Congregationalist (President of the National Free Church Council in 1927) said that it created a new epoch.[52] Frank Weston was pleading with all his fellow-Catholics to make it their guiding vision for years to come. The sympathetic attitude of Weston meant that many Anglo-Catholics supported it. T. A. Lacey welcomed it in a pamphlet.[53] But Darwell Stone, Principal of Pusey House, did not approve, and with Father Puller wrote a long pamphlet in criticism of it.[54] Headlam, soon to follow Gibson as Bishop of Gloucester and to play a very considerable part in reunion, thoroughly approved of it in the *Church Quarterly Review*, saying that

> the claims of the episcopate are put forward on grounds which no historian could condemn. There is no attempt to justify the episcopate as of divine institution, nor is it stated that it is the exclusive channel of grace. The Church of England is an episcopal Church and we do not think that its belief in episcopacy could be stated in a more moderate and reasonable manner.[55]

Major and Rashdall in the *Modern Churchman* both approved of the Conference but Rashdall felt that the bishops had not been bold enough on reunion.[56] The Bishops of Peterborough, Zanzibar, and Hereford (Linton Smith) produced in 1921 a book *Lambeth and Reunion. An*

---

[51] See E. S. Woods and F. B. Macnutt, *Theodore, Bishop of Winchester*, p. 144.

[52] These judgements are given in J. G. Lockhart, *Cosmo Gordon Lang*, p. 271.

[53] T. A. Lacey, *The Universal Church. A Study in the Lambeth Call to Union.*

[54] *Who are members of the Church?* A Statement of evidence in criticism of a sentence in the Appeal to all Christian People by Darwell Stone and F. W. Puller (Pusey House Occasional Papers No. 9). See also F. L. Cross, *Darwell Stone*, pp. 147–8.

[55] *Church Quarterly Review*, vol. xci, p. 151.

[56] See *Modern Churchman*, vol. x, pp. 149–50 and 518ff.

Interpretation of the Mind of the Lambeth Conference of 1920 which sought to get a sympathetic hearing for what the Conference had said.[57]

What followed after the Appeal? There were, first of all, the Malines Conversations which owed so much to Lord Halifax and Cardinal Mercier and in which Gore, Frere, and Armitage Robinson played a part. They were attacked by Hensley Henson, ended in 1928, and proved abortive.[58] There were also talks with Nonconformists. The Free Church Federal Council issued a provisional statement in September 1920. In March 1921 came a more detailed statement, *The Free Churches and the Lambeth Appeal*. In November 1921 the Anglicans and Nonconformists met together for discussion in the first of a series of conferences. There were twenty-five Nonconformists and nine diocesan bishops – later ten – together with the two Archbishops. The main work was done by a subcommittee consisting, on the Anglican side, of Lang, Gibson (the Bishop of Gloucester), Woods (Bishop of Peterborough), Strong (Bishop of Ripon), Ridgeway (Bishop of Salisbury), Headlam, and Frere; and, on the Free Church side, of Dr P. Carnegie Simpson (Presbyterian), Dr Scott Lidgett (Wesleyan), Dr A. E. Garvie (Congregationalist), Dr J. H. Shakespeare (Baptist), Dr J. D. Jones (Congregationalist), and Professor A. S. Peake (Primitive Methodist). Their first report came out in May 1922 and was favourably received. However, questions were raised about the status of the existing Free Church ministry. The Free Churchmen conceded the point that, after reunion, all ministers should be episcopally ordained but found themselves unable to agree to the re-ordination of non-episcopally ordained ministers. Discussion continued until 1925 and then came to an end. It was clear that a majority of the Anglicans felt that Nonconformist ministers should be conditionally re-ordained. Again the rock of episcopacy had proved a stone of stumbling. Discussions were not resumed until after the 1930 Lambeth Conference.[59]

We have seen that the subject of modernism did not crop up at the Lambeth Conference of 1920. Yet in the year following the Lambeth Conference modernism became a topic of conversation because of the

[57] *Theology* published a whole series of reviews of the Conference Report. There were also pamphlets from J. R. Cohu, J. J. Willis, A. P. S. Tulloch, and papers by H. J. Wotherspoon, R. S. Kirkpatrick, and James H. Leishman (see p. 318).

[58] See G. K. A. Bell, *Randall Davidson*, vol. ii, pp. 1254ff.

[59] For a discussion of Lambeth 1920 by a Liberal Evangelical, Bishop A. W. T. Perowne, and the Presbyterian P. Carnegie Simpson see *The Call for Christian Unity*, ed. V. F. Storr and G. H. Harris.

famous (or infamous) Girton Conference. This raised a great deal of controversy and brought the issue of modernism before the Canterbury Convocation. One of its results was the setting up in 1922 of the Archbishops' Commission on Doctrine. Burge was chairman, succeeded later by William Temple. Its Report did not emerge until 1938, long after the 1930 Conference. It is possible that the Report might have been discussed had there been a Lambeth Conference in 1940. The Second World War, however, postponed that Conference until 1948, by which time the Report on Doctrine had been quietly forgotten. However, the 1930 Conference discussed the doctrine of God and the 1948 Conference discussed the doctrine of man. Modernism, however, has never come on to the agenda.

10

COSMO LANG AND
THE CONFERENCE OF 1930

Though stalemate arose in discussions with the Roman Catholics and the Nonconformists after the Lambeth Conference of 1920, progress was made in relations with the Swedish Church and with the Orthodox. After Lambeth 1920 both Anglicans and Orthodox engaged in intensive study of each other's church. The Orthodox Professor Komnenos, one of the delegates to the Lambeth Conference, in a study of Anglican ordinations pronounced in their favour. In July 1922, Meletios, Patriarch of Constantinople, with the Holy Synod adopted a Declaration that

> as before the Orthodox Church, the ordinations of the Anglican Episcopal Confession of bishops, priests, and deacons, possesses [sic] the same validity as those of the Roman, Old Catholic and Armenian Churches possess, inasmuch as all essentials are found in them which are held indispensable from the Orthodox point of view for the recognition of the 'Charisma' of the priesthood derived from Apostolic succession.[1]

This prepared the way for future advance. The Patriarch of Jerusalem and the Church of Cyprus took similar action. Meletios also appointed Archbishop Germanos, the Metropolitan of Thyateira, as his representative in London for communications with the Archbishop of Canterbury. In 1925 came a notable demonstration of Christian unity in London, when the Archbishop of Canterbury, the Patriarchs of Alexandria and Jerusalem, the Archbishop of Uppsala, and the Patriarch of the Assyrian Church joined in celebrating the 1500th anniversary of the Nicene Creed, which they recited together in Westminster Abbey.

Four conferences must now be mentioned as forming a background to the Conference of 1930. In April 1924 there took place in Birmingham a Conference on a large scale, which became known as

---

[1] See G. K. A. Bell, *Documents on Christian Unity*, 1920–4, No. 19. See also Chapter 4 of G. K. A. Bell, *Christian Unity. The Anglican Position.*

C.O.P.E.C., a short title for 'Conference on Christian Politics, Economics, and Citizenship'. There were 1,500 delegates, of whom eighty came from outside the British Isles. Six European countries and China and Japan were represented. Its purpose was described by its secretary, Miss Lucy Gardner, as the establishing of a 'norm of Christian thought and action for the further working out of Christian order'. William Temple, then Bishop of Manchester, took a large part in the proceedings. It may be difficult to assess the precise effects of the Conference, but it influenced Christian thought. There was nothing like it again until the Malvern Conference of 1941.[2]

In 1925 there took place at Stockholm a World Conference on Life and Work, after six years of preparation. Five hundred delegates came from thirty-seven countries. No ecumenical Christian conference of such magnitude had taken place since the Council of Nicaea, sixteen hundred years before. There was, however, no representation from the Church of Rome and the Conference lacked representatives from the younger Churches in Africa and Asia. But it was the first large-scale contact between British, French, and German churchmen since the Great War. G. K. A. Bell was a leading Anglican present.[3] Two years later (1927) there met at Lausanne the first World Conference on Faith and Order. Gore, Headlam, and Temple were present among the Anglicans. The two main points on which the Conference reached agreement were that the faith of the Church is that to which the Apostles' and Nicene Creeds bear witness, and that, if unity of order is to be achieved, it must rest on the basis of the historic episcopate. There was also a classic statement of the Gospel, drafted by a group led by Adolf Deissmann, the German New Testament scholar.[4] Then, in the following year, 1928, came the Ecumenical Missionary Conference at Jerusalem, which had developed out of the Edinburgh 1910 Conference and the setting up in 1921 of the International Missionary Council. The result of this Conference can be seen in the words of Dean Iremonger:

> The 'Messages and Recommendations' of the Conference were set out in *The World Mission of Christianity*, and it is not too much to say that the fellowship of these leaders of the Christian forces in fifty countries, which deepened as they spent their Passiontide in prayer and counsel on the Mount of Olives within sight of Calvary, marked the beginning of a new missionary

[2] On C.O.P.E.C. see F. W. Dillistone, *Charles Raven*.

[3] See Ronald Jasper, *George Bell, Bishop of Chichester*, pp. 60–5.

[4] See F. A. Iremonger, *William Temple*, p. 401. The Lausanne Conference is being commemorated this year (1977).

outlook in many Churches: 'An atmosphere was generated,' wrote Dr. Mott, 'in which serious difficulties and conflicting views, while never ignored but frankly expressed, were transcended': misunderstandings were removed, the way to even closer co-operation was opened, and the younger Churches experienced the stimulus of being treated not as pupils on whom the teachers of the Western world were seeking to impose the stamp of fixed ecclesiastical forms and practices, but as partners in a great enterprise for the Kingdom of God to which they could contribute something of their own genius and their own racial culture. The presence of a much larger proportion of delegates from the younger Churches when the next missionary conference was held at Tambaram, near Madras, shows that this confidence in them was not misplaced.[5]

Archbishop Davidson, who had been present at every Lambeth Conference since 1878, retired in November 1928, just after the second rejection in Parliament of the Deposited Book. He was succeeded at Canterbury by Cosmo Gordon Lang, Archbishop of York. William Temple was translated from Manchester to York: the 1930 Conference was the only one he attended. Lord Davidson of Lambeth (as he became on retirement) was asked to play some part in the 1930 Conference, but he died on 24 May of that same year.

Lang's first years at Canterbury were made difficult through illness. Struck down by severe internal pains on Advent Sunday 1928, not long after his enthronement, he had a lengthy recuperation at Bognor. Then he went on a voyage through the Mediterranean in April 1929, visited the Holy Land, and contacted representatives of the Orthodox Church. He returned in good health, but in June 1930, just before the Lambeth Conference was due to begin, illness came upon him again and once more he was forced to retreat to Bognor, and there prayed for the forthcoming assembly. 'Afterwards', says his biographer, 'he was grateful for the respite, irksome as at first he found it. "I tremble to think", he wrote, "what might have happened, apart from health, if I had emerged into the Conference from that overcrowded June." As it was he entered it with collected thoughts and weathered it without illness or even undue fatigue.' The Archbishop was worried about the Conference, especially regarding the tricky issue of the South Indian scheme, but as things began to go well 'he grew better and strong himself'.[6] It was the South Indian scheme of reunion which was to be the major issue facing the bishops.[7]

[5] Ibid., pp. 398–9.
[6] See J. G. Lockhart, Cosmo Gordon Lang, p. 343.
[7] Cf. N. P. Williams's book written in 1930, Lausanne, Lambeth and South India.

We must now note some of the changes in the episcopate. Theodore Woods had gone from Peterborough to Winchester, in succession to E. S. Talbot, who had retired. E. W. Barnes, the notorious modernist, author of *Should such a faith offend?* (1927), was at Birmingham, in succession to Henry Russell Wakefield. H. A. Wilson, Rector of Cheltenham, the scene of the Church Congress of 1928 on 'The Anglican Communion, Past, Present and Future', had become Bishop of Chelmsford in 1929.[8] A. C. Headlam had been Bishop of Gloucester since 1923 and E. J. Palmer had returned from Bombay to be his Assistant Bishop. G. K. A. Bell, who as Archbishop Davidson's chaplain had acted as assistant secretary in 1920, had become Bishop of Chichester in 1929, and was the episcopal secretary of the Conference, assisted by Mervyn Haigh, the chaplain at Lambeth.[9] T. B. Strong had succeeded Burge at Oxford and C. M. Blagden had succeeded Theodore Woods at Peterborough.[10] The Mirfield monk, W. H. Frere, had succeeded at Truro F. G. Guy Warman, who had gone to Manchester in place of Temple. A. A. David, a Liberal Evangelical, ex-Headmaster of Rugby, was at Liverpool, and E. A. Burroughs, another Liberal Evangelical, had succeeded Strong at Ripon.[11] St Clair Donaldson had come home from Australia to be Bishop of Salisbury. Cyril Garbett was at Southwark, having become Bishop there in 1919. The Archbishop of Armagh, as in 1920, was C. F. D'Arcy and the Archbishop of Dublin, J. A. F. Gregg. The best-known of the Scottish bishops was Kenneth Mackenzie of Argyll and the Isles. The Archbishop of Wales was A. G. Edwards. From America there came the Presiding Bishop, J. de W. Perry of Rhode Island, and Bishop Gailor of Tennessee, who had been Acting-Presiding Bishop in 1920. Bishops Brent and Lawrence had both died. Bishop Westcott of Calcutta and Bishop Azariah of Dornakal came again. The most outstanding of the Canadian bishops was Bishop C. J. Farthing of Montreal. Bishop Walter Carey was at Bloemfontein and Neville Talbot at Pretoria. The Archbishop of the West Indies was E. Hutson. Seven bishops came from Japan, including one native one, P. Y. Matsui of Tokyo. Nine bishops came from China, including H. W. K. Mowll, Bishop in Western China.[12] M. N. Trollope came from Korea; from the

---

[8] See H. A. Wilson (ed.), *The Anglican Communion. Past, Present and Future.*
[9] See F. R. Barry, *Mervyn Haigh.*
[10] See C. M. Blagden, *Well Remembered.*
[11] See H. G. Mulliner, *Arthur Burroughs.*
[12] See Marcus L. Loane, *Archbishop Mowll.*

Niger came the black Bishop, A. W. Howells; from Persia, Bishop Linton and from Uganda, Bishop J. J. Willis of Kikuyu fame. There had been further Conferences at Kikuyu in 1922 and in 1927. Progress in reunion had gone forward though no United African Church was formed.[13] Frank Weston now dead had been succeeded at Zanzibar by T. H. Birley.

At the time of the Conference the leading lights among the Anglo-Catholics were Frere of Truro, Furse of St Albans, Mosley of Southwell, and Bishop Pearce of Derby (brother of the Bishop of Worcester), sometime Master of Corpus Christi College, Cambridge, and Bishop Seaton of Wakefield. The Evangelical leaders were Guy Warman of Manchester, Wilson of Chelmsford, Burroughs of Ripon, Pollock of Norwich, and David of Liverpool. Bishop Henson considered that the outstanding personalities of the Conference were Lang, Palmer, Temple, and Headlam. To these we must add the name of Henson himself and also that of Bell.

J. G. Lockhart mentions some of the domestic details of this Conference. In 1930 for the first time financial assistance (£2,000) was granted to the Archbishop for running the Conference by the Church Assembly, but this sum was inadequate, as the expense of entertaining the bishops to lunch and tea every day for five weeks ran into £1,400. The catering became the problem of the Archbishop's other chaplain, Lumley Green-Wilkinson, who 'discovered some racecourse caterers, who accepted the contract and carried it out to the general satisfaction, the waitresses subsequently declaring that they "preferred Bishops to bookies".'[14]

The theme of the Conference was the word 'Witness'. Its programme was headed with the title, 'The Faith and Witness of the Church in this Generation'. It was divided into five sections as follows:

I The Christian Doctrine of God:
   a in relation to modern thought;
   b in relation to non-Christian religions and ideals;
   c as determining the character of Christian worship;
   d to be realized throughout the Church by teaching and study.

(There was thus introduced a new feature – the attempt to consider

---

[13] See Roger Lloyd, *The Church of England 1900–1965*, pp. 426ff., and J. J. Willis, etc., *Towards a United Church*.

[14] J. G. Lockhart, *Cosmo Gordon Lang*, p. 344.

an important topic of theology. In 1948 the bishops looked at the Doctrine of Man.)

    II The Life and Witness of the Christian Community, individual and corporate, in the fulfilment of the Divine prupose, with special reference to questions of:
        a marriage;
        b sex;
        c race;
        d education and governments;
        e peace and war.
    III The Unity of the Church.
        a Report of results of the Lambeth Appeal, 1920; World Conference of Faith and Order (Lausanne).
        b Schemes and proposals of Union.
        c Relations of the Anglican Communion with particular Churches.
    IV The Anglican Communion:
        a its ideal and future;
        b its organization and authority;
          1 central
          2 national and provincial
          3 missionary dioceses, under the jurisdiction of the Archbishop of Canterbury (Questions of Church order with regard to forms of worship and rules of marriage).
    V The Ministry:
        a supply of men for Holy Orders, and the Church's duty to provide for it;
        b the training of clergy before and after ordination;
        c supplementary ministries;
          1 deaconesses
          2 voluntary clergy
        Reports: Women's Work, Resolution 54, Lambeth Conference 1920.
                Ministry of Healing, Resolution 63, Lambeth Conference 1920.
                Communities, Resolution 57, Lambeth Conference 1908.
    VI Youth and Its Vocation.

'Youth' was a new subject.

The Quiet Day at Fulham on Friday, 4 July, with which the Conference started is well described by Bishop Henson.

I made my way quite easily by bus to Fulham Parish Church, where the services and addresses were arranged. The Bishop of London celebrated the

Holy Communion at 8.30 a.m. There were, I suppose, about 150 bishops present. We had breakfast in a parish room hard by the church. The readings were from Church's 'Pascal', the sermon on Bishop Andrews, but the acoustics of the room were so bad that many of the feeding bishops heard little. Old Bishop Talbot, now in his eighty-seventh year, was the conductor, but he was more impressive than coherent, and was heard with difficulty. In the interval between the addresses we sate about in the Palace Grounds, which are very beautiful.[15]

Lockhart remarks that Talbot, 'almost the last survivor of those who had had personal links with the Oxford Movement and the friend and disciple of Dean Church' had recently fallen and broken his thigh; hence he was practically carried in by his large son, Neville, Bishop of Pretoria.[16]

On the next day, Saturday, 5 July, came the customary visit to Canterbury. When the bishops arrived at Canterbury in the morning by train from London they were received by the Dean, Dick Sheppard, and, after offering prayers at the grave of Lord Davidson, were entertained to lunch in the Coleridge Museum of St Augustine's College.[17] The bishops were welcomed in the cathedral and especial honour was paid to the Orthodox delegation which was headed by Meletios, the Patriarch of Alexandria. Lang stood at St Augustine's chair to receive them all and then from it gave his address. Though Henson found this 'most dignified, but rather too long and elaborate', he thought the hymns 'were excellently chosen, and excellently sung; but the Te Deum, sung by the Cathedral Choir, sounded thin and inadequate.'[18] Afterwards came the usual garden party. Then they returned to London.

The next day there was a service of Holy Communion, not in Westminster Abbey (as in 1888, 1897, 1908, and 1920) but in St Paul's Cathedral. Presumably this was to mark the completion of the restoration of St Paul's.[19] The preacher in St Paul's was William Temple. The text of his sermon, on the majesty of God, was Revelation 1.8. It included the oft-quoted words:

---

[15] *Retrospect of an Unimportant Life*, vol. ii, p. 258.
[16] J. G. Lockhart, *Cosmo Gordon Lang*, p. 344.
[17] See *The Times*, 7 July 1930.
[18] *Retrospect of an Unimportant Life*, vol. ii, p. 258.
[19] St Paul's had been reopened after restoration on 25 June. See W. R. Inge, *Diary of a Dean*, p. 148.

While we deliberate, He reigns; when we decide wisely, He reigns; when we decide foolishly, He reigns; when we serve Him in humble loyalty, He reigns; when we serve Him self-assertively, He reigns; when we rebel and seek to withhold our service, He reigns – the Alpha and the Omega, which is and was, and which is to come, the Almighty.[20]

Temple remarked that he would not have been in the pulpit at all, but for the death of Lord Davidson, who had originally been engaged to preach. Henson, no easy one to please, said that the sermon was 'excellent and excellently delivered'. He added,

Less than half the bishops communicated, but even so, the Archbishop had to consecrate twice. The singing of the hymn *'Glorious things of Thee are spoken'*, at the close of the service was most moving, the whole of the vast congregation joining with much religious ardour. If our problems could be solved by well-arranged pageants, we should do well enough even now![21]

Bishop E. S. Woods also wrote of the service in *Theodore, Bishop of Winchester*:

It was an impressive sight as the scarlet-robed procession of Bishops – 308 of us – moved round outside the great Cathedral and in at the West Door: a procession so long that its head had reached the top of the aisle while the last files were still descending the steps of the South Door.[22]

The service in St Paul's was attended by the Orthodox delegation but not by the Nonconformists. The latter felt aggrieved at their treatment. Headlam, who had just published his little book on *Christian Unity*, reiterating the arguments of his Bampton Lectures, contended that all the delegations should have been present in the cathedral.[23] He preached the sermon at St Paul's at Evensong on the Sunday with 'Unity' as his subject.

On Monday, 7 July, the Conference began to get down to business. Henson again described the scene:

The Library seemed rather congested. However, as a seat had been reserved for me, I had no personal inconvenience. The President, Lang, made references to his predecessor, and did so in felicitous words and at no undue length. Then Bell, the Bishop of Chichester, who is the Secretary of the Conference, made a series of anouncements, after which we fell to work. The subject was 'The Christian Doctrine of God'. Archbishop D'Arcy opened

---

[20] This passage is quoted in *The Times*, Monday, 7 July.
[21] *Retrospect of an Unimportant Life*, vol. ii, p. 259.
[22] Op. cit., p. 333.
[23] See R. Jasper, *A. C. Headlam*, p. 204.

with an admirable speech, and was followed by a rather disappointing speech from Archbishop Temple. The Bishop of Oxford (Strong) had something useful to say, and said it in his worst manner. The Bishop of Goulburn [L. B. Radford] was fluent and copious, evidently giving the substance of his commentary on the Colossians, which, he told the Conference, had engaged his leisure for years past.[24]

Radford's *Commentary* came out in the Westminster Series in 1931.

On Tuesday, 8 July, the Conference dealt with 'The Life and Witness of the Christian Community'. In the morning marriage and sex were debated. Theodore Woods of Winchester gave the first speech, followed by Henson. Garbett of Southwark, interested in all social questions, came next. In the afternoon the heat was so intense that 'many of the bishops fell asleep'.[25] Henson began to feel that the bishops 'were generally disposed to go far towards accepting the modern horrors, 'contraceptives', 'sterilization' etc.'[26] The race question brought forth 'fluent incoherence (loudly applauded) from Bishop Howells, of the upper Niger'. Bishop Karney of Johannesburg castigated the white population of South Africa for their un-Christian temper. On this day the Orthodox delegation was officially received.[27]

On Wednesday, one of the bishops, G. M. Long of Newcastle, New South Wales, collapsed and died. The subject of the discussion that day was reunion with particular reference to South India. Temple and Bell spoke but were both cautious. Headlam's speech was well received. Henson said, 'It is plain that his books have been read, and have impressed the bishops, and certainly he counts as one of the weightiest factors in the Conference. Yet the speech lent itself to much hostile criticism, and could have been "torn to ribbons" by a competent opponent.'[28] Henson was referring to Headlam's contention that reunion with the Orthodox Church and with the Nonconformists could go hand in hand. In the afternoon, both Bishop Azariah of Dornakal and Bishop Linton of Persia spoke in favour of the South Indian Scheme.

On Thursday, 10 July, the bishops got down to a discussion on 'The Anglican Communion'. As in 1920 this subject interested Henson least of all. The bishops were given a fair amount of buffoonery from the

[24] *Retrospect of an Unimportant Life*, vol. ii, p. 259.
[25] Ibid., p. 260.
[26] Ibid., p. 260.
[27] See J. G. Lockhart, *Cosmo Gordon Lang*, p. 346.
[28] *Retrospect of an Unimportant Life*, vol. ii, p. 261.

Bishop of Colorado (Johnson) and a large number of stutters from Bishop Palmer. Archbishop Carter of Capetown raised the difficult question of the name of the Anglican Communion, which had, in fact, ceased to be 'Anglican'. At the end of the afternoon the bishops were photographed in their robes.[29]

Friday, 11 July, witnessed a discussion on 'The Ministry of the Church'. Henson was impressed by the speeches of Bishop Waller of Madras, Bishop Garbett of Southwark on faith-healing, and Bishop Frere of Truro on religious communities. Of Frere, he wrote, 'looking very ascetic' he 'impressed the Conference with a speech on communities, in the course of which he said that but for unction preceded by prayer and confession, he would not have been with us. This allusion to recent illness, made with conviction and simplicity, was very moving. He is, and looks, the perfect monk.'[30]

On Saturday, 12 July, the bishops were introduced to the subject of 'Youth and Its Vocation'. The English bishops did much of the speaking – Winnington-Ingram of London, Furse of St Albans, Lovett of Portsmouth, Burroughs of Ripon, and Woolcombe of Whitby. Most of the bishops then went off to Liverpool for a function in the uncompleted cathedral.

Now the committees got to work under their various chairmen. These were as follows:

1 The Christian Doctrine of God. Archbishop D'Arcy of Armagh.
2 The Life and Witness of the Christian Community. Bishop Theodore Woods.
3 The Unity of the Church. Archbishop Temple.
4 The Anglican Communion. Bishop St Clair Donaldson of Salisbury.
5 The Ministry of the Church. Bishop F. R. Phelps of Grahamstown.
6 Youth and Its Vocation. Bishop Winnington-Ingram.

The committee work went on from Monday, 14 July, until Friday, 25 July. The President left them to work undisturbed, though paying occasional visits to committees in difficulties, and was thus free to entertain. Again, there were the customary social events. On Wednesday, 23 July, the bishops went to Buckingham Palace to be received by the King, George V, who was presented with a loyal address penned by Henson at Lang's request. The Archbishop of Canterbury suggested to the King that 'the visit had been a good lesson in

[29] Ibid., p. 261.
[30] Ibid., p. 262.

geography; to which His Majesty replied: "I know more about it than you – you see, I collect stamps." [31] The next day there was a royal garden party at Buckingham Palace. 'There was an immense concourse,' Henson wrote in his diary, 'the refreshment tent was besieged, but many could not get "bite or sup".' [32]

The two most important and crucial committees were (2) on 'The Life and Witness of the Christian Community' and (3) on 'The Unity of the Church'. Bishop Henson was on both of these committees, but, in the end, resigned from 'Life and Witness' and confined himself to 'Reunion'. Woods was chairman of 'Life and Witness' – a natural choice, as he had long shown special interest in social questions, having led the British delegation to the Stockholm 'Life and Work' Conference in 1925. There were subcommittees on 'Marriage and Sex', 'Race', and 'Peace and War'. Woods was also chairman of the subcommittee on 'Marriage and Sex'. Again, he was an expert in the subject. His biographer writes:

> He had, before this, given considerable attention to the problem of Birth-Control. He had not only written a pamphlet on the subject as an aid to the deliberations of the committees, but had also produced, privately, other literature to help and guide the opinions of the English Bishops. He had, before Lambeth, made up his mind fairly conclusively along the lines which were ultimately approved by the great majority of the committee and of the Conference itself. He saw quite clearly the moral issues involved as they appeared to him, and he saw how the advice which he wished to be given fitted into the whole Christian treatment of marriage and sex. [33]

In the report itself there were nearly three pages devoted to birth control.

Henson was present at some of the deliberations of the reunion committee on Monday, 14 July, and wrote that 'Temple was in the chair, but Headlam was in command'. Ten days later, however, Henson wrote 'Temple is an excellent Chairman, good-tempered, resourceful, and very industrious'. The reunion committee was compelled to separate into two subcommittees – one to study relations with non-episcopal churches, under Temple, the other relations with episcopal churches, under Headlam. Amongst the episcopal church delegates were the Old Catholics, the Archbishop of Utrecht and the Bishops of

[31] J. G. Lockhart, *Cosmo Gordon Lang*, p. 346. For Henson's address, see *Retrospect of an Unimportant Life*, vol. ii, pp. 259 and 261.

[32] *Retrospect of an Unimportant Life*, vol. ii, p. 270.

[33] *Theodore, Bishop of Winchester*, p. 337.

Haarlem and Deventer, who were welcomed on 16 July. Lang entertained them to dinner bewailing the rustiness of his French and German.[34] The Orthodox delegation, which has already been mentioned, consisted of Archbishop Meletios, Patriarch of Alexandria; Archbishop Germanos of Thyateira, representing Constantinople; the Metropolitan of Epiphania; Ignatius, from the Patriarchate of Antioch; the Archbishop of Jordan (Timotheos) from the Patriarchate of Jerusalem; the Archbishop of Corcyra (Athenagoras) from the Church of Greece and with him the Archimandrite, Michael Konstantides of the Orthodox Community in London; the Archimandrite Sabbas Sovietoff, the Metropolitan of Warsaw from Poland; and from Cyprus, the Archimandrite Leontius, Bishop Designate of Paphos; from the Patriarchate of Rumania, the Archbishop of the Bucovina; from the Patriarchate of Yugoslavia, the Metropolitan of Novi Sad.[35] Headlam, who found the discussions with the Orthodox very absorbing, wrote:

> The discussions with the Orthodox were most interesting. I was in the Chair and had to carry on the whole thing. The Committees were extraordinarily good – the best Committees I have ever worked with. They never spoke unnecessarily but only when they could help matters out. The point was to get an agreed statement of belief on Orders and the Eucharist, which should contain nothing which should be difficult for an Evangelical. Then I had to explain all our efforts with Non-conformists and South India to them, and put a sort of modified approach, so that it would be no longer possible to say that South India would make Union with the Orthodox impossible. I always took care to explain carefully anything which represented another point of view from theirs, so that there might be nothing conceded.
>
> Meletios was very helpful. He wanted to come to terms, so he put his questions in a way that was easy to answer them. They had a good many conferences together and had a good deal of trouble with one or two of their people. The Roumanian Archbishop was inclined not to be conciliatory; the Roumanians are unlike the others – not Philo-Anglican – and are a good deal under Romanist intrigues. If we had had one or two more days it would have been completely satisfactory.[36]

Headlam's subcommittee also dealt with the Old Catholics. The Archbishop of Utrecht welcomed the idea of a Joint Commission on Doctrine; he also expressed a hope that both Anglicans and Orthodox

[34] J. G. Lockhart, *Cosmo Gordon Lang*, p. 346.
[35] See *The Times*, 27 June, p. 19; and *Report 1930*, pp. 132–3.
[36] R. Jasper, *A. C. Headlam*, pp. 208–9. Headlam's letter was written on 3 August. See also L. W. Barnard, *C. B. Moss*, pp. 77–85.

would come to discuss the question of reunion at the International Old Catholic Congress at Vienna in 1931. The subcommittee also met with Armenian, Moravian, and Swedish delegations. Because of the political situation, it was impossible to proceed far with the Armenians. It was hoped that negotiations would be taken up again with the Moravians where they had been left off in 1924. Bishop Rhode of Lund suggested, now that relations between the Anglican and Swedish churches were close, that the Church of England might seek for closer relations with the Church of Finland.

The most difficult question was that of reunion with the non-episcopal churches and, in particular, the South Indian scheme. This came before the larger committee on reunion. Henson gives details of some of the discussions on this issue. A great deal of hostility to the scheme came from the Scottish bishops and from Archbishop Hutson of the West Indies. Henson wrote on 16 July:

> There can be no doubt that the scheme lends itself to effective criticism; but, if the proposals of the conference of 1920 are not to be shown to be utterly unmeaning, the scheme must be generally approved. I think that this is becoming evident to the bishops, and that it will finally determine their decision; but there is plainly a considerable opposition, which will not be easily defeated.[37]

Eleven Nonconformists came before the committee on 15 July, among them Carnegie Simpson, who, according to Henson, 'spoke brusquely and effectively'. Henson did not feel that the bishops treated the delegation in the right way. Neville Talbot inflicted a long and irrelevant speech on them. On Thursday, 17 July, there was a visit from Dr John White and Lord Sands. 'They were not', wrote Henson,

> as they were careful to emphasize, commissioned to represent the Church of Scotland, but, none the less, they were admirable examples of the Presbyterian polity. We had agreed upon a number of questions which should be addressed to them, and thus we succeeded in avoiding the fiasco which happened when the Nonconformist deputation appeared. Both the Presbyterians made an excellent impression, especially Dr White. He was straightforward, informing and humorous. More than one bishop observed what an excellent type of bishop he would have exhibited, had his lot been cast in an episcopal church.[38]

Friday, 18 July, and Saturday, 19 July, were spent by the reunion

---

[37] *Retrospect of an Unimportant Life*, vol. ii, p. 265.
[38] Ibid., pp. 265–6.

committee in dealing with a draft report produced by Temple. Henson did not like it. It was far more Catholic than he approved, and he found 'very little concession in all the impressive volume of conciliatory, and even flatterous, speech which is addressed to non-episcopalians'. Some of the lack of conciliation seemed to be the work of Neville Talbot, who was upset on Saturday, when Henson succeeded in carrying some corrections mitigating the over-rigid episcopalianism of the draft.

The reunion committee went to work again from Monday, 21 July, until Friday, 25 July. On the Monday Henson drew their attention to a false leakage about their work in the *Morning Post*. Headlam agreed that a totally wrong impression had been given. Lang referred to the matter 'in strong terms'. Carnegie Simpson came before the committee again and

> challenged the sub-Committee to tell him what there was that we could add to the ministry which he already possessed. For our episcopal orders are as decisively, nay, far more decisively, rejected by the Church of Rome than are his Presbyterian orders by the Church of England. The most that can be said for Anglican episcopacy is that it is a real ministry of the Word and Sacraments in the Universal Church, and that is what we are not prepared to deny to the Presbyterian polity. Indeed, it is difficult to rebut the contention that non-Roman episcopacy introduces its adherents to a smaller section of the Christian family than Presbyterianism; a contention which many non-episcopalians do not hesitate to urge against the Anglican claim.[39]

Tuesday, 22 July, saw vehement speeches against the South Indian scheme from the Bishops of Indianopolis (J. M. Francis) and Kootenay (A. J. Doull). Headlam answered the first effectively and the last was not very successful, according Henson who went on in his diary:

> Headlam's performances in the Conference are very interesting. He has certainly made a considerable figure both as a theologian, and as a negotiator with the Easterns. He has also 'cut in' on behalf of the South Indian Scheme very effectively. His attitude on episcopacy has been greatly modified since the days when he used to 'correct' my use of Lightfoot's 'Dissertation'.[40] He is apt to intervene too often, and, perhaps, with too pontifical a manner. There is always a bludgeon up his sleeve; he is a hesitating speaker, but it must be admitted that he has done well.[41]

[39] *Retrospect of an Unimportant Life*, vol. ii, p. 269.

[40] The famous dissertation on 'The Christian Ministry' in J. B. Lightfoot, *Saint Paul's Epistle to the Philippians*.

[41] *Retrospect of an Unimportant Life*, vol, ii, p. 269.

Wednesday, 23 July, found a considerable rally of the Anglo-Catholics on the committee which dashed the excessive hopes of the Evangelicals. 'However,' Henson wrote,

> we shall give some sort of a blessing to the South Indian Scheme. . . . It is very doubtful whether the modest advance towards a Christian attitude which was made at the Conference of 1920 will be maintained. The truth is that, under the description 'the Anglican Communion', there are gathered two mutually contradictory conceptions of Christianity.[42] How long the divergence of first principles can be concealed remains to be seen. Sometimes I think the rupture is very near.[43]

Thursday, 24 July, saw the die-hard Anglo-Catholics battling hard, but William Temple kept them in order. On Friday, 25 July, Henson had a brush with Headlam, whose 'characteristic brusqueness of manner was noted with repugnance'.[44]

The last fortnight of the Conference came with the final plenary sessions from Monday, 28 July, until Thursday, 7 August. The Monday saw the bishops dealing with the Report of the Committee on Ministry, when some discussion took place on the ministry of women. Henson recalls a speech by the Bishop of Birmingham.

> Barnes interposed a curious and characteristic speech advocating complete equality – he could even look forward to female bishops – on the ground of the latest biological science. He is a striking figure, the very model of a 'heresiarch'. He might have been Huss in front of the fathers of Constance, or Luther at the Diet of Worms. Tall, pallid with much study, with stooping shoulders, and a voice at once challenging and melancholy, he commands attention as well by his manner and aspect as by his opinions, which are almost insolently oppugnant to the general mind. He is a good man, but clearly a fanatic, and in a more disciplined age, could not possibly have avoided the stake![45]

Henson supported a motion of Bishop Farthing of Montreal authorizing bishops to allow lay readers to administer the chalice. This is in Resolution 65, which also deals with the subject of auxiliary priests, a style of ministry which is now much in vogue.

Resolution 65.
The Conference for reasons given in the Report of its Committee on the

[42] Cf. Max Warren, *Crowded Canvas* (1974), p. 171.
[43] *Retrospect of an Unimportant Life*, vol. ii, p. 270.
[44] Ibid., p. 271.
[45] Ibid., p. 272.

ministry cannot recommend a widespread adoption of the proposal that men of mature age and assured position might be called by authority, and if willing, ordained to the priesthood without being required to give up their present occupation. But while declaring that ordination to the priesthood involves full and lifelong service, not to be made subservient to any other interests, it sees no insuperable objection to the ordination, with provincial sanction and under proper safeguards, where the need is great, of such *Auxiliary Priests*.

Further, in order to meet the present pressing need, the Conference would not question the action of any Bishop who, with the sanction of the national, regional or provincial Church concerned, should authorise such licensed *Readers* as he shall approve to administer the chalice at the request of the parish priest.[46]

On Tuesday, 29 July, there was a further debate on deaconesses.[47] Then the bishops got down to the Report on the Life and Witness of the Church. Bishop Kempthorne of Lichfield introduced the resolutions dealing with peace and war. Resolution 25 read, 'The Conference affirms that war as a method of settling international disputes is incompatible with the teaching and example of Our Lord Jesus Christ.' Henson criticized this, but it was passed. This day the archbishops and bishops of England gave a garden party in Lambeth Palace grounds.

On Wednesday, 30 July, the bishops proceeded to deal with sex and marriage. Bishop Theodore Woods introduced the Report 'at great length'. Bishop Furse of St Albans attacked it. Garbett of Southwark defended it, though not, according to Henson, very effectively. More opposition came from Bishop R. G. Shedden of Nassau. The discussion continued on Thursday, 31 July. The Bishop of Exeter (Lord William Cecil) delivered a passionate diatribe against contraceptives 'which he clearly placed in the same category as abortions and infanticide'. Henson then defended them and was followed by Bishop Walter Carey of Bloemfontein who made an impassioned appeal against them. The Report, at the suggestion of Headlam, was sent back for recasting. At this point it will be as well to set out the resolution (15) which the Conference in the end passed, much to the disgust of Walter Carey, who abandoned the bishops, with many anathemas, and refused to take part in the final service:

Where there is a clearly felt moral obligation to limit or avoid parenthood,

[46] *Lambeth Conference 1930 Report*, p. 60.

[47] Ibid., p. 273. For Charles Raven's criticism of Lambeth 1930 on deaconesses see F. W. Dillistone, *Charles Raven*, p. 261.

the method must be decided on Christian principles. The primary and obvious method is complete abstinence from intercourse (as far as may be necessary) in a life of discipline and self-control lived in the power of the Holy Spirit. Nevertheless, in those cases where there is such a clearly-felt moral obligation to limit or avoid parenthood, and where there is a morally sound reason for avoiding complete abstinence, the Conference agrees that other methods may be used, provided that this is done in the light of the same Christian principles. The Conference records its strong condemnation of the use of any methods of conception-control from motives of selfishness, luxury, or mere convenience.

(Carried by 193 to 67).

The bishops passed on to race problems and then after lunch Temple and Headlam introduced the Report on Unity.

Reunion continued to be discussed on Friday, 1 August. Headlam had an easy course, the only opposition to the Report of the Committee on the Orthodox Church coming from Bishop Burroughs of Ripon. Henson remarked that Burroughs

is not well liked by the Conference. He is polemical, garrulous, and humourless. The bishops were in no mood for a *réchauffé* of the Prayer Book controversy. So the Orthodox Churches came to harbour very easily, and Headlam was loudly cheered. It was in my opinion a notable personal triumph, which he had honestly earned.

Temple now brought forward the resolutions dealing with the South Indian scheme. 'These passed', said Henson,

with hardly a shadow of dissent, and when the decisive vote had been unanimously favourable, the Conference allowed itself to indulge in some complimentary speeches. The President called for silent prayer, and after an interval read some collect. Then somebody started the Doxology which was sung with feeling and fervour. How precarious the position is, however, was disclosed by the brisk opposition offered to a mild resolution which gave a tiny measure of recognition to the not infrequent practice of liberal-minded Anglicans, viz. receiving the Holy Communion in the Churches of the non-episcopalians when they had access to none of their own. However, this resolution [42] was finally adopted by a large majority.[48]

---

[48] *Retrospect of an Unimportant Life*, vol. ii, p. 275. Resolution 42 reads:
'*Special Areas.* The Conference, maintaining as a general principle that intercommunion should be the goal of, rather than a means to, the restoration of union, and bearing in mind the general rule of the Anglican Churches that "members of the Anglican Churches should receive the Holy Communion only from ministers of their own Church," holds, nevertheless, that the administration of such a rule falls under the

The resolutions on South India are contained in Resolution 30 (*a*) to (*f*). (*a*) says the Conference has heard the proposals for the scheme with the deepest interest. (*b*) notes that no new province of the Anglican Communion is proposed under new conditions, but a new province of the Universal Church, giving the Indian expression of the spirit. (*c*) notes that complete agreement over doctrine will not be reached before the inauguration of the Union. (*d*) Members of the South Indian Church in the future will be amenable to the regulations of the province and diocese of the Anglican Communion in which they happen to be staying. They will be treated as similarly circumstanced individuals unless a province changes its regulations. (*e*) The Conference leaves it to the bishops of the Church of India, Burma, and Ceylon to work out the principles embodied in the scheme. (*f*) The Conference gives its approval to the suggestions on the scheme in the Reunion Report.

So the South Indian business was successfully dealt with. Much credit was due to William Temple. Henson wrote,

> Before the meeting of the Conference, the South Indian Scheme had been the subject of vehement controversy. A polemical literature of considerable extent had been produced, and many alarming prophecies of disruption had been made. Much credit for the successful piloting of the scheme through the Conference is due to the Indian bishops, and much to the skill, good temper, and resource of the Chairman of the Committee, Archbishop Temple. He has gained great popularity in the process; and will emerge from the Conference with greatly enhanced reputation. Bishop Palmer has done well. His valorous efforts to get the better of his woeful stutter, and his evident devotion to his cause did much to commend his arguments.[49]

Saturday, 2 August, saw the bishops engaged on the Report on 'The Organization of the Anglican Communion'. Henson called it 'a subject of portentous dullness' which was presented

---

discretion of the Bishop, who should exercise his dispensing power in accordance with any principles that may be set forth by the national, regional or provincial authority of the Church in the area concerned. The Bishops of the Anglican Communion will not question the action of any Bishop who may, in his discretion so exercised, sanction an exception to the general rule in special areas, where the ministrations of an Anglican Church are not available for long periods of time or without travelling great distances, or may give permission that baptized communicant members of Churches not in communion with our own should be encouraged to communicate in Anglican churches, when the ministrations of their own Church are not available, or in other special or temporary circumstances.'

[49] *Retrospect of an Unimportant Life*, vol. ii, p. 275.

with boring prolixity by the Bishop of Salisbury. St Clair Donaldson is one of the best of men – simple, unselfish, good-tempered, and conscientious – but with something of the smugness of a pattern Sunday School scholar, and the reverent pettiness of an Anglo-Catholic zealot! He finds his soul's hunger wholly satisfied by Anglicanism, and every part of our silly conventional make-believe is, for him, rich in spiritual significance! He speaks too fast, has a curiously uninteresting voice, and is intolerably verbose.[50]

It was a field day for the colonial bishops. The Indian bishops impressed Henson, but he was far less satisfied with the Australian and Canadian bishops. He thought the Scottish bishops counted for nothing. The Welsh ones scarcely said a word.

Monday, 4 August, was again devoted to the Anglican Communion. Tuesday, 5 August, was devoted to the Report on Youth which Henson found 'unnecessarily windy and platitudinous'. He suggested that it should be called 'Childhood by a Second Childhood'. Lang was also disappointed by it.[51] This was the last day that Henson spent at the Conference as he had to return to Auckland Castle. On the Wednesday and Thursday the Report on the Christian Doctrine of God was covered and the revised Report on 'The Life and Witness of the Christian Community'. Archbishop Lang felt that the treatment of the Christian doctrine of God was disappointing.[52]

On Friday, 8 August, the bishops discussed the encyclical, which had been drafted on the theme of witness by Bishop Palmer and Mervyn Haigh. The latter's part in it is told by Bishop Barry in his biography of Haigh.

The principal report of the Conference was on the Christian Doctrine of God. When it came to drafting the Encyclical Letter, the committee responsible produced two draft attempts to expound and commend this, both of which Lang felt to be inadequate. It was then Wednesday afternoon and the Letter had to go to the printer on Thursday morning for final endorsement by the assembled bishops. But nothing was yet written to be laid before them. With the consent of the drafting committee, the Archbishop then asked Mervyn to try his hand. He agreed, not only as an obvious duty but as a God-given opportunity to express some of those

[50] Ibid., p. 277. On St Clair Donaldson see C. T. Dimont and F. de Witt Batty, *St Clair Donaldson* (1939).

[51] J. G. Lockhart, *Cosmo Gordon Lang*, p. 347. Lang thought that there had been weak handling by the chairman, Winnington-Ingram.

[52] Ibid. Not everyone shared Lang's opinion.

theological insights which he and I had long shared together. The job was finished at 2 a.m. on Thursday, and the whole Encyclical was in print in the bishops' hands the following afternoon.

Mervyn displayed much virtuosity in using that rather plummy, stilted style which was thought to be suitable for episcopal utterances. But through that medium he wrote from his heart. . . . It was for him, a *confessio fidei*, if not yet an *apologia pro vita sua*. It set forth the conviction by which he lived and by which his whole ministry was directed.[53]

On the Friday Bishop Palmer piloted it through 'with great vigour and his usual patience and sometimes humour', according to Lang. An appeal to youth incorporated by Bishop Woods was cut short and other alterations made. Later Lang wrote,

The Letter had a more favourable reception from the leading newspapers than I expected, and it has some merits. But it is too long and wordy. Ten years hence the character of this Letter should be reconsidered. That of 1920 and this of 1930 fall between the two stools of exhortation or edification and information — too much of the former, too little of the latter. When this Letter of 1930 is read, ordinary people (who won't read or can't really understand the Resolutions as a whole) will have little idea of what the Conference actually did. I think that the main things which the Conference really decides should be tersely stated in a framework of exhortation.[54]

The plenary sessions came to an end on Saturday, 9 August. Theodore Woods in his *Diocesan Chronicle* said,

The scene on the last morning of the Conference will not easily be forgotten by those who were present. The night before, Lady Davidson, with characteristic graciousness, had brought the silver and ebony cross which had been presented to the late Archbishop at the close of the Conference ten years ago. It lay on the table last Saturday as the Conference drew to its end. It is to be an heirloom of the Archbishops of Canterbury for the future. Many words of thanksgiving were spoken, and a presentation of a pastoral staff (which the craftsman is to produce in due course) was made to the Primate in recognition of his untiring patience as well as the ability with which he had presided. Taking Lord Davidson's cross in hand, he pronounced the final Benediction, to be repeated next day in Westminster Abbey.[55]

Bishop Walter Carey was not present at the concluding service at

[53] F. R. Barry, *Mervyn Haigh*, p. 107.
[54] J. G. Lockhart, *Cosmo Gordon Lang*, p. 352.
[55] *Theodore, Bishop of Winchester*, pp. 340–1.

Westminster Abbey, but Lang was not much worried by his absence, and afterwards wrote to Mervyn Haigh, 'I see the sensation-mongering Press makes the most of Carey – as if he counted for anything!' Carey, however, does not seem to have been the only absentee. Bishop Trollope of Korea absented himself over the passing of Resolution 42. Lang tells the story:

> Meanwhile a trouble had been brewing, leading to the most awkward incident in the Conference. It arose over Resolution 42. . . . York conveyed to me an intimation from the Metropolitans and Presiding Bishops that several Bishops had told them they were so greatly concerned about the passing of that Resolution that they meditated withdrawal and absence from the final Service in the Abbey. The only inkling I had of this was a letter from Korea (Dr Trollope) written from Cuddesdon, saying he had gone and could take no further part.
>
> Apparently some thirty or forty Bishops were feeling uncomfortable and wanted the Resolution reconsidered. When Lang objected, pointing out that it had been carried by a large majority, the Bishops replied that the atmosphere created by the South Indian Resolution had 'rather hypnotised' them. After some parleying with the Metropolitans, Lang decided he would not try to reason with the 'rebels', but would leave it with the Conference to settle whether the question was to be reopened. The Conference, after hearing a very forthright speech from its President, agreed with him by a large majority, an explanatory note was added to placate the malcontents, and there were no further withdrawals.[56]

In Westminster Abbey the Archbishop of Canterbury celebrated the Holy Communion. The Bishop of Rhode Island (J. de Wold Perry, Presiding Bishop of PECUSA) preached, a fact which can be gleaned from *The Times*. None of the episcopal biographies mentions the sermon and Henson was not present to make any biting comment upon his efforts. During the administration of the Communion the hymn 'Alleluia, sing to Jesus' was sung. So ended the Seventh Conference. Lang probably imagined that he would see another in 1940. He wrote to Mervyn Haigh thanking him for what he had done. 'If I am spared and am not too old to tackle another Conference ten years hence, I shall look forward to your being the *Episcopal* Secretary!'[57] Mervyn Haigh did indeed prove to be the episcopal secretary at the next Lambeth Conference, held in 1948. Some might have imagined that Bell would

[56] J. G. Lockhart, *Cosmo Gordon Lang*, pp. 350–1.

[57] F. R. Barry, *Mervyn Haigh*, p. 106. The date of the letter is given as 16 May – which is quite impossible. Probably it should be 18 August.

then be Primate, but that was not to be.[58] There were others who suggested that Haigh would end his days at Canterbury, but that, too, was not to be. William Temple succeeded Lang in 1942, but did not live to call the next Conference. He was succeeded by Geoffrey Fisher in 1945. Fisher called the next Lambeth Conference in 1948, and also that of 1958.

What was the net result of the 1930 Lambeth Conference? Roger Lloyd in his *The Church of England, 1900–1965* felt that it left unhappy memories. 'But memories of the 1930 conference,' he wrote, 'were not happy. In more ways than one it had been the least successful of the whole series, and the whole body of the American bishops, and some of the Canadian ones as well, had not found it a very happy experience because it seemed to them to be managed too exclusively by the English episcopate.' The domination of the English bishops is readily apparent from the diary of Henson, who wrote on 2 August:

> A striking feature of this Conference to those who know the previous history of the persons concerned, is the solidarity created by their academic experience. Lang, Palmer, and Temple are Balliol men, Lang and Headlam have been All Souls Fellows, Headlam as Regius Professor of Theology had been the official chief and colleague of Temple. It is ever the sway of unperceived and unacknowledged personal forces which determines the courses of public affairs. These four men – Lang, Temple, Palmer, and Headlam – have been the most potent figures in the Conference, and the fact is not *solely* due to their official positions and personal ability, though of course these are very considerable. The habit of personal association and the common loyalty to institutions have counted for much.[59]

Henson himself had been quite a personality at the Conference and he had also been a Fellow of All Souls.

Lang was obviously not held in the same affection in the eyes of the American bishops as Randall Davidson. No doubt he was too pontifical for them, and so we do not find the bishops making him a presentation in the way they had done to Frederick Temple and Davidson. Fortunately, Fisher had a more acceptable approach.

Yet the Lambeth Conference of 1930, though Stephen Neill suggests that there was a feeling that it had been less courageous than that of 1920 on the subject of reunion, was not without its achievements.[60]

[58] See R. Jasper, *George Bell*, pp. 284–5, and D. MacKinnon, *The Stripping of the Altars*, pp. 83–94.

[59] *Retrospect of an Unimportant Life*, vol. ii, p. 276.

[60] See Dewi Morgan, *The Bishops Come to Lambeth* (1958), p. 114.

9. The bishops at the Conference of 1930, outside Lambeth Palace

10. The bishops of the 1948 Conference in session in the Library Hall, Lambeth Palace

Some measure of endorsement had been given to the South Indian scheme and good progress had been made with the Orthodox and Old Catholics. Some advance had been made in the partial blessing given to birth control – a blessing which was met with disapproval by High Churchmen and Roman Catholics.[61] Headlam in his article in the *Church Quarterly Review* on 'The Lambeth Conference and Reunion' certainly felt pleased. He evidently thought that the Report on the Christian Doctrine of God was the Conference's most important work, for it reminded men and women of the fundamental Christian belief, the revelation of God in Christ, the basis of all religious life.[62] There were quite a number of pamphlets written on the Conference afterwards, including one by T. S. Eliot. He was not without his criticisms but felt that the Conference 'has affirmed, beyond previous Conferences, the Catholicity of the Church; and in spite of defects and dubious statements in detail, the Report will have strengthened the Church both within and without.'[63] George Malcolm Thomson also wrote a pamphlet and the magazine *Theology* published a whole series of articles on the Conference Report by such writers as Francis Underhill, E. G. Selwyn, K. E. Kirk, A. E. J. Rawlinson, W. G. Peck, and Mabel Phillips. James Nisbet and Co. published a series of pamphlets on the Conference by protagonists at it, like Archbishop D'Arcy and Bishops Palmer and Theodore Woods, and others who had been onlookers, like Charles Raven, whose *Looking Forward* (1931) is not mentioned by Dillistone.

[61] See George H. Tremenhere, *Resolution 15 of the Lambeth Conference of 1930*. See also K. E. Kirk in *Church Quarterly Review*, vol. iii, p. 96.

[62] See *Church Quarterly Review*, vol. iii, pp. 205–26.

[63] T. S. Eliot, *Thoughts after Lambeth*. A critique of the Reports of the Lambeth Conference 1930.

11

GEOFFREY FISHER
1948 AND SOUTH INDIA

The Conference of 1930 had not been happy for relations with the English Nonconformists, who thought the Orthodox delegation had been more warmly received than themselves by the Anglican bishops. However, they were asked to renew the discussion which had broken down in 1925. Something did develop and in 1936 came *A Sketch of a United Church*, published from Lambeth Palace, with a foreword by Archbishop Lang. This was the report of a commission of thirty-eight ministers and clergy, equally divided between the Church of England and the Free Churches.[1] This commission pictured a united church involving Congregational, Presbyterian, and Episcopal elements. On the particular question of episcopacy they said this:

> The agreement formerly reached, that episcopal ordination in practice should be generally accepted, was subject to the understanding that such acceptance 'would not imply the acceptance of any theory as to its origin or character'. Experience has shown that this phrase raises certain difficulties of interpretation. Accordingly it seems better to say that in agreeing to include the Episcopate, together with the Presbyteral and Congregational elements of Church order, we also agree that the constitution of the united Church must leave room for, and recognise as permissible, various theories of the origin and nature of the Episcopate.

Then they outlined the two theories of episcopacy, (*a*) the view that bishops were appointed, as it were, from above, by Apostles and (*b*) the view that the episcopate emerged by elevation of members of the presbyterate. The authors of *A Sketch* felt both views allowable and that a united church could emerge without deciding which was correct. However, Crown appointment of the episcopate (abhorrent to Free Churchmen) was ruled out.

In 1938 there was published another document, *Outline of a Reunion Scheme for the Church of England and the Free Churches in England*. This provided for an episcopally organized Church with a General

[1] See Erik Routley, *Creeds and Confessions*, p. 151.

Assembly, diocesan synods, and local congregational councils. It was felt that there could be more than one bishop in each diocese, and an ex-Anglican bishop and an ex-Free Church bishop could share the duties. It was stated that

> the acceptance of episcopal ordination for the future would not imply the disowning of past ministeries (*sic*) of Word and Sacrament otherwise received. . . . It would allow for various theories regarding the origin and character of the Episcopate. It would imply the continuity of the Episcopate of the united Church with the historic Episcopate in its succession from ancient times. It neither affirms nor excludes the view that Apostolic Succession determines the validity of the Ministry and Sacraments.

However, the *Outline* did not commend itself to Free Churchmen so progress was halted, until after the Second World War.[2]

On 3 November 1946 Archbishop Geoffrey Fisher, who had succeeded Temple in 1945, preached a famous sermon in Great St Mary's at Cambridge, on John 10.9 and 10, in the course of which he asked the Free Churches 'to take episcopacy into their system'.

> The Church of England is in full communion with the Old Catholics on the Continent: and its relations with the Orthodox Churches on the one hand, and with the Churches of Sweden and Finland on the other, already approach, if they do not yet reach, full communion. My longing is, not yet that we should be *united* with other churches in this country, but that we should grow to *full communion* with them.
>
> As I have said and as negotiations have shown, no insuperable barrier to that remains until we come to questions of the ministry and government of the Church. Full communion between churches means not that they are identical in all ways, but that there is no barrier to exchange of their ministers and ministries. Every Church's ministry is effective as a means by which the life of Christ reaches His people. Every Church's ministry is defective because it is prevented from operating in all folds of His flock. For full communion between churches there is needed a ministry mutually acknowledged by all as possessing not only the inward call of the Spirit but also the authority which each church in consequence requires.
>
> At the Lausanne Conference of Churches in 1927, it was said that in view of the place which the Episcopate, the Council of Presbyters, and the Congregation of the Faithful, respectively had in the constitution of the early Church, in view of the fact that these three elements are each today and have been for centuries accepted by great communions in Christendom, and that they are each believed by many to be essential to the good order of

---

[2] In 1941 there came the official reply from the Free Churches, *A Reply of The Free Church Federal Council*.

the Church, 'We recognize that these several elements must all . . . have an appropriate place in the order of life of a reunited Church.'

Every constitutional scheme has proceeded on those lines. The non-episcopal churches have accepted the principle that episcopacy must exist along with other elements in a reunited Church. For reasons obvious enough in Church history, they fear what may be made of episcopacy. But they accept the fact of it. If they do so for a reunited Church, why not also and earlier for the process of assimilation, as a step towards full communion?

It may be said that in a reunited Church they could guard themselves in the constitution against abuses of episcopacy. But they could do so far more effectively by taking it into their own system. The Church of England has not yet found the finally satisfying use of episcopacy in practice: nor certainly has the Church of Rome. If non-episcopal churches agree that it must come into the picture, could they not take it and try it out on their own ground first?

It is of course not quite as simple as all that. There are requirements and functions which Catholic tradition attaches to the office of a bishop in the Church of God, which, if our aim is assimilation and full communion, must be safeguarded. Negotiators in the past have been able to agree upon them, and could with hope inquire into them further, if our non-episcopal brethren were able to contemplate the step I suggest.

As it seems to me, it is an easier step for them to contemplate than that involved in a union of churches: and if achieved, it would immensely carry us forward towards full communion, without the fearful complexities and upheavals of a constitutional union. In such a giving and receiving of episcopacy, there would be a mutual removal of a barrier between the folds.[3]

Fisher's Cambridge sermon was part of the background to the Lambeth Conference of 1948.

So much for the Free Churches. Now we turn to the Orthodox. The Orthodox delegates went back from the 1930 Lambeth Conference to report to their churches. The Patriarch and Holy Synod of Alexandria soon declared their acceptance of the validity of Anglican ordinations. In 1931 the Joint Doctrinal Commission, which had been appointed in November 1930, met in London. Headlam was chairman and with him on the Anglican side were the Archbishop of Dublin (J. A. F. Gregg), the Bishop of Gibraltar (F. C. N. Hicks), the Bishop of Fulham (B. S. Batty), the Bishop of Northern Indiana (C. Gray), Drs Goudge and Grensted of Oxford, Canon Douglas and the Rev. Philip Usher. The discussions can be read today in *Lambeth Occasional Reports 1931–8*.

[3] See R. P. Flindall, *The Church of England 1915–1948*, pp. 438–9, and *The Archbishop Speaks*, pp. 68–9.

The Evangelicals viewed the discussions with some apprehension. The Conference was not easy and not a great deal of advance was made. However, some progress was now made later in the thirties with the Rumanian church. A delegation of the Anglican Church, with Bishop Hicks of Lincoln as chairman, met at Bucharest in June 1935. Agreements were reached not only on the doctrine and significance of the sacred ministry, but also upon the Eucharist, tradition, and justification. The Rumanian Commission decided to recommend the Rumanian Holy Synod to accept the validity of Anglican orders. The Report of the talks was presented to Canterbury Convocation and in due course approved.[4] In 1939 came the Second World War. May 1940 saw conferences between Anglicans and theologians of the Serbian church and an Anglican delegation in Belgrade, an account of which is given in Jasper's *Arthur Cayley Headlam*. More fruitful was a visit which was made by the same delegation to Sofia. Representatives of the Holy Synod of the Church in Bulgaria accepted Anglican ordination in principle. There were further contacts in 1943 when Archbishop Garbett of York visited the Russian Patriarch, Sergius.[5] In 1945 the Metropolitan of Kiev, Nicolai, visited Lambeth. In 1946 the Bishop of Hereford (R. G. Parsons) visited Belgrade and Archbishop Garbett of York made a similar visit in 1947.

There was a fruitful outcome from the Lambeth Conference of 1930 with respect to the Church in Finland. A special committee was appointed to investigate the position of the Church in Finland and a report was issued in 1934.[6] The Church of Finland had had a gap in the apostolic succession in 1884 when all the Finnish bishops died and a new bishop was consecrated by presbyters. However, the Convocations adopted resolutions which promised a relationship which would lead to the achievement, in due course, of 'complete intercommunion, based on a common episcopal ministry'. As a means towards this both Houses of both Convocations agreed that 'if the Archbishop of Turku (Åbo) shall

---

[4] See *Report of the Conference at Bucarest from June 1st to June 8th, 1935, between the Rumanian Commission on Relations with the Anglican Communion and the Church of England Delegation appointed by the Archbishop of Canterbury* in *Lambeth Occasional Reports 1931–38*.

[5] See Charles Smyth, *Cyril Foster Garbett*, ch. 12.

[6] *The Church of England and the Church of Finland. A Summary of the Proceedings at the Conferences held at Lambeth Palace, London, on October 5th and 6th, 1933, and at Brando, Helsingfors, on July 17th and 18th, 1934*. This is in *Lambeth Occasional Reports, 1931–38*.

invite the Archbishop of Canterbury to appoint a Bishop to take part in the consecration of a Bishop in the Church of Finland, he may commission a Bishop for such purpose'. The Upper and Lower Houses of York and the Upper House of Canterbury added that, if the Archbishop of Canterbury should ask the Archbishop of Turku (Åbo) to take part in the consecration of a bishop in the Church of England, it was hoped that he would be willing to commission a bishop for such a purpose. They further agreed 'that members of the Church of Finland may be admitted to Communion in the Church of England, provided that they are at that time admissible to Communion in their own Church.' They also asked that Finnish bishops be requested to confer at Lambeth Conferences and on other occasions.

There were also difficulties over apostolic succession in regard to the Lutheran Churches of Latvia and Estonia. In 1936 and 1938 representatives of the Church of England met with representatives of the Evangelical Lutheran Churches of Latvia and Estonia at Lambeth, Riga, and Tallinn. These Churches found themselves able to take a stronger line on episcopacy and happy relationships developed. Headlam had much to do with this. Then came the war. Headlam tried to keep in touch with them, but when the countries emerged from the war they were in the hands of Russia.

With the Old Catholics also progress was made after 1930. In July 1931 Anglicans and Old Catholics met at Bonn. Bishop Headlam led the Anglicans, who consisted of the Bishop of Fulham (S. Batty), the Dean of Chichester (A. S. Duncan-Jones), Professor N. P. Williams, Canon J. A. Douglas, G. F. Graham-Brown (Principal of Wycliffe Hall), C. L. Gage-Brown, C. B. Moss, and Philip Usher. The Old Catholics were represented by the Bishop of Deventer (Mgr J. J. Berends), the Bishop of Berne (Dr A. Kury), the Bishop of Bonn (Dr G. Moorg), Professor E. Gaugler of Berne, and Professor A. Rinkel of Amersfoort – though in the end Usher and Gaugler were unable to attend. At length this brief statement was agreed upon:

1 Each Communion recognizes the catholicity and independence of the other and maintains its own.

2 Each Communion agrees to admit members of the other Communion to participate in the sacraments.

3 Intercommunion does not require from either Communion the acceptance of all doctrinal opinion, sacramental devotion, or liturgical

practice characteristic of the other, but implies that each believes the other to hold all the essentials of the Catholic faith.[7]

This agreement was ratified by the Episcopal Synod of the Old Catholic Churches at Vienna in September 1931 and in Canterbury Convocation in 1932. York Convocation followed suit and then the rest of the Anglican Communion. In June 1937, Bishop Headlam and the Bishop of Fulham went on a visit to Utrecht. By that date Old Catholic and Anglican bishops had already taken part in episcopal consecrations in each other's churches. In November 1939, just after the outbreak of war, Headlam went to Utrecht again.

Such, then, were the fruits of the Lambeth Conference of 1930. The outbreak of the war meant that holding a Lambeth Conference in 1940 was out of the question. It had to be postponed till the end of hostilities. This country emerged from the war with Geoffrey Fisher at Canterbury after the brief archiepiscopate of William Temple. Lambeth Palace had been heavily damaged and its restoration took a decade, 1945–55. One of Fisher's most important tasks was to develop friendly relations with the American Episcopal Church. In 1946, visiting the United States for the first time, he attended the General Convention at Philadelphia. Fortunately during the war he had got to know Henry Sherrill, elected Presiding Bishop at that General Convention. Sherrill had been in England during the war overseeing the chaplains to the United States forces. Fisher remarked:

> I remember that we first met in the south aisle of St Paul's Cathedral, and fell into each other's arms at sight. From then onwards we were completely devoted to each other, with no barriers of any kind, able to talk freely, to laugh freely, to think together along the same lines of sanctified common sense and eager to promote the common welfare of the Anglican Communion in every possible way. And we each possessed a certain amount of drive, to get things moving. So we were poised for this great enterprise.[8]

The occasion of this meeting in St Paul's Cathedral was the service in memory of President Roosevelt. The next day Sherrill was present at Fisher's enthronement in Canterbury. A few days later he presented gifts to Archbishop and Mrs Fisher from the American chaplains in England.

[7] See *Report of the Meeting of the Commission of the Anglican Communion and the Old Catholic Churches held at Bonn on Thursday, July 2, 1931*, p. 7. See also L. W. Barnard, *C. B. Moss*, pp. 86–99.

[8] William Purcell, *Fisher of Lambeth*, pp. 174–5.

Fisher was the second Archbishop of Canterbury to visit the U.S.A. while in office. The Davidsons had attended the General Convention in Boston in 1904. The Fishers crossed the Atlantic in the *Mauretania*, and found an entertaining companion in Field-Marshal Montgomery, also making the crossing. At Winnipeg, Fisher addressed in St John's Church all the bishops and the whole synod of the Church of Canada. From there they went to Philadelphia, and spoke to the American church on the Anglican tradition. Bishop Stanley Eley, who was then Fisher's chaplain, said that

> this lengthy tour really broke the ice with the Americans. They had always had a great love and affection for the Mother Church, but somehow or other, I don't think they thought that they really belonged, that they were an integral part of it. From that moment onwards, however, they knew they were, and his speeches and sermons out there were of first-rate importance in preparing for the spirit of the Lambeth Conference of 1948.[9]

Fisher returned home to start dealing with all the aspects of the Conference from agenda to hospitality. The 1948 agenda was based largely on that proposed for 1940. The subjects were

a The Christian Doctrine of Man.
b The Church and the Modern World.
c The Unity of the Church.
d The Anglican Communion.
e The Church's Discipline in Marriage.
f Baptism and Confirmation.

A lot of literature on the Anglican Communion was published in connection with the 1948 Lambeth Conference. Bishop Wand of London edited for the Oxford University Press *The Anglican Communion. A Survey*, a comprehensive survey of the Communion, with articles by Dean Malden of Wells (on 'The Church of England and its Offshoots'), Bishop Stephen Neill (on 'The Church of India, Burma and Ceylon'), Archbishop Philip Carrington (on 'The Church of England in Canada and Newfoundland'), the Rev. R. W. Stopford, later Bishop of Peterborough and then of London (on 'Tropical Africa'), the Rev. C. B. Moss (on 'The Disestablished Home Churches'), and Canon Roger Lloyd (on 'The Mission of the Church of England'). Bishop Wand in the preface to the book referred to Canon McLeod Campbell's *Christian History in the Making* (1945) and added, 'We wish to take up the story where he left it, and to present a bird's-eye view of the finished

[9] William Purcell, *Fisher of Lambeth*, pp. 179–80.

product, or at least of that product at the stage of development it has reached today.'[10]

There also was published *The Mission of the Anglican Communion*, edited by Bishop E. R. Morgan of Southampton (later Bishop of Truro) and Canon Roger Lloyd of Winchester. This contained a chapter by Bishop Michael H. Yashiro of Kobe on 'Church and State: The Suffering of the Church in Japan'. Canon G. W. O. Addleshaw (then a Canon of York, now Dean of Chester) wrote on 'The Law and Constitution of the Church Overseas'. Oliver S. Tomkins, then Assistant General Secretary of the World Council of Churches and of the Faith and Order Continuation Committee wrote on 'The Anglican Communion and the Oecumenical Movement'. Canon W. F. France, Warden of St Augustine's College, Canterbury, wrote on 'The Place of Missionary Societies within the Church'. Henry de Candole, then Vicar of Henfield, a leader in the Parish and People movement, wrote on 'Giving and Receiving' and was well in advance of his time in his contention that the younger churches had much to offer the Mother Church.

In 1947 Canon McLeod Campbell, General Secretary of the Missionary Council of the Church Assembly, had written *Lambeth Calls*, a sequel to his *Christian History in the Making*, and to which Archbishop Fisher contributed an introduction. McLeod Campbell had a chapter on 'The Anglican Communion and the War'.

Bishop F. R. Barry of Southwell, one of those bishops asked to produce preliminary papers for the forthcoming Lambeth Conference, wrote on 'The Christian Doctrine of Man'. However, he gathered together far more material than was needed and so produced a book, *Recovery of Man*.[11] The year 1948 saw also the publication of *Lambeth and Unity* by Louis A. Haselmayer for the American Church Union by Morehouse-Gorham Co. in New York and Dacre Press in Westminster. It was a plea for a high doctrine of episcopacy on the lines of *The Apostolic Ministry* edited by Bishop Kenneth Kirk in 1946.

The episcopal secretary for the 1948 Conference was Mervyn Haigh of Winchester who had been groomed for this task in 1930 when he was Lang's chaplain at Lambeth and acted as assistant secretary to George Bell of Chichester.[12] His assistant was Stanley Eley, Archbishop

[10] J. W. C. Wand (ed.), *The Anglican Communion. A Survey*, p. vii.

[11] See F. R. Barry, *Period of My Life*, for the genesis of the book.

[12] It is very odd that there is no reference to the part played by Haigh in the 1948 Conference in F. R. Barry's *Mervyn Haigh*.

Fisher's chaplain. Haigh edited the official *Handbook of the Lambeth Conference*, which was published as a supplement to the 1948 *Official Year Book of the Church of England*. In this publication Haigh had some reference to the grief of the South Indian bishops in not being allowed to send representatives to the Conference. Haigh went on:

> If the great venture towards Christian reunion in South India works out, as all should hope and pray, successfully and happily, and if it is followed by other such ventures in other lands, the Lambeth Conferences of the Anglican Communion will inevitably and happily decrease in importance, and some form of General Council of Churches increasingly united in their respective areas, will come more and more to the front.

This line of thought was taken up critically by the *Church Times* which wrote, 'The Catholic principles of Anglicanism must not be discarded for the sake of achieving a working compromise with Protestantism, which may have false semblances of unity.' It made out that there was 'an English episcopal caucus which is apparently prepared to jettison the principles of Prayer Book, Ordinal, etc.' Mervyn Haigh said in the following week's *Church Times* that this suggestion was mischievous and was supported by Bishop Morgan of Southampton, his suffragan. But Bishop Walter Carey, whose *The Church of England's Hour* (1946) had contained the words, 'Of course, episcopacy (not prelacy) is of the *esse* of Church Order' (p. 73), supported the attitude of the *Church Times*.

As there had not been a conference for eighteen years a very large number of bishops had not attended one before. The Archbishop of Canterbury himself had not done so, not having become Bishop of Chester until 1932. In contrast, Archbishop Garbett of York had attended the Conferences of 1920 and 1930 as Bishop of Southwark. The big names amongst the episcopate were Bishop Wand of London, who was President of the Anglo-Catholic Congress, which took place concurrently with the Lambeth Conference, Bishop Rawlinson of Derby, Bishop Barry of Southwell, Bishop Hunkin of Truro, Bishop Blunt of Bradford, Bishop Kirk of Oxford, Bishop Chavasse of Rochester, and Bishop Bell of Chichester. R. G. Parsons was at Hereford, E. R. Morgan at Southampton, G. C. L. Lunt at Salisbury, C. M. Blagden at Peterborough, L. S. Hunter at Sheffield, G. A. Chase at Ripon, W. D. L. Greer at Manchester, E. W. Barnes at Birmingham, and C. A. Martin at Liverpool. J. A. Fitzgerald Gregg was now Archbishop of Armagh and Bishop J. C. H. How was Primus of

Scotland and Bishop of Glasgow. The Bishop of Brechin was Eric Graham. H. K. Sherrill came as the Presiding Bishop of the American Episcopal Church, and there were sixty-five other bishops from the U.S.A.

The Primate of All Canada was G. F. Kingston and Philip Carrington was Archbishop of Quebec and Metropolitan of the Province of Canada. There were eleven bishops from India including the Assistant Bishop of Colombo.[13] H. W. K. Mowll was Primate of Australia and G. H. Clayton Bishop of Johannesburg. Three bishops came from Japan, Bishop Yashiro of Kobe, Bishop T. M. Makita of Tokyo, and Bishop S. Yanagihara of Osaka. There were no less than ten bishops from China, including Bishop Hall of Hong Kong and South China. Bishop Cooper came from Korea, Bishop J. L. Wilson from Singapore, Bishop Gelsthorpe from the Sudan, Bishop Geoffrey Allen from Egypt and Bishop Horsley from Gibraltar. It was expected that the Metropolitan of South Africa, Bishop Darbyshire of Cape Town, would be present but he died in England on 30 June. Wilfrid Parker, Bishop of Pretoria and grandson of Archbishop Longley, was present. Bishop Stephen Neill, a man with a wide-ranging mind, was present as Assistant Bishop of Canterbury.

The meeting of the bishops was preceded by the well-known Lambeth Walk, i.e. the visitation of the overseas bishops up and down the country. I well remember Bishop Mervyn Haigh of Winchester coming to Southampton with three of the overseas bishops, including one of the Japanese, who spoke to us through an interpreter. The biographer of Bishop Blunt remarks how that prelate appreciated the visitation.

Preceding the Conference four overseas Bishops visited Bradford for the 'Lambeth Walk' and three thousand people took part in a public procession. Thousands more attended two rallies. After the 'Lambeth Walk' Blunt said, 'Well, this has been a real reward for seventeen years' work; and believe me, the encouragement which it gave me will long stay in my mind.'[14]

'Nemo' in the *Church Times* complained that the bishops came to the Conference somewhat overworked by the Lambeth Walk. That, however, was not his only complaint. He also had something to say about the way in which hospitality was arranged for the bishops. 'The housing arrangements', he said,

[13] This was H. L. J. de Mel who gained fame at the 1968 Conference.
[14] J. S. Peart-Binns, *Blunt*, p. 216.

seem to have been made with little imagination or sympathy. One bishop and his wife were sent to a house in Chislehurst, with the result that they had to queue every morning for a bus to the station, fight for a place on the train and then queue for a bus to Lambeth. Add to this there were functions in the evening which they had to attend and it will be seen how late they got to bed after making their journeys and how much was the extra strain imposed upon them.[15]

1948 was a pretty severe year in post-war Britain; rationing was still on and there were all sorts of restrictions. Mrs Frances Temple, the widow of William Temple, who was in charge of hospitality, defended the action of her committee vigorously in a letter to the *Church Times*.[16]

The 1948 Conference kept up the old tradition of making a start at Canterbury, and at St Augustine's College (which was celebrating its centenary) Canon W. C. France welcomed the bishops to lunch. There were 230 of them present, and there were guests from foreign churches. The Red Dean (Dr Hewlett Johnson) welcomed the bishops at the door of Canterbury Cathedral for the afternoon service of inauguration. Fisher, speaking to the assembly from the historic chair of St Augustine, said that the community to which they belonged was no longer English or Anglo-Saxon. It included churches of many other nations, races, and tongues, in every continent. But though the word 'Anglican' was no longer altogether appropriate for that diverse family of autonomous churches, it bore witness to a truth of the past and a task of the present. Every one of the churches represented there traced its ancestry back to the church of these islands and so to Canterbury and St Augustine. After the service cheques were presented to the Archbishop from Australia (by the Archbishop of Sydney) and from Canada (by the Bishop of Nova Scotia) on behalf of the Canterbury Cathedral Appeal Fund.

Another great opening service took place at St Paul's Cathedral on 4 July. On this occasion Fisher for the first time wore the famous cope which had been given to him by the Christians of Japan. It had been brought to this country by Bishop Michael Yashiro to try to obliterate the memories of the war, and been impounded at the docks on his arrival until a two hundred pound import fee was paid. Fisher had gone to the Chancellor of the Exchequer and arranged for the fee to be cancelled. Later he chose to wear this cope at the coronation of Queen Elizabeth.

[15] *Church Times*, 13 August 1948, p. 471.
[16] *Church Times*, 27 August 1948, p. 499.

The bishops were welcomed by Dean Matthews of St Paul's who came there just before the service from Westminster Hospital where he was receiving treatment for his throat. It was appropriate for the American bishops to be at St Paul's on 4 July – Independence Day – and Fisher had felicitously asked Bishop H. K. Sherrill, the Presiding Bishop, to preach at this Holy Communion service. Bishop Yashiro and Bishop T. Lindel Tsen of Honan (the chairman of the House of Bishops in China) assisted with the distribution of the elements. Then the Conference proceeded to Lambeth to get down to business in the Great Library, which had been hastily restored. *The Times* published a picture of Fisher receiving the prelates. While they were at work there was a conference for bishops' wives arranged by the Central Council for Women's Church Work, with Mrs Frances Temple and Mrs Michael Ridley as hostesses, and Hugh Ashdown, Provost of Southwark, as chaplain. The members of the Lambeth Conference were received by the King at Buckingham Palace on 13 July and in spite of its being an austerity conference there was a reception at the Mansion House on 14 July. The C.M.S. also held a reception at 6 Salisbury Square, and Prebendary Treacher and his wife gave a dinner for a hundred bishops at the headquarters of the Church Army in Bryanston Street. So the usual social side of the proceedings was not in abeyance.

In the Conference itself a great spirit of unity prevailed. In their encyclical the bishops gave utterance to this theme. 'Meeting again in Conference after a long interval of eighteen years, and after the grievous separations of war, we declare our thankfulness to Almighty God for the profound and joyful experience, in this meeting, of our unity in the faith of Christ and in the fellowship of the Holy Spirit.' This sense of unity was remarked on by a writer in the *Official Year Book of the Church of England 1949*.

Many bishops attending the Conference felt that they had rediscovered how much they shared in common and how great was their unity of mind and spirit. In the opinion of the senior Bishops there was no question, as compared with the Lambeth Conference of 1930 (when so many of the English and American bishops seemed to have different interests), that on this occasion they had all been considering much the same issues and were more equally well informed on the range of subjects coming before the Conference. Even where there was agreement to differ on some aspects of the South India Scheme, the difference seemed less important owing to the range of agreement and the growth of a world-wide ecumenical outlook. The bishops went away immensely encouraged and feeling that they were backed by world-wide prayer and understanding.[17]

Dewi Morgan points in contrast to the disunity in the contemporary world. 'As the bishops were meeting, English and American aeroplanes were relieving the Soviet blockade of Berlin; North Korea was proclaiming itself a People's Republic; Communist rule was being established in Czechoslovakia; Israel was being proclaimed independent; Gandhi was assassinated; and Malan was becoming Prime Minister of South Africa.'[18]

Item No. I on the agenda was the Doctrine of Man. Bishop Wand of London chaired the committee dealing with this, but the part played by Bishop Barry of Southwell was immense. 'The report on the Christian doctrine of Man', writes Barry in *Period of My Life*,

> most of which, as it happened, I wrote myself, has been criticised as unsatisfactory. So it is, twenty or more years later, in a radically changed context. The strongly humanist tone of the report must be understood against the background of the 'savage and inhuman theologies' of the then dominant 'neo-orthodoxy'. I do not think it was too bad at the time, and it received quite a warm welcome. . . . The Church's task today, as never before, is to vindicate the humanity of man against all that is threatening to dehumanise it. But the whole situation has changed since then; and if I were asked now to draft a document on Christian anthropology in the present context, it would have to be written in very different terms.[19]

The Report on 'The Church and the Modern World' was the work of a committee chaired by G. Ashton Oldham, Bishop of Albany. It dealt with human rights and referred to the commissions at Lake Success which were considering a Declaration of Human Rights. It dealt with the Church and war and reaffirmed what the 1930 Conference had said. It added, 'Despite brave and glorious deeds by individuals, war itself has always been beastly, costly, and horrible, and to-day the atom bomb lifts it into a new dimension, multiplying its destructive power a thousandfold and making civilians its chief victims'. It went on to deal with the Church and the State and with Communism, condemning the Church in the past for being too identified with the ruling classes. Christian education was also treated and then 'The Church Militant'.

Bishop Bell of Chichester chaired the committee on 'The Unity of the

[17] Op. cit., p. 299.
[18] *The Bishops Come to Lambeth*, p. 121.
[19] *Period of My Life*, p. 171.

Church', and made a good impression. 'His introductory speech' wrote Jasper,

> was a masterly and succinct survey of the whole problem. He pointed out that the search for Christian unity could not follow a single uniform pattern. In some cases there would be an attempt to secure organic unity; but in others the aim would be intercommunion, and even here the degree of finality or completeness might vary. He then went on to consider the views of Hooker and other divines on episcopacy. In various reunion schemes affecting the Church of England it had always been accepted as a necessary principle: but that the method by which it became accepted should differ in different schemes, according to the variety of conditions, need cause little surprise. The question facing the Anglican Communion was this: if non-episcopal Churches, agreeing on points of fundamental doctrine, were to accept episcopacy for the future, should we welcome that acceptance and exercise a reasonable tolerance regarding temporary anomalies?[20]

Bell then went on to refer to the World Council of Churches which was shortly to be created at Amsterdam. Some of the bishops would go on from Lambeth to Holland. In the end the Conference welcomed the creation of a World Council of Churches. On the question of South India the Conference was divided. It was clear from the outset that there would be no uniformity of opinion here. After much discussion the Conference agreed that former Anglicans who had joined the Church of South India still retained full communion with the Anglican Communion, but non-episcopally ordained ministers of the Church of South India had not acquired any new rights or status in relation to the Anglican Communion. A majority of the bishops (137) believed that ministers ordained after the inauguration should be accepted as true ministers in the Church of Christ; but a substantial minority (97) believed that it was not yet possible to make any decision on their status.[21] The total number of bishops attending the Conference was 329 so it would appear that about 100 did not vote. We know that Archbishop Garbett and Bishop Kirk were in the minority.

In the Report on Unity there was a section on current schemes. It was

[20] Ronald C. D. Jasper, *George Bell*, p. 348.

[21] See R. Jasper, *George Bell*, p. 349. E. W. Kemp in his *Kenneth Escott Kirk*, p. 178, gives the majority figure as 135.

Bishop Stephen Neill wrote to me on 7 May 1976 to say: 'On 1948 I could a tale unfold! Who would guess that the greater part of the South India report was written by a sub-committee composed of Kenneth Oxon (Kirk), myself, and George Cockin of Bristol, to see that Kenneth did not twist me round his little finger! A process to which I do not readily submit. Nor shall I ever be given the credit for my steady insistence that

reported that no progress had been made with the Church of Scotland since 1934 but there was a prospect of new initiatives. Similarly, though the Conference welcomed at the opening session delegates from the Free Churches, no progress had been made on that front since the talks of the thirties. Information was given on reunion schemes in Ceylon, North India, Iran, and Nigeria. There was also a section on the Philippine Independent church, which had broken away from Rome in 1902, and had been given bishops consecrated by the two Anglican bishops in the Philippines and the Bishop of Honolulu. Something was said about the Church of Rome, but things did not look very bright in that direction in 1948.

> We believe that there is considerable willingness on the part of members of the Anglican Communion to enter into a fruitful co-operation with Roman Catholics on a common ground. But we are frankly puzzled by the apparent contradiction between these repeated general invitations to co-operation which the Pope himself has issued and the attitude of many Roman Catholics in particular countries when it comes to definite programmes.[22]

On the Orthodox Church they pointed to the happier situation of the Russian church in 1948 compared with 1930. The Lambeth Fathers felt the need of a pan-Orthodox Synod before relationships between Anglicans and Orthodox could progress much further. Relations'with the Old Catholics were in a most happy state and the Conference welcomed the presence of Dr Andreas Rinkel, Archbishop of Utrecht, at the opening of its sessions. The committee also welcomed the contact with the churches of Denmark and Iceland which had been inaugurated at Chichester in October 1947, and expressed satisfaction at welcoming Archbishop Lehtonen of Finland, Bishop Aulén (the notable theologian) of Strangnas, and Bishop Fuglsang-Damgaard of Copenhagen, and Bishop Sigurgeir Sigurdsson of Iceland at the opening session. The committee wanted more information on the Spanish Reformed Church and the Lusitanian Church, which had not had a bishop since the death of Bishop Canbrera in 1916.

At the 1948 Conference we see a first expression of a desire for a

---

full weight must be given to the Anglo-Catholic difficulties which rested far more on anxiety about possible syncretism in the church than simply on the question of the ministry – this is what lay behind the divided vote – not a triumph of Anglo-catholics, but a deliberate and charitable concession granted by the supporters of S. India out of true Christian concern for the anxieties of their brethren.'

[22] Report, Part II, pp. 67f.

meeting of what has now become known as the 'wider episcopal fellowship', i.e. a meeting of bishops of the Anglican Communion and of bishops of those episcopal churches with which they hold communion. They ended by saying, 'We cordially welcome the establishment of the World Council of Churches.'

Archbishop Carrington of Quebec presided over the committee on the Anglican Communion. This produced one or two very important suggestions. First there was the suggested formation of an Advisory Council on Missionary Structure, which could deal with such things as the grouping of dioceses into provinces and other kindred matters. There was also the idea of having a Central College for the Anglican Communion; and it was suggested that this should be based at St Augustine's College, Canterbury. Then there was a proposal of another Anglican Congress – there had not been one since 1908 – the date of June 1953 being suggested for this. All these ideas were subsequently implemented, though the Congress took place in 1954 not 1953.

Another committee dealt with the Church's discipline in marriage. This group was chaired by Bishop Herbert of Norwich. They reaffirmed what the Conferences of 1920 and 1930 said about marriage being lifelong and indissoluble, but referred to the possibility of a form of prayer that could be used after a civil marriage. Nothing whatsoever was said on the question of contraception.

The committee on baptism and confirmation was chaired by the Bishop of Grahamstown (the Rt Rev. A. H. Cullen) and its secretary was Bishop Chase of Ripon. They were in the advantageous position of being able to use the recently published report *The Theology of Christian Initiation.* They did not desire to see any change in the established order of baptism, confirmation, and first communion, but suggested the need for a new order of infant baptism 'shorter and expressed in simpler language than the present Prayer Book provides. It has also been suggested that it would add reality to the administration of Baptism if in the Service godparents were called on to make confession of their own repentance, faith and obedience rather than make promises on behalf of the child.'

While the Lambeth Conference went on there also took place the Sixth Anglo-Catholic Congress on the subject of 'The Church', which had, like the Lambeth Conference, originally been planned for 1940. Bishop Wand of London was its President and many of the other bishops took part in it, like Kirk of Oxford, Wynn of Ely, and Hudson of Newcastle. It was woven around the pattern of the Lambeth

Quadrilateral. There were four speakers on the Bible (Canon A. M. Ramsey of Durham, Canon F. W. Green of Norwich, Fr Gabriel Hebert, and Fr Jonathan Graham of Mirfield), four on the creeds (Dean E. G. Selwyn of Winchester, Canon Frederic Hood, Dom Augustine Morris, and the Rev. Tom Parker of Pusey House), four on the ministry (Dom Gregory Dix, Mrs T. G. Jalland, the Rt Rev. K. D. Mackenzie, formerly Bishop of Brechin, and the Rev. A. H. Couratin, Principal of St Stephen's House), and four on the sacraments (Canon R. C. Mortimer, Donald MacKinnon, Dr E. L. Mascall, and the Rev. G. B. Bentley of Lincoln). It was a notable gathering and probably not since then has the Anglo-Catholic party met together with such unity. By the next Lambeth Conference, Ramsey was to be Archbishop of York and Canon Mortimer Bishop of Exeter.

The Conference of 1948 ended on 8 August with a great service in Westminster Abbey; 300 bishops were present, the Americans wearing black and the English red. Archbishop Garbett of York preached the sermon in the course of which he said, 'Within a few years our civilization might utterly pass away. . . . Only a united Church can hope to stand firm against the united front of Islam, Hinduism, or of an aggressive and atheistic communism.' A few days later Fisher gave a broadcast on the Conference for the B.B.C. 'The Lambeth Conference of 1948,' he said, 'had said nothing startling; it had said much that was true, and it went to the heart of the matter.'

There can be no doubt that Fisher made a far better impression upon the American bishops in 1948 than had Lang upon their predecessors in 1930. A comment of Bishop Sherrill is given in Purcell's *Fisher of Lambeth*:

> He seldom interfered from the Chair, but he followed the discussions and the reports of the various committees with meticulous care, which must have meant long hours of study after the day's work was apparently over. I cannot recall hearing an unhappy or critical remark by any of our bishops or their wives — no small achievement in itself.[23]

Bishop Blagden in his *Well Remembered* says that the figures who stood out in 1948 were Bell, Rawlinson, Clayton, Gregg of Armagh, and Garbett.

> There was no commanding group of Bishops, but we were conscious of a new attitude in the American episcopate. The Presiding Bishop was listened to with close attention and respect at both Conferences [1930 and 1948],

[23] Op. cit., p. 186.

but whereas in 1930 so many from U.S.A. seemed to come to England just for a holiday – I sat among them at every full session, and observed how lightly many of them were attached to the Conference – in 1948 they were true participators in it, realising that these questions which were being argued out before them were their questions as well as ours, and that what we faced in Southern India they were beginning to face much nearer home.[24]

He then went on to praise the President.

And, as for the present Archbishop, who had never been at a Lambeth Conference before, and now found himself presiding over this great host from every part of the world – he, never tired, always accessible, rarely at a loss, won the hearts of all our visitors, making them feel that there was nothing cold or clammy in the welcome which England gave them, and keeping the Conference alive with his vigour and energy and unfailing humour. This, the foreigner felt, was one of those with whom you could do business, who spoke the same tongue and followed the same lines as yourself, and a ripple of delighted laughter ran round the whole Conference when, after many hecklings from the Bishop of Truro at one critical meeting, he called to his objector, who though small was very vocal, 'Come up here and stand upon the platform,' just as if he were still Head Master of Repton and Hunkin a fourth-form boy in his class. No one laughed more heartily at himself than the Archbishop. This is what endeared himself to us all.[25]

Looking back now over the pages of the *Church Times* one finds mostly words of approval for the Conference. On 27 August the late Canon Frederic Hood described the Report on Unity as 'masterly, perhaps the best thing produced from a Lambeth Conference this century'. An earlier issue had been sorry that the Conference had said nothing about the modernists, one of whom, Bishop Barnes of Birmingham, was enjoying the notoriety occasioned by his now forgotten book *The Rise of Christianity*, but there was not even a private condemnation of the book such as the condemnation of Colenso at the Lambeth Conference of 1867. One might also have expected the bishops to say something about the *Report on Doctrine in the Church of England*. This had been the work of a high-powered committee appointed after the famous Girton Conference of 1921 by Archbishop Davidson. It had reported in 1938, but then been forgotten. Lambeth 1948 drew no attention to it, but recently Dean Matthews (who served on the commission) and Bishop Barry (who also served upon it) have pointed to the value of the document, which is generally thought of as

---

[24] *Well Remembered*, p. 264.
[25] Ibid., p. 265.

too liberal and accommodating, a criticism voiced for example by Leslie Paul in his book, *A Church by Daylight*. Bishop Wand wrote by no means disparagingly of the document in his *Anglicanism in History and Today* (1961):

> It was typically Anglican in that it did not endeavour to rest its findings in profound philosophical principles, about which no one would ever agree. It was content to point out what was the general consensus among scholars on the subjects discussed – which ranged, in point of fact, over the whole creed – and revealed how wide a range of opinion on controversial matters was consonant with Anglican loyalty. The volume did a vast amount of good in providing a *vade mecum* for the clergy and in assuring the laity that there was an Anglican mind on these matters. Unfortunately, the outbreak of war in the year following its publication diverted attention; and by the time the war was over it had been forgotten by the majority. It is probable, however, that those of the older generation who have retained their copies and have had reason to refer to them in recent years have been surprised how good and useful a book it is.[26]

This is a remarkable testimony from an Anglo-Catholic, especially when one considers some of the Anglo-Catholic opposition to the document in 1938, as is witnessed by the *Memorandum on the Report of the Archbishops' Commission on Christian Doctrine* written by Father Gabriel Hebert of Kelham and published with the authority of the council of the Church Union.

Another report to which one might have expected some allusion to be made in the Lambeth Conference of 1948 was that called *Towards the Conversion of England* which had been published in June 1945 and which was reprinted several times in that year and in 1946. Bishop Chavasse of Rochester chaired the members of the commission that produced the report and on the committee were future Bishops of Lichfield (Reeve), Bristol (Tomkins), and Southwark (Stockwood).

Archbishop Fisher remarked that nothing very controversial had been uttered at the 1948 Conference and this possibly accounts for the small amount of pamphlet literature which it provoked. The one notable review of the 1948 Report was that produced by the members of the theological and liturgical committee of the Church Union, which came out in April 1949.[27] This was the work of the group which had been behind the organization of the Anglo-Catholic Congress. Yet though

[26] Op. cit., p. 141.
[27] *Lambeth 1948 Reviewed*. A Report of the Theological and Liturgical Committee of the Church Union April 1949. Published by the Church Union.

the Conference had been hardly controversial (apart from the South Indian church) yet it had been valuable. Indeed Dewi Morgan in his *The Bishops Come to Lambeth* says that 'in many ways, it proved one of the most successful of all'.

12

MINNEAPOLIS AND
THE CONFERENCE OF 1958

One of the minor results of the 1948 Conference was the drawing up by Archbishops Fisher and Garbett of some Rules for Churchmen, in accordance with a subsection of the Report on the Christian Doctrine of Man. There were seven rules which were in due course adopted in Convocation.

1 To follow the example of Christ in home and daily life, and to bear personal witness to him.
2 To be regular in private prayer day by day.
3 To read the Bible carefully.
4 To come to church every Sunday.
5 To receive the Holy Communion faithfully and regularly.
6 To give personal service to church, neighbours, and community.
7 To give money for the work of the parish and diocese, and for the work of the Church at home and overseas.

Another outcome was the creation of an Anglican Cycle of Prayer, in which each day of the year was assigned to a particular province or diocese. This has become a stimulus to the search for information about other parts of the Communion.

The Advisory Council of Missionary Strategy was set up and the Central College of the Anglican Communion started at St Augustine's, Canterbury. The Anglican Congress, the most important Anglican event between the Conferences of 1948 and 1958, was arranged to be held at Minneapolis, Minnesota, 4–13 August 1954, thanks to an invitation received from the General Convention of the Protestant Episcopal Church in 1949.

Fisher left the Conference of 1948 to go to Amsterdam for the first meeting of the World Council of Churches, which had arisen out of the joining together of the old 'Life and Work' and 'Faith and Order' Movements. In fact, Fisher was in the chair at Amsterdam at the historic moment of inauguration on 23 August. In 1952 he was in the

United States once again for the General Convention of the Protestant Episcopal Church of the United States of America at Boston, Massachusetts. Fisher returned once again to the United States in 1954 for the Anglican Congress at Minneapolis in August. The theme in this 'Year of Hope' – for people were writing on the subject of hope, which was the theme of the Evanston Conference of the World Council of Churches which followed Minneapolis – was 'The Call of God and the Mission of the Anglican Communion'. The Congress began at 8 p.m. on Wednesday, 4 August, in the Minneapolis Auditorium, when addresses were given by Archbishop Fisher and Bishop Sherrill. The next day they started on the first topic, 'Our Vocation', with a lecture on 'The Position of the Anglican Communion in History and Doctrine' by Bishop William Wand of London in the morning and another by Archbishop Carrington in the afternoon on 'The Structure of the Anglican Communion', which included the remark that the 'Lambeth Conference is the best *formal expression* of our unity'. The next day there were group discussions on this first topic. Then on Friday, 7 August, the Congress turned to the second topic, 'Our Worship', with lectures by the Rev. Massey H. Shepherd on 'Our Anglican Understanding of Corporate Worship' and by Bishop Colin Dunlop, Dean of Lincoln, on 'The Liturgical Life of the Anglican Communion in the Twentieth Century'. On Sunday the Congress listened to sermons from the Rev. Roland Koh of Hong Kong and later from Bishop Howells of Lagos, Bishop William J. Gordon of Alaska, and Bishop Lakdasa Jacob de Mel of Kurunagala. On Monday there were group discussions on Topic 2 and then on Tuesday the Congress embarked upon Topic 3, 'Our Message'. Bishop John S. Moyes of Armidale spoke on the 'Individual', Bishop Ambrose Reeves of Johannesburg on the 'Family' and Dr Kathleen Bliss on the 'Citizen'. Wednesday saw group discussions on Topic 3 and then in the evening the Congress listened to addresses on Topic 4, 'Our Work'. Senator Charles P. Taft spoke on 'The Role of the Laity', Bishop Bravid W. Harris of Liberia spoke on 'The Missionary Task', and Bishop Leslie Hunter of Sheffield spoke on 'A Church in Action'. Group discussion followed on Thursday, 12 August. Friday saw the end of the Congress, with two General Sessions and a closing service in the Cathedral Church of St Mark, when the sermon was preached by Archbishop Arthur W. Barton of Dublin. There were 657 delegates to this Congress – 201 bishops, 242 priests, and 214 lay delegates, 65 of whom were women. The Report of the Congress was edited by Professor Powel Mills Dawley and in that volume Bishop

Walter H. Gray of Connecticut, the episcopal secretary of the Congress, wrote as follows:

> The Anglican Congress of 1954 marks a new era in the history of the Anglican Communion in that it is the first representative gathering of the Church held outside the British Isles. This is a recognition both of the worldwide character of our Communion, and that the Anglican Communion is now an international family of Churches, independent in government, but unified in fellowship and in adherence to common traditions of faith and order, and the Book of Common Prayer.

The issue of *Pan-Anglican*[1] in the following October had half of its pages devoted to the 1954 Congress and gives valuable photographs of the various personalities, services, and gatherings.

From Minneapolis a number of the delegates went on to the Second Assembly of the World Council of Churches which was held at Evanston, Illinois, from 15 to 31 August. Bishop Sherrill was one of the six Presidents of the World Council. The main theme of the Assembly was 'the Christian Hope' and a large amount of literature had been written on this subject, including J. E. Fison's *The Christian Hope* and C. F. D. Moule's *The Meaning of Hope*. Dr Michael Ramsey, Bishop of Durham, was present and wrote a critique of Evanston later. He felt the assembly was too large, the American publicity rather overdone and vulgar, and the programme overloaded. Ramsey made two acute and prophetic observations:

> Two impressions particularly came to me. 1. The primacy and poignancy of the question of Race for the Christian conscience. On one occasion there came to the platform a Bantu Christian pleading for the end of racial obstruction to brotherhood in Christ, and a delegate of the Dutch Reformed Church whose members sometimes defend segregation (including segregation in Church worship) by arguments from the Bible akin to those which were once advanced on behalf of negro slavery. In the latter delegate the struggles of conscience were observable: but what of the conscience of all Christians everywhere? 2. The growing leadership of the Churches in Asia already, and perhaps of the Churches in Africa very soon. Their need for resources and technical help from the West remains, just as the countries wherein they are set need the help of the West to meet terrible poverty. But neither the Churches nor the countries will suffer western domination: they are rising to adult stature, they are the teachers and we the learners.[2]

---

[1] This was an excellent magazine published half-yearly at Hartford, Connecticut, which started in 1950. It performed a valuable service in making Anglicans conscious of other parts of the Communion.

[2] A. M. Ramsey, *Durham Essays and Addresses*, pp. 83–4.

This was written in 1954. Two years later Trevor Huddleston's *Naught for your Comfort* hit the headlines.

The period between Fisher's first Conference and his second was one of great activity in the Church of England. 1950 saw the publication of the report *Church Relations in England*, being the Report of Conversations between Representatives of the Archbishop of Canterbury and Representatives of the Evangelical Free Churches in England, which was prefaced by Fisher's Cambridge sermon. Rawlinson, the Bishop of Derby, was the Anglican chairman and Nathaniel Micklem, the Congregationalist, the Free Church chairman. Out of this report there developed the talks of the Church of England with the Methodists, which started in 1956.

In 1949 the Church of England also commenced talks with the Church of Scotland. Again the Bishop of Derby chaired the Anglican delegates; Dr William Manson, the notable New Testament scholar, chaired the Presbyterians. Their first report was issued in 1951. In 1957, in the year before the Lambeth Conference, the S.P.C.K. published *Relations between Anglican and Presbyterian Churches. A Joint Report*. Dr Donald Baillie, the famous theologian, author of *God was in Christ*, was chairman of the Presbyterians in these conversations until his death in 1954. This report was commended in Convocation in May 1957 but further discussion deferred until after the Lambeth Conference.

The year 1954 saw the publication of the report of a commission on the ecclesiastical courts set up by Convocations in 1951. In that same year there was a sequel to the report of the Archbishops' commission on canon law which had first reported in 1947. This second report was entitled *The Revised Canons of the Church of England further considered*. This work of the revision of canon law went on right through Fisher's primacy and was almost complete when he retired. The final revision was published in 1969. 1954 brought the publication of *Baptism and Confirmation Today*.

In 1957 came the publication of the report on *Prayer Book Revision in the Church of England*, which was the work of the liturgical commission under the chairmanship of Bishop Colin Dunlop, with Geoffrey Willis as secretary. This was produced with a definite view to the meeting of the Lambeth Conference in 1958. A much smaller group produced a valuable report *The Commemoration of Saints and Heroes of the Faith in the Anglican Communion*. The decade between the two Lambeth Conferences saw also a report on the question of Church and

State under the chairmanship of Sir Walter Moberly. This was the
successor to the report of 1935. One of its most notable members was
Professor Norman Sykes, the distinguished historian of the eighteenth-
century church.

The question of the nullity of marriage had come up for the first time
in a Lambeth Conference in 1948 and in the very next year a
commission was appointed by the two Archbishops 'to examine the
laws of Nullity, ecclesiastical and civil, and questions relating thereto, in
their general and practical bearings'. The chairman was Bishop Wand.
Bishop Chavasse of Rochester and Bishop Askwith of Gloucester
served upon it.

Thus the years between 1948 and 1958 were years of immense
activity under the leadership of an indefatigable archbishop. It was a
decade of positivism in Anglicanism. Liberalism and modernism were
at a discount. The spirit of Barth and Brunner prevailed. There was little
inkling of what the sixties were going to produce and the theological
erosion that would then take place. The Anglican Communion seemed
in a strong position.

When the bishops came together again in 1958 they came together as
friends. Many of them had met in 1948 and had renewed their
acquaintance in 1954 at the Anglican Congress. Thus Fisher's task was
considerably eased. However, there were some changes. Wand had left
London and been succeeded by H. C. Montgomery Campbell; Bishop
Haigh of Winchester had retired and been replaced by Bishop Alwyn
Williams from Durham; R. P. Wilson had taken the place of Bishop Bell
at Chichester; H. J. Carpenter had succeeded Kirk at Oxford; R. W.
Stopford was Bishop of Peterborough in place of Spencer Leeson; and
the notorious Bishop Barnes of Birmingham had been replaced by
Leonard Wilson; at Lichfield, Stretton Reeve had taken the place of
E. S. Woods; at Lincoln, Kenneth Riches was Bishop in the stead of
Maurice Harland now translated to Durham. The Archbishop of York
was A. M. Ramsey, translated there after a short time at Durham. He
was now one of the most outstanding bishops in the Anglican
Communion, already regarded as the natural successor to Fisher at
Canterbury. A. E. Morris had superseded D. L. Prosser as Archbishop
of Wales and T. Hannay was Primus of Scotland in place of J. C. H.
How. Archbishop Gregg was still Primate of All Ireland and Bishop
Sherrill remained the Presiding Bishop in the U.S.A. Bishop A. N.
Mukerjee was Bishop of Calcutta and Metropolitan of India, R. H.
Owen was Bishop of Wellington and Primate of New Zealand, and

Joost de Blank was Archbishop of Cape Town and Metropolitan of South Africa. Ambrose Reeves was Bishop of Johannesburg, Stephen Bayne was Bishop of Olympia, and W. L. S. Fleming Bishop of Portsmouth.

Preparations for the 1958 Conference were made by several publications in 1957, some of which we have already noted. The Spring 1958 *Pan-Anglican* devoted a special edition to the forthcoming Conference. Dewi Morgan wrote his little book *The Bishops Come to Lambeth*, which proved popular, although the professional historian will find in it things to criticize. Just before the start of the Conference the report on *The Family in Contemporary Society* came out, drafted by Professor G. R. Dunstan.[3]

Bishop Robert Stopford of Peterborough was the episcopal secretary in 1958 and the assistant secretary was Eric Jay, the Archbishop's chaplain, who has become well known as the author of a *New Testament Greek. An Introductory Grammar*.[4] The programme for the Conference consisted of five subjects:

1 The Holy Bible. Its Authority and Message.
2 Church Unity and the Church Universal.
3 Progress in the Anglican Communion.
    a Missionary Appeal and Strategy.
    b The Book of Common Prayer.
    c Ministries and Manpower.
4 The Reconciling of Conflicts between and within Nations.
5 The Family in Contemporary Society.

One of the most controversial aspects of the 1958 Conference was the invitation to Archbishop Makarios of Cyprus to attend as one of the Orthodox delegates. Times were troublous for the British in Cyprus where Archbishop Makarios was the political as well as the religious head. On 22 May *The Times* announced Makarios had been invited. The next day it added that the invitation was of a purely ecclesiastical nature. Both the Colonial Office and the Foreign Office had been informed. The Greek press began to see in the invitation an attempt to lure the Archbishop to Britain by the British Government. Many churchmen were upset by the whole business. Major-General Spears sent a letter to Fisher strongly objecting and said that the relatives of British soldiers killed in Cyprus might reasonably apply for a warrant

---

[3] See Max Warren, *Crowded Canvas*, p. 173.
[4] He is now Professor of Theology at Montreal, Canada.

for the arrest of Makarios. On 4 June Makarios announced that he would come but twenty days later he had decided against it. Instead he would be represented by Archbishop Athenagoras of Thyateira, Exarch of the Oecumenical Patriarch in West and Central Europe. When Richard Dimbleby interviewed Archbishop Fisher on television, Fisher said he viewed with abhorrence Makarios's political behaviour and his association with terrorism. He added, 'I know as well as anybody what a bad character he is.' This hardly commended Fisher in Orthodox circles and later he had to send a cable to the Archbishop of Athens: 'Archbishop Makarios's ecclesiastical office highly honoured by me. My remarks expressly excluded reflections on his personal character. Criticisms confined strictly to certain political aspects.' The Greek Orthodox Patriarch in Alexandria recalled his delegation and would not be represented at the Conference. In the end there were no Greek Orthodox delegates present, though Constantinople, Russia, Rumania, Bulgaria, and the Armenian Church were represented.

The Conference began on Thursday, 3 July, with the customary service in Canterbury Cathedral. Fisher, seated in the chair of St Augustine which had been moved to the steps before the screen, and wearing the cope and mitre presented to him in 1948 by the Japanese, received the representatives of the other Christian communions, the Baptists, the Congregationalists, the Lutherans, the Eastern Orthodox, and the Old Catholics, and then the bishops of the Anglican Communion. 'For twenty minutes', reported *The Times*, 'the long procession wound its way up the nave from the great west door, the sun lighting the full robes of the Russian prelates, the sombre habit of the Lutherans, like figures from a Rembrandt painting and the splash of red and white as the first Anglican bishops followed.' Amongst the representatives was Bishop Otto Dibelius of Berlin. There were no Anglican bishops from China apart from Bishop Hall of Hong Kong. The service was for the first time televised and many of us remember very vividly the broadcast and the sermon of the Archbishop, and its references to the circumstances of the calling of the First Lambeth Conference.[5]

On the next day, Friday, 4 July, the assembly got down to business at Lambeth at 2.30 p.m. after a morning of Mattins, Litany, and Holy Communion in Lambeth Parish Church. An amusing incident marked the beginning of the proceedings. A young man, tall, bearded, and dressed as a bishop, and a girl stood up at the end of the Great Hall and

[5] See *Pan-Anglican*, Spring 1959, pp. 11–14.

proceeded to address the Conference. But they were ushered out before they had said a sentence or two. They were members of the League of Empire Loyalists. A photograph of this episode appeared in *The Times*. Then the delegates from the Scandinavian Churches, the German Evangelical Church, the Church of Scotland, and the Free Church Federal Council of England were officially received. On Saturday, 5 July, the morning was devoted to meetings of committees. In the afternoon the Mayor and Mayoress of Lambeth were received and then the Old Catholic, Orthodox, and Armenian delegates. On Sunday, 6 July, there was a Solemn Eucharist and then from Monday, 7 July, to Friday, 11 July, the plenary sessions took place. From 14 July to 25 July the committees met at Lambeth and Church House, Westminster. From 28 July until 8 August came the final plenary sessions.

One notable absentee from the visiting delegates was Don Santos Molina who had been consecrated as Bishop of the Spanish Episcopal Reformed Church at Madrid in 1956 by the Bishop of Meath (representing the Archbishop of Armagh), and two American bishops. Refused an exist visa from Spain to attend the consecration of Bishop Ferreira Fiandor of Portugal, he was debarred from coming to the Lambeth Conference as well.

The usual social activities took place. There was a reception at the Mansion House, and Queen Elizabeth the Queen Mother gave a party at St James's Palace. Toc H gave a reception at 42 Trinity Street, to which the guests went by river. Mr M. T. Mbu, the Commissioner for Nigeria, gave a dinner party for the West African bishops. The British Council of Churches gave a reception at Sarum Chase, Hampstead. The Prime Minister, Harold Macmillan, gave a dinner for the archbishops and metropolitans at 10 Downing Street. The Queen received over 300 bishops at Buckingham Palace in the State Ballroom on 5 August (an event that had had to be postponed because of her illness). 'Mr Butler, Home Secretary, was present', said *The Times*, 'on the dais with the Queen, who before entering the ballroom, had passed through the picture gallery, where the wives of the delegates were assembled. The Lord Chancellor and the Speaker of the House of Commons also held a reception in the Royal Gallery of the Palace of Westminster.'

The main subject of the Conference was the Bible. The chairman of the committee on 'The Holy Bible. Its authority and message' was Dr Michael Ramsey, Archbishop of York. Its deputy-chairman was Dr Philip Carrington, Archbishop of Quebec. Ramsey, who had held professorships at Durham and Cambridge, was a notable biblical scholar and theologian, disciple of Sir Edwyn Hoskyns and exponent of biblical theology. There can be little doubt that he penned the Report, which castigated evolutionary liberalism and said that the Bible could not be understood apart from the supernatural activity of God in history. Bultmann and the scholars of his school were obviously (though not by name) criticized. The Report indicates the importance of the duty of expounding the Bible and looks with favour upon modern translations. 1958 is the first year that a Lambeth Conference referred to the value of modern translations. Ramsey made a great impression through his chairing of the committee. 'The Archbishop of York', wrote Archbishop Carrington, 'was one of the dynamic figures in the Conference, both in his occasional words of warning or guidance, and in his Chairmanship of the Committee on the Bible.'[6]

The second committee dealt with the subject of 'Church Unity and the Church Universal'. The Chairman was Falkner Allison, Bishop of Chelmsford (later translated to Winchester). There were subcommittees on 'Unity and the Ecumenical Movement' (Kenneth Riches, Bishop of Lincoln, chairman), on 'Particular Churches' (chairman, H. J. Carpenter, Bishop of Oxford), and on 'Relations with the Presbyterians' (chairman, A. E. J. Rawlinson, Bishop of Derby). One of the important things coming out of this committee was the formulation of what became Resolution 14 on Full Communion and Intercommunion.

> The Conference endorses the paragraph in the Report of the Committee on Church Unity and the Church Universal which refers to the use of the terms 'full communion' and 'intercommunion', and recommends accordingly that where between two Churches not of the same denominational or confessional family, there is unrestricted *communio in sacris*, including mutual recognition and acceptance of ministries, the appropriate term to use is 'full communion', and that where varying degrees of relation other than 'full communion' are established by agreement between two such Churches the appropriate term is 'intercommunion'.

This committee had the difficult task of dealing with two schemes of reunion – the *Scheme of Church Union in Ceylon* or Lanka and the *Plan of Church Union in North India and Pakistan*. This issue was to the 1958 Conference what the issue of South India was to that of 1948. In the end resolutions were passed in which the Anglican Communion

---

[6] For more detail see my article 'The Bible and the Lambeth Conferences' in *Theology*, July 1975, pp. 361–70.

was advised that, subject to minor alterations, it could enter into communion with the proposed Church of North India and advised that the provinces of the Anglican Communion should enter into full communion with the church of Lanka. Later, however, the Convocations in England and some provincial synods elsewhere, were not at first prepared to be guided by the Lambeth Conference.[7]

The committee spoke about the Roman Catholic Church. Though that Church retained its conviction that the only goal of reunion must be submission to the papacy, there were some welcome signs of an increasing Roman awareness of the importance of the ecumenical movement. Regarding the Spanish Reformed Episcopal Church and the Lusitanian Church of Portugal, they welcomed the consecration of Bishops Molina and Fiandor. They drew attention to the closer relations with the Philippine Independent Church since the consecration of three bishops there by Anglican bishops from the U.S.A.

The Committee on 'Progress in the Anglican Communion' was chaired by Walter H. Gray, Bishop of Connecticut. There were three subcommittees:

A Missionary Appeal and Strategy (chairman, Walter Gray, Bishop of Connecticut).
B The Book of Common Prayer (chairman, George Simms, Archbishop of Dublin).
C Ministries and Manpower (chairman, H. W. Bradfield, Bishop of Bath and Wells).

Committee A recommended the appointment of a full-time secretary of the Advisory Council on Missionary Structure which had been brought into being in 1948. Eventually Bishop Stephen Bayne, Bishop of Olympia, was appointed to this office. The committee on the Prayer Book went into every aspect of its revision, making use of the two preparatory reports. The subcommittee on ministries and manpower wanted greater emphasis on post-ordination training. Some good resulted from this. The Report also added a Memorandum on Auxiliary Priests which had been submitted by Bishop Hall of Hong Kong.

The Conference as a whole recommended the holding of another Anglican Congress, in view of the success of that held at Minneapolis in 1954 and suggested the date 1963 and the topic 'The World-wide Mission of the Church'.

[7] See further Barry Till, *The Churches Search for Unity*, pp. 319–20.

The committee on 'The Reconciling of Conflicts between and within Nations' was chaired by Joost de Blank, Archbishop of Cape Town. Their Report said much on the Church's task of reconciliation, commending the work of the United Nations. There was a great deal of discussion and debate over Resolution 106 on 'Modern Warfare and Christian Responsibility'. This declared war incompatible with the teaching and example of Jesus Christ. Governments should be pressed for the abolition by international agreement of nuclear weapons. The Conference urged governments to devote their utmost efforts at once to framing a comprehensive international disarmament treaty. But it is clear from the encyclical that there was deep division. Some of the bishops regarded the use of nuclear weapons as indefensible in any circumstances, while others thought that so long as these weapons existed there were circumstances in which their use was preferable to political slavery. The actual voting on this matter was not published in the Report and on 2 October a circular 'Voting at Lambeth' by Archbishop Fisher was published by the Church Information Board. On conflict within nations, the Report dealt with the problem of racialism in the United States, in Israel and the Arab world, and in India, Pakistan, Burma, and Ceylon.

The most far-reaching and important report came from the committee on 'The Family in Contemporary Society', chaired by Bishop Stephen F. Bayne of Olympia, an excellent piece of writing. It outlined the purposes of God in marriage between a man and a woman, which were clearly discernible both from scriptural authority and the testimony of the family of the Church: (a) the procreation of children; (b) the binding of a husband and a wife together as one flesh and one spirit through the love that they hold each for the other; and (c) the responsible creation of home life in which the lessons of discipline and forgiveness and the recognition of the rights of others are learned as prerequisites for the discharge of the wider family obligations to which men are for ever called in this world. A marriage which unbalances this tripartite structure runs the risk of doing serious damage to the concept of marriage as our Lord proclaimed it. There is no reason for Christian marriage to stumble over the sexual relationship so essential and so rich in its possibilities. From it, as a gift from God, children are born into the world. Yet the marriage in which the sexual function finds expression only for breeding children as fast as possible would be a distortion of true marriage. And, by the same token, a marriage is untrue which perverts the sexual act to self-gratification and sensuality alone. What is

11. The disturbance at the beginning of the 1958 Conference

12. The bishops in Canterbury Cathedral at the opening service, 1968

true marriage, and therefore that to which we are called to witness as Christians, is marriage in depth as our Lord reveals it wherein our highest love and our profoundest responsibility are joined in the creation both of new lives (where possible) and new life. The report says this on sexual intercourse:

> But the procreation of children is not the only purpose of marriage. Husbands and wives owe to each other and to the depth and stability of their families the duty to express, in sexual intercourse, the love which they bear and mean to bear to each other. Sexual intercourse is not by any means the only language of earthly love, but it is, in its full and right use, the most intimate and the most revealing; it has the depth of communication signified by the biblical word so often used for it, 'knowledge'; it is a giving and receiving in the unity of two free spirits which is in itself good (within the marriage bond) and mediates good to those who share it. Therefore it is utterly wrong to urge that, unless children are specifically desired, sexual intercourse is of the nature of sin. It is also wrong to say that such intercourse ought not to be engaged in except with the willing intention to procreate children.

The Report went on to condemn the wilful withholding of one partner from intercourse with the other, 'sometimes misnamed "continence"'. It also condemned 'any means which interrupts or prevents the fulfilment of *coitus* and thus precludes, in husband or wife, the full completion of the sexual act'. It then rejected the practice of induced abortion, or infanticide, which involves the killing of a life already conceived (as well as a violation of the personality of the mother) save at the dictate of strict and undeniable medical necessity. It also spoke on artificial human insemination and drew attention to the 1948 Report on this subject. 'Artificial insemination by any other one than the husband raises problems of such gravity that the Committee cannot see any possibility of its acceptance by Christian people.' There is a great deal in this Report which is gloriously positive and creative. Indeed, Dewi Morgan remarks in his *Lambeth Speaks*, 'Perhaps no Lambeth Conference has ever reached a more sustained and positive note.'[8] This courageous document did not go without criticism. Father Robert Wingfield Digby, the Jesuit, preaching in the church of the Immaculate Conception in Farm Street, remarked, 'There is nothing admirable in the idea of Christian leaders shedding their traditional principles to suit the demands of modern paganism.' It is rather interesting to note that Marie Stopes, who must have rejoiced at the way the Anglican wind

[8] Op. cit., p. 51.

was blowing, lived long enough to hear what the bishops had said. She died in October 1958.

The final set of plenary sessions took place between Monday, 28 July, and Friday, 8 August, at Lambeth Palace. Bishop Sherrill recalled the final session of the Lambeth Conference:

At the closing session of the 1958 Conference, it was my privilege to present a gift to the Archbishop on behalf of all the bishops. I said incidentally that, as I had watched His Grace preside, I had wondered what he had done before becoming Bishop of Chester, and that all at once an inspiration came to me: 'He must have had something to do with a boys' school.' The Archbishop in replying said that he never understood why people tried to belittle or denigrate what was meant by being the headmaster of a school, and went on to make an interesting and amusing defence of schoolmasters. Then came the closing prayers and Benediction. The last words of the Archbishop were 'Class dismissed'.

The final service took place at Westminster Abbey at 10.30 a.m. on Sunday, 10 August. The Rev. Michael Adie, who was Archbishop Fisher's chaplain, describes it in *Pan-Anglican*, Spring 1959, but as he in a previous paragraph says something about the worship and other arrangements of the Conference it will be as well to quote him at length:

The bishops stayed in hotels and hostels. In the hostels daily services were held; even so some Bishops felt that their programme was so full that they did not have the time they wanted for unhurried waiting prayer. Yet they were surely borne up by the prayers of the faithful throughout the world!

Twice a week at Lambeth Palace a different group of a dozen or so Bishops came to spend two nights as the personal guests of the Archbishop and Mrs Fisher, and in the Palace Chapel each day a different Bishop celebrated the Holy Communion, each using his own order of the liturgy. One morning the congregation prayed with the Bishop of Calcutta for 'relief from famine'; another day the Bishop of Kurunagula celebrated the Ceylon Liturgy and broke into his native Singhalese for the blessing; the Arab Bishop in Jordan, Lebanon and Syria significantly asked our prayers for international peace. When Bishop Yashiro, the Presiding Bishop of Japan, celebrated, one Englishman in the congregation found himself kneeling next to the Metropolitan of India to receive Communion. As the English and Indian hands were held up to receive from Japanese hands the Sacrament of the Body of our Lord, the Englishman reflected on this symbol of peace as he recalled that fifteen years before his hands had been used in war in India against the Japanese. So each nationality recognised the reconciliation which God gives and which the Church strives to effect in the world.

The final act of worship was in Westminster Abbey. . . . In 1958 they were readily welcomed by the Dean and Chapter. Once again the crowds saw the line of Bishops in scarlet and white moving through the streets and into church. The Bishops went to their seats by the high altar as the choir sang. Then the Archbishop of Canterbury, passing the very spot where five years before he had crowned Queen Elizabeth II, went to the altar to celebrate the Holy Communion. The Epistle was read by the Presiding Bishop of Japan, and the Gospel by the Primate of Canada. Then the retiring Presiding Bishop of the Episcopal Church in the United States, Bishop Sherrill, preached to his brethren and to many Christians throughout the world, and he recalled us to the pastoral work of the Church, that care and concern for every individual which Christ the Good Shepherd showed supremely to His flock.[9]

Fisher found the final service very moving. 'Never in my life', he said,

have I been so moved as at the closing service in Westminster Abbey at the end of the Conference, when Henry Sherrill preached the sermon, and we went in procession from the Abbey to the Chapter House, all the Bishops of the Anglican Communion. [There were actually 313 bishops present in the Abbey.] Then I bade them farewell. There immediately in front of me was Owen, Archbishop of New Zealand, who had been up at Oxford with me, and then headmaster at Uppingham when I was headmaster at Repton. There were all the others. I knew that I should never see Owen or many of them again. I did just say a few words of farewell to them all, a word of gratitude and love and affection, and had to turn away as they ended, because I could not trust myself to say more.[10]

When the Lambeth Conference Report was published, Fisher gave a press conference at Church House, Westminster. Asked whether this was the first time that the Church had actually supported family planning, he replied, 'It is the first time, I think, they have considered it. [!] In 1930 there had been a resolution solely on the limitation of families. That was a very narrow little view.' He was asked, 'Do you advocate Family Planning?' He replied, 'What the Conference says, is that it is necessary and I agree.' Miss Juanita Francis, Secretary of the Married Woman's Association, said that the Bishops had given a 'realistic and human approach to birth control'. Dr Norman Snaith, the well-known Old Testament scholar and the 1958 President of the Methodist Conference felt that the Lambeth Report was 'very good and very sensible and very practical'.

Bishop Bell, though he had retired from Chichester, was present at

[9] Op. cit., pp. 77–8. Bishop Sherrill's sermon is on pp. 78–81.
[10] W. Purcell, *Fisher of Lambeth*, p. 200.

the Conference. It was his fourth, and there were not many in 1958 who could remember the Conference of 1920. His biographer recalls Bell's reluctance to leave the Abbey after the closing service. 'It was a sad little figure who was almost the last bishop to leave the Abbey.' Bell's general impression of the Conference was that it had tried to do too much, and that there were too few outstanding leaders. 'No doubt about *fellowship*', he said,

> but main comment is far too large an Agenda. Too many subjects of importance in the time, or men to do them justice. *Few outstanding figures.* Ebor certainly. Dublin on his subject also. Exeter carried weight on Unity affairs. Chelmsford did well as chairman of Unity Committee. Olympia did well as Chairman of Family Committee. But very few weighty bishops: and it was noted that the English bishops failed to give leadership. Too little of supernatural or spiritual or (if preferred) too little of theological approach anywhere. Some of the newer English bishops disappointed with their first Lambeth. The pace of the Conference was far too swift. With all my criticisms I must bear testimony to the spirit of genuine brotherhood and friendship: and sense of Anglican Communion much deeper and stronger than at any previous Conference (partly due to Anglican Congress at Minneapolis 1954).

George Bell died later in this same year.

Dr Ramsey, the Archbishop of York, did not preach one of the Conference sermons, though he played a prominent part in the Conference. He also gave the inaugural address at the Eucharistic Congress, which took place while the Lambeth Conference was in progress to mark one hundred years of the Church Union, and was the fifth of the Church Congresses organized by the Church Union since 1920. Princess Margaret became the first member of the Royal Family to support such a congress when she attended the opening Evensong in Westminster Abbey.

Literature followed upon the end of the Conference. A large number purchased the official Report. More bought the popular summary of it, published by the S.P.C.K. and entitled *Lambeth and You*. Eric Mascall, then a Student of Christ Church, published a controversial pamphlet criticizing the Conference, *Lambeth and Church Unity*. Dewi Morgan, the editorial secretary of the S.P.G., followed up his book *The Bishops Come to Lambeth* with a commentary on the 1958 Conference, *Lambeth Speaks*. In his concluding 'Epilogue', he said:

> The ninth Lambeth Conference has gone into the history books. Without a

trace? No, because it has left us with a great body of ideas. And those ideas must now find their expression and realization through the group of human beings which is the earthly end of the Church. It is a large group, permeating every race and culture. But the ideas it is to express are larger still, for we handle not words but the Word, source of all wisdom. It now remains for every part of the Mystical Body to offer itself as the means whereby that Word becomes known, accepted, loved, adored.[11]

[11] Op. cit., pp. 133–4.

13

MICHAEL RAMSEY
PREPARATION FOR THE
CONFERENCE OF 1968

The 1958 Conference spoke of the appointment of an Anglican Executive Officer. In March 1959 an appointment was announced – that of Stephen Bayne, the American Bishop of Olympia, who had made his mark at the Conference as chairman of the committee on 'The Family in Contemporary Society'. It is now apparent from John S. Peart-Binns's *Ambrose Reeves* that Bayne was not the first bishop to be offered the post. He writes:

> After considerable consultation the Archbishop of Canterbury (G. F. Fisher) invited Reeves to become the first Anglican Executive Officer. This would have meant Reeves leaving South Africa [where he was Bishop of Johannesburg] and making his headquarters in London as the base for world-wide travel and activity. It seems possible if not probable that this was a move to prise Reeves away from South Africa. Whatever the position it is fascinating to speculate what would have happened if Reeves had accepted. The Anglican Communion might be a slightly different shape, if not colour, today. But Reeves declined and the Bishop of Olympia (Stephen F. Bayne Jr) was offered the post and accepted it in March 1959.[1]

Archbishop Fisher announced this appointment of Bishop Bayne in these terms:

ANGLICAN EXECUTIVE OFFICER

At the request of the Lambeth Conference, 1958, the Metropolitans of the Anglican Communion have appointed a new officer with the title of Anglican Executive Officer.

The chief duties are on the one hand to act as controller of the Anglican Advisory Council on Missionary Strategy, and on the other hand to exercise a general supervision on behalf of the Consultative Body of the Lambeth

---

[1] J. S. Peart-Binns, *Ambrose Reeves*, pp. 149–50. Peart-Binns notes that for Reeves the 1958 Lambeth Conference was 'one of the richest experiences of his life'.

Conference on all matters affecting the Anglican Communion which call for attention between the decennial Conferences.

As the office is a new one it will be for the first holder of it to discover how best to fulfil these duties and to render his best service to the various Provinces of the Anglican Communion in their joint concerns.[2]

Before this official announcement was made, Geoffrey Fisher, in a letter to Bishop Bayne, expanded upon the brief official announcement.

Only one other word: you mention your strong feeling that there ought to be a certain degree of looseness in the new post making it clear that this is not an English invention, nor merely an extension of my office. With that I wholly agree. I might have been guilty of describing it as a kind of auxiliary office to me: I really never meant that, but I did realize that I should be unloading many things on to you to my own great relief which at present I carry almost entirely on my own shoulders. But, of course, in this office you are entirely your own master, responsible to the Anglican Advisory Council on Missionary Strategy for any tasks that you take on at their request, and responsible to the Consultative Body of the Lambeth Conference for any assignments you take on at their request (which means in effect at my request): so there we are.[3]

The choice of Stephen Bayne was inspired. He made an immense success of the new office, and soon became a well-known figure both in this country and throughout the whole Anglican Communion, where he travelled very widely. 'His personality,' wrote the late Roger Lloyd, 'was exactly suited to the task he had accepted. Pleasant and easy in manner, he was most likeable, and he had the gift of bestowing on all others the ease he had himself in all manner of conversation. There was depth and often profundity in his speeches and his writing.' He was soon, for example, writing a regular column in the *Church Times*.

Pan-Anglican for Spring 1959 published a review of the Lambeth Conference of the previous year and contained the announcement that the next Anglican Congress would be held at Toronto in 1963. Before Fisher retired he made an historic journey to Jerusalem, Istanbul, and Rome. At Jerusalem, after going to the Church of the Holy Sepulchre, he visited the Orthodox Patriarch, the Latin Patriarch, and the Armenian Patriarch. Then on 29 November he arrived at Istanbul and greeted the Oecumenical Patriarch, the Armenian Patriarch, and the Apostolic Delegate. From there he proceeded to Rome, where on 2 December he visited the Pope – John XXIII, who had succeeded Pius

---

[2] Stephen F. Bayne, *An Anglican Turning Point*, p. 11.
[3] *An Anglican Turning Point*, p. 11.

XII in the year of the last Lambeth Conference, and was to be a notable reformer. Fisher recalled one interesting item in his informal talk with the Pope, how

at one point he said: 'I should like to read to you a passage from an address that I recently gave.' He read, in English, a passage which included a reference to 'the time when our separated brethren should return to the Mother Church.' I at once said: 'Your holiness, not *return*.' He looked puzzled and said, 'Not return? Why not?' I said: 'None of us can go backwards. We are each now running on parallel courses; we are looking forward, until, in God's time, our two courses approximate and meet.' He said, after a moment's pause, 'You are right.' From that moment, as far as I know, he and the Vatican never talked about our returning to a past situation, and looking backwards for our objective. That was, in fact, a very notable conversion.[4]

On 17 January 1961 the resignation of Archbishop Fisher was announced. The see of Canterbury was declared vacant from 31 May. Fisher thought that the time had come to lay down his burden. He felt he could not put himself wholeheartedly into certain things – like the Third Assembly of the World Council of Churches at New Delhi, due to take place in November of 1961. Then there was the Anglican Congress looming up in 1963. Bishop Henry Sherrill, Fisher's old friend, had retired after the Lambeth Conference of 1958, and had been succeeded by the Rt Rev. Arthur C. Lichtenberger, Bishop of Missouri, who was due to serve until 1970. In the event he died in the year 1968. Fisher felt he could not face Toronto 1963 without Sherrill. So at the age of 73 he resigned.

It was natural that Mr Macmillan should have chosen Michael Ramsey to succeed Fisher, though the move was opposed by the *Church of England Newspaper*. It was thought at the time that Fisher favoured the Bishop of Peterborough, Stopford, who had been the episcopal secretary of the 1958 Lambeth Conference. The name of Dr Coggan was also mentioned. In the end Coggan followed Ramsey to York, and eventually to Canterbury. Those who did not favour Ramsey's appointment presumably regarded him as too much of a High Churchman and a pure theologian. 'He was, in fact, the only serious runner' remarks Trevor Beeson in *The Church of England in Crisis*,

but there were questions in some minds (especially Fisher's) about his administrative skill and his vigour. His arrival on the national scene

---

[4] W. Purcell, *Fisher of Lambeth*, p. 283.

occasioned some surprise among the general public who found it difficult to believe that he was not older than the outgoing Primate and who wondered why the leadership of the national church in the 20th century had been entrusted to someone who appeared to have been resurrected from a distant ecclesiastical past. But television viewers quickly came to recognize in the new Archbishop a man of formidable intellect, simple faith, utter integrity and warm humanity – qualities not lightly to be dismissed in any public figure. As the years have passed, so he has grown in stature until he now has an unrivalled position in the life of the Church of England.[5]

Ramsey's appointment as the hundredth Archbishop of Canterbury was announced on 19 January 1961. His formal election took place at Canterbury on 5 June and the confirmation of the election at St Paul's Cathedral on 21 June. A short time later he returned to York for the marriage ceremony of the Duke of Kent and Katharine Worsley, the first royal marriage in York since that of Edward III in 1328. He was enthroned at Canterbury on 27 June. After his enthronement the first person he received in his study at Lambeth was the general secretary of the World Council of Churches, Dr W. A. Visser 't Hooft. The following morning he saw the Anglican Executive Officer, Stephen Bayne. Then began the preparations for the Third Assembly of the World Council of Churches at New Delhi in November. There he made his major address to the Assembly on the evening of the sixth day. 'Just as our mission is unity, holiness, truth, all three,' he declared,

so our scandal is the distortion of unity, holiness, truth, all three. . . . The world does not hear the call to holiness, and does not care for the truth in Christ. But the world has its own care for unity, albeit conceived in a secular way: longing for peace, it desires that men and nations should be joined to each other and the forces which separate them removed. And the world, caring thus for unity, is shocked when the Church fails to manifest it.

Ramsey received communion with about fifteen hundred other people at the first ever 'open' Eucharist conducted by Anglicans at a meeting of the World Council. While the meeting was still in progress some leaders praised it as 'the second Reformation' and 'the greatest gathering of Christians since the sixteenth-century Council of Trent', but Ramsey was more realistic: 'New Delhi is a symbol; a milestone on a journey, but also a signpost telling us to go on.' From this event Ramsey returned

[5] Op. cit., pp. 163–4.

to England to baptize the infant son of Princess Margaret, born while he was in India.[6]

In 1962 there began that ferment in the Church which was to mark the period of Ramsey's primacy. In the Church of England the theological dovecotes were caused to flutter by the publication of *Soundings* in that year, a work edited by Dr Alec Vidler, then Dean of King's College, Cambridge. In the following year the ferment reached a greater pitch with the publication by the S.C.M. of Dr John Robinson's *Honest to God*. The change that was coming about in the Church and the contrast to the primacy of Archbishop Fisher are well painted by Dr John Robinson in the 1969 edition of his book *On Being the Church in the World*.

> After the shaking of the foundations experienced in the forties it [the period of the fifties] was a time of reconstruction and renewal. Economically the Prime Minister could say at its close, 'You've never had it so good', ecclesiastically the Archbishop of Canterbury could report that the Church of England was 'in good heart'. Indeed, through Dr Fisher's primacy the assumption still held that the past would continue, basically as it had been, into the future. By tory reformist measures the Church of England could be refurbished for a flourishing and relevant future. New canons and new courts were created, revised lectionaries, catechisms and psalters rolled out. Commissions were appointed to re-order the Church's government, worship and pastoral machinery. The Church Commissioners prospered. Christian Stewardship caught on, ordinations crept up, and new theological colleges and Church training colleges were the order of the day. By 1960 the *Church of England Newspaper* was able to announce (and I remember the words because I quoted them in hope): 'A new Church of England is being born, a Church efficient, sophisticated and progressive, a Church with money enough to spare.' Indeed, I find that my first Confirmation sermon in 1959 contained the peroration: 'You are coming into active membership of the Church at a time when great things are afoot. I believe that in England we may be at a turning of the tide. Indeed, in Cambridge, where I have recently come from, I am convinced that the tide has already turned.'
>
> How wrong can one be? The tide was indeed imperceptibly on the turn. But 1960 was to represent the high-water mark not the low-water mark! From about 1961 onwards the vital statistics of organized religion in this country (and not only in this country) – for baptisms, confirmations, ordinands, conversions to Roman Catholicism, etc. – began to show a dramatic decline. Theologically, too, the climate rapidly changed.[7]

---

[6] He was later a choirboy at my own church of Milton, Oxfordshire.

[7] J. A. T. Robinson, *On Being the Church in the World*, pp. 8–9.

This period saw the growth of interest in the writings and theological viewpoint of Pierre Teilhard de Chardin, whose *The Phenomenon of Man* had come out in 1959. Another equally influential work was Dietrich Bonhoeffer's *Letters and Papers from Prison*, which was published in hardback in 1953, and then in paperback in 1959. Another part of the theological background was the assault on some of the presuppositions of the biblical theologians which came with James Barr's *The Semantics of Biblical Language*. In England the form-critical method in Gospel criticism was used with a vengeance by Dennis Nineham in his *Gospel of St Mark* published in 1963. Also in 1963 came Van Buren's *The Secular Meaning of the Gospel*, and Werner and Lotte Pelz's *God is No More*. In 1964 came Douglas Rhymes's *No New Morality*. In 1965 John Robinson wrote another book *The New Reformation*, Leslie Weatherhead wrote *The Christian Agnostic*, and James A. Pike, the American radical bishop, wrote *A Time for Christian Candour*. But more influential than this trio was Harvey Cox's *The Secular City*. Then in 1966 came the 'Death of God' movement,[8] while in 1967 came two radical works from Christian theologians on sex.[9]

The Church of Rome was in no less a ferment than the Church of England. Pope John had unexpectedly announced his calling of the Twenty-first Ecumenical Council on 25 January 1959 (when he had been Pope but ninety days). On 11 October 1962, after four years of preparation the Council opened. The first period of deliberations ended on 8 December 1962. Pope John's successor Pope Paul VI opened the second session on 29 September 1963 and it ended on 4 December. Then on 5 January 1964 Pope Paul visited and embraced Athenagoras, the Oecumenical Patriarch. The third session of the second Vatican Council took place from 14 September to 21 November 1964. The final session extended from 14 September to 8 December 1965. The Council's deliberations were watched over by observers from various other churches. The Church of England was represented by the Bishop of Ripon (Dr John Moorman) and Canon Pawley. From the years of

---

[8] See T. J. Altizer and William Hamilton, *Radical Theology and the Death of God* and Thomas W. Ogletree, *The 'Death of God' Controversy*. Note also the work of the Roman Catholic, Robert Adolfs, *The Grave of God*.

[9] Norman Pittenger, *Time for Consent. A Christian's Approach to Homosexuality*, and Leonard Hodgson, *Sex and Christian Education*. Pittenger's book has since been enlarged (1970).

the Council Dr Hans Küng emerged as one of the leading Roman Catholic reforming theologians.[10]

In the midst of Vatican II came the third Anglican Congress at Toronto from 13 to 23 August 1963. In preparation for it appeared the publication *The Church in the 60's*, edited by the Rev. P. C. Jefferson, editorial secretary in the Department of Religious Education in the Anglican Church of Canada. This had an article on the Congress by the Most Rev. Howard H. Clark, Archbishop of Rupert's Land and the Primate of Canada, who said that

> the Anglican Congress will in 1963 come to Canada, a young country which has grown, without revolution, from colony to nation; to a young church, still learning to use the great resources that, in Christ, it possesses; to Toronto, a bustling city, in appearance almost American, in population increasingly multi-racial, and yet the strongest center of Anglicanism in Canada.

Dr E. R. Fairweather wrote on the Anglican Congress at Minneapolis of 1954. In Part 2, on Frontiers of the Church, Dr R. H. L. Slater wrote on 'Reaching the non-Christian Faiths', and Dr D. R. G. Owen on 'Understanding the other Philosophies of Life'. Dr J. G. Rowe wrote on 'Accepting the Political Challenges' and Bishop W. R. Coleman (of Kootenay in the Anglican Church of Canada) on 'Confronting the Cultural Challenges'. Part 3 was on Facing the Frontiers. Here Dr Eric Jay, Principal of Montreal Diocesan Theological College, wrote on 'Mobilizing the Manpower' and Stephen Bayne on 'Organizing for Action'. The final two chapters were on 'The Anglican Communion' by Canon H. M. Waddams and (as he then had become) Lord Fisher of Lambeth.

Another pre-Congress publication was *Anglican Mosaic* edited by William E. Leidt, and with a foreword by Lakdasa J. de Mel, Bishop of Calcutta and Metropolitan of India. This volume was a survey of the Anglican Communion and did for the nineteen-sixties what Bishop Wand's *The Anglican Communion* had done in 1948. After an initial section on 'The Anglican Mosaic' by Bishop Stephen Bayne, there were sections on 'The Church in the New Nations of Africa', 'The Church in the Cradle of Religion', 'The Church in the South Pacific', 'The Church in the New World' and 'Where it all began' (an article on the Church in the British Isles by Dewi Morgan). Dewi Morgan also produced his own book in preparation for Toronto – *Agenda for Anglicans* (1963) with a

[10] In 1977 his most famous book, *On Being a Christian*, was published.

preface by Stephen Bayne – and Canon Howard A. Johnson wrote *Global Odyssey. Visiting the Anglican Churches.*

Pan-Anglican, published at Easter 1963 (the first number since Spring 1961), gave final details of the Congress. The general theme was to be 'The Church's Mission to the World'. Bishop Dean of Cariboo announced in an article that these sub-titles had been selected:

The Church's Mission to the World on the Religious Frontier
The Church's Mission to the World on the Political Frontier
The Church's Mission to the World on the Cultural Frontier
The Challenge of the Frontiers – Training for Action
The Challenge of the Frontiers – Organizing for Action
The Vocation of the Anglican Communion.

The many speakers and panellists were announced. These included Canon Max Warren, Archbishop Coggan, Bishop Sadiq of Nagpur, Archbishop MacInnes, Miss Janet Lacey, Mr (now Sir) John Lawrence, Bishop Wickham of Middleton, the Rev. Malcolm Boyd, Canon F. C. Synge, Dr Alan Richardson, Bishop Lakdasa de Mel, Canon Howard A. Johnson, Bishop Stopford, Dean Eric Abbott, Archbishop Simms, Canon H. M. Waddams, Bishop Roland Koh of Kuala Lumpur. Joost de Blank, Archbishop of Cape Town, was booked as preacher at the closing service. The Congress was to take place at the Royal York Hotel, the largest hotel in the Commonwealth, with 1,600 guest rooms and an assembly hall holding 2,200 people.

Before the Congress took place there were various gatherings for consultation at London, Ontario. One was a gathering of the primates and metropolitans of the Anglican Communion, with advisers, meeting in the Advisory Council on Missionary Strategy and the Lambeth Consultative Body. Out of this came an important document with the heading 'Mutual Responsibility and Interdependence in the Body of Christ', which was presented to the Congress by Dr Coggan, the Archbishop of York, on Saturday, 17 August, and 'stole the show'. The document outlined six objectives.

1 The undertaking of a comprehensive study of the needs and resources throughout the Anglican Communion.

2 Without waiting for the results of such a long-range study, we must ask each church to join in an immediate commitment to increased financial support.

3 We ask for a parallel commitment as to manpower.

4 We must continue and extend the whole process of inter-Anglican consultation.

5 Each church must radically study the form of its own obedience to mission and the needs it has to share in the single life and witness of the Church everywhere.

6 We must face maturely and without sentimentality the nature of the Anglican Communion, and the implications for us all of the one Lord whose single mission holds us together in one Body.

Archbishop Ramsey went on to speak about the document and its authority, which was 'technically none, morally considerable'. He ended with these words:

What is immediately going to happen is this, that if all of you who are here, laity and priests and bishops and primates of the Anglican churches, find this document and its convictions coming home to your mind and conscience, to your judgment as well as your heart – and again I ask, 'If it doesn't, what does?' because that is really the perplexity – then you are going home not just to report on what a jolly time we all had (utterly true though that is), but to be ambassadors within your own church of a new way of looking at your church's past and privileges. It means burdens. It means the bearing of one another's burdens, so fulfilling the law of Christ. But it isn't just burden, and it isn't just law. 'None of us liveth to himself, and no man dieth to himself' is the very essence of spiritual health. It is a victorious way, it is Christ's own way, and what is so terrible, there is no other way.[11]

There followed speeches from Bishop David M. Goto of Tokyo, Richard Roseveare of Accra, Bishop Sadiq of Nagpur, and then Stephen Bayne, the Executive Officer.

Thus out of Toronto came the initials MRI which were to sound round the Anglican Communion for years to come. The Congress programme became dwarfed by this document. There were some, like Canon Max Warren, who felt that this was wrong and called it 'the major tactical mistake of the Congress'. However, nothing could alter the fact that a great call for the reformation and rebirth of Anglicanism had been made in this document.

The *Proceedings* of the Toronto Congress were edited by Dr Eugene Fairweather, who wrote an introduction in which he said:

It may be instructive to compare the Congress just ended with the Minneapolis Congress of 1954. Many critics have already remarked that on the whole the speeches at Minneapolis were better than the speeches at Toronto. In a way, they are quite right. The Congress of 1954 was assigned

---

[11] *Report of Proceedings*, p. 125.

the task of expounding an august tradition – the theological and liturgical tradition of the Church of England and the Anglican Communion – and those who spoke to its great theme were in a position to exploit their scholarly resources to the full. The Congress of 1963 went on to ask what the Anglican Communion must do in the present and the future and how it must go about doing it, and its leaders were compelled by their terms of reference to speak tentatively rather than magisterially, to explore possible lines of action rather than to interpret received truths. As a result, much of what they had to say naturally seems incomplete and untidy, long on questions and short on answers. The enduring value of the Toronto Congress will therefore be determined primarily by the readiness of Anglicans, first to think their way into the problems which the Congress felt so deeply, and then to work together towards sound solutions. This assessment applies (I think) to the way in which each of the great issues that we have been considering was handled at Toronto. . . .

The Congress was a moving, disturbing, exciting experience, and even the least sensitive could hardly remain untouched by what he saw and heard. But it was an unfinished enterprise, a summons to further thinking and planning, a call to the churches to take new and daring steps towards the fulfilment of the Christian mission to the world. That means that the most important chapters in the story of Toronto have still to be written – by us.

For the next few years the idea of 'Mutual Responsibility and Interdependence in the Body of Christ' was taken up on all sides in the Anglican Communion.[12]

Some of the Toronto delegates had already been present in Canada at another Conference, the World Council of Churches, Faith and Order Conference at Montreal, which was the successor of Lausanne 1927, Edinburgh 1937, and Lund 1952. This had been held from 12 to 26 July.[13]

In the Church of England Barry Till, who had recently returned from the deanery of Hong Kong, was commissioned to make known the theme of MRI. In November 1964 his little book *Change and Exchange: Mutual Reponsibility and the Church of England* was published by the Church Information Office, with a foreword by Sir Kenneth Grubb, Chairman of the Missionary and Ecumenical Council of the Church Assembly. In 1965 came the 'No Small Change' Campaign which occupied the attention of many parishes in the Church of England during Lent. In the Fall of 1965 *Pan-Anglican* published its

---

[12] See Stephen Bayne, *Mutual Responsibility and Interdependence in the Body of Christ* (1963).

[13] See P. C. Rodger and L. Vischer, *The Fourth World Council on Faith and Order*.

MRI number with a leading article by the new Anglican Executive Officer, Ralph Dean, Bishop of Cariboo (unlike Stephen Bayne, he did not resign his see), and another by the Deputy Executive Officer, the Rev. W. W. Jackson. There were various other articles on MRI and how it was working in various parts of the world. The Rev. D. M. Paton, the Regional Officer for the British Isles, wrote on MRI and the Church of England and said, 'No Small Change was, as these things go, a considerable success. Some think it penetrated more deeply into the Church of England than anything has done for several decades.' The theme was continued in the Church of England with booklets like Mutual Responsibility. Questions and Answers, edited by John Wilkinson[14] and Douglas Webster's Mutual Irresponsibility. In the same year Barry Till edited another book, Changing Frontiers in the Mission of the Church, which dealt with Mutual Responsibility in various parts of the word and a number of representative Anglicans contributed.

As the MRI campaign went on everyone was considering the question of the union of the Anglican and Methodist Church. In February 1963 there was published Conversations between the Church of England and the Methodist Church. This was a Report to the Archbishops of Canterbury and York and the Conference of the Methodist Church by certain Anglicans under the Chairmanship of Bishop H. J. Carpenter of Oxford and certain Methodists under the chairmanship of Dr Harold Roberts, Principal of Richmond College, Surrey, who had been President of the Methodist Conference in 1957. The Anglicans included Bishop Martin of Liverpool, Bishop Allison of Winchester, and Bishop Taylor of Sheffield. Bishop Bell had been a member of the commission but died in 1958. Dean Norman Sykes had also been a member, but he died in 1961. The Report was not signed by all the Methodists, for C. K. Barrett, T. E. Jessop, T. D. Meadley, and Norman H. Snaith dissented from it. The main proposals of this 1963 Report were these:

That there should be union in two stages. Stage one would be intercommunion, followed by a period of increasing co-operation between the two distinct Churches. Then, in stage two, union with one another in one Church. This would be brought about by:

a A Service of Reconciliation which would inaugurate stage one and

---

[14] This contained essays by Alan Richardson, H. G. G. Herklots, Douglas Webster, C. K. Sansbury, G. F. Allen, John Lawrence, A. M. Allchin, J. C. Vockler, R. W. Woods, and F. D. Coggan.

would reconcile the two Churches and unify their ministries, as each prayed that God would give to the other the distinctive characteristics which it believed it had received from Him.

b The acceptance by the Methodist Church of the ministry of bishops in continuity with the historic episcopate and of the future invariable practice of episcopal ordination of its ministers.

c The provision of means for growing together during stage one.

The four who disagreed with the scheme felt that too much store was set by tradition, and too much claimed for the historic episcopate. To them the laying on of hands in the Service of Reconciliation looked suspiciously like ordination. They did not like the use of the term 'priest'. Also they opposed the denial of lay administration of Holy Communion and were afraid of the absorption of Methodism by the Church of England.

After long discussions the Convocations of Canterbury and York and the Methodist Conference set their general approval on the scheme. However, they realized there were questions which had to be clarified. So a new commission was set up to revise the Service of Reconciliation and to prepare forms of service to be used at ordinations in both Churches.

In 1967 came the next Report, *Towards Reconciliation.* This provoked criticism from Archbishop Lord Fisher of Lambeth in his pamphlet *Covenant and Reconciliation. A Critical Examination.* Evangelical Churchmen had already voiced their criticisms in *The Church of England and the Methodist Church* edited by James Packer and published in 1963.

In 1968, the year of the next Lambeth Conference came further Reports, *Anglican-Methodist Unity. 1 The Ordinal,* and *Anglican-Methodist Unity. 2 The Scheme.* Again there was considerable opposition, notably from two High Churchmen, Margaret Deanesly and Geoffrey G. Willis who wrote *Anglican-Methodist Unity. Some Considerations Historical and Liturgical.* This then was a very important background to the Lambeth Conference of 1968.

Another episode in the period between the Ninth and the Tenth Lambeth Conferences was the famous Paul report of 1964. This was the document *The Deployment and Payment of the Clergy* by Leslie Paul, commissioned by the Central Advisory Council of the Ministry. It had a great deal to say about the unequal distribution of clergy in the dioceses and expressed a desire for the abolition of the freehold. At length a commission was set up to take into consideration the Paul report and make recommendations as to how much of it should be implemented. So there was issued from the Church Information Office in 1967 *Partners in Ministry*. Gerald Ellison, the Bishop of Chester, was critical of this document and published in 1968 *Progress in Ministry*. His pamphlet had a commendation by the Bishops of Ely, Exeter, Leicester, Peterborough, Sheffield, Winchester, and Taunton, all of whom supported moderate, rather than radical, reform.

Yet another issue confronting the Church was the question of the ordination of women. On this subject an Archbishops' Commission reported in 1966. Its chairman was Bishop Ellison of Chester and two canons of Christ Church were upon it – Henry Chadwick and V. A. Demant – and Dean Richardson of York. Demant led the opposition to the ordination of women; Miss Kay M. Baxter gave the case for their ordination; Alan Richardson expressed the view that 'there are no sound theological reasons why women should not be ordained to the priesthood, but that it is nevertheless inexpedient to take such a step at the present time.' In the next year, 1967, a working party, set up by A.C.C.M. and the Council for Women's Work in the Church, considered the question and reported in 1968. This was chaired by Michael Hollis, Assistant Bishop of St Edmundsbury.

The sixties was also a period of considerable liturgical renewal. The year 1966 saw the publication of *Alternative Services. First Series* and *Alternative Services. Second Series*. The first series was largely based on the 1928 Prayer Book. The second series was the work of the Church of England Liturgical Commission. By the time that the Lambeth Conference of 1968 took place a great number of English parish churches were using the Series 2 Service of Holy Communion for many of their celebrations of the sacrament.

We have seen how Archbishop Fisher visited Pope John just before his retirement. Things did not stand still during the archiepiscopate of Michael Ramsey. In 1963, the year of Toronto, the former Archbishop of Milan, Giovanni Batista Cardinal Montini came to the papal throne as Paul VI. It was in the very next year that Lambeth received its first visit from a cardinal since 1558. The German born Jesuit Augustus Cardinal Bea, an active octogenerian, who, at Pope John's prompting, had founded the Vatican Secretariat for Christian Unity, came and met Archbishop Ramsey on an official visit to Lambeth. In March 1966 the Archbishop of Canterbury visited the Vatican for a three-day visit, in spite of some Protestant objections. The climax was a service at St Paul's Outside the Walls when Pope Paul, accompanying Archbishop

Ramsey to the door of the basilica, removed his pontifical ring and placed it on Canterbury's finger. At the end of their meeting the two leaders announced their intention of inaugurating between the Roman Catholic Church and the Anglican Communion a serious dialogue which, founded on the gospels and on the ancient common traditions may lead to that unity in truth for which Christ prayed. In January 1967 a Joint Preparatory Commission met at Gazzada, near Milan. The outcome was a series of recommendations which reshaped existing practices of collaboration and discussion between the two Churches. The Joint Preparatory Commission met again in September 1967 at Huntercombe Manor in England. Their discussions were more doctrinal and centred upon the authority of the Bible. In due course a permanent Joint Commission was set up.[15]

Talks were also going on in the sixties between the Anglicans and Presbyterians in the United Kingdom. There were four panels, one from the Church of England, one from the Church of Scotland, one from the Presbyterian Church of England, and one from the Episcopal Church of Scotland. From these discussions there emerged a Report in 1966, out of which came a new chapter, since the two Churches in Scotland and the two Churches in England were encouraged to engage in bilateral talks. In 1968 came the Report *Relations between the Church of England and the Presbyterian Church of England*. This expressed a hope that the plan for union between the English Presbyterian Church and the Congregational Church would come about and the 'Reformed Church' would result and that the Anglican–Methodist scheme would come into existence. They went on, 'We think that it would be absurd and even scandalous to allow the "Reformed Church" to settle down into a separate life while the Church of England and the Methodist Church for their part proceeded on their own towards Stage Two of Organic Unity.'

From all this one can readily see what an active period the years between 1958 and 1968 were. This decade saw some important books published on Anglicanism and Anglican history. In 1961 the late Canon H. G. G. Herklots published *Frontiers of the Church. The Making of the Anglican Communion*; in 1966 he wrote *The Church of England and the American Episcopal Church. A Study in Relationships*, with a preface by Bishop Stephen Bayne. In 1965 had appeared his popular short study, *Some Heroes of the Anglican*

[15] See Alan C. Clark and Colin Davey, *Anglican/Roman Dialogue. The Work of the Preparatory Commission*.

Communion. 1965 also saw the publication of a provocative book by Professor A. T. Hanson, *Beyond Anglicanism.* A study of *The Anglican Church in South Africa* was produced by Professor Peter Hinchliff in 1963 and in the same year Archbishop Philip Carrington published *The Anglican Church in Canada. A History.* There also came out that year from the pen of Bishop H. R. McAdoo *The Spirit of Anglicanism, A Survey of Anglican Theological Method in the Seventeenth Century.*[16] Canon Roger Lloyd brought out in 1966 a revision of his earlier two volumes *The Church of England in the Twentieth Century,* and added to them a section on the Church from 1939 to 1965. Marion Lochhead wrote on *Episcopal Scotland in the 19th Century.* A much less known book is *Anglicanism in Ecumenical Perspective* by William H. van de Pol, published in 1965 by Duquesne University Press, Pittsburgh. Its author was born in 1897, baptized into the Dutch Reformed Church, and worshipped in the Lutheran Church until 1919, when he was confirmed as an Anglican. In 1940, after twenty years as an Anglican, he was received into the Church of Rome and became a priest in 1944.

[16] His previous book was *The Structure of Caroline Moral Theology.*

14

THE 'NEW STYLE'
CONFERENCE OF 1968

Some wondered whether the next Conference would be brought
forward to take place in the centenary year 1967. This was considered
but rejected. It was held in 1968 – very much a revolutionary year. The
theological revolution was still going on. People were studying John
Robinson's latest (and perhaps his best) book, *Exploration into God*
(1967). But in the fog and uncertainty a more positive note was uttered
by John Macquarrie, whose *Principles of Christian Theology*,
published by the S.C.M. Press in 1966, was now being widely read.[1] A
ferment was going on in the theological colleges as a committee under
Sir Bernard de Bunsen considered their reorganization. The whole
business of pastoral reorganization was still subject to debate, the fruits
of which were to be seen in the Pastoral Measure of 1968. The question
of synodical government was also very much in the air since the
publication of the report *Synodical Government in the Church of
England* (1966) and this led to the Synodical Government Measure of
1969. Another much discussed element of reorganization was that of
diocesan boundaries: the report *Diocesan Boundaries* had come out in
1967.

In 1968 there were a number of new episcopal personalities. There
was Ian Ramsey, who had gone straight from being Nolloth Professor
of the Philosophy of Religion at Oxford to the Prince-Bishopric of
Durham, and whom many expected to succeed Michael Ramsey as
Archbishop of Canterbury.[2] There was Cyril Eastaugh, Bishop of
Peterborough, a leader of the rather depleted Anglo-Catholic party.
Leslie Brown, Archbishop of Uganda at the time of the Toronto
Congress, was now Bishop of St Edmundsbury and Ipswich. George
Reindorp, made Bishop of Guildford in 1961, had not yet participated
in a Lambeth Conference. The notorious Bishop Robinson of
Woolwich also had not yet been heard at a Lambeth Conference.

[1] A revised edition of this has just been published (1977).
[2] Cf. Michael De-la-Noy, *A Day in the Life of God*, p. 89.

Donald Coggan, the Archbishop of York, had been Bishop of Bradford in 1958. Oliver Tomkins had become Bishop of Bristol, Mervyn Stockwood Bishop of Southwark, John Moorman Bishop of Ripon, and Launcelot Fleming Bishop of Norwich in the year after the last Lambeth Conference. A notable English suffragan, who like John Moorman was a leader in the Anglo-Catholic party, was Graham D. Leonard, Bishop of Willesden.[3] At Liverpool the new bishop since 1966 was the Evangelical Stuart Blanch.[4] In Wales the new Archbishop was Glyn Simon, Bishop of Llandaff, a New Testament scholar. K. M. Carey was Bishop of Edinburgh. In Ireland the Archbishop of Armagh was James McCann and George Simms Archbishop of Dublin. In the United States the Presiding Bishop was John E. Hines, as Arthur Lichtenberger had been obliged to retire, stricken by Parkinson's disease, in 1964. (Lichtenberger was to die just after the 1968 Conference.) The Primate of All Canada was Howard H. Clark, who had made a name for himself at Toronto. A notable and controversial Canadian bishop was George N. Luxton, Bishop of Huron, who like the late Dr John Heuss, Rector of New York City's Trinity Parish, wished the Lambeth Conference to become an Anglican Council, carefully controlling the Anglican Communion. In India, the Metropolitan was the Bishop of Calcutta, H. Lakdasa J. de Mel, who had come to the fore at Toronto. The Primate of Australia was P. N. W. Strong, Archbishop of Brisbane, who in 1958 had been Bishop of New Guinea. In New Zealand the new Primate (in place of Owen) was Norman A. Lesser, Bishop of Waiapu, who, though he had been a bishop since 1947, had not been to a Lambeth Conference before. In South Africa, Joost de Blank was no longer at Cape Town; he had returned to England through ill-health and was now a canon of Westminster. His successor was Robert S. Taylor. E. G. Knapp-Fisher, a former Principal of Cuddesdon, was Bishop of Pretoria.[5] Oliver Green-Wilkinson was Archbishop of Central Africa and Campbell MacInnes, Archbishop in Jerusalem. Stanley Eley, once chaplain to Archbishop Fisher at Lambeth, was now Bishop of Gibraltar. Henry R. McAdoo, the author of *The Spirit of Anglicanism*, was Bishop of Ossory. Stephen F. Bayne was now Vice-Chairman of the Executive Council of PECUSA and Director of the Overseas Department. James Pike, the notorious American liberal bishop, author of *A Time for Christian Candour*

---

[3] Now Bishop of Truro.
[4] Now Archbishop of York.
[5] He has now been appointed a canon of Westminster.

(1964), had ceased to be Bishop of California in 1966. George Appleton, an authority on non-Christian religions, who has recently retired as Archbishop in Jerusalem, was in 1968 Archbishop of Perth in Australia.[6]

The year 1968 besides being a Lambeth year was also the year of an Assembly of the World Council of Churches. The first assembly had been held at Amsterdam following the 1948 Lambeth Conference; the second had been at Evanston, Illinois, in 1954, following after the Anglican Congress at Minneapolis. The third General Assembly was at New Delhi in 1961 – one of the first events which Michael Ramsey attended as Archbishop of Canterbury. The Lambeth Conference was to be preceded by the Fourth World Assembly at Uppsala, in Sweden, in July. The theme of the Uppsala Assembly was 'Behold, I make all things new'. The words 'renewal' and 'revolution' were the key words. Archbishop Ramsey attended as one of the six presidents; other bishops from Great Britain and Ireland were Archbishop Simms, Bishop Oliver Tomkins of Bristol, Bishop Blanch of Liverpool, and Bishop Williams of Bangor. This World Assembly met with a background of controversial issues like Nigeria–Biafra, Vietnam, and Czecho-slovakia's fight for freedom from the Iron Curtain tyranny. One of the advances made at Uppsala was the inclusion of nine Roman Catholic theologians among the 135 members of the Faith and Order Commission of the World Council – even though the Roman Catholic Church was not a member of the parent Council. The Pope and Cardinal Bea both sent a message to Uppsala, as also did the Oecumenical Patriarch, Athenagoras I of Constantinople. Among those who addressed the Assembly on 'Rich and Poor Nations' was Kenneth Kaunda of Zambia, and the Roman Catholic laywoman, Barbara Ward, Professor of International Economic Development at Columbia University, New York. Mr James Baldwin, the American negro writer, spoke on 'White Racism or World Community'. In its message to the world the Uppsala Assembly made these four points:

1 All men have become neighbours to one another. Torn by our diversities and tensions, we do not yet know how to live together. *But God makes new.*

2 Scientific discoveries and the revolutionary movements of our time open new potentialities and perils for men. Man is lost because he does not know who he is. *But God makes new.*

---

[6] George Appleton now lives at Ginge, near Wantage, not far from where these words are written.

3 The ever-widening gap between the rich and the poor, fostered by armament expenditure, is the crucial point of decision today. *But God makes new.*

4 These commitments demand the worship, discipline, and mutual correction of a world-wide community. In the World Council of Churches and its regional, national and local counterparts only the beginning of this community has been given to us. *But God makes new.*

Archbishop Michael Ramsey gave a press conference at Uppsala and it was chiefly significant for some references to a recent statement by Pope Paul strongly defending papal infallibility[7] and the immaculate conception. Dr Ramsey remarked,

> After all the emphasis by the Vatican Council on collegiality, I regretted that there was no reference to collegiality in the reference to infallibility.
>
> Also since the Vatican Council began to distinguish between the more fundamental dogmas and the less fundamental ones, I was surprised that particular Roman Catholic dogmas, like the Immaculate Conception and the papal infallibility, were inserted along with the tenets of the Nicene Creed.

The Archbishop returned from Uppsala to face immediately the Lambeth Conference. Preparation for this had been thorough. Preparatory papers had been written by a number of 'consultants' who were to take part in the Conference (though they were not bishops) and others. (A selection from these papers was published after the Conference in 1969 by the S.P.C.K.) Here then is the programme:

Section I The Renewal of the Church in Faith
Chairman: The Archbishop of Rupert's Land (The Most Rev. Howard Clark)

   a The Language of Faith
     1 The Nature of Theological Language
       Chairman: The Bishop of Michigan (Rt Rev. R. S. Emrich)[8]
       Preparatory Paper by Professor John Macquarrie
     2 The Debate about God
       Chairman: The Bishop of Saskatoon (Rt Rev. S. C. Street)
       Preparatory Paper: The Rev. David Jenkins

---

[7] The *Church Times*, Friday, 12 July 1968, printed the phrase 'paper infallibility' for papal infallibility!

[8] In the event the chairman was Bishop K. C. Evans of Ontario. Bishop Emrich was not present at the Conference.

3 The Finality of Christ
      Chairman: The Bishop of St Edmundsbury and Ipswich (Rt Rev.
      L. W. Brown)
      Preparatory Paper: Professor Henry Chadwick
4 Dialogue with other Faiths
      Chairman: The Archbishop of Perth (Most Rev. George Appleton)
      Preparatory Paper: Canon A. K. Cragg
5 The Varieties of Unbelief
      Chairman: The Bishop of Masasi (Rt Rev. Trevor Huddleston)
      Preparatory Paper: Dr Charles C. West
6 Confessing the Faith Today
      Chairman: The Bishop of Ossory, Ferns, and Leighlin (Rt Rev. H.
      R. McAdoo)
      Preparatory Paper: The Rev. David Edwards
b The Experience of Faith
7 The Psychology of Faith
      Chairman: The Bishop of Edinburgh (Rt Rev. K. M. Carey)
      Preparatory Paper: The Rev. Owen Brandon
8 Faith and Society
      Chairman: The Presiding Bishop of PECUSA (Rt Rev. J. H.
      Hines)[9]
      Preparatory Paper: Dr D. Kitagawa
9 Spirituality and Faith
      Chairman: The Bishop of Barking (Rt Rev. W. F. P. Chadwick)
      Preparatory Paper: The Rev. A. M. Allchin
10 Faith and Culture
      Chairman: The Bishop of Norwich (Rt Rev. W. L. S. Fleming)
      Preparatory Paper: Dr F. W. Dillistone
c The Faith and Secular Society
11 Christian Appraisal of the Secular Society
      Chairman: The Bishop of Ottawa (Rt Rev. E. S. Reed)
      Preparatory Paper: Dr D. L. Munby
12 International Morality Today
      Chairman: The Bishop of Chichester (Rt Rev. R. P. Wilson)
      Preparatory Paper: Sir Kenneth Grubb
13 The Technological Society.
      Chairman: The Bishop of Middleton (Rt Rev. E. R. Wickham)
      Preparatory Paper: Canon R. S. O. Stevens
14 Urbanization and the Metropolis
      Chairman: The Bishop of New York (Rt Rev. H. W. B.
      Donegan)[10]
      Preparatory Paper: The Rev. Gibson Winter.

[9] In the event the Bishop of Auckland, the Rt Rev. E. A. Gowing, became chairman.
[10] In the event the Bishop of Newcastle (N.S.W.), the Rt Rev. J. A. G. Housden, acted
as chairman.

Section II. The Renewal of the Church in Ministry

Chairman: The Archbishop of York

a The Ministry of the Laity
   15 Laymen in Mission
      Chairman: The Bishop of Coventry (Rt Rev. C. K. N. Bardsley)
      Preparatory Paper: Canon Douglas Webster
   16 Laymen in Society
      Chairman: The Bishop of Natal (Rt Rev. T. G. V. Inman)
      Preparatory Paper: Miss E. Molly Batten
   17 Laymen in Ministry
      Chairman: The Bishop of Southwark (Rt Rev. A. M. Stockwood)
      Preparatory Paper: Mr J. Mark
b Forms of Ordained Ministry
   18 The Priesthood
      Chairman: The Bishop of Pretoria (Rt Rev. E. S. Knapp-Fisher)
      Preparatory Paper: The Rev. J. Leslie Houlden
   19 Voluntary and Part-time Ministries
      Chairman: The Bishop of Barrackpore (Rt Rev. R. W. Bryan)
      Preparatory Paper: Canon Eric James
   20 The Diaconate
      Chairman: The Bishop of Nassau and the Bahamas (Rt Rev. B. Markham)
      Preparatory Paper: The Bishop of St Andrews (Rt Rev. J. Howe)
   21 Women and the Priesthood.
      Chairman: The Bishop of Nova Scotia (Rt Rev. W. W. Davis)
      Preparatory Paper: Dr Alan Richardson
c The Episcopate
   22 The Nature of the Anglican Episcopate
      Chairman: The Bishop of Lagos (Rt Rev. S. I. Kale)
      Preparatory Paper: Canon R. P. C. Hanson (who later became Bishop of Clogher)
   23 See III*b* below
   24 Oversight and Discipline
      Chairman: The Bishop of Huron (Rt Rev. George N. Luxton)[11]

Section III. The Renewal of the Church in Unity

Chairman: The Metropolitan of India

a The Pattern of Unity
   25 Christian Unity and Human Unity
      Chairman: The Bishop of California (Rt Rev. G. K. Myers)
      Preparatory Paper: Professor C. F. D. Moule of Cambridge

---

[11] In the event Bishop Gresford Jones of St Albans acted as chairman.

26 Principles of Union
        Chairman: The Bishop of Bristol (Rt Rev. O. S. Tomkins)
        Preparatory Paper: The Archbishop of Canterbury
27 Intercommunion in a Divided Church
        Chairman: The Bishop of Dunedin (Rt Rev. A. H. Johnston)
b A Review of Schemes
28 Current Schemes
        Chairman: The Bishop of Oxford (Rt Rev. H. J. Carpenter)
29 Relations with the Roman Catholic Church
        Chairman: The Bishop of Ripon (Rt Rev. J. R. H. Moorman)
23 The Papacy and the Episcopate
        Chairman: The Bishop of Milwaukee (Rt Rev. D. H. V. Hallock)
30 Relations with the Eastern Orthodox Church
        Chairman: The Bishop of Western New York (Rt Rev. L. L. Scaife)
        Preparatory Paper: Dr Nikos Nissiotis
c The Wider Episcopal Fellowship
31a Inter-Anglican Structures
        Chairman: The Archbishop of Cape Town (Rt Rev. R. S. Taylor)
        Preparatory Paper: The Bishop of Cariboo
31b The Role of the Anglican Communion in the Families of Christendom
        Chairman: The Bishop of South Dakota (Rt Rev. C. H. Gesner)[12]
        Preparatory Paper: Dr D. T. Niles
32 The Positive Idea of a Wider Episcopal Fellowship
        Chairman: The Bishop of Connecticut (Rt Rev. W. H. Gray)
        Preparatory Paper: Canon David Paton

It can be seen immediately from this list, that, though there were but three main topics, The Renewal of the Church in Faith, in Ministry, and in Unity, there were no less than thirty-three committees. This large number was the idea of the planning or steering committee which consisted of Archbishop Simms, Bishop Stopford of London, Bishop Mortimer of Exeter, Bishop Eley of Gibraltar, and Bishop Stephen Bayne, the Vice-President of the Executive Council of PECUSA (as he was now) and Bishop Ralph Dean of Cariboo, who was the Anglican Executive Officer and also the episcopal secretary for the Conference – he was in fact the first bishop from outside England to be the episcopal secretary. The large number of committees was part of the new look which the Archbishop of Canterbury encouraged the committee to give to the Lambeth Conference of 1968. Ralph Dean felt that the idea was completely justified. 'In little groups of fifteen or so, each bishop had a chance to speak at this level, even if some, with becoming modesty, refrained from speaking at plenary sessions.'[13]

[12] In the event the chairman was Bishop G. E. Gordon of Sodor and Man.
[13] *Pan-Anglican*, Fall, 1968, p. 9.

Another innovation was that of having consultants and observers. There were no less than twenty-four consultants: the Rev. A. M. Allchin, then Librarian at Pusey House; Dr P. B. Anderson, consultant in PECUSA on co-operation with Eastern churches; Miss Molly Batten, Research Officer of the Board for Social Responsibility; Archdeacon Edward Carpenter of Westminster; Professor Henry Chadwick; Canon A. K. Cragg; the Rev. H. L. J. Daniel, Presbyter of the South Indian Church; Dr P. Day, Ecumenical Officer of the Executive Council of PECUSA; Professor E. R. Fairweather of Trinity College, Toronto; Canon John Findlow, the Archbishop of Canterbury's representative at the Holy See; the Rev. W. Fletcher, of the Centre de Recherches et Etudes at Geneva; the Rev. E. M. B. Green, of the London College of Divinity; the Rev. Martin Jarrett-Kerr, the Mirfield father; the Rev. David Jenkins, Chaplain of Queen's College, Oxford, author of the Bampton Lectures, *The Glory of Man*; the Rev. John Macquarrie, author of *Principles of Christian Theology* and Professor at Union Theological Seminary; the Rev. John Mbiti, Lecturer at Makerere University College, Uganda; Canon Basil Moss of A.C.C.M.; the Rev. Dennis Nineham, Regius Professor of Divinity at Cambridge; Canon David Paton, Secretary of the Missionary and Ecumenical Council of the Church Assembly (MECCA), a position from which he was shortly to retire; the Rev. C. Powles, a member of the external relations committee of the National Council of the Nippon Sei Ko Kai; the Rev. H. E. Root, Professor of Theology at Southampton and an observer at Vatican II; Canon John Satterthwaite, general secretary of the Council on Foreign Relations and the Archbishop of Canterbury's Commission on Roman Catholic Relations; Canon John Taylor, general secretary of the Church Missionary Society;[14] Canon Douglas Webster, Professor of Missions at Selly Oak College.

In addition to the consultants there were also a large number of observers (an idea filched from Vatican II). These churches sent observers – the Armenian Church, the Assemblies of God, the Baptist World Alliance (the Rev. Dr Ernest A. Payne), the Coptic Church, the Evangelical Church in Germany (Bishop Hanns Lilje), the International Congregational Council (the Rev. Dr Norman Goodall and the Rev. John Huxtable), the Lusitanian Church (the Rt Rev. Dr Luis C. R. Pereira), the Lutheran World Federation (Dr Einar Molland, author of *Christendom*), the Mar Thoma Church, the Old Catholic Church, the

[14] Now Bishop of Winchester.

Orthodox Church (representatives from Constantinople, Alexandria, Jerusalem, Moscow, Serbia, Rumania, Bulgaria, Cyprus (Bishop Kallinikos of Amathus), the Orthodox Church of France and Western Europe, and the Russian Orthodox Church in Exile), the Philippine Independent Catholic Church, the Religious Society of Friends, the Roman Catholic Church (Bishop Christopher Butler, Father John Coventry, and Father Josef A. Dessain), the Salvation Army (Brigadier William G. Brown), the Spanish Reformed Episcopal Church (the Rt Rev. Ramon Taibo), the Syrian Orthodox Church, the World Convention of Churches of Christ, the World Council of Churches (Dr Eugene Carson Blake, Dr Nikos A. Nissiotis), the World Methodist Council (the Rev. A. Raymond George and Dr Harold Roberts), and the World Presbyterian Alliance. Invitations were given to some other churches from which observers were not sent – The Church of the East (Assyrian), the Ethiopian Church, the Orthodox Patriarchates of Antioch and Georgia, and the Church of Greece.

The summoning of large number of observers was as happy an event as the bringing in of the Anglican consultants. Bishop Dean wrote afterwards in *Pan-Anglican*, Fall, 1968,

The idea of having Consultants and Observers proved to be a huge success. The twenty-five Consultants found themselves in great demand at the meetings of Sections and Sub-Committees, as did the sixty or so Observers from other Churches, who did much more than merely observe, and gladly accepted the invitation to participate in the discussion and the debates at every level. It is probably true to say, in fact, that the level of speeches in plenary sessions from the Consultants was higher than that of the episcopal speeches, but that is no criticism of the bishops. The Consultants, after all, were specially chosen for their expertise – which the Observers also manifested – while the bishop is, and ought to be, a general practitioner.

Yet another innovation at the 1968 Conference was a substantial volume entitled *Lambeth Conference 1968. Preparatory Information*, published by the S.P.C.K., a most valuable piece of work, produced under the direction of Bishop Ralph Dean. There were full statistics on the Anglican Communion; then a chapter on liturgical revision since 1958 was followed by a long section (a formidable undertaking) giving 'Statements of Previous Conferences on Matters on the Agenda'. The last section was a considerable one on 'Christian Unity and the Anglican Communion'.

A more ephemeral pre-Lambeth production was the slim booklet of twenty-four pages, *Lambeth '68*, the work of the Archbishop of Canterbury's press officer, Michael De-la-Noy, which featured a cover showing the Bishop of Masasi, Trevor Huddleston, in his shirt sleeves, surrounded by black children, a picture unrelated to the Conference. Many were offended by the caricature pictures of bishops on each page – two were rather portly ones with umbrellas – and by the list of 'Places to Eat', which seemed to be in rather a high price range and included Claridges. In *The Times*, the Provost of Southwell wrote, 'We shall not support this scale for the expenses of our episcopate'. But a lady from Nottinghamshire replied, 'I defend the right of our bishops to have a slap-up meal if they want to. Even our Lord did not disdain a feast occasionally.' Michael De-la-Noy says something about the brochure in his book *A Day in the Life of God* (1971):

In view of the poverty in which some of the bishops, particularly those from Africa and the Middle East, are accustomed to work, and the question of world poverty in general with which the Conference was due to concern itself, it was considered by some people that the inclusion of the list of restaurants was insensitive, a point of view I can certainly understand; and in view of the righteous indignation to which I should have realised the brochure would give rise I certainly believe now that to have published the list of restaurants was bad P.R. In defence, it was said by others that this particular entry was symptomatic of the tensions within Christianity, focused in the fact that plenty of wealthy American bishops would most certainly be eating out in the West End, and that it was hypocritical to pretend otherwise. . . .

The Archbishop had no comment to make on the brochure until he began to receive a few private complaints. Then he said he wanted the offending page deleted in some way or other. I pointed out that the brochure was already printed and that to start re-designing it or obliterating an entry once it had been seen by the press would only cause additional publicity and comment. He accepted this advice, but said that if the brochure came under attack in Conference he might have to denounce it. I asked him not to do anything so rash; everyone knew I had been the editor, and I should be asked what it felt like to be denounced in public by my boss. I pointed out that this could only result in embarrassment for both of us. The Archbishop saw the point, and kept quiet. Not so the Archbishop of York, who went on the wireless to call the brochure a major P.R. blunder. Sure enough, the next morning I was telephoned by *The Evening News*, who wanted to know what it felt like to be denounced by Dr Coggan! For the first and last time in my three years as a press officer I gave that fatuous reply 'no comment'.[15]

15 Op. cit., pp. 53–4.

It was becoming clear that the Lambeth Conference of 1968 was going to be very different from any of its predecessors. The public got a reminder of what previous Conferences had been like by the republication of Dewi Morgan's *The Bishops Come to Lambeth* with an account of the 1958 conference added, by my book *The First Lambeth Conference 1867* (1967) and by my article '100 Years of Lambeth' in the *Church Times Supplement*, 19 July 1968. Another notable difference from previous Conferences was the holding of this one in Church House, Westminster, and not at Lambeth Palace. Obviously Lambeth would no longer have a room big enough for the plenary sessions. To begin with there was the largest number of bishops ever present at a Conference – 462. (In 1958 there had been 310 present.) In addition there were the 26 consultants and 76 observers. Besides a difference of place there was also a difference of attitude towards the press and public, who for the very first time were admitted to some of the plenary sessions. Thus two American priests, James B. Simpson and Edward M. Story, were able to share in much of the Conference and write a readable account of it in 1969, *The Long Shadows of Lambeth X*. There they speak of the activities in Church House.

Inside Church House, on the second floor, activities centered in Hoare Memorial Hall, named for [sic] a prominent banker and churchman of the last century. Ringed with tables for registration, it was not unlike a hotel ballroom converted to the use of a convention. At the rear of the hall stood tiers of gray metal mailboxes – one for every three Bishops, numbered according to the Conference's official processional order. Many of the men were accustomed to a number that dictated their places in processions in their own national Churches as well as their seats in an assembly of bishops. All that was momentarily changed: the Bishop of Springfield [Illinois], for instance, ordinarily No. 588, became No. 271. One of his colleagues remarked, 'I'm in the 300s – don't know if I feel like a convict or a hymn'. Behind the registration desks were other tables bearing long rows of plastic briefcases issued for all Conference participants. Lightweight and practical, the bags zipped across the top and had *Lambeth Conference 1968* discreetly embossed in gold letters in the right corner.

The bright blue cases contained tickets to the official services, invitations to the parties, *Who's Who at Lambeth '68*, and several other booklets including lists by processional order, official observers, official consultants, and constitution of committees. The most immediately important items were the badges, small white cards encased in clear plastic with the color of the printing denoting the rank of its bearer – purple for bishops, gold for wives, blue for observers, black for consultants, green for staff, red for press.[16]

The bishops began signing in on Monday, 22 July. By the time they departed for the opening service 462 had signed in. A number of American bishops were absent from the Conference; they stayed at home in some cases because they were in areas of racial unrest.

On the afternoon of 25 July, the Tenth Lambeth Conference began with the usual service at Canterbury. Dr Michael Ramsey addressed the multitude of bishops from the throne of St Augustine. He used as his text the Epistle to the Hebrews 12.26–9. In the course of it he said:

> As Anglicans we ask ourselves: '*Quo tendimus?*' This Lambeth Conference faces big questions about our relations with one another as a world-wide Anglican family and about our role within a Christendom which is being called to unity in the truth. Can we do better than take to heart and apply to our tasks the counsel which Pope Gregory gave to St Augustine – '*non pro locis res, sed loca pro bonis rebus*', 'not things for the sake of places, but places for the sake of good things.' We shall love our own Anglican family not as something ultimate but because in it and through it we and others have our place in the one Church of Christ. The former, your Anglican family, is a lovely special loyalty: the latter is the Church against which our Lord predicted that the gates of death would not prevail. Now, as the work of unity advances there will come into existence united churches not describably Anglican but in communion with us and sharing with us what we hold to be the unshaken essence of catholicity. What then of the future boundaries of our Anglican Communion? We shall face that question without fear, without anxiety, because of our faith in the things which are not shaken. Perhaps the Anglican role in Christendom may come to be less like a separate encampment and more like a color in the spectrum of a rainbow, a color bright and unself-conscious.[17]

After giving his blessing in the choir, the Archbishop came down to bless those in the nave. So long was the procession of bishops, etc., that some of the archbishops had taken off their robes and were standing outside the cathedral while the rest of the procession was still emerging. A garden party followed. The sunshine alone was lacking. The *Church Times* reported that 'Some members of "CHURCH" distributed leaflets, but there was nothing that could really be called an incident.' CHURCH was a group of about two hundred radical Christians, one of whose leaders was the Rev. David Hart, bearded assistant curate at St

---

[16] Op. cit., p. 36.
[17] *The Long Shadows of Lambeth X*, p. 285.

Michael's, Highgate. The Archbishop invited them to meet him in his study on Tuesday, 2 July. The group had forty-five minutes with him. Dr Ramsey afterwards said that Hart was 'a good liberal Christian', while Hart said that 'The Archbishop was a very nice man. We had a very good dialogue.'

Business began on Saturday, 27 July, in Church House. At that meeting a message was received from the Pope; never before had a Lambeth Conference been so honoured. The message was read by Bishop J. G. M. Willebrands, head of the Vatican's Secretariat for promoting Christian Unity.[18] Archbishop Athenagoras of Thyateira read a statement from the Oecumenical Patriarch. Dr Eugene Carson Blake read messages of greetings from the World Council of Churches. After this the chairmen of the three sections into which the programme was divided said an introductory piece.

There now came a controversial note. The Pope had recently issued the encyclical *Humanae Vitae* which reiterated a prohibition of all artificial methods of birth control. The first days of the Lambeth Conference were very much occupied with this issue. At a press conference on the first Tuesday the Archbishop said that the teaching of the Pope was widely different from that of the Anglican Communion. The judgement of the Anglican Communion was agreed at the Lambeth Conference of 1958 and was expressed in Resolution 115. The Archbishop went on to say that 'The changes in human society and world population, as well as the development in the means available for contraception which have occurred since 1958, seem to me to reinforce rather than to challenge the argument employed and the conclusions reached at the Lambeth Conference of 1958.' In due course this 1968 Anglican attitude, reiterating that of 1958, was incorporated into Resolution 22 of the Conference.

Sunday, 28 July, saw the bishops participating in a Sung Eucharist at Westminster Abbey at 10.30 when there were present some 'primates now retired' including Geoffrey Fisher, Philip Carrington, and William Wand. Simpson and Story remarked, 'Geoffrey Fisher walked last, heavier and slightly lame but otherwise little changed in appearance since completing his seventeen years as the ninety-ninth successor to Augustine.'[19] Music was used that had been especially composed for Princess Margaret's wedding in 1960. The preacher was Dr Leonard

---

[18] Cardinal Bea had died.
[19] *The Long Shadows of Lambeth X*, pp. 77–8.

Beecher, Archbishop of East Africa. Abbey clergy assisted with the administration.

On Monday, 29 July, in the afternoon the Queen entertained all the bishops at a garden party at Buckingham Palace. This was their second garden party; there had been one at Lambeth the previous Saturday. 'There were some surprises:' wrote Simpson and Story,

> the observer from the World Methodist Council chose a black cassock, but the Bishop of Milwaukee dressed in a business suit and gray topcoat. One of the Japanese bishops wore a pinkish cassock with a discernible flower pattern and slit at the side in the style of the Far East. African bishops had floppy-brimmed businessmen's hats and long overcoats that contrasted oddly with their cassocks. One bishop turned up wearing a mortarboard. The most striking costume among the women was the kimono of pale green and gold worn by the wife of the Bishop of Tokyo.

With the Queen were the Duke of Edinburgh, Princess Margaret, and Princess Alice, Countess of Athlone, one of the last surviving granddaughters of Queen Victoria.[20]

The Monday morning had been devoted to business (non-agenda matters) in plenary sessions as also was the afternoon of Friday, 2 August. In between there were three days for committee work. The second week of the Conference saw three days, August 7–9 (Wednesday to Friday), devoted to plenary sessions on preliminary reports from each section of the Conference. During the following week sectional groups (combinations of subcommittees) worked on drafts of section reports. These were finally approved by the sections on Friday, 16 August, and presented to the Conference in the plenary sessions from Tuesday, 20 August, to Saturday, 24 August. Some more non-agenda matters were considered on 20 August. Such was the pattern of business.

There was a missionary weekend over Saturday, 10 August, and Sunday, 11 August. The bishops were in various parts of the country. In Northumbria, Bishop Ashdown of Newcastle led a procession of bishops including Trevor Huddleston to the Holy Island of Lindisfarne. Some 3,000 people took part in the Eucharist in the ruins of the twelfth-century Benedictine abbey and later in the day there was Solemn Evensong in the parish church. On Monday, 12 August, there was a vast concourse of people at the White City Stadium for a great service of

---

[20] She is still alive at 94 and was present at the Jubilee Service in St Paul's on 7 June 1977.

Holy Communion. The celebrant was Angus Campbell MacInnes, Archbishop in Jerusalem. The sermon was preached by the Bishop of Iran (H. Dehqani-Tafti). 'The timetable' write Simpson and Story,

> for the processions from the grandstands and field, usually the scene of dog races, was immediately tucked in cassock pockets as a collector's item. It reflected the careful planning necessary for a ceremonial that combined the complexities of the Feeding of the Multitude with D-day landings in Normandy.
>
> The congregation rose to its feet as the procession came into view, swelled in numbers by the dozens of deacons chosen to assist at the Eucharist. Red stoles sashed across their snowy surplices, the deacons carried chalices, patens, and ciboria that dated back to the 1400s and had been especially removed from sacristy safes all over London for use at the White City Eucharist.[21]

At the end of the service, as the Royal Air Force Band played, the bishops approached the grandstands to greet the congregation. 'It was Lambeth's finest moment of fellowship with its people, who, even in the extraordinary setting of a summer night on a playing field, felt something of the same intimacy of a greeting at the door of a parish church.'[22]

There was the customary reception by the Lord Mayor of London at the Guildhall – the only formal evening of the Conference, when a good many of the wives turned up in long dresses. Most of the bishops wore cassocks 'but one came in the odd eighteenth-century outfit owned by some English bishops, a violet suit with gold braid, lace, and knee breeches.' Another evening event was a visit to the theatre – it was the first time the Lambeth fathers had done this – in order to see Hadrian VII at the Mermaid Theatre, much to the surprise of Alec McCowen the leading actor.

Dr Ramsey's entertaining was kept simple.

> Instead of continuing the custom of inviting bishops and their wives to spend a night at Lambeth, the Ramseys restricted their entertaining to small sherry parties and dinners at Lambeth Palace and weekend parties at the Old Palace in Canterbury; even that amounted to a heavy load of entertaining, but it was warmly hospitable. Four evenings a week, guests came for Evensong in Lambeth Palace Chapel and remained for dinner. Coffee

[21] Op. cit., p. 80.
[22] Op. cit., p. 81.

followed in the drawing room, and by nine o'clock the guests were departing through the Tudor gateway.[23]

This was a great contrast to the First Lambeth Conference when feasting at Fulham and Addington went on till midnight. Another contrast was that this was the first gaiterless conference. 'The debonair Bishop of Chester turned up in gaiters at the registration and Lord Fisher wore gaiters at the Lambeth Palace garden party but otherwise the newspapers were correct in referring to Lambeth X as "the first gaiterless Lambeth Conference".'[24] Another change was over the photograph. This was not taken at Lambeth but in Dean's Yard and for the first time the bishops wore their convocation robes. The man who took the photograph was T. H. Everitt, the great-grandson of the gentleman who had taken the photograph in 1867.[25]

We must now look at the three Reports on Faith, Ministry, and Unity. The discussions on Faith were assisted by the presence of John Macquarrie, now, since 1965, an Anglican priest, and one of the foremost theologians of the Anglican Communion, and David Jenkins, who 'established himself as one of the keenest intellects among the observers'.[26] Dr John Robinson, author of *Honest to God*, evidently did not shine at the Conference. On the 'Debate about God' the bishops said:

a Since God is its subject, it is a basic debate, having a seriousness and hence possibilities for good far beyond those of more familiar debates about church institutions.

b The Debate has helped many to recognize that faith is not merely assent to propositions but also demands commitment, and calls for action.

c The Debate has reminded us that our understanding of truth is always incomplete and that our ideas of God may be 'dated' or inappropriate. New exploration can in the end be fortifying and enriching.

In a section on 'The Sickness of the Contemporary World' the Report thus characterized the world of 1968:

a The contemporary world is a world so acquainted with social revolution that men are beginning to accept the idea that violence of any kind is inevitable and even good for its own sake.

b It is a world of rapidly and radically changing moral values, often

---

[23] *The Long Shadows of Lambeth X*, p. 101.
[24] Ibid., p. 22 fn.
[25] Ibid., p. 71.
[26] Ibid., p. 115. Jenkins was a consultant rather than observer.

resulting in a 'permissive' society. The values of secular man are becoming relative. This can, and sometimes does, lead to ethical anarchism.

c It is a world of widespread fear deriving from the massive achievements of technology and the misdirection of scientific discovery – fear of nuclear, biological, and chemical warfare and the manipulation of men's minds.

d It is a world characterized by lack of unity and wholeness. Whether viewed on the local, national, or international level, society appears divided and fragmented.

To such a world as this the Church has to offer the gospel with understanding and relevance.

On prayer they said:

In order to learn and teach different techniques of prayer we need:

a To reappraise traditional methods, which have a greater value than they are sometimes credited with.

b To learn to keep still and listen to God. This means fostering each man's capacity for contemplation. In this field there is much to learn from the approach of oriental religions to silence.

c To develop new and modern methods, such as those of Michel Quoist.[27]

There was something on other religions. 'In dialogue with Judaism, Hinduism, Buddhism, Islam, African and other religions, Christians must be prepared to listen and to learn.'

Under the heading of 'International Morality Today' came a paragraph condemning racism.

Racial discrimination, as represented in the ghettos, opposition to inter-racial marriage, unfair employment practices, social ostracism, and lack of equal economic opportunities, must be overcome. This requires justice within communities and the acceptance of responsibility on the part of those who exercise power within such institutions as industry, law enforcement, and education. Nevertheless, the major responsibility and final decision remains with the individual in the person to person relationship demanded by Christian discipleship. The Church must educate itself, reform its practices, and support its members energetically when they act in obedience to the principles demanded by the gospel.

The last section of the Report was on 'The Achievement of Peace'. This referred to contemporary violence.

Christians need to understand the causes of these social upheavals and the reasons that lead men to change the existing order in the countries by violent

[27] Michel Quoist's *Prayers of Life* had been published in English in 1963 and was fairly well known.

means. In specific situations, circumstances of such extreme oppression may arise that some justice-loving Christians may conclude that the lesser of two evils is to join in armed revolt. Christians who are unable to endorse such action must find non-violent ways of changing the existing order. We commend in particular the non-violent approach so ably embodied in recent times by the late Dr Martin Luther King. We call upon the Church to reflect deeply, and in a theological manner, upon the issues raised in revolutionary situations.

A matter relevant to faith was the question of the Thirty-nine Articles. While the Conference was in progress the report *Subscription and Assent to the 39 Articles* came from the Archbishops' Commission on Doctrine, under the chairmanship of Ian Ramsey of Durham. The subject had been to the fore since January 1967, when David Edwards had published an article in *The Modern Churchman*, 'The Thirty-nine Articles: One Last Heave'. At a news conference on this Report, Ian Ramsey explained, 'We do not want to sweep the Thirty-nine Articles under the carpet but to send them to a stately home in England where we can visit them from time to time.'[28] In this sort of spirit the Lambeth Conference of 1968 passed Resolution 43 (though there were 37 dissentients to it):

43 The Conference accepts the main conclusions of the report of the Archbishops' Commission on Christian Doctrine entitled *Subscription and Assent to the Thirty-nine Articles* (1968) and in furtherance of its recommendation
   a suggests that each Church of our communion consider whether the Articles need be bound up with its Prayer Book;
   b suggests to the Churches of the Anglican Communion that assent to the Thirty-nine Articles be no longer required of ordinands;
   c suggests that, when subscription is required to the Articles or other elements in the Anglican tradition, it should be required, and given, only in the context of a statement which gives the full range of our inheritance of faith and sets the Articles in their historical context.

In the discussions on creation Bishop Fleming of Norwich was responsible for getting through a resolution (7) on the conservation of the seabed, which in view of the importance of the whole question of environment and conservation is worth quoting.

The Conference endorses the initiative of Dr Pardo, leader of the Maltese delegation at the United Nations, urging that steps be taken to draft a treaty embodying the following principles:

[28] *The Long Shadows of Lambeth X*, p. 145.

That the seabed beyond the limits of present national jurisdiction

- a be conserved against appropriation by nations or their nationals, so that the deep ocean floor should not be allowed to become a stage for competing claims of national sovereignty;
- b be explored in a manner consistent with the principles and purposes of the charter of the United Nations;
- c be exploited economically or made use of with the aim of safeguarding the interests of mankind;
- d be conserved exclusively for peaceful purposes in perpetuity.

The Report on Faith seems to have fallen short of the Archbishop's hopes, but this was undoubtedly because there were so many issues to handle – more than could be dealt with in the time.

We now turn to the subject of the Renewal of the Church in Ministry, that section of the agenda under the directorship of Donald Coggan, Archbishop of York. They began with the importance of consulting the laity. Resolution 24 said that 'no major issue in the life of the Church should be decided without the full participation of the laity in discussion and decision'.

The question of Christian initiation was discussed. Some wanted baptism delayed and a service of blessing of a child used soon after birth. But there was much disagreement here. In the end each province was asked to explore the theology of baptism and confirmation. There was much discussion on the question of the diaconate and the result was Resolution 32.

32 The Conference recommends:

- a That the diaconate, combining service of others with liturgical functions, be open to
  - i men and [women] remaining in secular occupations
  - ii full-time church workers
  - iii those selected for the priesthood
- b That Ordinals should, where necessary, be revised:
  - i to take account of the new role envisaged for the diaconate;
  - ii by the removal of reference to the diaconate as 'an inferior office';
  - iii by emphasis upon the continuing element of *diakonia* in the ministry of bishops and priests.
- c That those made deaconesses by laying on of hands with appropriate prayers be declared to be within the diaconate. (*For*, 221, *Against*, 183)
- d That appropriate canonical legislation be enacted by provinces and regional Churches to provide for those already ordained deaconesses.

There was some debate by letter after the Conference over the wording of *a* i since the words 'and women' should not be in the Report. The Archbishop of Canterbury wrote to all the archbishops afterwards indicating this.

The subject of the ordination of women to the priesthood was obviously bound to create great discussion and disagreement. The Archbishop of Canterbury said afterwards that he would like to have seen passed a resolution that there were no overwhelming theological objections to the admission of women to the priesthood. In the end they passed a resolution to say that 'the theological arguments as at present presented for and against the ordination of women to the priesthood are inconclusive'. The other resolutions on this issue were these:

35 The Conference requests every national and regional Church or province to give careful study to the question of the ordination of women to the priesthood and to report its findings to the Anglican Consultative Council (or Lambeth Consultative Body) [on this more will be said below] which will make them generally available to the Anglican Communion.

36 The Conference requests the Anglican Consultative Council (or Lambeth Consultative Body)
   a to initiate consultations with other Churches which have women in their ordained ministry and with those which have not.
   b to distribute the information thus secured throughout the Anglican Communion.

37 The Conference recommends that, before any national or regional Church or province makes a final decision to ordain women to the priesthood, the advice of the Anglican Consultative Council (or Lambeth Consultative Body) be sought and carefully considered.

38 The Conference recommends that, in the meantime, national or regional Churches or provinces should be encouraged to make canonical provision, where this does not exist, for duly qualified women to share in the conduct of liturgical worship, to preach, to baptize, to read the epistle and gospel at the Holy Communion, and to help in the distribution of the elements.

The failure of the Lambeth Conference to endorse the belief that there were no theological objections to the ordination of women was a victory for the conservatives – almost their only victory, according to Simpson and Story. But, as these two gentlemen remark, 'If Lambeth X did not open the door for women to be admitted to the priesthood, it surely unfastened the latch.' In another place they say that the conservatives' 'valiant efforts may have been little more than a holding action, overshadowed as they were by the recommendation that deaconesses should be considered within the diaconate.'

On the question of the episcopate there was the suggestion that some provision should be made for the training of bishops, that co-adjutor, assistant, and suffragan bishops should exercise every function of a bishop, and that the bishops should examine their style of living and their titles.

We come now to the section on the Renewal of the Church in Unity. Here under the title of 'Principles of the Anglican Quest for Unity' the members of this section put forward the famous Lambeth Quadrilateral but in a revised form.

1 Common submission to Scripture as the Word of God, the uniquely authoritative record of God's revelation of himself to man.

2 Common profession of the faith derived from that revelation, especially as witnessed to in the primitive Creeds.

3 Common acceptance of the divinely instituted sacraments of baptism and the Holy Communion.

4 Common acknowledgement of a ministry through which the grace of God is given to his people.

Obviously this is somewhat different from the Quadrilateral of 1888, with which we have dealt in an earlier chapter. When it was discussed the Bishop of Leicester (R. R. Williams) immediately said that it seemed to exclude the historic episcopate, and obviously that is the natural interpretation. Bishop Stark of Newark replied that it was true that the Quadrilateral had been rewritten but was it not about time? Bishop Leonard of Willesden strongly objected. Bishop Tomkins of Bristol said that it was an attempt to paraphrase the Quadrilateral rather than to quote it with the changes made in it by Lambeth Conferences since 1888. The Archbishop of Canterbury suggested the idea of a footnote with the exact wording of the 1888 Quadrilateral. This was added to the Report in due course.

The next very controversial matter was that of Anglican–Methodist relations. There was great trouble over Resolution 51:

51 The Conference welcomes the proposals for Anglican–Methodist unity in Great Britain and believes that the proposed Service of Reconciliation is theologically adequate to achieve its declared intentions of reconciling the two Churches and integrating their ministries.

There was a long discussion on this resolution, notably from Bishop

Eastaugh of Peterborough, who did not want the resolution to be put, since he felt that many of the overseas bishops had not studied the question of the link-up of Anglicanism and Methodism in England. Archbishop Simms on the next day came up with an alternative resolution:

> This Conference welcomes the progress made since 1952 towards unity between the Church of England and the Methodist Church in Great Britain along the issues recommended by the Lambeth Conference of 1958, and hopes that the Churches will be able to proceed to full communion and eventually to organic union.

This, however, though the work of the steering committee, was not acceptable. Bishop Hamilton of Jarrow then proposed that the original resolution be amended as follows:

> 51 The Conference welcomes the proposals for Anglican–Methodist unity in Great Britain and notes with satisfaction the view expressed in the report of Section III that the proposed Service of Reconciliation is theologically adequate to achieve its declared intentions of reconciling the two Churches and integrating their ministries.

The Bishop of Peterborough was willing for Archbishop Simms's motion to go forward. When Canterbury asked the bishops whether they wanted the Simms resolution or the Hamilton one to be put, uproar developed. Archbishop de Mel turned the scales. He called the Simms resolution 'a toothless, bloodless, colourless thing'. 'A little more of this behaviour,' he said 'and the Anglican Communion will get such a magnificent reputation for double-talk that we will become utterly disreputable. Our very honour will be challenged.' He sat down amid the most thunderous applause of the whole Conference. So Hamilton's resolution was put and only five or six bishops voted against it. Nevertheless some ill feeling had been created. Trevor Huddleston called de Mel's actions 'utterly un-Christian' and they were condemned by Russell, Assistant Bishop of Zanzibar. Bishop Eastaugh was outraged. On 13 September he wrote this letter to the *Church Times* in relation to their report on the matter:

> Sir,
>
> I have just returned to Peterborough to find your issue of the 30th August containing a report of the Lambeth debate on the scheme for Church of England/Methodist union. This report is misleading in what it states, even more misleading in what it omits, and your editorial comment on page three and in the leading article grotesque in view of the facts.

The bishops were asked in the original resolution to affirm that the proposed service of reconciliation in the scheme now before the Church of England 'is theologically adequate to achieve its declared intention of reconciling the two Churches and integrating their ministries.'

As the text of the scheme had not been circulated with the Lambeth papers it is certain that at least half, and more likely three-quarters, of the bishops had never read the scheme, much less considered it, and certainly were not in a position to pronounce on its theological adequacy.

My motion therefore that 'the question be not put' was a perfectly proper attempt to save the bishops from overseas from an impossible position. It was certainly not a 'parliamentary dodge'. I should welcome an informed and responsible theological judgment of the Lambeth fathers on the service of reconciliation, but not a snap vote without papers, even on the recommendation of one third of their number.

I notice that you describe the speech of Bishop De Mel on this subject as 'a personal triumph'. It was in fact not a speech which should be heard in any civilised assembly, let alone an assembly of Christians. It was a torrent of abuse, insult and hysteria – a rabble-rouser – rightly castigated in the Conference by Bishop Trevor Huddleston as 'utterly unChristian' – a fact not reported in your paper.

It certainly succeeded; and, if there could have been anything more sickening than the speech itself, it was the tumult of applause with which it was received. This classic instance of mass-reaction and non-thought was utterly disillusioning about the judgment of the Conference.

It is important that these facts should be widely known. The resolution on this matter passed by the Lambeth Conference must not be taken as a considered and reponsible decision of the bishops.

✠ Cyril Petriburg:
The Palace, Peterborough.

One can see from this letter (written some time afterwards) how high feeling must have run at the time. Simpson and Story note:

During the next few days feelings against de Mel ran so high that several bishops sent their regrets to Canterbury, saying that they could not be present at the closing Eucharist at St Paul's, at which de Mel was to be the preacher. In the end, almost all of them were persuaded to attend, but, even so, the man who once had been regarded as the most jovial of bishops came to the end of his last Lambeth under a heavy cloud of disapproval.

The next subject was the Roman Catholic Church. The permanent Joint Commission was welcomed and the principle of 'collegiality' was approved and endorsed. The Conference expressed its willingness to support the Anglican Centre at Rome.

The most far-reaching proposals were those in the section of the Report which dealt with 'Inter-Anglican Structures'. Here it was suggested that instead of the Lambeth Consultative Body (which went back to the last century) and the Anglican Council on Missionary Strategy, which went back to 1948, there should be an Anglican Consultative Council. 'We therefore propose' said the Report,

> the formation of an *Anglican Consultative Council*, which would continue the responsibilities hitherto entrusted to the L.C.B. and the A.C.M.S., and the replacement of the office of Anglican Executive Officer by a Secretary General appointed by, and responsible to, the Council.

This section went on to say something about Lambeth Conferences.

> In view of the historic importance of the *Lambeth Conference* over the past hundred years and the undoubted value of the present meeting, the Archbishop of Canterbury should be asked to decide, on the advice of the Anglican Consultative Council, upon the calling of future Conferences and on their time, place, and agenda.

In addition, it seemed to see the end of Anglican Congresses.

> *Worldwide Anglican Congresses* should be replaced by (*a*) *a joint meeting*, at the time of an Assembly of the World Council of Churches, of the Consultative Council and of Anglican participants in the Assembly in or near the place where the Assembly is held. This Anglican meeting should receive a report from the Consultative Council on its work and on that of the Secretary General and should consider other matters brought to it by the Council. (*b*) *regional meetings* of representatives of Anglican Churches, if possible in association with meetings of Area Councils of Churches.

The Report also suggested that the office of Regional Officer which had been born at Toronto should be discontinued, but regional churches should be ready to allow their qualified staff to collaborate with the office and work of the Secretary General, especially in the field of study and research.

The functions of the Anglican Consultative Council were given as eight in Resolution 69 of the Lambeth Conference:

> 1 To share information about developments in one or more provinces with the other parts of the communion and to serve as needed as an instrument of common action.
>
> 2 To advise on inter-Anglican, provincial, and diocesan relationships, including the division of provinces, the formation of new provinces and of regional councils, and the problems of extra-provincial dioceses.

3 To develop as far as possible agreed Anglican policies in the world mission of the Church and to encourage national and regional Churches to engage together in developing and implementing such policies by sharing their resources of manpower, money, and experience to the best advantage of all.

4 To keep before national and regional Churches the importance of the fullest possible Anglican collaboration with other Christian Churches.

5 To encourage and guide Anglican participation in the Ecumenical Movement and the ecumenical organizations; to co-operate with the World Council of Churches and the world confessional bodies on behalf of the Anglican Communion; and to make arrangements for the conduct of pan-Anglican conversations with the Roman Catholic Church, the Orthodox Churches, and other Churches.

6 To advise on matters arising out of national or regional church union negotiations or conversations and on subsequent relations with united Churches.

7 To advise on problems of inter-Anglican communication and to help in the dissemination of Anglican and ecumenical information.

8 To keep in review the needs that may arise for further study and, where necessary, to promote inquiry and research.

The membership of the Council was to be as follows:

a The Archbishop of Canterbury.
b Three from each of the following, consisting of a bishop, a priest or deacon, and a lay person:
    The Church of England
    The Episcopal Church in the United States of America
    The Church of India, Pakistan, Burma, and Ceylon
    The Anglican Church of Canada
    The Church of England in Australia.
c Two from each of the following, consisting of a bishop, and a priest, deacon or lay person:
    The Church in Wales
    The Church of Ireland
    The Episcopal Church in Scotland
    The Church of the Province of South Africa
    The Church of the Province of West Africa
    The Church of the Province of Central Africa
    The Church of the Province of East Africa
    The Church of the Province of Uganda, Rwanda, and Burundi
    The Church of the Province of New Zealand
    The Church of the Province of the West Indies
    Nippon Sei Ko Kai

The Archbishopric in Jerusalem
The Council of the Church of South-East Asia
The South Pacific Anglican Council
Latin America
any Province of the Anglican Communion not at present represented.[29]

d Co-opted members. The Council shall have power to co-opt up to six
additional members, of whom at least two shall be women and two lay
persons not over 28 years of age at the time of appointment.

This point was somewhat revolutionary!

The Archbishop of Canterbury was to be President of the Council,
and when present should preside at the inaugural meeting of each
Council. He would be *ex officio* a member of its committees. The
Council would elect a chairman and vice-chairman, who were to hold
office for six years. The Council would meet every two years. There
would be a standing committee appointed by the Council which would
include chairman and vice-chairman. The meetings would take place in
various parts of the world.

Resolution 69 in which all this is contained is the longest resolution of
the whole Conference. The resolution had the support of the Bishop of
Huron who had been campaigning for an Anglican Council with
executive powers. Though it was not quite what he wanted, the fact that
he supported it assisted its progress.

It will be remembered what a major issue that of MRI had been at the
Toronto Congress and since. It was therefore natural that the
Conference should say something on this important subject. What it
said is contained in Resolution 67:

a The Conference records its gratitude for the concept of Mutual
Responsibility and Interdependence in the Body of Christ, and for the
renewed sense of responsibility for each other which it has created within
our communion.

b The Conference believes that a developing M.R.I. has a vital
contribution to make to our relationships within the whole Church of God.
It therefore summons our Churches to a deeper commitment to Christ's
mission through a wide partnership of prayer, by sharing sacrificially and
effectively their manpower and money, and by a readiness to learn from
each other.

c The Conference urges that serious attention be paid to the need for co-

---

[29] Brazil should have been mentioned. In fact an amendment to the resolution was
passed to change the provision for representatives of Latin America to 'Council of
Anglican Bishops in South America', but this did not get into the final Report.

operation, at every level of Anglican and ecumenical life, in the planning, implementing, and review of all work undertaken, along the lines set out in the Report of Section III (para. 6 on p. 146).

d The Conference believes that the time has come for a reappraisal of the policies, methods, and areas of responsibility of the Anglican Communion in discharging its share of the mission of Christ and that there is a need for a renewed sense of urgency.

The Lambeth Conference of 1968 did not endorse any long encyclical letter, as all the previous Conferences had done. Instead the steering committee had devised a much shorter thing – a message. Running through this message, which was printed on the front page of the *Church Times* of 30 August, were words about God. . . . 'God is . . . God reigns . . . God loves . . . God speaks.' When the message was read out it was greeted with but perfunctory applause. Dr Ramsey asked what the Conference wanted done with it. It could be sent out in the name of the Conference, or the steering committee or torn up! Some suggested that it should go out from the Archbishop of Canterbury but it became obvious he did not want this. In the end the bishops voted their approval of the document – though the Bishop of Southwark held up his hand in opposition. The last session of the Conference came to and end with thanks by Bishop Stephen Bayne to Bishop Ralph Dean, which was seconded by the Bishop of London. Then Bishop Dean presented Canterbury with a Prayer Book bearing all the bishops' signatures.

The final service on the next day, Sunday, in St Paul's Cathedral, was a Eucharist at a freestanding altar beneath the dome. The preacher was Bishop de Mel. The Archbishop of Canterbury celebrated, but was joined at the prayer of consecration by all the metropolitans. 'Seldom' wrote Alan Shadwick in the *Church Times*,

> could there have been such a wonderful block of colour under Wren's great dome, but the same could be said of the gaiety of the scene in front of the façade as bishops and congregation poured out. Bishops were giving interviews into tape-machines behind pillars, cameras were clicking, and everybody seemed to be shaking hands or exchanging chaste Oriental salutations.

Undoubtedly Ramsey's reputation as a theologian came through at the Conference. It was the first time that the Conference had been presided over by a theologian since Frederick Temple or Edward White Benson. We may quote what Simpson and Story write:

Canterbury's brilliance as an articulate theologian maintained the Conference's personal respect for him beyond the regard it accorded his office. After his brief address of welcome and some comments during the debate on birth control, he generally refrained from speaking until the discussions narrowed down to such topics as the integrity of the Church and preservation of Catholic doctrine. He thrice addressed the bishops, taking them by surprise as he rose and spoke extemporaneously for five to ten minutes. Invariably, he was warmly applauded and on one occasion the Conference asked for and received the text of his remarks.

Supplementing his quiet forcefulness was a sense of humor and a rather quaint, courtly manner of presiding. Canterbury was at first slow, then later somewhat too hasty in calling for a vote, but eventually he struck an even course in which he gently nudged the Conference to its decisions.[30]

After the customary interval the Report of the Lambeth Conference was duly published. With it the S.P.C.K. also published a shorter survey of the Conference. This was edited by Ian Ramsey, Bishop of Durham, with the assistance of Michael Perry of the S.P.C.K. (whom Dunelm was shortly to appoint Archdeacon of Durham), and contained various photographs and messages from bishops and other personalities. In 1969 James B. Simpson and Edward M. Story published their *The Long Shadows of Lambeth X* to which this chapter has been much indebted. *Pan-Anglican* for the Fall of 1968 was devoted wholly to the Lambeth Conference. From this document perhaps the best section to quote here is the assessment of Bishop Luxton of Huron – or rather 'Reassessment' as he calls it.

In reassessment of Lambeth '68 I am asking myself – what really happened at this Conference? My answer is that the Anglican Communion, at least in her Episcopal order, found a new measure of maturity and collegiality. We took full advantage of the experience of the second Vatican Council, and much of our progress can be traced back to the four years of travail of the Roman Catholic Bishops at Vatican II. The 'periti' of the Vatican Council with their theological, historical and ecclesiastical experience, became our twenty-five Consultants; and they were given a full and useful place in our company. The Observers of the Roman Council also became part of our family circle and had a more direct influence on our deliberations than Rome could allow in her much more populous assembly. And our movement from the library of Lambeth Palace to the superb Assembly Hall of Church House, Westminster, was in itself a movement from a confined and awkward council chamber to a house of parliament where debates

---

[30] *The Long Shadows of Lambeth X*, p. 59.

could be held with an effectiveness and openness impossible in the more ancient setting.

Also, after the first few days of meeting, we crossed the Rubicon, so far as the Press was concerned, and opened out our Conference to the world, or such part of the world as might be interested. . . .

Perhaps our new measure of maturity showed itself more clearly in the freedom of our debates . . . our President fostered this by his desire to have all points of view fairly presented. The new collegiality of the Roman Bishops seemed to reach and influence us here. There was a greater self-confidence in the House. Away from Lambeth Palace the debates were less personally orientated and the atmosphere less confining. . . .

The Bishops from the Americas, and from the other provinces outside the British Isles, were more comfortable in the debates of '68 than they seemed to be in '58. They had a larger share in the work of the Conference and in the discussions. And their English brethren seem on the whole to have accepted them *almost* as equals. I wish that I could make a full statement rather than this guarded and qualified one; but many of the English Bishops still live in an awesome atmosphere of first class citizenship that cannot be opened to those who are not members of 'the club'. Perhaps we mistake a shyness and reserve and a protection of privacy for an attitude of superiority. At any rate, great progress has been made in the past ten years, especially by those English Bishops who have travelled throughout the Communion; and the new sense of corporate unity in our wide household is good to experience.

Going on to ask whether there would be another Lambeth Conference in ten years' time, Bishop Luxton thought there would need to be another one before 1978. He felt the bishops would need to come together in 1973. This, however, they have not done. He suggested a Lambeth Conference every five years. 'My own opinion' he said,

is that the expense of a Lambeth Conference every five years would be among the best spent money in our Church life, and would bring many dividends to the life of our Church in diocese and province. In its lesser aspects, it repairs the friendships of the Bishops of the Church. . . . It also gives to each of us a sense of belonging to a world-wide fellowship. It recovers for us a vision of world servanthood that is needed if the local Churches are not to seem to the outsider to be (in the phrase of the fourth assembly of the World Council of Churches) 'remote and irrelevant, and busy to the point of tediousness with their own concerns. The Churches need a new openness to the world in its aspirations, its achievement, its restlessness and its despair.' For one, I have found at Lambeth '68 a wonderful measure of that openness; and for my successors in office I plead for a more frequent application of the same.

15

ANGLICANISM
SINCE LAMBETH 1968

Our survey of the ten Lambeth Conferences is now complete. We have seen how Archbishop Longley courageously called the first of them in 1867, and how, in spite of a wish from overseas that it should be a synod of bishops, presbyters, and laymen – laywomen not then entering the picture – it was a conference, not a synod, and confined to the episcopate. In 1878 Archbishop Tait, who had been decidedly adverse to the Conference of 1867, was encouraged to call a second, and did so, in spite of some continuing opposition in various quarters. Archbishop Benson needed no persuasion to call the Conference of 1888, for, being a High Churchman, he was favourably disposed to conciliar and synodical action. He also planned a conference for 1897; his successor, Frederick Temple, presided over it. By now this decennial episcopal conference was recognized as a permanent feature of Anglicanism. Moreover, out of this last Conference of the nineteenth century emerged the Lambeth Consultative Body, which functioned until 1968. Archbishop Davidson, who had attended all the Conferences except the first, called another in 1908, notable in that it was immediately preceded by the first Pan-Anglican Congress. His second conference of 1920, soon after the Great War, earned more fame than all the rest, because of its 'Appeal to All Christian people'.

The Conference of 1930 was, perhaps, marred somewhat by Archbishop Lang's prelatical character and the feeling which it engendered among the Americans and others that they were second-class citizens. Archbishop Fisher had to disperse this distrust before the successful renewal of the Conferences after the Second World War, in that 'age of austerity', 1948. He was a notable leader at the 1954 Anglican Congress at Minneapolis and then, like Davidson, presided for a second time at a Lambeth Conference in 1958. Out of this emerged the Anglican Executive Officer. There followed in Michael Ramsey's archiepiscopate the Anglican Congress at Toronto in 1963, which was enacted before the backcloth of the Second Vatican Council. That

Council had such repercussions upon the Anglican Communion that the Lambeth Conference of 1968 was quite different from its predecessors, with the presence of press and public in Church House, Westminster, and with the expert assistance of observers and consultants. From this Conference emerged the Anglican Consultative Council, taking the place of the Lambeth Consultative Body.

Since 1968 there have been three meetings of the Anglican Consultative Council, the first in Kenya in 1971, the second at Dublin in 1973, and the third in Trinidad in 1976. These meetings, which might be described as 'Mini-Lambeths', have all taken place under the secretaryship of Bishop John Howe, whose appointment as Anglican Executive Officer was announced before the end of 1968. John Howe had been Bishop of St Andrews since 1955 and had written the preparatory paper on the diaconate for the 1968 Conference. Before his elevation to the episcopate, Howe, a bachelor, had been Vice-Principal of Edinburgh Theological College. He had taken a prominent part in conversations between Anglicans and Presbyterians in Scotland. He took up office on 1 May 1969, when Bishop Ralph Dean returned to Cariboo, from which diocese he had been seconded for five years. Before returning to Canada, Dean, after paying tribute to the pioneer work done by Stephen Bayne, expressed a belief that Howe was the right man to be the third Anglican Executive Officer. 'He has an independent and well-informed mind,' he said, 'a sense of humour, a missionary outlook and a theological point of view.'

In November 1969 Howe announced that all but three of the twenty churches in the Anglican Communion had given their approval to the proposal of an Anglican Consultative Council.[1] He made it known that the new Council, which would replace the Lambeth Consultative Body and the Advisory Council on Missionary Strategy, would meet for ten days early in 1971.[2] The position of Executive Officer would cease to exist and the Council would appoint a Secretary-General. The Council would subsequently meet every two years and its standing committee annually. The Council would be a permanent means of communication between the churches of the Anglican Communion, have the responsibility of developing agreed policies in the world mission of the Communion, and encourage and guide the participation of the Communion in the ecumenical movement.

[1] These three were the churches of Uganda, Rwanda, and Burundi; the Church of the Province of West Africa; and Latin America.

[2] Kenya had not then been decided upon as the place of meeting.

With the Anglican Consultative Council now fast becoming a reality, George Luxton, Bishop of Huron, pleaded with the English church to be less parochial. 'The attention' he said

> the English Church pays to the Anglican Communion and the Anglican Consultative Council through the seventies will be decisive not only for the survival of the Anglican Communion but for its effectiveness as well . . . The first two Executive Officers frequently supported the possibility of the *disappearance* of our Communion. They were pointing, of course, to the 'incident in history' quotation from the Lambeth Conference of 1930, which anticipated that we should lose our life in the Church Universal.[3] Many, however, have taken the Executive Officers' words to imply something else – a movement towards a full stop, towards a complete loss of identity. Some took it to mean the process of the merger of our member Churches with other denominations to form national Christian Churches throughout the world. I shudder at the thought of the upsurge of nationalism that would accompany such a disappearance . . . The Anglican Communion can survive and possibly will survive if the Consultative Council comes into lively being and gives to the Communion the leadership in thought and action that we so sorely need. Here's where the attitude of the English Church is all-important.

These words come from the last article that George Luxton wrote for the *Church Times*.[4] He died the following year.

The first meeting of the Anglican Consultative Council took place at Limuru in Kenya from 23 February to 5 March 1971. Later in the year a full report about it was published by the S.P.C.K. under the title *The Time is Now*. 'Throughout the meeting', wrote John Howe,

> the Council lived together as a community at Limuru. Not in London or New York, but in the Kenya countryside. Neither north nor south, but virtually on the equator. Not as senders or receivers, but as representatives of equal partner Churches in the Body of Christ.

> Each member Church has two or three members of the Council. Representatives of western countries were in a minority at Limuru, and the balance between members of European and non-European extraction was about even. The suggestion has been made that a central council of a world Church without a majority from European cultures is something that has not happened since before the Council of Nicaea – a speculation which, however, may be disproved. Our youngest delegate was twenty, our oldest seventy, our average age fifty-four and a half. We were 68% clergy (35% in episcopal orders) and 32% lay.

[3] See *Lambeth Conference Report 1930*, p. 153.
[4] *Church Times*, 3 October 1969, p. 11.

Bishop John Howe was elected Secretary-General and the office of Executive Officer came to an end. Sir Louis Mbanefo, the representative of West Africa and one of Nigeria's leading Anglicans, was elected Chairman of the Council.[5] Mrs Marion Kelleran from the U.S.A. was elected vice-chairman. It was decided that the first chairman should hold office until 1974 and the first vice-chairman for six years, as it seemed undesirable that both offices should end at the same time. The delegates to the Council from England were Bishop Brown of St Edmundsbury, Father Hugh Bishop, and Professor J. N. D. Anderson. Ralph Dean, Bishop of Cariboo, came as a Canadian delegate. Archbishop George Appleton came from Jerusalem. His successor at Perth, Archbishop G. T. Sambell, represented Australia. The Presiding Bishop, J. E. Hines, came from the U.S.A. Bishop Janani Luwum, martyred in 1977, was the delegate from Uganda, Rwanda, and Burundi. There were six consultants: Professor John Mbiti, Bishop Lesslie Newbigin, David M. Paton (who wrote an account of the Council for the *Church Times*), Mr Curtis Roosevelt from the United Nations Economic and Social Council, Canon John Taylor of the C.M.S., and Mr Francis Wilson of the University of Cape Town. There were also observers, including Dr Philip Potter of the World Council of Churches and Canon William Purdy of the Roman Church. A standing committee had to be appointed to deal with any emergencies arising before the next meeting. This consisted of the Rev E. D. Cameron (Australia), Bishop Dean (Canada), Mr Martin Kaunda (Zambia), Professor J. N. D. Anderson (England), the Rev R. T. Nishimura (Japan), Mr J. C. Cottrell (New Zealand), and Bishop G. C. M. Woodroffe (West Indies).

The Council met at the Limuru Conference centre, eighty miles from the equator, but over 6,000 feet above sea level. Those who came from the northern winter were refreshed by the sunshine, while those who came from lands of oppressive heat were refreshed by the cool breezes. Limuru is situated in the diocese of Mt Kenya whose Bishop welcomed them and whose theological college, St Paul's, entertained the delegates to tea. The most impressive service of the meeting was that held in All Saints Cathedral, Nairobi, when they were welcomed by the Provost, and the Archbishop and bishops of Kenya, and the sermon was preached by the President, Dr Ramsey, who was received by President Kenyatta.

[5] He died in 1977.

After five plenary sessions, the Council divided into sections for several days to discuss four subjects:

1   Unity and ecumenical affairs
2   Renewal – Church and Society
3   Renewal – Order and Organization in the Anglican Church
4   Mission and Evangelism.

It is not surprising that the controversial World Council of Churches programme to combat racialism, which had been inaugurated in the year after the Lambeth Conference, should have been an issue at the first Anglican Consultative Council and give rise to dissension. Bishop Paul Burrough, who had been present at the 1968 Lambeth Conference, left in dismay when he could not assent to Resolution 17:

1   That individuals, Churches, and other institutions be encouraged to re-examine, in penitence, their lives and structures with a view to eradicating all forms of discrimination;
2   That the Churches of the Anglican Communion urgently seek ways of implementing LCR 16 [Lambeth Conference Resolution 16] and the World Council of Churches' programme to combat racism, on the understanding that the grants made thereunder will not be used for military purposes;

The Archbishop of Cape Town, the Most Rev R. S. Taylor, also cast a dissenting vote. Bishop Burrough of Mashonaland argued that the resolution could only be interpreted as supporting groups actively engaged in violence against Rhodesia. Before withdrawing and returning to Salisbury, he said that he did so regretfully, because 'I have much love and thanksgiving for the Council but I dissociate myself from this resolution.' After sharing in communion the next day he departed.

Another divisive issue was that of the ordination of women. It will be remembered that the Lambeth Conference of 1968 had asked the Churches to study this question.[6] Eight Anglican Churches had done so, but had not yet sent in reports. The question now arose because Gilbert Baker, Bishop of Hong Kong since 1966, had asked for advice in view of the fact that his diocesan synod had approved in principle the ordination of women to the priesthood. Hong Kong was the diocese where Bishop Hall, Baker's predecessor, had ordained a woman to the priesthood in 1944. Resolution 28 was now passed at Limuru:

[6] See *Lambeth Conference Report 1968*, Resolution 35.

a   Many of the Churches of the Anglican Communion regard the question of the ordination of women to the priesthood as an urgent matter. We therefore call on all Churches of the Anglican Communion to give their consideration to this subject as requested by LCR 35, and to express their views in time for consideration by the Anglican Consultative Council in 1973.

b   In reply to the request of the Council of the Church of South-East Asia, this Council advises the Bishop of Hong Kong, acting with the approval of his Synod, and any other bishop of the Anglican Communion acting with the approval of his Province, that, if he decides to ordain women to the priesthood, his action will be acceptable to this Council; and that this Council will use its good offices to encourage all Provinces of the Anglican Communion to continue in communion with these dioceses.

(This was carried by 24 votes to 22).

c   In the terms of LCR 36, the Secretary General is asked to request the metropolitans and primates of the Churches of the Anglican Communion to consult with other Churches in their area in the matter of the ordination of women and to report to him in time for the next meeting of the Anglican Consultative Council.

In the twenty-two votes against *b* were those of Dr Michael Ramsey and Sir Louis Mbanefo.

The question of Anglican–Methodist Reunion also came up at Limuru, but before relating what happened there we must indicate what had taken place in England since Lambeth '68. The year 1969 will go down in the annals of the Church of England as the year of the rejection of the Anglican–Methodist Reunion Scheme – or, rather, the failure of the scheme to get a sufficient majority in the Convocations. At the Methodist Conference that year in Birmingham the scheme received a vote in favour of 77·4 per cent. This was above the needed 75 per cent. There followed the voting in Canterbury and York Convocations, which went as follows.

Canterbury Convocation. Upper House: for 27, against 2 (93 per cent majority).

Canterbury Convocation. Lower House: for 154, against 77 (67 per cent majority).

York Convocation. Upper House: for 11, against 3 (78 per cent majority).

York Convocation. Lower House: for 71, against 34 (68 per cent majority).

The five bishops who voted against the scheme were Peterborough (Eastaugh), Leicester (Williams), Ripon (Moorman), Carlisle (Bulley), and Sheffield (Taylor).

This defeat had been brought about by a combination of High Church and Evangelical opposition, united against the scheme in the way that they had a century before united against *Essays and Reviews*. Professor Mascall joined forces with Colin Buchanan and Dr J. I. Packer. There followed disappointment on the part of many – a disappointment shared by Dr Michael Ramsey, who remarked, 'It is certain that this so-far negative result will cause a great deal of restlessness, impatience and unwillingness to be patient with ecclesiastical rules. Yes, there will be bitterness, anger and cynicism – especially among those on the fringe of the Church of England who are going to have reason for being disillusioned about institutional religion.' Later, a notable ecclesiastical spokesman, David Edwards, addressing the Modern Churchmen's Conference at Culham, remarked bitterly,

> 1969 will, I am quite sure, turn out to have been one of the blackest years in the history of the Church of England. Methodism must be embittered because, having been more or less forced out in the eighteenth century, it has been led up the garden path in the twentieth. That must make the eventual union harder. Of course, more co-operation and intercommunion will come in the parishes, for more and more people are being driven by their own experience – to say nothing of historical theology – to see that the Evangelical understanding of the priorities in church order is right. But that is no substitute for a sense of direction, affirmed in public. The public will not forget in a hurry all that was implied in the headlines of 9th July 1969. Besides reports of starvation in Nigeria, riots in Kenya, war in Vietnam, clashes between Israel and Egypt, Russia and China, £38 million spent on sending a monkey into space, drug addiction in Britain, ANGLICANS REJECT CHURCH UNITY. Is God's memory more merciful? It is, we are told, to those who repent?[7]

Dr Ramsey now began to wonder whether a more successful result might have been accomplished if the voting had been left until after the introduction of the new synodical government in 1970. He told the Methodists this when he thanked them for voting for the scheme with a sufficiently large majority. In June 1970 the Methodist Conference voted again for the scheme, this time with a percentage of 79·4. The Anglicans who had fought against the scheme now brought out a rival

[7] See Alan M. G. Stephenson (ed.), *Liberal Christianity in History*, p. 134. With reference to the monkey in space note that before many days were passed man had walked on the moon.

one of their own which entailed more local growing into union. Two Anglo-Catholics, the renowned theologian E. L. Mascall and Bishop Leonard of Willesden, and two Evangelicals, Colin Buchanan and J. I. Packer, published *Growing into Union. Proposals for forming a United Church in England.* Dr Ramsey was sceptical about the new approach but thought that the book should be properly studied, since it contained some valuable discussions of ways of synthesis between Catholic and Evangelical positions in theology. He felt, however, that the liberal strain in Anglicanism received short shrift in the document and hence it suffered from lack of balance.

When the question of Anglican–Methodist reunion now came up before this representative gathering of Anglicans at Limuru a resolution was passed with one dissentient – that of the Evangelical Professor Anderson. Resolution 6 reads:

> Believing the Scheme for union between the Church of England and the Methodist Church to be theologically adequate, and the procedure in two stages to be appropriate in English circumstances, and noting its bearing upon church union elsewhere in the Anglican Communion, the Council hopes that Stage One will be implemented as soon as possible and that every opportunity will be fostered of co-operative growth into the organic union of Stage Two.

The Council's hopes, however, were not fulfilled when the matter came up at the General Synod. The synodical system of the Church of England had changed in 1970, when the General Synod had commenced its career in the presence of the Queen at Westminster Abbey. In place of the old Church Assembly, which ended after fifty years, there was a General or National Synod consisting of about 537 bishops, priests, and laity. Below this came the Diocesan Synods, to which certain diocesan clergy and laity were elected. The old Diocesan Conferences, which had involved all the clergy, came to an end. Below the Diocesan Synod came the Deanery Synods with their joint chairmen, one lay and one clerical (the rural dean). In May 1972 General Synod voted upon Methodist union. Dr Coggan, as chairman, announced the figures which were as follows:

Bishops 34 for, 6 against (85 per cent in favour).
Clergy 152 for, 80 against (65·52 per cent in favour).
Laity 147 for, 87 against (62·82 per cent in favour).

Thus two houses lacked the necessary 75 per cent majority. It could hardly be said that the bishops were dragging their feet! Dr Ramsey had been present and made a memorable speech in favour of the scheme.[8] Passions again were roused. One supporter of the scheme threatened to throw a stone at the window of the Bishop of Willesden, one of those who led the opposition. He carried out his threat, but the bishop had moved to another house! So the long negotiations between Anglicans and Methodists came to an end. Later, as we shall see, talks began again with the Methodists, in conjunction with other churches and from these a different sort of approach has emerged.

Out of the Limuru meeting there came in April 1973 a short book of statistics of the Anglican Communion, published by the Anglican Consultative Council. Though it was mainly the work of the Rev. D. B. Barrett of the Church of the Province of Kenya, Bishop Howe contributed a preface, which indicated that since 1600 the Anglican Communion had expanded from the 47 dioceses of the British Isles, with 4.2 million Anglicans, to 360 dioceses all over the world in 1972, with a total membership of 65.4 millions. Bishop Howe added that 'in 1971–2 for the first time, the number of Anglicans outside England (32.9 million) is greater than the number in England (32.5 million).' The whole object of the statistics was really to assist MRI. 'There has been and is,' wrote the Bishop,

> much that is haphazard in the Anglican Communion. Enthusiasm and lack of planning can beget unhappy progeny. For example, there are dioceses in the Anglican Communion with great opportunities, but which because they are under-staffed and under-financed are never able to tackle the task before them, but simply survive by the skin of their teeth from decade to decade. Meanwhile, new dioceses are started elsewhere, similarly under-financed, which will soon be in the same condition. It might have been better to do the one job well. But right choices in such matters require more knowledge of the facts and figures of the Anglican Communion than has generally been available.

The difficulty of being really up to date was revealed in the document. Since the statistics had been drawn up early in 1972, diocesan changes had taken place. In the Province of Central Africa the new diocese of Botswana had been created by the division of the diocese of Matabeleland. In South America the diocese of Paraguay and North Argentina had been divided into two – a diocese of Paraguay and a diocese of North Argentina. The Province of Uganda, Rwanda, and

---

[8] For the text see A. M. Ramsey, *Canterbury Pilgrim*, pp. 99–105.

Burundi had now become the Province of Uganda, Rwanda, Burundi, and Boga-Zaire. The new diocese of Boga-Zaire had been created and also new dioceses of Bukedi, Bunyoro, and Busoga, by division of existing dioceses.

A second meeting of the Anglican Consultative Council took place at Dublin, 17–27 July 1973. The delegates met in the new Church of Ireland Training College. The newly elected President of the Irish Republic, Mr O'Dailaigh, an Anglican, joined the assembly in Christ Church Cathedral and at a reception given by the Anglican Church of Ireland. At the Government reception in the state apartments of Dublin Castle, Dr Michael Ramsey was seen deep in conversation with the late Cardinal Conway. Mrs Marion Kelleran, upon the resignation of Sir Louis Mbanefo, became Chairman. Her place as vice-chairman was taken by Bishop Woodroffe of the Windward Islands. It was agreed that the next meeting of the Council should be held at Perth, Western Australia, 15–21 August 1975, following upon the Fifth Assembly of the World Council of Churches at Djakarta, 20 July–10 August. Most of the personnel at Dublin were the same as at Limuru. There were different consultants; among them were Professor E. Fairweather and Dr Eric Kemp.

There were first two plenary sessions, in which no decisions were taken; then the Council broke into sections:

1 Unity and Ecumenical affairs
2 Church and Society
3 Order and Organization in the Anglican Communion
4 Mission and Evangelism.

The crucial issue of racism came up. Two notable Anglicans had been exiled from Africa. In 1971 G. A. ffrench-Beytagh, Dean of Johannesburg, had been arrested, but eventually freed after trial and allowed to return to England. His experiences are chronicled in his book *Encountering Darkness*. In March 1972 Bishop Colin Winter of Damaraland was expelled from South-West Africa and remains today a bishop in exile, living in the diocese of Oxford.[9] These events were an obvious background to the Dublin meeting. A memorandum of some length came to the Council from the Church of the Province of South Africa, though it would hardly have satisfied Colin Winter. It included these words:

---

[9] Later his suffragan, Richard Wood, was also exiled.

Black leadership has now been given a constitutional role in the Reserves or Bantustans in South Africa. This means that black people are now able to use constitutional channels for giving expression to their desire for change. This is inadequate machinery for bringing about immediate and dramatic changes, but it does give Blacks an opportunity to struggle to liberate themselves.

The council, replying to this Memorandum, quoted the 1968 Lambeth resolution on Racism and then went on:

We reaffirm the Limuru decision to support the WCC Programme to Combat Racism. We note the information from the bishops of the province that there have been changes in the situation in two years when they say, 'Black leadership has now been given a constitutional role in the Reserves or Bantustans in South Africa', and 'successful strikes are evidence of the effective use of economic power by Africans who now find some support for their demands from leaders in their Bantustan governments'. However, we are also aware that there are other Black leaders who have been banned or placed under house arrest and are also aware of the sinister circumstances concerning the trial of the former Dean of Johannesburg and of the banishment of Bishop Winter from South West Africa.

We would urge that the Programmes be further extended to include a concern for poor and powerless groups, including minorities in parts of the world other than South Africa. Furthermore, additional grants should be made available through the Programme to Combat Racism, as well as other agencies, to help the families of political and war prisoners in numerous countries. Minority and oppressed groups in many parts of the world are engaged in a struggle for their legitimate social, legal, economic, and cultural rights, and many families of political and war prisoners are suffering.

While the initial Programme was intended to express a primary concern for white racism, we should remember racism includes conflict between black and white, white and black, brown and yellow, black and black.[10]

This reply was carried by 41 in favour and two against, with four abstentions. The two opponents were Bishop Burrough of Mashonaland and Bishop Burnett of Grahamstown.

Referring to the situation in Northern Ireland, the Council made this comment:

We are thankful for all the efforts being made to achieve reconciliation in Northern Ireland by sensitive Christian people and leaders. We hope that the effect of these efforts in Church and State will be the achievement of peace with justice for the North Irish people.

[10] *Partners in Mission*, pp. 27f.

The other divisive issue, as at Limuru, was the ordination of women. Following upon Limuru there had been a startling development. Bishop Gilbert Baker of Hong Kong had ordained to the priesthood on Advent Sunday 1971 two women, Jane Hwang and Joyce Bennett. So this time the Council were obliged to say 'There are, therefore, two women priests in the Anglican Communion.' Then they went on:

> No Church or Province has ceased to be in communion with the diocese of Hong Kong. This is not to say that all of them approve the action taken. In fairness, it must be said, however, that remaining in communion indicates that the other Churches and Provinces respect the right of Hong Kong to its action, in the light of Limuru Resolution 28.

They then continued:

> A number of Churches and Provinces have prepared reports or papers on the Ordination of Women to the Priesthood. These are from the Church of England, the Church in Wales, the Church of the Province of New Zealand, the Church of the Province of South Africa, and the Protestant Episcopal Church in the USA. The Church of England in Australia and the Anglican Church of Canada have both carried out similar studies. These reports represent an enormous investment of time and effort, and bear witness to the seriousness with which the matter of the ordination of women to the Priesthood is regarded. Further, it is hard to imagine *any* aspect of this subject which has not been examined by competent scholars, committees, and boards. The report made to the General Synod of the Church of England is particularly recommended for study.

This was a reference to the Howard Report, so called since it was largely written by Miss Christian Howard, which came out in 1972. This was an 87-page document, admirably indexed and annotated and containing information and references not otherwise easily accessible. The Council went on to give information on what provinces were doing. The Church of the Province of Burma had accepted in principle the ordination of women and agreed to its introduction when circumstances required it. The Church of the Province of New Zealand had agreed to it in principle, as also had the Anglican Church of Canada. In England the Church was considering the Howard Report in the dioceses and later the General Synod would decide the question. In Wales a report of their doctrinal commission on the subject had been referred to the dioceses. In the USA in November 1972 the House of Bishops voted that it was in the mind of the House that women should be ordained to the priesthood and the episcopate (in favour 74, against 61, abstentions 5). It also voted to recommend the General Convention in October 1973 to introduce canons to enable the ordination of women to take place. In Australia a doctrinal commission had looked into the matter and this was being studied in the dioceses. The South Pacific Council and Central Africa were at the moment negative in their attitude; it was felt that the time was not yet ripe.

We must now proceed to the third meeting of the Anglican Consultative Council which had on its agenda the great question of a Lambeth Conference. In August 1975 the Standing Committee of the Council met and voted in favour of the proposal for a Lambeth Conference in 1978. By a majority of five to three, with one abstention, it was voted that this Conference should be confined to bishops, and that all diocesans should be invited and a limited number of assistant bishops from non-Western countries. It was believed that the cost would be £350,000 and felt that the Conference should be residential and last four weeks. England was suggested as the venue. The *Daily Telegraph* reported that the University of York, where the General Synod had met, had been suggested as a possible venue. However, the whole Council had to consider the matter before the final decision.

The third Anglican Consultative Council had originally been booked to take place at Perth 3–21 August 1975. When the World Council of Churches Fifth Assembly was moved from Djakarta to Nairobi and its date postponed until November 1975, the Third Council was moved from Perth to Trinidad and postponed until 23 March to 2 April 1976. This meeting was held in the Chaguaramas Convention Centre and the diocese of Trinidad and Tobago showed itself very hospitable. The Prime Minister, Dr Eric Williams, welcomed the delegates at a reception. The President, Dr Donald Coggan, who had succeeded Dr Ramsey in December 1974, preached a sermon at a great public evening service on the Savannah in Port of Spain. The delegates from England were Bishop Brown of St Edmundsbury, Canon Peter Boulton, and Mr John Smallwood. There were other changes in personnel. The Most Rev. Edward Scott, Primate of All Canada, represented the Canadian church and the new Primus, John Allin, represented PECUSA. The Rev. A. E. Harvey of St Augustine's, Canterbury, and Professor John Macquarrie were among the consultants. Discussions took place under six headings:

1 Unity and ecumenical affairs
2 Church and Society

3 Ministry
4 Mission and Evangelism
5 The Lambeth Conference
6 Finance, Membership, and other matters.

The question of the ordination of women came up once again under the heading of ministry. This topic had hit the headlines in July 1974 when eleven women were ordained priests by rebel retired bishops in the USA. A majority of the American bishops later ruled that these ordinations were invalid. In September 1975 four more women were ordained priests by a retired bishop. In England a new publication added fuel to the fire. This was *Women Priests? Yes – Now* with contributions from Joyce Bennett of Hong Kong, Professor Lampe, and others. On the other side came a remarkable pamphlet from an Oxford college chaplain, John Saward. The question had been thrashed out in the General Synod and the ordination of women was approved in principle in July. Anglicans in Canada, Scotland, Wales, the Indian Ocean, Ireland, and the USA had reached the same point. It was reported to the Council that the USA General Convention did not adopt canons to enable women to be ordained but that the question would arise at the General Convention in September. Singapore had voted against the ordination of women. The Report of the Council stated, 'It is evident from this listing that there is within Anglicanism an increasing acceptance of the principle that women may be ordained to the priesthood.'

Perhaps at this point it would be appropriate to pursue the question of the ordination of women down to the present time. In July 1976 the Pope in correspondence with Dr Coggan gave his verdict that the existence of women priests would be a grave obstacle to unity. In November 1976, an American woman priest, Alison Palmer, ordained in 1975, celebrated a Eucharist in the Unitarian church at Golders Green in spite of a ban by the English bishops. The *Church Times* on 3 December published a photograph of the celebration and an account by Susan Young. In the same issue came the report of the ordination of six women to the priesthood in the Canadian church. This became the first major Anglican church officially to ordain women. In the USA at the General Convention the Bishops voted 95 to 61 in favour of ordaining women and the House of Deputies passed this resolution too, but by a narrow majority. The Australian Church came out strongly in favour of women priests in August 1977.

Returning now to Trinidad and the Anglican Council, we find a great deal of discussion on the subject of violence, but the question of a Lambeth Conference hit the headlines. The Council had before it some preliminary discussions by an *ad hoc* committee which had met on 18 and 19 March at Trinidad. This had outlined two possibilities. One was a conference restricted to 300, not wholly confined to bishops, and including the Anglican Consultative Council which was due to meet again in 1978. The agenda would include items on the Church, twentieth-century world, ecumenics, mission, society, similar to previous A.C.C.s and Lambeth Conferences; a study of episcopacy, and its relation to the whole People of God and synodical government; the nature and structure proper for the Anglican Communion. A very rough estimate of the cost was £200,000. The second proposal was that of a Lambeth Conference of 500 members in a traditional pattern of all diocesan bishops and some assistant bishops. In that case the latter part of the above agenda would predominate. The rough cost of this would be £400,000. The Council decided upon the second possibility and voted for a Lambeth Conference in 1978, on the pattern of 1968, residential, either in London or Canterbury. It would consist of 400 diocesan bishops, 40 assistants, and 60 consultants and observers, including the Standing Committee of the Anglican Consultative Council. It would last $3\frac{1}{2}$ weeks. The final voting was 40 for this sort of Lambeth Conference, 5 against, and 4 abstentions. The four abstaining were the Church of England delegates. Arthur Hodgkinson from Scotland said he was unable to support a Lambeth Conference because of finance and the unbalanced representation. In due course the Archbishop of Canterbury announced that the Conference would probably take place in Canterbury.

We must now examine developments regarding the Lambeth Conference since Trinidad. In July 1976 came the announcement that the 1978 Lambeth Conference would be held at the University of Kent. Registration date would be 22 July and the Conference would continue till 13 August. It would begin and end with a service in Canterbury Cathedral. There would also be a service in Westminster Abbey. Diocesan bishops were sent out invitations at the end of July 1976. In them this agenda was outlined:

The accent will be on prayer and waiting upon God.

An emphasis on understanding episcopacy such as would make the exercise of ministry of a bishop today a major theme of the Conference.

Within this context study will include:

a The nature of episcopacy (episcopē)

b The relation of episcopacy –

    i to the Church as the People of God, including the understanding of the Church as family and community

    ii to Synodical Government.

c Theology and the 20th century: the implications of contemporary situations for ministry, ethics, and pastoral responsibility. (The emphasis is unlikely to be the same for all parts of the world. Examples of possible areas of concentration are: technology and medicine, or the theology of renewal, or living with 'other faiths'.)

d Contemporary shape and structure for the Anglican Communion.

Future developments in relating together Lambeth Conferences and the Anglican Consultative Council.

Regarding the assistant bishops invited, it was said, 'For the most part, these assistant bishops will be from parts of our Communion where an indigenous episcopate is fairly recent, and the emphasis will be on younger men, much of whose work lies ahead of them.' Regarding the traditional 'Lambeth Walk' Dr Coggan was moved to write, 'I know that a 3-week Conference of the kind we have in mind will be exhausting, and so bishops will want to be as fresh as possible at the start. I therefore suggest that any activities undertaken in the United Kingdom are so arranged that bishops are not tired when they begin the Lambeth Conference. And during the Conference, including the Sundays, I discourage bishops from undertaking engagements. Indeed, suitable sessions of the Conference may be held on Sunday afternoons. I shall be grateful for your co-operation in this matter.' This was all in accordance with some words of Dr Coggan which he gave soon after Trinidad when he indicated that the Lambeth Conference was taking on a somewhat new role. 'Lambeth Conferences should be less bodies making great ultimata, and more a chance for leisurely prayer and uninterrupted consultation – and even more, perhaps, training sessions for shepherds to look after sheep.' It was announced in December 1976 that 358 diocesan bishops had accepted the Archbishop's invitation.

As the bishops in 1978 are to be concerned with theology, we must briefly paint the theological scene of the last decade. The decade 1968–78 has witnessed the death of the most famous German theologian of the century, Karl Barth, and the most famous German

New Testament scholar, Rudolf Bultmann. Barth's death in 1968 came two years after the demise of Emil Brunner and Paul Tillich.[11] An English giant who departed from the scene was C. H. Dodd, whose most lasting monument will be the New English Bible, the New Testament of which was published in 1961 and the Old Testament and Apocrypha in 1970.[12] One of the great Continental theologians who remains with us in his nineties is Gustaf Aulén, famous for *Christus Victor*. Sir Walter Moberly, the last surviving contributor to *Foundations*, died at 92 in 1974. Other leading Anglican theologians who have passed from us were Leonard Hodgson, Austin Farrer, and F. L. Cross.

The decade has been characterized by an emphasis on Christology. The negative attitude to the doctrine of God, though still with us, is less pronounced.[13] The 'Death of God' School are no longer in business. There has been a growth of interest in meditation and the mystical approach to God, coupled with an increasing desire to know what other religions have to say about God and a willingness to learn from them. Chracteristic of this has been the proliferation of multi-faith services.

Many works have been written on the person of Christ, some of them notable symposia. In 1970 the American liberal theologian, Norman Pittenger, now resident in Cambridge, published *Christology Reconsidered*. In 1972 S. W. Sykes and J. P. Clayton edited *Christ: Faith and History* with contributions from both liberals and conservatives. Maurice Wiles wrote on 'Does Christology rest on a mistake?' – a theme he has since taken further – and John Robinson on 'Need Jesus have been perfect?' Robinson followed up this essay in 1973 with a large volume *The Human Face of God* which seemed to some excessively negative, as also did Maurice Wiles's *The Remaking of Christian Doctrine* in 1974. Christology remained a large issue in the work of the Doctrine Commission, of which Wiles was Chairman; its report, *Christian Believing*, which came out in 1976, was heavily criticized for its liberalism, even in the pages of the *Modern Churchman*! The biggest Christological bombshell came in 1977 with the symposium edited by John Hick, *The Myth of God Incarnate*,

---

[11] Some have been shocked by the revelations about Paul Tillich's personal life. See Hannah Tillich, *From Time to Time*.

[12] F. W. Dillistone's life of C. H. Dodd is as excellent as his biography of Charles Raven.

[13] In the sixties a prevalent theological approach seemed to be 'There is no God and Jesus Christ is his son.'

containing essays by a team of distinguished radical scholars including Dennis Nineham, Maurice Wiles, and Don Cupitt. Many people criticized this scholarly work before they had even read it! An orthodox reply, *The Truth of God Incarnate*, was hastily produced. Edited and largely written by the Evangelical Michael Green, it also contained critiques by Bishop Stephen Neill, Brian Hebblethwaite, the Anglo-Catholic John Macquarrie, and the Roman Catholic Bishop B. C. Butler. Some have called upon the Lambeth Conference to adjudicate on the controversy. If the bishops read the books they would also do well to read the recent work of the veteran New Testament scholar C. F. D. Moule, *The Origin of Christology*, with which they will doubt-less be more in sympathy. Even the nonagenarian Gustaf Aulén has made a notable contribution to Christological study.[14]

Perhaps the most notable general work in theology in this decade has been the book by the liberal Roman Catholic Hans Kung, *On Being a Christian*, which came out in England at the same time as the new edition of John Macquarrie's *Principles of Christian Theology*. One of the most valuable and worth-while theological works from an Anglican during the decade is John A. Baker's *The Foolishness of God* which exhibits a sane but critical approach to theology. Lesser in scope but equally valuable is Michael Ramsey's *God, Christ and the World*, a helpful discussion, written in 1969, of the negative and positive positions in theology. Ramsey makes much of the *dictum* of William Temple, 'God is Christlike and in Him is no unChristlikeness at all'. He gives a critique of the positions of Van Buren and Harvey Cox.

One of the most notorious books of liberal theology – if it can be called theology – was John M. Allegro's *The Sacred Mushroom and the Cross* which was quickly demolished by a formidable array of scholars learned in oriental languages. As it has been forgotten the bishops at Lambeth will not have the task of refuting it! Liberal theology even found its way into the Salvation Army. Fred Brown, not to be confused with William G. Brown the Observer at the 1968 Lambeth Conference, wrote *Secular Evangelism* and was duly disciplined by his religious superiors.

Clearly the uppermost question at the moment – and it will doubtless remain so in 1978 – is the Christological one. Can the Lambeth Fathers of 1978 affirm, like their predecessors of 1867, 'the Lord Jesus Christ' as 'our Saviour, very God and very Man, ever to be adored and worshipped'? One hopes they can reaffirm this and yet retain a critical faith in the face of an upsurge of fundamentalism.

[14] *Jesus in Contemporary Historical Research* (1977).

We turn now from the theological to the ecumenical scene, dealing first with the Ten Propositions and then with Anglican–Roman Catholic relations and finally Anglican–Orthodox relations. After the failure of the Anglican–Methodist Scheme 'talks about talks' were initiated. A more flexible approach began, involving other churches besides the Methodists. Prominent in the new endeavour was the conception of covenanting towards unity at a given date. The churches involved were the Baptist Church, the Churches of Christ, the Congregational Federation, the Methodist Church, the Moravian Church, the Roman Catholic Church, and the United Reformed Church. Ten propositions were evolved, of which the most crucial were 4, 5, and 6.

> 4 We agree to recognize, as from an accepted date, the communicant members in good standing of the other covenanting Churches as true members of the Body of Christ and welcome them to Holy Communion without condition.

> 5 We agree that, as from an accepted date, initiation in the covenanting Churches shall be by mutually acceptable rites.

> 6 We agree to recognize, as from an accepted date, the ordained ministries of the other covenanting Churches, as true ministries of word and sacraments in the Holy Catholic Church, and we agree that all subsequent ordinations to the ministries of the covenanting Churches shall be according to a Common Ordinal which will properly incorporate the episcopal, presbyteral and lay roles in ordination.

Proposition 4 is, in effect, an extension of welcoming Trinitarian Christians to Anglican altars in accordance with Canon B 15A, a canon whose passage through General Synod in the early seventies was a great step forward. These Ten Propositions were discussed in the General Synod in the summer of 1976 following their publication earlier in the year. A proposal by Bishop Hare of Pontefract that all of them should be accepted was defeated by 165 votes to 104, but the discussion of them has continued and much pamphlet literature about them has appeared. The Anglican Consultative Council at Trinidad examined them, outlining the genesis of the Ten Propositions and the Churches' Unity Commission. They then went on to make their comments which, as they have been little noticed, are worth quoting.

> The Ten Propositions may be showing us a new way forward in the quest for unity and perhaps a new model of unity. This is called in the propositions 'visible unity', and is intended to indicate a more flexible concept than what has usually been understood as 'organic unity', viz. the formation of one

ecclesial structure, usually within the boundaries of a single nation. What is here called 'visible unity' is understood as an open-ended and ongoing process. The aim of the Ten Propositions is to get this process going. No 'Scheme of union' is put forward, but a step by step process which will lead all the churches into an ever deepening unity. . . .

They envisage therefore a covenant or solemn undertaking which would ask the churches to take two important steps:

(i) To accept each other's baptised members in good standing, and to admit them without condition to Holy Communion. From the time that they agreed to do this all the churches would use 'mutually acceptable rites' of initiation. These could be quite varied, e.g. an integrated rite of initiation which could be administered in infancy (as with the Orthodox) or in adulthood (as with the Baptists), or a divided rite of baptism in infancy followed by confirmation at a later time. But there would be agreement on certain basic essentials of the rite.

(ii) There would be an integration of ministries leading, it is hoped, not just to mutual recognition but to full interchangeability. This would be secured by two steps, which are contained in the single proposition 6, to make clear they are part of one 'package'. Existing ministries, which are all defective in isolation, though in different ways, would come together in an act of reconciliation which would have both sacramental and juridical significance. From the date on which that happened, all future ordinations would include the appropriate lay, presbyteral and episcopal participation. A common ordinal or at least a common 'core', which might be expanded in different traditions, would be adopted. The proposed Anglican–Methodist Ordinal has been suggested as a model. To carry out this proposal about ministries, the present non-episcopal churches would need to have bishops consecrated.[15]

Since these words were written the Alternative Series 3 draft Ordination Services have been published and these are very relevant to the discussion. At any rate, though the Ten Propositions have arisen in England, clearly they are of value to the whole Anglican Communion.

We turn now to Anglican–Roman Catholic relations. Contacts with Roman Catholics went on during the decade. In January 1969 Cardinal Suenens of Belgium visited Archbishop Ramsey at Lambeth Palace and the two men exchanged their latest books; in April this remarkable man visited York and unveiled a plaque in memory of the famous Malines Conversations. In 1977 the Cardinal became the first Roman Catholic to conduct a mission in the University of Oxford.

[15] *A.C.C. 3 – Trinidad*, pp. 17f.

In February 1971 Dr Ramsey received a visit from Cardinal Marty, Archbishop of Paris, and took him to see the Queen, and then Westminster Abbey, the Community of the Resurrection, and other places. In October 1973 Cardinal Willebrands, President of the Vatican Secretariat for promoting Christian Unity, became the first Roman Catholic since the Reformation to celebrate mass in Lambeth Chapel.

The official talks between Roman Catholics and Anglicans continued and bore fruit. The Anglican Chairman was now Bishop Henry McAdoo, Bishop of Ossory, Ferns, and Leighlin, who has recently written about progress made in *Being an Anglican*. The other Anglicans were John Moorman, Bishop of Ripon, Edward Knapp-Fisher, Bishop of Pretoria, Geoffrey T. Sambell, Co-adjutor Bishop of Melbourne and later Archbishop of Perth,[16] Dr Henry Chadwick, the Dean of Christ Church, Oxford, the Rev. Julian Charley of St John's College, Nottingham, Harold Root, Professor of Theology at Southampton, A. A. Vogel, Bishop Co-adjutor of West Missouri, and Professor Eugene Fairweather from Toronto. The Secretary at first was Canon Satterthwaite but his place was soon taken by Colin Davey. The Chairman of the Roman Catholic delegates was the Rt Rev. Alan Clark, Auxiliary Bishop of Northampton. The first outcome of their discussions was *An Agreed Statement on Eucharistic Doctrine* published in 1972, but agreed upon at a meeting at Windsor in September 1971. The meeting of the Anglican–Roman Catholic Commission at Canterbury in September 1973 produced the agreed statement on Ministry and Ordination. From a subsequent meeting of the two sides at Venice in 1976 resulted the publication of the agreed statement on Authority in the Church, in January 1977. This was the most controversial of the three. It envisaged a future Church with a universal primacy in it. Something was said about the question of papal infallibility, a stumbling block to many Anglicans.

Anglicans find grave difficulty in the affirmation that the pope can be infallible in his teaching. It must, however, be borne in mind that the doctrine of infallibility is hedged round by very rigorous conditions laid down at the First Vatican Council. These conditions preclude the idea that the pope is an inspired oracle communicating fresh revelation, or that he can speak independently of his fellow bishops and the Church, or on matters not concerning faith and morals. For the Roman Catholic Church the pope's dogmatic definitions, which, fulfilling the criteria of infallibility, are preserved from error, do no more but no less than express the mind of the

[16] Sambell's place was later taken by Archbishop F. R. Arnott of Brisbane.

Church on issues concerning the divine revelation. Even so, special difficulties are created by the recent Marian dogmas, because Anglicans doubt the appropriateness, or even the possibility, of defining them as essential to the faith of believers.

The retired Archbishop of Canterbury, Dr Ramsey, is reported to have given his support of the statement on a recent tour of Australia.

1974 saw the publication of a useful account of Anglican–Roman Catholic relations by Bernard and Mary Pawley, while 1977 witnessed the publication of two valuable pamphlets on the subject by Roman Catholics. One was Dr Edward Yarnold's *Anglican Orders – A Way Forward*, which attempts to get round the Papal Bull *Apostolicae Curae*; the other is *Anglicans and Roman Catholics* by Richard L. Stewart. In April 1977 Dr Donald Coggan followed the example of Archbishops Ramsey and Fisher and visited the Pope at the Vatican. Dr Coggan stayed at the English College at Rome and visited the Pope on 28 April. Among other things he invited the Pope to send three observers to the 1978 Lambeth Conference.

We pass on now to Anglicans and Orthodox. Here there were valuable contacts and visits. In August 1969 Dr Ramsey received a visit from Archbishop German of the Serbian Orthodox Church. In July 1972 he went to Istanbul for the funeral of the Oecumenical Patriarch, Athenagoras I, who in 1967 had been the first Oecumenical Patriarch to visit Lambeth and whom Ramsey regarded as 'a dear friend and great Christian'. In place of Athenagoras, Demetrios, Metropolitan of Imbros in Tenedos, was installed as Oecumenical Patriarch and Archbishop of Constantinople. A month previous to this visit to Constantinople, Ramsey had been a guest of the Patriarch Maxim in Bulgaria, together with the Bishop of Fulham and Gibraltar (Satterthwaite) and Bishop Browning of the American churches in Europe. The Archbishop expressed a hope that a Theological Commission of the Orthodox Church and the Anglican Communion would soon start work. His hope was fulfilled in September 1973 when the first meeting took place at Oxford. This had been prepared for by a gathering at Chambesy, where there is an Orthodox centre, in September 1972. Dr Harry Carpenter, retired Bishop of Oxford, acted as Anglican Co-chairman. Other bishops were Falkner Allison, Bishop of Winchester, Robert Runcie, Bishop of St Albans, and Bishop Satterthwaite of Fulham and Gibraltar. H. R. T. Brandreth was Theological Secretary. Dr Ramsey paid the Commission a visit and joined in one of the discussions. It was decided to hold a further full meeting in 1976. In the meantime sub-committees would meet in 1974 and 1975 to prepare papers on (i) Inspiration and Revelation in the Holy Scripture; (ii) The authority of the Councils, and (iii) The Church as the eucharistic community. During the meeting the delegates attended a memorial service to the late Oecumenical Patriarch at Christ Church. They were also present at the new Orthodox Church in Oxford, whose minister, the Very Rev. Archimandrite Kallistos Ware (an ex-Anglican), was the Theological Secretary for the Orthodox Delegation. From 17–22 October the Patriarch of Bulgaria, Maxim, visited Lambeth.

In July 1976 the second full session of talks between Anglicans and Orthodox took place at Zagorsk, forty miles from Moscow. Bishop Runcie of St Albans led the Anglicans; Archbishop Stylianos of Australia deputized for Archbishop Athenagoras of Thyateira and Great Britain as Orthodox co-chairman. Both sides agreed that the *Filioque* clause was not an essential part of the Nicene Creed. The result was some agreement in a limited field.

On 30 April Dr Coggan visited the Oecumenical Patriarch Demetrios I after going to Rome to see Pope Paul VI. He also had talks with Schnork Kaloustian, the Armenian Patriarch. The great difficulty which they encountered in their discussions was that of the ordination of women which the Oecumenical Patriarch declared unacceptable to the Orthodox Church. The answer of the Archbishop of Canterbury was that the Anglican Communion did not seek the agreement of the Orthodox Church on the subject but was hoping for understanding of it. Dr Coggan later visited the Metropolitan Damaskinos of Tranoupolis at the Orthodox Centre at Chambesy on the occasion of his visit to Geneva. The most recent meeting of the Anglican–Orthodox Commission was at Cambridge in July 1977. After it Bishop Runcie told the *Church Times*, 'The talks were conducted in a friendly and Christian spirit, but were not tranquil'. The ordination of women was the great problem. It was announced that a special meeting would be held between Anglicans and Orthodox theologians just before the Lambeth Conference in 1978 in the hope of influencing the Conference in the matter of the ordination of women.

Turning now to the World Council of Churches, here the big event of the decade has been the Nairobi Assembly in 1975. But there are other things to note. Pope Paul VI visited the World Council of Churches at Geneva in June 1969 and joined in a service with the World Council leaders and members of other Churches. In May 1977 Dr Coggan visited Geneva after his visits to the Pope and the Oecumenical Patriarch. January 1973 saw a valuable ten-day conference on Salvation organized by the Commission on World Mission and Evangelism of the World Council of Churches. David Jenkins, now Director of the William Temple Foundation, Manchester, wrote of this Conference:

> I can only rejoice that meeting in Asia, the Asian delegates, together with their Third World colleagues were in a small numerical majority as far as influence and ideas went. We may be at the end of an era for the West, but Jesus Christ is not identified with that (even if the Western practices seem to support such a notion). The Church continues to grow and much as yet unexpected and unseen renewal is beginning to flow north, east, south and west.

The Fifth Assembly of the World Council of Churches had originally been scheduled to be held at Djakarta, Indonesia, in August 1975, but it was found inadvisable to hold it in a mainly Islamic country. So it was moved to Nairobi and the time altered to November and December. It took place amid an element of criticism. There was a feeling on the part of some that it was too concerned with combating racism and insufficiently concerned with preaching the Gospel. David Edwards was hostile in the *Church Times*. 'The World Council of Churches in recent years has had a feeble record in the consideration of basic doctrine and spiritual practice. It is revealing to ponder why, although the W.C.C. does not shirk controversy in the political field, it could not conceivably launch at Nairobi a Programme to combat Atheism.' Since Nairobi Bernard Smith has published a book, *The Fraudulent Gospel: Politics and the World Council of Churches*, which delivers a bitter attack on the World Council of Churches.

The Nairobi Assembly was held at the Kenyatta Conference Centre, not far from the smaller conference centre at Limuru where an Anglican Consultative Council meeting had taken place. Kikuyu is not far away. The fact that the World Council of Churches' General Secretary, Dr Philip Potter, was a coloured man indicated the move from Europe to the Third World. The theme of the meeting was 'Jesus Christ frees and unites' and was to be discussed under five sections:

1 Confessing Christ today
2 What unity requires
3 Seeking community

4 Education for liberation and community
5 Structures of injustice and struggles for liberation.

Pope Paul sent a message to Dr Potter and there were many observers appointed by the Vatican; three Roman Catholics addressed the assembly but there was no great advance on the Roman front. One tense moment in the assembly came through the appeal published in *Target*, the assembly's daily newspaper, by two members of the Russian Orthodox Church within the U.S.S.R. regarding the serious breaches of human rights and religious freedom.[17] Richard Holloway of the Scottish Episcopal Church asked why the U.S.S.R. was never mentioned in the World Council documents. There was much embarrassment in the Orthodox delegation. Kenneth Slack, who wrote an excellent account of the meeting, summed it up as follows:

> I do not think it is yet possible to identify a message that comes through the Nairobi assembly in the same direct way [as at Uppsala]. In some degree this is due to the fact that justice, the Uppsala word, if appallingly demanding, is simple and direct. There were signs at Nairobi that the daunting complexity of many of the problems was more fully realized. Thus Professor Birch, for all the urgency of his plea for a radically reordered international economic system, had to admit that it was still a matter of wide debate what kind of technology could help the poor without bringing in its train the same destruction as he described in the developed world. Canon Burgess Carr, for all his commitment to a free Africa, had to utter that heart-cry (at the end of Mr Manley's address) about an Africa where freedom was proving so elusive, and where so many had fled as refugees from their own newly-freed lands. I had a clear impression at Nairobi that some of the easier Utopianism that had currency at Uppsala seven years before did not carry the credibility that it once did. Uppsala met as the tragedy of the Nigerian-Biafran war moved to its horrible end. Each day's headlines in the secular press during Nairobi spoke of the Angolan civil war, with rival factions fuelled and armed by distant powers. The Angolan tragedy somehow proved more sobering than the Nigerian one.
>
> But there was no weakening of conviction in the assembly that God purposes a different community for mankind in which men shall be both free and united. Liberation rather than unity was the particular stress within the theme 'Jesus Christ frees and unites', but unity was not forgotten. I was struck by the comment of a shrewd young man who had been to many

[17] On Christians behind the iron curtain there have been at least two publications worth noting. One is Trevor Beeson, *Discretion and Valour. Religious Conditions in Russia and Eastern Europe.* The other is Georgi Vins, *Three Generations of Suffering.* Richard Wurmbrand has also written a large number of books on the subject.

secular conferences of importance. You could never doubt, he told me, that this was a Christian conference. That did not mean it was without its tensions, and indeed at times its ill temper. It does mean that somehow it was in the main held with a genuine sense of brotherhood, and again and again there came those startling moments of openness to others which are one of the striking manifestations of the Spirit at such gatherings.[18]

One of the results for Great Britain at the end of the Assembly was that she was left with no President in the World Council. It was understood that Dr Coggan would not allow his name to go forward.

Only brief reference can be made here to the charismatic and pentecostal movement which has been a marked phenomenon of the last decade. A full account of the whole pentecostal movement came from Walter J. Hollenweger in *The Pentecostals*. Dr Ramsey himself made a contribution to *The Charismatic Christ* which, among other things, has some shrewd comments on the musicals *Godspell* and *Jesus Christ Superstar*. Pentecostalism hit Rome as well as Protestant churches. Cardinal Suenens was the author of *A New Pentecost?* In South Africa the charismatic movement has become widespread and Bill Burnett, now Archbishop of Cape Town, has become a strong participant in it. Whatever we may think of the charismatic or pentecostal movement it has undoubtedly to be reckoned with.

Finally in our consideration of the ecumenical movement we must draw attention to two national unions. In November 1970 there was formed at Lahore the United Church of Pakistan which joined together Anglicans, United Methodists, and members of the Sialkot Church Council of the United Church in Pakistan (Scottish Presbyterians and the Pakistani Lutheran Church). In the same month the Church of North India was also inaugurated at Nagpur and brought together Anglicans, Methodists, Baptists, Presbyterians, Congregationalists, Brethren, and Disciples of Christ. In the inaugural service Lakdasa de Mel, ex-Metropolitan of India, Pakistan, and Ceylon, played some part.

We must turn now to the internal organization of the Anglican Communion and its progress. In the year after the 1968 Conference Timothy Wilson published *All One Body*, dedicated to Dr Ramsey, in which a large selection of bishops who were present at Lambeth '68 spoke about Anglicanism in various parts of the world. Bishops from overseas who participated in the venture were Trevor Huddleston, who at Lambeth '68 was transferring from Masasi to Stepney, Lakdasa de

[18] K. Slack, *Nairobi Narrative*, pp. 85f.

Mel, Gilbert Baker (Hong Kong), Leonard Beecher (Nairobi), Hassan Dehqani-Tafti (Iran), John Hines (U.S.A.), Oliver Allison (Sudan), Oliver Green-Wilkinson (Zambia), and Alphaeus Zulu (Zululand).[19]

Both Drs Ramsey and Coggan have carried out visitations of various parts of the Anglican Communion. In December 1970 Archbishop Ramsey visited South Africa and on that occasion had strong words to say to Mr Vorster; he also went to Uganda. In March 1973 the Ramseys visited the Far East – India, Singapore, Brunei and Sabah, Hong Kong, the Philippines, Korea, and Japan. While in Hong Kong he was able to speak to two Anglican women priests. In July 1974 the Archbishop visited the U.S.A. and in October came his last overseas tour as Archbishop when he visited South America. There he spoke out strongly on the question of human rights when he met the head of the Chilean military junta. Dr Coggan's first major overseas tour was to the Sudan in October 1976. In February 1977 he went on a visitation of the Far East, taking in Papua, New Guinea, Australia, New Zealand, and Fiji.

A number of new provinces have been inaugurated in the last decade. In 1970 there came into existence the Church of Burma when the Rt Rev. Francis Ah Mya became the first Archbishop (later to be succeeded by John Aung Hla). In July the new province of Tanzania was inaugurated and a month later the new province of Kenya, when in the presence of President Jomo Kenyatta, the Most Rev. Festo Olang' was enthroned as first Archbishop. Changes came about in Central Africa where the new province with four dioceses, Zambia, Malawi, Mashonaland, and Matabeleland, had been inaugurated by Archbishop Fisher in 1965. In May 1970 Oliver Green-Wilkinson, the Archbishop of Central Africa, and also Bishop of Zambia, wanted to withdraw Zambia from the group because of what he considered the unchristian regime in Rhodesia. Later he died tragically in a car accident. Today there is still one Province of Central Africa, with seven dioceses. In March 1973 the new Province of the Indian Ocean was instituted consisting initially of three dioceses, Madagascar, Mauritius, and the Seychelles. The organization of the Anglican Communion was considered at the Anglican Consultative Council at Dublin in July

---

[19] Two books on the Church of England published in the last decade were Leslie Paul's *A Church by Daylight* and Trevor Beeson's *The Church of England in Crisis*. Reference should also be made to Edward Carpenter's *Cantuar* and David Edwards's *Leaders of the Church of England 1828–1944* as valuable books on Anglicanism published in the last decade.

1973. A new disposition of dioceses in the Middle East was proposed, which was to comprise four dioceses:

1 Jerusalem (to include Israel, Jordan, Lebanon and Syria)
2 Cyprus and the Gulf
3 Egypt
4 Iran.

There was to be a new system for the election of a bishop for the diocese of Jerusalem, instead of an outside appointment of an archbishop in Jerusalem. Later in the year Dr Ramsey appointed Bishop Stopford, recently retired from London, to supervise the setting up of the new scheme. It was also agreed that the diocese of Sudan should revert to the jurisdiction of the Archbishop of Canterbury. In Melanesia, which had recently been celebrating the centenary of Bishop J. C. Patteson,[20] a new Province was recommended and has since come into being. The Episcopal Church of the Sudan was inaugurated in October 1976 and the new Province of Papua New Guinea was instituted in February 1977. Thus there have been considerable changes since 1968.

In the years between 1968 and 1977 there have been a great many changes in the leading personalities in Anglicanism and these we must now outline. Michael De-la-Noy, the flamboyant press officer of the Archbishop of Canterbury in 1968, responsible for the document *Lambeth '68*, which issued in a row, was dismissed from his post in July 1971 and in the following year wrote a book about his experience as press officer called *A Day in the Life of God*. Bishop Stephen Bayne, the first Anglican Executive Officer, to whom the Anglican Communion owed a great deal, and not least, his book *An Anglican Turning Point*, died in January 1974 when he was only 65. His successor, Ralph Dean, became Archbishop of Cariboo and Metropolitan of British Columbia. In 1969 he spoke of his years as Executive Office as 'wonderful years, but years for which you pay a very high price'. He was speaking at the Synod of the Anglican Church in Canada. He added, gloomily, 'as far as the world is concerned, it is too late for things such as inter-communion because nobody cares anymore'.[21] In 1973 he suddenly gave up his offices and was given by the Canadian church five years' leave of absence to join, at the age of 60, the staff of Christ Church, Greenville, South Carolina.[22]

[20] The decade has seen a new life of Patteson by Sir John Gutch.
[21] See *Church Times*, 19 September 1969.
[22] See *Daily Telegraph*, 24 July 1973.

Archbishop Geoffrey Fisher, who was present at the final service at St Paul's in 1968, died in the Yeatman Hospital at Sherborne, Dorset, in 1972 and was buried, not at Canterbury, but at Trent, where he had acted as priest-in-charge since his retirement. Before his death Canon Purcell of Worcester brought out his life, though Dr Edward Carpenter has since embarked on a definitive one. Archbishop Philip Carrington, another great Anglican, who also was present with Fisher in St Paul's in 1968, died in 1975. Another famous bishop and writer on Anglicanism, William Wand, died at the age of 92, in August 1977 and was quickly followed by Canon Max Warren. But perhaps the most notable death of 1977 was that of Archbishop Janani Luwum, who died as a martyr in Uganda, in the centenary year of Bishop Hannington.

Ian Ramsey, the philosopher Bishop of Durham, died in 1972 a few weeks after he had participated in the British Council of Churches Conference at Birmingham. David Edwards wrote a book about the Conference, *The British Churches turn to the Future* and also *Ian Ramsey – Bishop of Durham – a Memoir*. Another former Bishop of Durham, who died in 1968, was also commemorated in a life – Bishop Alwyn Williams.[23] Bishop F. R. Barry, a noted liberal Anglican, and Robert Mortimer, a great Anglo-Catholic, both died in 1976. A notorious American liberal, James Pike, died in the wilderness of Judaea in September 1968.

Emmanuel Amand de Mendieta, who told of his conversion to Anglicanism in *Rome and Canterbury* and wrote *Anglican Vision* in 1971 died in 1977. Other deaths we must note are those of Bishop William Greer of Manchester, R. O. Hall of Hong Kong, John Taylor of Sheffield, Joseph Fison of Salisbury, Robert Stopford (who after his post-retirement job in Jerusalem took on another as Bishop of Bermuda), Archbishop Chisholm of Melanesia, Lakdusa de Mel, Joost de Blank, and J. L. Wilson, whose life *John Leonard Wilson Confessor for the Faith* was written by Roy McKay.

There have been many changes in the episcopal bench. George Simms, who earned golden opinions as Archbishop of Dublin, was elected Archbishop of Armagh and Primate of All Ireland. John Robinson left episcopal work at Woolwich, returned to Cambridge as Dean of Trinity College, and has now made a name for himself for his attempt to attach an early date to every book in the New Testament. His successors at Woolwich were first David Sheppard, the Test cricketer and author of *Built as a City*, a book on urban ministry, and then, when

<hr>

[23] See C. H. G. Hopkins, *Bishop A. T. P. Williams.*

Sheppard moved to Liverpool, Michael Marshall, a leading Anglo-Catholic. Other leaders among the Anglo-Catholics are Eric Kemp, Bishop of Chichester, Graham Leonard, who was translated from the suffragan see of Willesden to the diocesan see of Truro, and John Tinsley, ex-Professor of Theology at Leeds, who became Bishop of Bristol in succession to Oliver Tomkins.[24]

Besides the two Primates there is quite a galaxy of Evangelicals – reminiscent of the Palmerstonian Evangelicals in the time of Archbishop Sumner. John Taylor, author of *Enough is enough*, a best-seller, and *The Go-Between God*, is now Bishop of Winchester; Maurice Wood is Bishop of Norwich; David Brown is Bishop of Guildford; Sheppard at Liverpool has already been noted.

Simon Phipps, notable for his work in Coventry, moved from Horsham to Lincoln. Stretton Reeve's successor at Lichfield was Kenneth J. P. Skelton, a man with much experience in Africa. John Habgood, writer in *Soundings*, succeeded Ian Ramsey at Durham, while Gerald Ellison moved from Chester to follow Stopford at London. Robert Runcie, Principal of Cuddesdon, followed Gresford Jones at St Albans and Kenneth Woollcombe, Principal of Edinburgh Theological College, and contributor to *The Historic Episcopate*, followed Harry Carpenter at Oxford. At Derby, Geoffrey Allen was followed by Cyril Bowles (an Evangelical) and at Birmingham, Laurence Brown succeeded Wilson. Patrick C. Rodger, Provost of Edinburgh Cathedral, was Greer's successor at Manchester. Robin Woods, whose father (Edward), uncle (Theodore), and brother (Frank) had played their parts in Lambeth Conferences, became Bishop of Worcester in succession to Mervyn Charles-Edwards. Gordon Fallows, penultimate Principal of Ripon Hall, was translated from Pontefract to Sheffield in succession to John Taylor and A. J. Trillo, another ex-Principal of a theological college (Cheshunt, now no more) is Bishop of Chelmsford. A notable suffragan is Hugh Montefiore, Bishop of Kingston. There are not many English bishops still on the bench who were present at Lambeth '68, but notable names which immediately suggest themselves are George Reindorp, who has now moved from Guildford to Salisbury, Mervyn Stockwood, still at Southwark, Ronald Williams of Leicester, David Say of Rochester, and Gerald Ellison, formerly of Chester and now of London. Trevor Huddleston at Stepney retires after the 1978 Conference.

Turning to the Anglican Communion in other parts, the Presiding

---

[24] Graham Leonard was chairman of the Commission which produced the Mothers' Union Report *New Dimensions*.

Bishop of the American Episcopal Church is now John Allin. Gwilym Williams is Archbishop of Wales and Allen Johnston Archbishop of New Zealand. Bishop A. I. M. Haggart of Edinburgh has now succeeded R. K. Wimbush as Primus of the Episcopal Church of Scotland. Moses Scott is Archbishop of West Africa and E. W. Scott Primate of Canada.

The most notable change has been that of the two Primates. Donald Coggan, Archbishop of York, succeeded Michael Ramsey at Canterbury and Stuart Blanch moved from Liverpool to York. Dr Ramsey retired on 14 November 1974, the very day that the Worship and Doctrine Measure passed the Lords. This freedom in worship was something upon which he had set his heart when he became Archbishop of Canterbury and his primacy has seen both the Series 2 and Series 3 communion services and many other changes in the liturgy of an experimental nature. To mark his retirement he published a number of his sermons and addresses under the title *Canterbury Pilgrim*. In his opening paper, 'Lessons of a Pilgrimage', he contrasted the scene in the seventies with that of the sixties.

> As he walks from the sixties towards the mid-seventies, this Canterbury pilgrim begins to find himself in a different scene and a different climate. The apathy about God and Christianity remains, morals are even more chaotic, and the world is even more cruel. Nor is the dislike of 'institutions' any less. But amongst the faithful there is a lively faith, worship has greater 'boldness of access', and the loss of nerve seems to belong to yesterday. The pilgrim sees more often not the spectre of atheism within the Church but powerful movements of spirituality of one kind and another, some without and some within the Churches, and his problem is what to do and say about *these*.[25]

Michael Ramsey remained to the end of his time at Canterbury convinced of the value of a Lambeth Conference. In May 1973 in his Presidential Address to the Diocesan Synod of Canterbury, he spoke of Lambeth and Anglicanism. He said he believed that the see of Canterbury was still a symbolic focus of Anglican unity, if only because it was impossible to define the Anglican Communion without it.

> Here I have found a certain ambivalence of attitude. Inevitably there are Anglican Churches overseas which are suspicious of the Church and State relation in this country and do not want to feel themselves in any way an English-led communion. Yet, I believe, that if an Archbishop of Canterbury will identify himself with the Communion as a whole and try to be less an

[25] Op. cit., p. 7.

English prelate than a servant of the Anglican Communion as widely as he can, then the see of Canterbury will continue to have its symbolic role. I believe, however, that no bond of our Anglican union is stronger than the fellowship between the Anglican bishops; and rightly so, as it is the historic role of the Bishop to represent unity between, as well as within, the Churches.[26]

He went on to speak of the Lambeth Conference.

Here I would deprecate the suggestion, of which we have heard a little in recent years, that the role of the Lambeth Conference is obsolete. The present Anglican Consultative Council which meets every two years, is no substitute, and was never designed to be a substitute, for the Lambeth Conference.

There is nothing sacrosanct about the name Lambeth or about the location where the bishops may meet. But I believe that, as a mode of association between the Anglican provinces, nothing is more characteristic or more necessary than the meeting from time to time of the bishops drawn from every province, together with bishops from sister Churches in communion with us.

As Ramsey went into retirement a volume of essays, edited by Christopher Martin, *The Great Centuries to Come*, was brought out in his honour. This contained a paper by Bishop John Howe on 'The Future of the Anglican Communion' and one by Canon Allchin on 'Approaches to Eastern Orthodoxy and to Rome'.

The succession of Donald Coggan to the see of Canterbury was announced in May 1974 and ended a great deal of speculation in which various names had been bandied about, including those of John Howe, Henry Chadwick, Owen Chadwick, and Kenneth Woollcombe. He was enthroned in January 1975 and in the following month Stuart Blanch was enthroned at York, a day or two after the death of Alan Richardson, the Dean of York, a notable theologian and protagonist of 'Biblical Theology'. Later in the year the two archbishops publicized a Call to the Nation which made some impression upon the country and is chronicled in *Dear Archbishop* by John Poulton. Mervyn Stockwood, the Bishop of Southwark, denounced the Call in the *Morning Star* and so an ecclesiastical row was engendered. David Perman in his *Change and the Churches*, a book well worth reading by the bishops before they

---

[26] In December 1970 the report of the Chadwick Commission on Church and State was published and offered two solutions, one radical, the other more conservative, to deal with the Church-State relationship. Miss Valerie Pitt could not agree with the report and wrote a paper in favour of disestablishment.

come to Lambeth,[27] is critical of the Archbishops' action: 'Archbishop Coggan's appeal was the first of its kind since William Temple's Malvern Conference in 1941, and he had the advantages denied to his predecessor – a fat, peacetime press, and television too. But it is doubtful if Dr Coggan's appeal will merit even the footnote in the history books which Temple achieved at a time when there was certainly no shortage of world news.' I myself think that a better comparison than the Malvern Conference, which did not get into the homes in the way that Coggan's appeal did, would be the Mission of Repentance and Hope initiated by Randall Davidson in 1916; that too was heavily criticized.

Dr Coggan has been as keen as Dr Ramsey on the idea of the Lambeth Conference. In his book *Convictions* he wrote:

Lambeth was a big and expensive operation – expensive in manhours, in energy and money. Many have asked: 'Was it all worthwhile?' I say 'Yes'. These conferences have been held roughly once a decade since their inception 101 years ago. No one can say what shape the next will take, but I hope greatly that there will be another. Some have spoken of Lambeth 1968 as the last; I consider such talk to be ill-conceived and premature. I believe in these conferences, not merely for the statements that come out of them, although these statements often read rather 'flatly', for they frequently are the work of more than one mind and bear none of the sparkle of the spoken word. But even these statements are valuable as distillations of hard thinking, and serve as the basis of preaching and discussion in ensuing months and years.

Perhaps the greatest benefits which come out of the Lambeth Conference are the friendships formed and deepened. I mean by this not merely that it can be said at the end of the conference that 'a good time was had by all'. I mean something much deeper. I mean that men (and women, for some hundreds of wives come to London) get to know one another, to understand the problems of areas which they had never visited, and, out of this deep fellowship in Christ, intelligent and constant prayer is bound to flow. This will enrich the life of the Anglican Communion as nothing else. *This* is our greatest need.[28]

So we look forward to the eleventh Lambeth Conference. It will not be an easy one. Difficult questions will have to be faced, in particular the very question of what bishops are for;[29] whether women should be

---

[27] As also is John Adair's *The Becoming Church*.

[28] Op. cit., pp. 153f. Cf. also Anne Arnott, *Wife to the Archbishop*, p. 126.

[29] Relevant here may be the report *Bishops and Dioceses* which came out in 1971.

ordained is another prominent issue. We know that Dr Coggan is keen that they should, but the divisive effect this will have and the damage it will do to Roman Catholic and Orthodox relations will have to be considered. There is also the question of the relationship of the races. As these words are written the bishop whose name is most often in the news is that of a Rhodesian, Abel Muzorewa, not an Anglican but a Methodist, the leader of the moderates in the fight for a just regime in Rhodesia. Also Bishop Colin Winter, exiled Bishop of Damaraland, wishes to return to his diocese in Namibia, and may call upon the Lambeth bishops to support him. He said recently in Westminster Abbey:

> To me, as spokesman from the Third World, the Lambeth Conference will be a shame and irrelevance unless many of us bishops in the West change – unless we can be liberated from the handicaps of privilege, wealth, environment and prejudice, it will fail. If we bishops from the West sit secure and at peace, unchallenged, removed and remote from the sufferings and the pain of the world around us, the pain that our society is causing the so called Third World, Lambeth will fail.[30]

There is also the question of the self-supporting ministry in these days of inflation. The new Christology has also to be discussed. The *Church Times* has expressed a hope that basic doctrine will be put firmly on the agenda of next year's Lambeth Conference. Here, however, the bishops, few of whom are theologians, will need to tread carefully and be guided by the consultants. There is also the ecumenical question.[31]

It seems unlikely that this eleventh Lambeth Conference will be the last. But it may be the last virtually confined to the episcopate and the twelfth may well involve bishops, presbyters, and laity in equal proportions.[32] Such a development would seem to be demanded by the spread of synodical government and in view of the fact that the bishops no longer have the monopoly of theological expertise. The Conference will no longer take place in secrecy and one wonders whether there is need any longer to keep secret the details of past deliberations of Lambeth Conferences!

[30] *Church Times*, 1 July 1977, p. 1.

[31] Among recent developments are the Archbishop's call for the resumption of talks between the Church of England and the Church of Scotland. For a trenchant comment on these talks see Ian Henderson, *Power without Glory*.

[32] I notice that this is the view of John Howe; see *Church Times*, 11 March 1977, p. 1.

BIBLIOGRAPHY

1 MANUSCRIPT SOURCES

The Longley Letters in Lambeth Palace Library
The Box of Lambeth Conference 1867 Papers
The Tait Papers for the Lambeth Conference 1867
The Box of Papers for the 1878 Lambeth Conference
Manuscript Diary of Bishop Charles T. Quintard of Tennessee for 1867
  (seen in Xerox)
Manuscript Diary of Bishop Nevill of Dunedin, 1878 (seen in Xerox)
Oxford B.D. thesis by Ronald G. Lunt on the life of his father, Geoffrey
  C. L. Lunt, Bishop of Ripon and Salisbury (1967)

2 NEWSPAPERS AND PERIODICALS

The Times
Guardian
Church Times
Chronicle of Convocation
Church Quarterly Review
Church Illustrated
Theology
Modern Churchman
Pan-Anglican
Anglican World
American Church Quarterly Review
Journal of Ecclesiastical History

3 PRINTED VOLUMES, PAMPHLETS, AND ARTICLES

Abbott, Walter M. (ed.), *The Documents of Vatican II*. London,
  Geoffrey Chapman, 1967.

Adolfs, Robert, *The Grave of God. Has the Church a Future?* London, Compass Books, Burns and Oates, 1967.

Aglionby, Francis Keyes, *The Life of Edward Henry Bickersteth. Bishop and Poet. Bishop of Exeter 1885–1900.* London, Longmans and Co., 1907.

Albright, Raymond W., *A History of the Protestant Episcopal Church.* New York, Macmillan Co., London, Collier-Macmillan Ltd., 1964.

Alexander, Eleanor, *Primate Alexander. Archbishop of Armagh.* London, Edward Arnold, 1913.

Allegro, John M., *The Sacred Mushroom and the Cross.* A Study of the Nature and origins of Christianity within the fertility cults of the ancient Near East. London, Abacus, 1973.

Alternative Services. First Series. Recommended by the Archbishops of Canterbury and York to be introduced to the Convocations and the House of Laity. London, S.P.C.K., 1966.

Alternative Services. Second Series. Recommended by the Archbishops of Canterbury and York to be introduced to the Convocations and the House of Laity. London, S.P.C.K., 1966.

Altizer, Thomas J. J., and Hamilton, William, *Radical Theology and the Death of God.* London, Penguin Books, 1968.

The Anglican Communion: Its Position and Prospects. Sermons preached in St James's Church, Piccadilly, in July and August 1897 by the Bishop of Kentucky, the Archbishop of Rupertsland, the Archbishop of Sydney, the Bishop of Calcutta, the Archbishop of Capetown. London, S.P.C.K., 1897.

The Anglican Communion. The Fact of the Matter. London, Church Information Office, 1962.

Anglican–Methodist Conversations. Speeches at the Joint Sessions of the Convocations of Canterbury and York by the Bishop of London and the Dean of Carlisle on the Interim Report – 'Towards Reconciliation' – 27 April 1967. London, Church Information Office, 1967.

Anglican–Methodist Unity. Report of the Anglican–Methodist Unity Commission. Part I The Ordinal. London, S.P.C.K. and Epworth Press, 1968.

Anglican–Methodist Unity. Report of the Anglican–Methodist Unity Commission. 2 The Scheme. London, S.P.C.K. and Epworth Press, 1968.

'Anglican–Methodist Unity: a Symposium'. L. W. Brown, Trevor T. Rowe, G. D. Leonard, C. O. Buchanan, C. K. Barrett, Lord Fisher of

Lambeth, Percy Scott, Henry St John in *The Church Quarterly*, vol. i, no. 2, October 1968.

Anglican–Methodist Unity. Report of the Joint Working Group. 1971 G. S. 40. London, Church Information Office, 1971.

The Anglican–Presbyterian Conversations. The Report of the panels appointed by the Church of Scotland, the Presbyterian Church of England, the Church of England and the Episcopal Church of Scotland. Edinburgh, St Andrew Press, and London, S.P.C.K., 1966.

Anglican World, July–August 1963, vol. iii, no. 4, 'Toronto 1963'.

Anson, Harold, *T. B. Strong. Bishop, Musician, Dean, Vice-Chancellor*. London, S.P.C.K., 1931.

Arnott, Anne, *Wife to the Archbishop*. London and Oxford, Mowbrays, 1976.

Arrowsmith, John Boulton, Peter, and Gibbs, Derek, *Visible Unity and the Ten Propositions*. London, Faith Press, 1976.

Authority in the Church. A Statement on the question of Authority, its nature, exercise, and implications. Agreed by the Anglican–Roman Catholic International Commission. Venice 1976. London, Catholic Truth Society, and S.P.C.K., 1977.

Baker, John Austin, *The Foolishness of God*. London, Darton, Longman and Todd, 1970.

Baptism To-day. Being the Schedule attached to the Second Interim Reports of the Joint Committees on Baptism, Confirmation and Holy Communion, as presented to the Convocations of Canterbury and York in October 1949. London, Press and Publications Board of the Church Assembly, 1949.

Baptism and Confirmation To-day. Being the Schedule attached to the Final Reports of the Joint Committees of the Convocations of Canterbury and York, together with the minority schedule submitted to the Canterbury Convocation in October 1952. London, S.P.C.K., 1955.

Barnard, L. W., *C. B. Moss (1888–1964). Defender of the Faith*. London, A. R. Mowbray and Co. Ltd., 1967.

Barnes, Ernest William, *The Rise of Christianity*. London, Longmans Green and Co., 1947.

—— *Should such a faith offend?* Sermons and Addresses. London, Hodder and Stoughton, 1927.

Barr, James, *The Semantics of Biblical Language*. London, Oxford University Press, 1961.

Barry, F. R., *Recovery of Man*. London, Nisbet and Co. Ltd., 1948.

—— *Mervyn Haigh*. London, S.P.C.K., 1964.

—— *Period of My Life*. London, Hodder and Stoughton, 1970.

Bateman, Doris, *Round the World to Lambeth*. London, S.P.G., 1957.

Bayne, Stephen Fielding, *An Anglican Turning Point. Documents and Interpretations*. Austin, Texas, The Church Historical Society, 1964.

—— *Mutual Responsibility and Interdependence in the Body of Christ with related background documents*. London, S.P.C.K., 1963.

Bazeley, J. S., 'Lambeth Conference Review. Liturgical Revision in the Anglican Communion' in *Theology*, vol ii, no. 9, March 1923, pp. 161–3.

Bedell, George Thurston, *The Canterbury Pilgrimage to and from the Lambeth Conference and the Sheffield Congress* by Rt Rev. G. T. Bedell, D.D., Bishop of Ohio. New York, Anson D. F. Randolph and Co., 1878.

Beeson, Trevor, *The Church of England in Crisis*. London, Davis-Poynter, 1973.

—— *Discretion and Valour*. Religious Conditions in Russia and Eastern Europe. London, Fontana Books, Collins, 1974.

Bell, G. K. A., 'The Malines Conversations' in *Church Quarterly Review*, no. ccxl, April 1928.

—— *Randall Davidson. Archbishop of Canterbury*. 2 vols., London, Oxford University Press, 1935.

—— *Christian Unity. The Anglican Position*. Olaus Petri Lectures at Uppsala 1946. London, Hodder and Stoughton, 1948.

—— *The Kingship of Christ. The Story of the World Council of Churches*. Penguin Books, 1954.

—— (ed.), *Documents on Christian Unity 1920–4*. London, Oxford University Press, 1924.

—— (ed.), *Documents on Christian Unity. Second Series*. London, Oxford University Press, 1930.

—— (ed.), *Documents on Christian Unity. Third Series 1930–48*. London, Oxford University Press, 1948.

—— (ed.), *Documents on Christian Unity. Fourth Series 1948–57*. London, Oxford University Press, 1958.

—— and Robertson, W. L., *The Church of England and the Free Churches. Proceedings of Joint Conferences held at Lambeth Palace 1921–25*. London, Oxford University Press, 1925.

Benham, William, 'The Lambeth Conference 1867' in *Guardian*, 19 and 26 June, 1878, pp. 857–9 and 889–98.

Benham, William, *Catharine and Craufurd Tait. Wife and Son of Archibald Campbell Tait Archbishop of Canterbury. A Memoir.* London, Macmillan Co., 1879.

Benson, Arthur Christopher, *The Life of Edward White Benson, sometime Archbishop of Canterbury.* 2 vols., London, Macmillan and Co., 1899.

Bevan, R. J. W. (ed.), *The Churches and Christian Unity.* London, Oxford University Press, 1963.

Bickersteth, M. G., *A Sketch of the Life of the Rt. Rev. Robert Bickersteth, D.D., Bishop of Ripon 1857–1888.* London, Rivingtons, 1887.

Bill, E. G. W. (ed.), *Anglican Initiatives in Christian Unity.* Lectures delivered in Lambeth Palace Library 1966. London, S.P.C.K., 1967.

Bishops and Dioceses. The Report of the Ministry Committee Working Party on the Episcopate. C.I.O., 1971.

Blagden, Claude M., *Well Remembered.* London, Hodder and Stoughton, 1953.

Blanch, Stuart, *Land of Hope and Glory.* London, B.F.B.S., 1976.

Bonhoeffer, Dietrich, *Letters and Papers from Prison.* London, Fontana Books, Collins, 1959.

Bosher, Robert S., 'The Pan-Anglican Congress of 1908' in *Historical Magazine of the Protestant Episcopal Church*, June 1955, pp. 126–42.

—— *The American Church and the Formation of the Anglican Communion 1823–1853.* The M. Dwight Johnson Memorial Lecture in Church History 1962. Evanston, Illinois, Seabury-Western Theological Seminary, 1962.

Brand, William Francis, *Life of William Rollinson Whittingham First Bishop of Maryland.* 2 vols., New York, 1883.

Brandreth, Henry T., *The Oecumenical Ideals of the Oxford Movement.* London, S.P.C.K., 1947.

—— *Unity and Reunion. A Bibliography.* Second edition with Supplement. London, Adam and Charles Black, 1948.

Brilioth, Yngve, 'The Church of Sweden in its Relation to the Anglican Church' in *Church Quarterly Review*, no. clxxix, April 1920.

Brown, Fred, *Secular Evangelism.* London, S.C.M., 1970.

Browne, George Forrest, *The Church Historical Society XXX. Glastonbury.* An Address given by the Bishop of Stepney (designate of Bristol) on Tuesday, August 3, 1897, in the Ruined Church of the Abbey. London, S.P.C.K., 1897.

Browne, George Forrest, *The Recollections of a Bishop*. London, Smith, Elder and Co., 1915.

Buchanan, C. O., Mascall, E. L., Packer, J. L., Leonard, G. D., *Growing into Union. Proposals for Forming a United Church in England*. London, S.P.C.K., 1970.

Burgon, John William, *Lives of Twelve Good Men*. 2 vols., London, John Murray, 1889.

Burroughs, E. A., *The Christian Church and War*. The Lambeth Series. London, James Nisbet and Co. Ltd., 1931.

Campbell, J. McLeod, *Christian History in the Making*. London, Church Assembly Publications Board, 1946.

—— *Lambeth Calls. The Anglican Communion To-day. A Unified Statement*. Published for the Missionary Council of the Church Assembly by the Press and Publications Board of Church House, Westminster, London, 1947.

—— *New Horizons. Christian Strategy in the Making*. London, Church Information Board, 1951.

Canon Law of the Church of England. Being the Report of the Archbishops' Commission on Canon Law. London, S.P.C.K., 1949.

Canons of the Church of England. Canons Ecclesiastical promulged by the Convocations of Canterbury and York in 1964 and 1969. London, S.P.C.K., 1969.

Carey, Kenneth M., *The Historic Episcopate in the Fullness of the Church*. Seven Essays by Priests of the Church of England. Westminster, Dacre Press, 1954.

Carey, Walter, *The Church of England's Hour. Death or Resurrection?* London and Oxford, A. R. Mowbray & Co. Ltd., 1946.

—— *Good-Bye to My Generation*. London and Oxford, A. R. Mowbray & Co. Ltd., 1951.

Carnegie, W. H., 'Lambeth Conference Reviews II (e) Peace and War' in *Theology*, vol. xxii, March 1931.

Carpenter, Edward, *Cantuar. The Archbishops in their Office*. London, Cassell, 1971.

Carpenter, S. C., *Winnington-Ingram. The Biography of Arthur Foley Winnington-Ingram, Bishop of London 1901–1939*. London, Hodder and Stoughton, 1949.

Carrington, Philip, *The Anglican Church in Canada. A History*. Toronto, Collins, 1963.

Carus, William, *Memorials of the Right Reverend Charles Pettit*

McIlvaine, D.D., D.C.L., Late Bishop of Ohio in the Protestant Episcopal Church of the United States. London, Elliot Stock, 1882.

Caswall, Henry, *Americans and the American Church*. London, John and Charles Mozley, 1851.

—— *The Jubilee, or What I saw and heard in London on the 15th and 16th of June, 1852*. London, Francis and John Rivington, 1852.

—— *A Pilgrimage to Canterbury in 1852*. London, Francis and John Rivington, 1852.

—— *The Western World Revisited*. Oxford, John Henry Parker, 1853.

Catholicity. A Study in the Conflict of Christian Traditions in the West. Being a Report presented to the Archbishop of Canterbury. London, Dacre Press, Westminster, 1947.

Chardin, Pierre Teilhard de, *The Phenomenon of Man*. London, Fontana Books, Collins, 1965.

Charnwood, Lord (ed.), *Discourses and Letters of Hubert Murray Burge, D.D., K.C.V.O., Bishop of Southwark 1911–1919, Bishop of Oxford 1919–1925*. London, Chatto and Windus, 1930.

Chase, F. H., *Belief and Creed, being an examination of portions of 'Faith of a modern churchman'*. London, Macmillan, 1918.

Chorley, E. Clowes, *Men and Movements in the American Church*. The Hale Lectures. Hamden, Connecticut, U.S.A., Archon Books, 1961.

Christian Unity being The Report of a Joint Conference held at Lambeth Palace together with a Preliminary Statement by the Archbishops of Canterbury and York and the Moderator of the Federal Council of the Evangelical Free Churches. London, S.P.C.K., 1922.

Church, Mary C., *Life and Letters of Dean Church*. Edited by his daughter. London, Macmillan and Co., 1894.

Church and State. Report of the Archbishops' Commission. London, Church Information Office, 1970.

The Church and the Law of Nullity of Marriage. The Report of a Commission appointed by the Archbishops of Canterbury and York in 1949. London, S.P.C.K., 1955.

Church and Empire. A Reprint of the Special Number of the Times, June 25, 1930. London, *The Times*, 1930.

Church Illustrated. Special Lambeth Conference Number, May 1958. London.

Church Illustrated. Prelude to Toronto July 1963. London.

Church of England and the Church of Sweden. Report of the Commission appointed by the Archbishop of Canterbury in pursuance of Resolution 74 of the Lambeth Conference of 1908. London, A. R. Mowbray and Co. Ltd., Milwaukee, The Young Churchman Co., 1911.

Church Relations in England. Being the Report of Conversations between Representatives of the Archbishop of Canterbury and Representatives of the Evangelical Free Churches in England together with the Sermon preached by the Archbishop of Canterbury, November 3rd 1946, entitled 'A Step Forward in Church Relations'. London, S.P.C.K., 1950.

Clark, Alan C., and Davey, Colin, *Anglican Roman Dialogue. The Work of the Preparatory Commission.* London, Oxford University Press, 1974.

Clarke, Henry Lowther, *Constitutional Church Government in the Dominions beyond the Seas and in other Parts of the Anglican Communion.* London, S.P.C.K., 1924.

—— 'The Lambeth Appeal and its Results' in *Anglican Essays* edited by W. L. Paige Cox. London, Macmillan and Co., 1923.

Coggan, Donald, *Convictions.* London, Hodder and Stoughton, 1975.

Cohu, J. R., *Addresses on the Lambeth Conference.* London, Skeffington and Son. Ltd., 1921.

Commemoration of Saints and Heroes of the Faith in the Anglican Communion. The Report of the Commission appointed by the Archbishop of Canterbury. London, S.P.C.K., 1957.

Common Prayer 1970. A Report submitted by the Church of England Liturgical Commission to the Archbishops of Canterbury and York October 1969. London, S.P.C.K., 1970.

Conference of Bishops of the Anglican Communion, holden at Lambeth Palace, September 24–27, 1867. Published by authority. London, Rivingtons, 1867.

Conference of Bishops of the Anglican Communion. Holden at Lambeth Palace, July 1878. Letter from the Bishops, including the Reports adopted by the Conference. London, Paris, and New York, Cassell, Petter and Galpin.

Conference of Bishops of the Anglican Communion Holden at Lambeth Palace in July 1888. Encyclical Letter from the Bishops and the Resolutions and Reports. London, S.P.C.K., 1888.

Conference of Bishops of the Anglican Communion Holden at Lambeth Palace in July 1897. Encyclical Letter from the Bishops with the Resolutions and Reports. London, S.P.C.K., 1897.

Conference of Bishops of the Anglican Communion. Holden at

Lambeth Palace July 27–August 5, 1908. Encyclical Letter from the Bishops with the Resolutions and Reports. London, S.P.C.K., 1908.

Conversations between the Church of England and the Methodist Church. A Report to the Archbishops of Canterbury and York and the Conference of the Methodist Church. London, Church Information Office and Epworth Press, 1963.

[Copleston, R. S., Bishop of Calcutta], *Addresses given at a Quiet Day to Bishops of the Lambeth Conference, Fulham, July 23rd 1908.* For strictly private circulation only. (Bodleian 1001e 817(10).)

Cox, Harvey, *The Secular City.* Secularization and Urbanization in Theological Perspective. London, Penguin Books, 1968.

Coxe, Cleveland, *Impressions of England or Sketches of English Scenery and Society.* 2nd edn, New York, Dana and Co., 1856.

Creighton, Louise, *Life and Letters of Mandell Creighton, D.D. Oxon and Cam. Sometime Bishop of London* by his wife. 2 vols., London, Longmans, Green and Co., 1904.

——— *The Anglican Communion.* Press and Publications Board, Church Assembly, Church House, Westminster, London, 1929.

Cross, F. L., *Darwell Stone. Churchman and Counsellor.* London, Dacre Press, Westminster, 1943.

Cunningham, B. K., 'Lambeth Conference Review III. V(a) The Supply and Training of Men for Holy Orders', in *Theology*, vol. xxi, no. 124, October 1930.

Curteis, G. H., *The Life of George Augustus Selwyn, Bishop of Lichfield and New Zealand.* London, Kegan Paul, 1889.

Curtis, William Redmond, *The Lambeth Conferences. The Solution for Pan-Anglican Organization.* Studies in History, Economics and Public Law edited by the Faculty of Political Science of Columbia University No. 488. New York, Columbia University Press; London, P. S. King and Son Ltd., 1942.

Dammers, A. H., 'Lectionary, Liturgy and Lambeth' in *Theology*, vol. lxii, no. 465, March 1959.

D'Arcy, C. F., *God in Science.* The Lambeth Series. London, James Nisbet and Co. Ltd., 1931.

——— *The Adventures of a Bishop: A Phase of Irish Life. A Personal and Historical Narrative.* London, Hodder and Stoughton, 1934.

Dark, Sidney, *Archbishop Davidson and the English Church.* London, Philip Allan and Co. Ltd., 1929.

——— *The Lambeth Conferences. Their History and their Significance.* London, Eyre and Spottiswoode, 1930.

David, A. A., and Furse, M. B., *Marriage and Birth Control*. The Lambeth Series. London, James Nisbet and Co. Ltd., 1931.

Davidson, Randall T. (ed.), *The Lambeth Conferences of 1867, 1878, and 1888 With the Official Reports and Resolutions, together with the Sermons preached at the Conferences*. Edited by Randall T. Davidson, Dean of Windsor. London, S.P.C.K., 1889.

—— *Origin and History of the Lambeth Conferences of 1867 and 1878, with the Official Reports and Resolutions*. London, S.P.C.K., 1888.

—— *The Five Lambeth Conferences*, compiled under the direction of the Most Rev. Randall T. Davidson, D.D., Archbishop of Canterbury. London, S.P.C.K., 1920.

——(ed.), *The Six Lambeth Conferences 1867–1920*. Compiled under the direction of the Most Reverend Lord Davidson of Lambeth, Archbishop of Canterbury 1903–1928. London, S.P.C.K., 1929.

—— and Benham, William, *Life of Archibald Campbell Tait, Archbishop of Canterbury*. 2 vols., London, Macmillan and Co., 1891.

Dawley, Powel Mills (ed.), *Report of the Anglican Congress 1954*. London, S.P.C.K., 1955.

Deanesly, Margaret, and Willis, Geoffrey G., *Anglican–Methodist Unity. Some Considerations Historical and Liturgical*. London, Faith Press, 1968.

De Lancey, William Heathcote, *The Mission to the Jubilee. Bishop de Lacey's Report to the Convention of the Diocese of Western New York of the Mission to England to attend the Closing Services of the Third Jubilee of the Society for the Propagation of the Gospel 1852*. Utica, U.S.A., Curtiss and White, 1852.

De-la-Noy, Michael, *A Day in the Life of God*. Derby, The Citadel Press, 1971.

Deployment of the Clergy. The Report of the House of Bishops' Working Group. G.S. 205. London, Church House, 1974.

Diggle, John W., *The Lancashire Life of Bishop Fraser*. London, Sampson Low, Marston, Searle and Rivington, 1889.

Dillistone, F. W., *Charles Raven. Naturalist, Historian, Theologian*. London, Hodder and Stoughton, 1975.

Dimon, C. T., and Batty, F. de Witt, *St Clair Donaldson, Archbishop of Brisbane 1905–1921, Bishop of Salisbury 1921–1935*. London, Faber and Faber, 1939.

Diocesan Boundaries. Being the Report of the Archbishop of

Canterbury's Commission on the Organisation of the Church by Dioceses in London and the South-East of England 1965/1967. C.A. 1653. London, Church Information Office, 1967.

Doctrine in the Church of England. The Report of the Commission on Doctrine Appointed by the Archbishops of Canterbury and York in 1922. London, S.P.C.K., 1938.

Duffield, G. E. (ed.), *The Paul Report Considered*. Marcham, Berks., Marcham Manor Press, 1964.

Eden, G. R., and Macdonald, F. C., *Lightfoot of Durham. Memories and Appreciations*. London, Cambridge University Press, 1932.

Edwards, David L., 'The Thirty-nine Articles: One last Heave' in *Modern Churchman*, January 1967, vol. x, no. 2, pp. 135–41.

—— *Religion and Change*. London, Hodder and Stoughton, 1969.

—— *Leaders of the Church of England 1828–1944*. London, Oxford University Press, 1971.

—— *The British Churches Turn to the Future*. One Man's View of the Church Leaders Conference, Birmingham 1972. London, S.C.M., 1973.

—— *Ian Ramsey Bishop of Durham*. London, Oxford University Press, 1973.

Edwards, James George, *Progress of Religious Thought in the XVIII and XIX Centuries*. Taunton: Printed for private circulation by Barnicott and Pearce at the Athenaeum Press, 1904.

Eliot, T. S., *Thoughts after Lambeth. A Critique of the Reports of the Lambeth Conference 1930*. London, Faber and Faber, 1930.

Ellison, Gerald, *Progress in Ministry. An Examination of the Proposals contained in the Report 'Partners in Ministry', with suggestions for a Better Way forward*. London, The Faith Press, 1968.

—— *The Anglican Communion. Past and Future*. Greenwich, Connecticut, U.S.A., Seabury Press, 1960.

'Episcopal Comments on the Lambeth Conference' in *Church Quarterly Review*, no. lv, April, 1889.

Evans, John H., *Churchman Militant. George Augustus Selwyn. Bishop of New Zealand and Lichfield*. London, George Allen and Unwin Ltd.; Wellington, New Zealand, A. H. and A. W. Reed, 1964.

Evanston to New Delhi. 1954–1961. Report of the Central Committee to the Third Assembly of the World Council of Churches. Geneva, World Council of Churches, 1961.

The Evanston Report. The Second Assembly of the World Council of Churches. London, S.C.M. Press, 1955.

Fairweather, Eugene R. (ed.), *Anglican Congress 1963. Report of Proceedings*. London, S.P.C.K., 1963.

—— and Hetlinger, R. F., *Episcopacy and Reunion*. London, A. R. Mowbray and Co. Ltd., 1953.

The Family in Contemporary Society. A Report. London, S.P.C.K., 1958.

Fey, Harold E. (ed.), *The Ecumenical Advance. A History of the Ecumenical Movement*. vol. ii 1948–68. London, S.P.C.K., 1970.

ffrench-Beytagh, Gonville, *Encountering Darkness*. London, Collins, 1973.

Fisher, Geoffrey F., *The Archbishop Speaks. Addresses and Speeches by the Archbishop of Canterbury, The Most Reverend Geoffrey Francis Fisher, P.C., G.C.V.O., D.D.* Selected by Edward Carpenter. London, Evans Brothers Ltd., 1958.

—— *A Survey of Church Relations 1920–67*. London, S.P.C.K., 1967.

—— *Covenant and Reconciliation. A Critical Examination*. London, Mowbray and Co. Ltd., 1967.

—— (ed.), *The Lambeth Conferences (1867–1930). The Reports of the 1920 and 1930 Conferences, with selected resolutions from the Conferences of 1867, 1878, 1888, 1897 and 1908*. London, S.P.C.K., 1948.

Fitzgerald, Maurice H., *A Memoir of Herbert Edward Ryle, K.C.V.O., D.D. Sometime Bishop of Winchester and Dean of Westminster*. London, Macmillan and Co., 1928.

Flindall, R. P., *The Church of England 1814–1948. A Documentary History*. London, S.P.C.K., 1972.

Fouyas, Methodios, *Orthodoxy, Roman Catholicism and Anglicanism*. London, Oxford University Press, 1972.

Fowler, J. H., *Edward Lee Hicks*. London, Christophers, 1922.

Fletcher, Joseph, *Situation Ethics*. London, S.C.M., 1966.

France, W. F., *The Oversea Episcopate. Centenary History of the Colonial Bishoprics Fund 1841–1941*. The Colonial Bishoprics Fund, Tufton St., Westminster, London, 1941.

Free Churches and the Lambeth Appeal. Being the Report of a Committee appointed by the Federal Council of the Evangelical Free Churches of England and the National Free Church Council. London, The Religious Tract Society, 1921.

Fulford, Francis, *Sermons, Addresses, and Statistics of the Diocese of Montreal*. Montreal, Dawson Bros., 1865.

—— *A Pan-Anglican Synod*. A Sermon Preached at the General

Ordination held by the Right Reverend the Lord Bishop of Oxford in the Cathedral Church of Christ in Oxford on Sunday, December 23rd, 1866 by Francis Fulford, D.D. Lord Bishop of Montreal and Metropolitan of Canada. With an Appendix. Oxford, Rivingtons; Montreal, Dawson Brothers, 1867.

Garbett, Cyril, *The Claims of the Church of England.* London, Hodder and Stoughton, 1947.

Gardiner, Dorothy, *The Story of Lambeth Palace. A Historical Survey.* London, Constable and Co. Ltd., 1930.

Gibbard, Mark, 'Catholics in the World Church' in *Catholic Anglicans Today*, edited by John Wilkinson. London, Darton, Longman and Todd, 1968.

Glazebrook, M. G., *The Faith of a Modern Churchman.* 2nd edn revised and enlarged. London, John Murray, 1925.

—— *The Letter and the Spirit. A Reply to the Bishop of Ely's Criticisms of the Faith of a Modern Churchman.* London, John Murray, 1920.

Glubokovsky, Nicolas N., 'Union, Intercommunion and the Lambeth Conference' in *Church Quarterly Review*, vol. xcv, October 1922.

Goodall, Norman, *The Ecumenical Movement. What it is and What it does.* London, Oxford University Press, 1964.

—— *Ecumenical Progress. A Decade of Change in the Ecumenical Movement 1961–71.* London, Oxford University Press, 1972.

Gore, Charles, 'Reunion in South India' in *Church Quarterly Review*, vol. ccxix, July 1930.

—— *The Prevention of Conception commonly called Birth Control*, London, Mowbray and Co. Ltd., 1930.

Goudge, H. L., *The Church of England and Reunion.* London, S.P.C.K., 1938.

—— *The Admission of Nonconformists to Communion.* A Paper read to the Oxford Branch of the English Church Union, April 27, 1932. London and Oxford, A. R. Mowbray and Co. Ltd., 1932.

—— *The Question of Contraception. A Lecture delivered to some clergy of the diocese of Manchester with a criticism of some points in the December, 1930 number of Theology.* London, League of National Life, 1931.

Gray, Charles, *Life of Robert Gray, Bishop of Cape Town and Metropolitan of Africa.* 2 vols., London, Oxford and Cambridge, Rivingtons, 1876.

Gray, G. F. S., *The Anglican Communion. A Brief Sketch.* London, S.P.C.K., 1958.

Grubb, Sir Kenneth, *Crypts of Power. An Autobiography.* London, Hodder and Stoughton, 1971.

Gummer, Selwyn, *The Chavasse Twins.* London, Hodder and Stoughton, 1963.

Gutch, Sir John, *Martyr of the Isles. The Life and Death of John Coleridge Patteson.* London, Hodder and Stoughton, 1971.

Hales, E. E. Y., *Pope John and His Revolution.* London, Eyre and Spottiswoode, 1966.

Handbook of the Lambeth Conference 1948 Being a Supplement to the Official Year Book of the Church of England 1948. Press and Publication Board of the Church Assembly, Church House, Westminster and London, S.P.C.K., 1948.

Hanson, Anthony Tyrrell, *Beyond Anglicanism.* London, Darton, Longman and Todd, 1965.

Harrison, Hall, *Life of the Right Reverend John Barrett Kerfoot, D.D., LL.D., First Bishop of Pittsburgh., With Selections from his Diaries and Correspondence.* 2 vols., New York, James Pott and Co., 1886.

Haselmayer, Louis A., *Lambeth and Unity.* New York, Morehouse Gorham Co., and London, Dacre Press, Westminster, 1948.

Headlam, Arthur Cayley, 'The Lambeth Conference and the Union of the Churches' in *Church Quarterly Review*, no. cxxxii, July 1908.

—— 'The Lambeth Conference' in *Church Quarterly Review*, no. cxxxiii, October 1908.

—— 'The Lambeth Conference' in *Church Quarterly Review*, no. clxxxi, October 1920.

—— 'Lambeth Conference and Reunion' in *Church Quarterly Review*, no. ccxxii, January 1931.

—— *The Doctrine of the Church and Reunion* being the Bampton Lectures for the year 1920. London, John Murray, 1920.

—— *Christian Unity.* London, S.C.M. Press, 1930.

—— *The Anglicans, Orthodox and Old Catholics. Notes on the Lambeth Report on Unity.* London, S.P.C.K., 1930.

Headlam, Maurice, *Bishop and Friend. Nugent Hicks, Sixty-fourth Bishop of Lincoln.* London, Macdonald and Co. Ltd., 1944.

Hebert, A. Gabriel. *Memorandum on the Report of the Archbishops' Commission on Christian Doctrine.* Published for the Church Union by S.P.C.K., London, 1939.

Henderson, Ian, *Power without Glory*. Richmond, Virginia, John Knox Press, 1969.

Henson, H. Hensley, *Anglicanism and Reunion. Sermon preached in Westminster Abbey on Trinity Sunday, June 14, 1908, being the eve of the Pan-Anglican Congress*. London, Hugh Rees, 1908.

—— *Reunion and Intercommunion. Two Lectures on the Report of the Lambeth Conference*. London, Hugh Rees, 1909.

—— *The Creed in the Pulpit*. London, Hodder and Stoughton, 1912.

—— *Retrospect of an Unimportant Life*, vol. i 1863–1920 and vol. ii 1920–39. London, Oxford University Press, 1946.

Herklots, H. G. G., *Frontiers of the Church. The Making of the Anglican Communion*. London, Ernest Benn Ltd., 1961.

—— *The Church of England and the American Episcopal Church. A Study in Relationships*. London, A. R. Mowbray and Co. Ltd., 1966.

—— *Some Heroes of the Anglican Communion*. Church Information Office, Church House, Westminster, London, 1965.

—— 'Mutual Responsibility and Interdependence in the Anglican Communion: an eighteenth Century Version' in *Church Quarterly Review*, vol. clxv, no. 357, October–December 1964.

—— 'The Origins of the Lambeth Quadrilateral' in *Church Quarterly Review*, vol. clxvii, January to March 1968.

Heywood, B. O. F., *About the Lambeth Conference*. London, S.P.C.K., 1930.

Hick, John (ed.). *The Myth of God Incarnate*. London, S.C.M., 1977.

Hickin, L. C., 'Towards a United Church' in R. R. Osborn (ed.), *Grounds of Hope*. Cambridge and London, James Clarke and Co. Ltd., 1968.

Hinchliff, Peter, *The Anglican Church in South Africa. An Account of the History and Development of the Church of the Province of South Africa*. London, Darton, Longman and Todd, 1963.

Hind, John, 'The Development of the Lambeth Conference' in *Theology*, vol. li, no. 336, June 1948.

Hobhouse, Walter, *A Short Sketch of the First Four Lambeth Conferences, 1867–1897*. London, S.P.C.K., 1908.

Hodgson, Leonard, *Sex and Christian Freedom. An Enquiry*. London, S.C.M., 1967.

Hogg, William Richey, *Ecumenical Foundations. A History of the International Missionary Council*. New York, Harper and Bros., 1952.

Holland, Henry Scott, *A Bundle of Memories*. London, Wells Gardner and Co. Ltd., 1915.

Hooft, W. A. Visser 't, *Memoirs*. London, S.C.M., and Philadelphia, Westminster Press, 1973.

Hopkins, C. H. G., *Bishop A. T. P. Williams. Headmaster, Dean, Bishop. Winchester, Oxford, Durham*. Great Wakering, Mayhew-McCrimmon, 1975.

[Hopkins, John Henry], *Life of the Right Reverend John Henry Hopkins, First Bishop of Vermont and Seventh Presiding Bishop* by One of his sons. New York, F. J. Huntington and Co., 1873.

Hopkins, John Henry, 'The Next Lambeth Conference' in *American Church Quarterly Review*, vol. xxvi, July 1874, pp. 417ff.

How, Frederick Douglas, *William Conyngham Plunket, Fourth Baron Plunket and Sixty-first Archbishop of Dublin. A Memoir*. London, Isbister and Co. Ltd., 1900.

—— *Archibald Maclagan. Being a Memoir of the Most Revd. the Right Honble. William Dalrymple Maclagan, D.D., Archbishop of York and Primate of England*. London, Wells Gardner, Darton and Co. Ltd., 1911.

Howe, John, *Partners in Mission. Anglican Consultative Council*. Second Meeting, Dublin, 1973. London, S.P.C.K., 1973.

—— *The Time is Now. Anglican Consultative Council*. First Meeting, Limuru, Kenya 1971. London, S.P.C.K., 1971.

—— *ACC 3 Anglican Consultative Council*. Third Meeting. Trinidad. London, 1976.

—— and Barrett, D. B., *Membership, Manpower and Money in the Anglican Communion. A Survey of 27 Churches and 360 Dioceses*. London, S.P.C.K. for the Anglican Consultative Council, 1973.

Hughes, Thomas, *James Fraser, Second Bishop of Manchester. A Memoir 1818–1885*. London, Macmillan and Co. Ltd., 1887.

Huntington, William Reed, *The Church-Idea. An Essay towards Unity*. New York, Charles Scribner's Sons, 1899.

Hutton, William Holden, *Letters of William Stubbs, Bishop of Oxford 1875–1901*. London, Archibald Constable and Co. Ltd., 1904.

Inge, W. R., *Diary of a Dean. St Paul's 1911–1934*. London, Hutchinson and Co. (n.d.).

Iremonger, F. A., *William Temple, Archbishop of Canterbury. His Life and Letters*. London, Oxford University Press, 1948.

Istavridis, Vasil T., *Orthodoxy and Anglicanism*. Translated from the Greek. London, S.P.C.K., 1966.

Jacob, Edgar (Bishop of St Albans), 'The Lambeth Conference and the

Pan-Anglican Congress' in *Church Quarterly Review*, no. cxxx, January 1908, pp. 257–77.

Jagger, Peter J., *Bishop Henry de Candole. His Life and Times 1895–1971*. Leighton Buzzard, Faith Press, 1975.

Jasper, Ronald C. D., *Arthur Cayley Headlam. Life and Letters of a Bishop*. London, Faith Press, 1960.

—— *George Bell, Bishop of Chichester*. London, Oxford University Press, 1967.

Jefferson, P. C. (ed.), *The Church in the 60s*. The Anglican Congress, 1963. Toronto. Anglican Book Centre, London, S.P.C.K., Connecticut, U.S.A., Seabury Press, 1963.

Jennings, D. A., *The Revival of the Convocation of York, 1837–1861*. Borthwick Papers no. 47, St Anthony's Hall, York, 1975.

Jesus Christ Frees and Unites. Preparatory Booklet for the Fifth Assembly of the World Council of Churches. London, S.C.M., 1974.

Johnson, David Enderton (ed.), *Uppsala to Nairobi 1968–1975*. Report to the Central Committee of the Fifth Assembly of the World Council of Churches. New York, Friendship Press. London, S.P.C.K., 1975.

Johnson, Hewlett, *Searching for Light. An Autobiography. Hewlett Johnson, Dean of Canterbury 1931–1963*. London, Michael Joseph, 1968.

Johnson, Howard A., *Global Odyssey. Visiting the Anglican Churches*. London, Geoffrey Bles, 1963.

Johnson, Humphrey J. T., *Anglicanism in Transition,* London, New York and Toronto, Longmans, Green and Co., 1938.

Journal of the Proceedings of the Bishops, Clergy and Laity of the Protestant Episcopal Church in the United States of America Assembled in a General Convention, held in the city of New York from Oct. 7th to Nov. 3rd inclusive 1874. Printed for the Convention. Hartford, Connecticut, 1875.

Keeton, Barry, *Some Observations on Anglican–Roman Catholic Relations*, London, Faith Press, 1976.

Kemp, Eric Waldram, *The Life and Letters of Kenneth Escott Kirk, Bishop of Oxford 1937–1954*. London, Hodder and Stoughton, 1959.

Kirk, K. E., 'Lambeth Resolutions on Marriage and Sex' in *Church Quarterly Review*, vol. cxi, October 1930.

—— (ed.), *The Apostolic Ministry. Essays on the History and Doctrine of Episcopacy*. London, Hodder and Stoughton, 1946.

Kirk, Peter, *One Army Strong*. London, Faith Press, 1958.

Kitchin, G. W., *Edward Harold Browne D.D. Lord Bishop of Winchester. A Memoir*. London, John Murray, 1895.

Knox, Edmund Arbuthnott, *Reminiscences of an Octogenarian 1847–1934*. London, Hutchinson and Co. (n.d., 1935?).

Lacey, T. A., *The Universal Church. A Study in the Lambeth Call to Union*. London and Oxford, A. R. Mowbray and Co., 1921.

Lambeth 1948 Reviewed. A Report of the Theological and Liturgical Committee of the Church Union, April, 1949. The Church Union, Lord Halifax House, London, 1949.

Lambeth Appeal. Australia and Reunion Being the Official Report of Proceedings of Reunion Conference between Representatives of the Australian Presbyterian, Methodist, and Congregational Churches in Australia, Holden at the Chapter House, St Andrew's Cathedral, Sydney on March 28–29, 1922. Sydney, Angus and Robertson Ltd., 1922.

'Lambeth Conference of 1888' in *Church Quarterly Review*, no. liii, October 1888.

The Lambeth Conference and Church Reform in Spain and Portugal. Being the Substance of an Address delivered by the Archbishop of Dublin at the Annual Meeting of the Spanish and Portuguese Church Aid Society, August 7, 1888. Dublin, 1888.

'The Lambeth Conference of 1897' by Darwell Stone, in *Church Quarterly Review*, vol. xlv, October 1897.

Lambeth Conference 1930. Encyclical Letter from the Bishops with Resolutions and Reports. London, S.P.C.K., 1930.

Lambeth Conference 1948. Encyclical Letter from the Bishops together with the Resolutions and Reports. London, S.P.C.K., 1948.

Lambeth Conference 1958. The Encyclical Letter from the Bishops together with the Resolutions and Reports. London, S.P.C.K., and Greenwich, Connecticut, Seabury Press, 1958.

Lambeth '68. London, Church Information Office, 1968.

Lambeth Conference 1968. Preparatory Information. London, S.P.C.K., 1968.

Lambeth Conference 1968. Resolutions and Reports. London, S.P.C.K.; New York, Seabury Press, 1968.

Lambeth. What's That? An answer in word pictures for young people. London, C.M.S. and S.P.G., 1958.

Lambeth and Our Times. A Guide for Speakers and Study Group Leaders in connection with the Lambeth Conference of 1958.

Church Information Board, Church House, Westminster, London, 1957.

Lambeth and You. London, S.P.C.K., 1958.

Lambeth Occasional Reports 1931–8. With a Foreword by the Bishop of Winchester (Mervyn Haigh). London, S.P.C.K., 1948.

Lambeth Encyclical and other Proposals Considered. Scottish Church Society Conference 1920. Edinburgh, Andrew Eliot, 1920.

Lang, Cosmo Gordon, *The Unity of the Church of England.* London, S.P.C.K., 1925.

Lawrence, William, *Fifty Years.* London, S.C.M. Press, 1924.

Leidt, William E., *Anglican Mosaic.* The Anglican Congress 1963. Toronto, Anglican Book Centre, London, S.P.C.K., and Connecticut, Seabury Press, 1963.

Leonard, Graham, *'to everyman's conscience' Comments on the Report of the Anglican Methodist Unity Commission.* (Published by the Bishop of Willesden. No date).

Liddon, Henry Parry, *Life of Edward Bouverie Pusey.* Edited and prepared by the Rev. J. C. Johnston and the Rev. Robert J. Wilson. 4 vols., London, Longmans Green and Co., 1893.

Lightfoot, J. B., 'The Christian Ministry' in *Saint Paul's Epistle to the Philippians. A Revised Text with Introduction, Notes and Dissertations.* London, Macmillan and Co., 1881.

Lilley, A. L., 'Lambeth Conference Reviews. The Christian Doctrine of God as determining the character of Christian Worship' in *Theology,* vol. xxi, no. 125, November 1930.

Lloyd, Roger, *The Church of England 1900–1965.* London, S.C.M. Press, 1966.

Loane, Marcus L., *Archbishop Mowll. The Biography of Howard West Kilvington Mowll, Archbishop of Sydney and Primate of Australia.* London, Hodder and Stoughton, 1960.

Lockhart, J. G., *Cosmo Gordon Lang.* London, Hodder and Stoughton, 1949.

Louth, Andrew, *Commentary on the Agreed Statement on Ministry and Ordination* 1973. London, C.L.A., 1977.

Lunn, Sir Henry, *A Free Church Impression. Lambeth Series.* London, James Nisbet and Co. Ltd., 1931.

—— *Reunion at Lambeth. John Wesley's Message to the Bishops in Conference, July 1920,* with an Introductory Letter by Sir Henry S. Lunn. London, The Epworth Press, 1920.

McAdoo, H. R., *The Structure of Caroline Moral Theology. An*

Investigation of Principles. London, New York, Toronto, Longmans, Green and Co., 1949.

—— *The Spirit of Anglicanism. A Survey of Anglican Theological Method in the Seventeenth Century.* London, A. and C. Black, 1963.

Macdonnell, John Cotter, *The Life and Correspondence of William Connor Magee, Archbishop of York, Bishop of Peterborough.* 2 vols., London, Isbister and Co., 1896.

Mackarness, Charles Coleridge, *Memorials of the Episcopate of John Fielder Mackarness, D.D., Bishop of Oxford from 1870 to 1888.* Oxford and London, John Parker and Co., 1892.

McKay, Roy, *John Leonard Wilson Confessor of the Faith.* London, Hodder and Stoughton, 1973.

MacKinnon, Donald, *The Stripping of the Altars. The Gore Memorial Lecture, delivered on 5 November 1968 in Westminster Abbey and other papers and essays on related topics.* London, The Fontana Library, Collins, 1969.

Macmorran, Kenneth M., *Reunion and the Lambeth Conference. A Charge Delivered at the Easter Visitation 1930 in the Church of S. Andrew, Farnham, S. Mary, Guildford and S. Martin, Dorking.* London and Oxford, A. R. Mowbray and Co., 1930.

McNabb, Vincent M., 'Lambeth Conference Review. The Lambeth Conference and Reunion. A Roman Catholic View' in *Theology*, vol. ii, no. 8, pp. 107–10, 1921.

McNeile, E. R., 'Christianity and Theosophy' Lambeth Conference Reviews IV in *Theology*, vol. i, no. 5, November 1920, pp. 307–10.

Macquarrie, John, *Principles of Christian Theology.* London, S.C.M., 1966.

—— *Christian Unity and Christian Diversity.* London, S.C.M., 1975.

Major, H. D. A., 'The Lambeth Conference' in *Modern Churchman*, vol. x, no. 4 and 5, August 1920.

—— 'The Theology of the Lambeth Conference' in *Modern Churchman*, vol. xx, no. 8, November 1930.

—— 'Lambeth and Reunion' in *Modern Churchman*, vol. xxxviii, no. 4, December 1948.

Malone, Dumas (ed.), *Dictionary of American Biography.* New York, Charles Scribner's Sons, 1928– [1936] and 1943—.

Marriage, Divorce and the Church. The Report of the Commission on the Christian Doctrine of Marriage. London, S.P.C.K., 1970.

Mascall, E. L., *The Convocations and South India. What did the Convocations decide, and how does their decision affect the*

Catholicity of the Church of England? London, A. R. Mowbray and Co. Ltd., 1955.

Mascall, E. L., *The Recovery of Unity. A Theological Approach.* London, Longmans Green and Co., 1958.

—— *Lambeth and Christian Unity.* London, The Faith Press, 1958.

—— 'Lambeth and Unity' in *Church Quarterly Review* April–June 1959, pp. 158–72.

Mason, Arthur James, *Life of William Edward Collins, Bishop of Gibraltar.* London, Longmans Green and Co., 1912.

Matthews, W. R., *Memories and Meanings.* London, Hodder and Stoughton, 1969.

Meacham, Standish, *Lord Bishop. The Life of Samuel Wilberforce 1805–72.* Cambridge, Massachusetts, U.S.A., Harvard University Press, 1970.

Meeting of the Adjourned Conference of Bishops of the Anglican Communion – holden at Lambeth Palace, December 10, 1867. I. Reports of Committees appointed by the Conference. II. Resolutions of the Adjourned Conference. London and Oxford and Cambridge, Rivingtons, 1867.

Mendieta, Emmanuel Amand de, *Anglican Vision.* London, S.P.C.K., 1971.

Mews, Stuart P., 'Kikuyu and Edinburgh. The Interaction of Attitudes to Two Conferences' in *Studies in Church History*, vol. vii, Councils and Assemblies, ed. G. J. Cuming and Derek Baker. London, Cambridge University Press, 1971.

Middleton, R. D., *Dr. Routh.* London, New York and Toronto, Oxford University Press, 1938.

M[ary] C. S. M[ills], *Edith Davidson of Lambeth.* London, John Murray, 1938.

Moberly, C. A. E., *Dulce Domum. George Moberly. His Family and Friends.* London, John Murray, 1911.

Modern Eucharistic Agreement. London, S.P.C.K., 1973.

Montgomery, H. H., 'Randall Thomas Davidson' in *Church Quarterly Review*, vol. cxi, October 1930.

M.M. [Maud Montgomery], *Bishop Montgomery. A Memoir.* London, S.P.G., 1930.

Moorman, John, *Vatican Observed. An Anglican Impression of Vatican II.* London, Darton, Longman and Todd, 1969.

Morgan, Dewi, *The Bishops come to Lambeth.* London, A. R. Mowbray and Co. Ltd., 1967.

Morgan, Dewi, 'The Man who did not like the Lambeth Conference' [i.e. Dean Stanley] in *Church Illustrated*, June 1958.

—— *Lambeth Speaks*. London, A. R. Mowbray and Co. Ltd., 1958.

—— *Agenda for Anglicans*. London, S.C.M., 1963.

—— *The Church in Transition. Reform of the Church of England*. London, Chatto and Windus, 1970.

Morgan, E. R., 'Lambeth Conference Reviews. The Unity of the Church, A' in *Theology*, vol. xxi, no. 125, November 1930.

—— 'A Central College for the Anglican Communion' in *Theology*, vol. lii, no. 348, June 1949.

—— and Lloyd, Roger, *The Mission of the Anglican Communion*. London, S.P.C.K. and S.P.G., 1948.

Morris, Edwin, *The Lambeth Quadrilateral and Reunion*. London, Faith Press, 1969.

Moss, C. B., *The Old Catholic Movement. Its Origins and History*. London, S.P.C.K., 1964.

The Moving Spirit. A Survey of the Life and Work of the Anglican Communion. Church Information Board, Church House, Westminster, London, 1957.

Mozley, J. K., 'Lambeth Conference Reviews. The Christian Doctrine of God' in *Theology*, vol. xxii, no. 127, January 1931.

Mulliner, H. G., *Arthur Burroughs. A Memoir*. London, Nisbet and Co. Ltd., 1936.

Mylne, Louis George, *The Counsels and Principles of the Lambeth Conference of 1888. A Charge delivered to the Clergy and Church Committee men of the Diocese of Bombay in S. Thomas's Cathedral, on Wednesday, Jan. 9th 1889*. Byculla, Bombay, Education Society's Press, 1889.

Neill, Stephen, *Towards Church Union 1937–1952. A Survey of Approaches to Closer Union among the Churches*. Published on behalf of the Faith and Order Commission of the World Council of Churches, London, S.C.M. Press, 1952.

—— *Anglicanism*. London, Penguin Books, 1958.

—— *Men of Unity*. London, S.C.M., 1960.

New Dimensions. The Report of the Bishop of Willesden's Commission on the Objects and Policies of the Mothers' Union. London, S.P.C.K., 1972.

Nineham, D. E., *The Gospel of St Mark*. London, Penguin Books, 1963.

Norman, E. R., *Church and Society 1770–1970. A Historical Study*. Oxford, Clarendon Press, 1976.

Northcott, Cecil, *Evanston World Assembly. A Concise Interpretation*. London, United Society for Christian Literature, Lutterworth Press, 1954.

Norwood, Frederick Wm., *Nonconformity and the Lambeth Conference. An Address from the Chair of the Congregational Union of England and Wales on October 7th 1930*. London, Independent Press, 1930.

Oecumenical Patriarch in England, 9–14 November 1967. London, S.P.C.K., 1968.

Official Year-Book of the National Assembly of the Church of England 1949. Lambeth Number. London, Press and Publications Board of the Church Assembly and S.P.C.K.

Ogletree, T. W., *The 'Death of God' Controversy*. London, S.C.M., 1966.

Oliver, John, *The Church and Social Order. Social Thought in the Church of England 1918–1939*. London, Mowbray, 1968.

On Dying Well. An Anglican contribution to the debate on euthanasia. London, Church Information Office, 1974.

Ordination of Women to the Priesthood. A Consultative Document presented by the Advisory Council for the Church's Ministry. G.S. 104. London, Church Information Office, 1970.

Ordination of Women. Official commentary from the Sacred Congregation for the Doctrine of the Faith on its declaration Inter insigniores 'Women and the Priesthood' of 15 October 1976 together with the exchange of correspondence in 1975 and 1976 between Dr Coggan and Pope Paul VI. London, C.T.S., 1976.

Outline of a Reunion Scheme for the Church of England and Evangelical Free Churches of England. London, S.C.M. Press, 1936.

'Overseas Echoes of the Lambeth Conference. 1. The United States, Burton Scott Easton. 2. Canada, Bishop of Montreal. 3. Australia, Bishop of Willochra.' in *Theology*, vol. ii, no. 12, June 1921.

Overton, John Henry, and Wordsworth, Elizabeth, *Christopher Wordsworth, Bishop of Lincoln 1807–1885*. London, Rivingtons, 1888.

Oxenden, Ashton, *The History of My Life*. London, Longmans Green and Co., 1891.

Packer, J. I. (ed.), *The Church of England and the Methodist Church. A Consideration of the recent Anglican Methodist Report*. Marcham, Abingdon, Marcham Manor Press, 1963.

Paget, Elma K., *Henry Luke Paget. Portrait and Frame*. London, Longmans Green and Co., 1939.

—— 'Lambeth Conference Reviews. V. The Ministry of Women' in *Theology*, vol. i, no. 6, Dec. 1920, pp. 355–8.

Paget, Stephen, and Crum, J. M. C., *Francis Paget Bishop of Oxford, Chancellor of the Garter, Honorary Student and Sometime Dean of Christ Church*. London, Macmillan and Co., 1913.

Palmer, Edwin James, 'The Proposed Union of Churches in South India' in *Church Quarterly Review*, vol. ccxix, July 1930.

—— *The Great Church Awakens. Ideas and Studies concerning Union and Reunion*. London, Longmans, Green and Co., 1920.

—— *The Destiny of the Anglican Churches. A Short Study of the History, Principles and Prospects of the Anglican Communion*. Lambeth Series. London, James Nisbet and Co., Ltd., 1931.

Pan-Anglican Congress 1908, vol. i General Report with the addresses at the Devotional Meeting, London, S.P.C.K., 1908.

Pan-Anglican Congress 1908, vol. vii. Sections F. and G. The Anglican Communion (Section F) Duty of the Church to the Young. (Section G) Speeches and Discussions together with papers published for the consideration of the Congress. London, S.P.C.K., 1908.

Paton, David M. (ed.), *Essays in Anglican Self-Criticism*. London, S.C.M., 1958.

—— 'Secular Ecumenism and the Anglican Future' in the *Modern Churchman*, New Series, vol. xii, no. 3, April 1969, pp. 190–200.

—— (ed.) *Breaking Barriers. Nairobi 1975*. London, S.P.C.K., 1976.

—— and Latham, Robert, *Point of Decision*. London, S.P.C.K. and Epworth Press, 1967.

Paul, Leslie, *The Development and Payment of the Clergy*. London, Church Information Office, 1964.

—— *A Church by Daylight. A Reappraisal of the Church of England and its Future*. London, Geoffrey Chapman, 1973.

Pawley, Bernard, *Looking at the Vatican Council*. London, S.C.M., 1962.

—— and Margaret, *Rome and Canterbury through Four Centuries. A Study of the Relations between the Church of Rome and the Anglican Churches 1530–1973*. London and Oxford, Mowbrays, 1974.

Peart-Binns, John S., *Blunt*. Queensbury, Yorkshire, The Mountain Press (n.d.).

—— *Ambrose Reeves*. London, Victor Gollancz Ltd., 1973.

Peck, W. G., 'Lambeth Conference Reports. The Unity of the Church. B' in *Theology*, vol. xxi, no. 125, Nov. 1930.

Pelz, Werner and Lotte, *God is no More*. London, Penguin Books, 1968.

Perry, William Stevens, *The Reunion Conference at Bonn, 1875. A Personal Narrative*. Privately printed 1876. (Copy in Lambeth Palace Library.)

—— *The Second Lambeth Conference. A Personal Narrative*. Davenport, Iowa, 1879.

—— *The Third Lambeth Conference. A Personal Narrative by the Bishop of Iowa*. Privately printed 1891.

Petitpierre, Robert, *Exorcism. The Findings of a Commission convened by the Bishop of Exeter*. London, S.P.C.K., 1972.

Phillips, Mabel, 'Lambeth Conference Reviews, V (c) Deaconesses' in *Theology*, vol. xxii, March 1931.

Pike, James A., *A Time for Christian Candour*. London, Hodder and Stoughton, 1965.

Pilgrim for Unity, London, Catholic Truth Society and S.P.C.K., 1977.

Pittenger, Norman, *Time for Consent? A Christian's Approach to Homosexuality*. London, S.C.M., 1967 and new enlarged edn, London, S.C.M., 1970.

Pol, William H. van de, *Anglicanism in Ecumenical Perspective*. Pittsburgh, Duquesne University Press, 1965.

Pollock, Bertram, *A Twentieth Century Bishop, Recollections and Reflections*. London, Skeffington and Co. Ltd (n.d.).

Pornography: The Longford Report. London, Coronet Books, Hodder Paperbooks Ltd., 1972.

Potter, Henry Codman, *Reminiscences of Bishops and Archbishops*. New York and London, G. P. Putnams and Co., 1906.

Poulton, John, *Dear Archbishop*. London, Hodder and Stoughton, 1976.

Prayer and the Departed. Report of the Archbishops' Commission on Christian Doctrine. London, S.P.C.K., 1971.

Prayer Book Revision in the Church of England. A Memorandum of the Church of England Liturgical Commission. London, S.P.C.K., 1957.

Prestige, G. L., *The Life of Charles Gore. A Great Englishman*. London, William Heinemann, 1935.

Purcell, William, *Fisher of Lambeth. A Portrait from Life*. London, Hodder and Stoughton, 1969.

Pusey, E. B., *Habitual Confession not discouraged by the Resolution accepted by the Lambeth Conference*. A Letter to His Grace the Lord

Archbishop of Canterbury. Oxford, James Parker and Co., London, Oxford and Cambridge, Rivingtons, 1878.

Quoist, Michel, *Prayers of Life*. Dublin and Melbourne, Gill and Son, 1963.

Ramsey, Arthur Michael, *God, Christ and the World. A Study in Contemporary Theology*. London, S.C.M., 1969.

—— *Lambeth Essays on Faith*. London, S.P.C.K., 1969.

—— *Lambeth Essays on Ministry*. London, S.P.C.K., 1969.

—— *Lambeth Essays on Unity*. London, S.P.C.K., 1969.

—— *Canterbury Pilgrim*. London, S.P.C.K., 1974.

—— *Durham Essays and Addresses*. London, S.P.C.K., 1956.

—— *Canterbury Essays and Addresses*. London, S.P.C.K., 1964.

Ramsey, Ian, and Perry, Michael, *Faith Alert. The Lambeth Conference 1968*. London, S.P.C.K., 1968.

Rashdall, Hastings, 'Reunion and the Lambeth Proposals' in the *Modern Churchman*, vol. x, No. 10, January 1921.

Raven, Charles, *Looking Forward*. The Lambeth Series. London, James Nisbet and Co. Ltd., 1931.

Rawlinson, A. E. J., 'Lambeth Conference Review. IV The Anglican Communion' in *Theology*, vol. xxii, no. 128, February 1931.

—— *The Anglican Communion in Christendom*. London, S.P.C.K., 1960.

Relations between Anglican and Presbyterian Churches. A Joint Report. London, S.P.C.K., 1957.

Relations between the Church of England and Presbyterian Church of England. A Report. London, S.P.C.K., 1968.

Reply of the Free Church Federal Council to the Joint Conference of Representatives of the Church of England and the Free Churches regarding the three Documents presented to it by the Conference of 1938. London, 1942.

Report of the First Anglo-Catholic Congress. London, S.P.C.K. 1920.

Report of the Sixth Anglo-Catholic Congress. Subject: The Church. London, July 1948. Dacre Press, Westminster, n.d.

Reunion. The Lambeth Conference and the Free Churches. London, S.P.C.K., 1924.

Revised Canons of the Church of England Further Considered. London, S.P.C.K., 1954.

Rickards, Edith, *Bishop Moorhouse*. London, John Murray, 1920.

Ridding, Lady Laura, *George Ridding. Schoolmaster and Bishop*.

Forty-third Headmaster of Winchester 1866–1884, First Bishop of Southwell 1884–1904. London, Edward Arnold, 1908.

Rivers, W. H. R., 'Christian Science and Spiritual Healing' in *Theology*, vol. ii, no. 7, January 1921, pp. 37–41.

Robinson, John A. T., *On Being the Church in the World*. London, Penguin Books, 1969.

—— *Honest to God*. London, S.C.M., 1963.

—— *Exploration into God*. London, S.C.M., 1967.

—— *Christian Freedom in a Permissive Society*. London, S.C.M., 1970.

Robinson, J. Armitage, *The Vision of Unity*. London, Longmans Green and Co., 1908.

—— 'Lambeth Conference Reviews. VIII. The Lambeth Conference and the Call to Unity' in *Theology*, vol. ii, no. 7, 1921, pp. 41–6.

Rodger, Patrick C., and Vischer, L., *The Fourth World Conference on Faith and Order. The Report for Montreal 1963*. London, S.C.M., 1964.

Ross, Kenneth N., *The Necessity of Episcopacy. 'The Historic Episcopate' considered*. London, The Church Union, 1955.

Ross, Philip J., *Toronto Diary*. Impressions of the Anglican Congress, Toronto. London, C.M.S., 1963.

Rouse, Ruth, and Neill, S. C. (eds.), *A History of the Ecumenical Movement 1517–1948*. London, S.P.C.K., 1954.

Routley, Erik, *Creeds and Confessions. The Reformation and its Modern Ecumenical Implications*. London, Gerald Duckworth and Co. Ltd., 1962.

Sandford, E. G. (ed.), *Memoirs of Archbishop Temple by Seven Friends*. 2 vols., London, Macmillan and Co., 1906.

Saward, John, *The Case against the Ordination of Women*. London, C.L.A., 1975.

Scharlieb, Mary, 'Lambeth Conference Reviews III. Problems of Marriage and Sexual Morality. Lambeth Conference 1920. Resolutions 66, 67, 68, 69, 70' in *Theology*, vol. i, no. 5, Nov. 1920, pp. 301–6.

Schwarze, W. N., 'The Moravian Church and the Proposals of the Lambeth Conference' in *Church Quarterly Review*, no. cxxxvii, October 1909.

Scottish Church Society Conferences, 1920. The Lambeth Encyclical and other Proposals Considered (Papers by H. J. Wotherspoon, R. S. Kirkpatrick, James H. Leishman). Edinburgh, Andrew Elliott, 1920.

Seaver, George, *John Allen Fitzgerald Gregg, Archbishop*. London, Faith Press, 1963.

Selbie, W. B., 'Lambeth Conference Reviews. II A Free Church View' in *Theology*, vol. i, no. 4, October 1920, pp. 243–5.

Selwyn, E. G., 'Lambeth and Marriage' in *Theology*, vol. xxi, December 1930.

—— 'Preludes to Lambeth' in *Theology*, vol. xxi, no. 122, August 1930.

—— 'The Lambeth Conference' in *Theology*, vol. i, no. 4, October 1920, pp. 211–21.

—— 'The Free Churches and Lambeth' in *Theology*, vol. ii, no. 11, May 1921.

—— 'The Lambeth Agenda' in *Theology*, vol. xx, no. 119, May 1930.

Sheppard, David, *Built as a City. God and the Urban World Today*. London, Hodder and Stoughton, 1974.

Sheppard, H. R. L., *The Impatience of a Parson. A Plea for the Recovery of Vital Christianity*. London, Hodder and Stoughton, 1927.

Short Guide to the Lambeth Conference of 1958. Articles Reprinted from The Official Year Book of the Church of England 1958. London, Church Information Board, 1958.

Signet, 'Lambeth and Uppsala 1968' in *Modern Churchman*, N.S., vol. xi, no. 2, January 1968, pp. 65–7.

Simpkinson, C. H., *The Life and Work of Bishop Thorold. Rochester 1877–91. Winchester 1891–95*. London, Isbister and Co. Ltd., 1896.

Simpson, James B., *The Hundredth Archbishop of Canterbury*. New York and Evanston, Harper and Row, 1962.

—— and Story, Edward M., *The Long Shadows of Lambeth X*. New York, McGraw-Hill Book Company, 1969.

Simpson, J. G. (ed.), *The Lambeth Joint Report on Church Unity. A Discussion by the Archbishop of York, the Rev. W. B. Selbie, the Rev. J. Scott Lidgett, the Rev. P. Carnegie Simpson, the Bishop of Gloucester, Members of the Lambeth Joint Conference*. With an Introduction by J. G. Simpson, Canon and Treasurer of St. Paul's Cathedral. London, Hodder and Stoughton, 1923.

Sketch of a United Church. London, S.P.C.K., 1936.

Slack, Kenneth, *The Ecumenical Movement*. London, Edinburgh House Press, 1960.

—— *Nairobi Narrative*. London, S.C.M., 1976.

Smith, H. Maynard, *Frank Bishop of Zanzibar. Life of Frank Weston D.D., 1871–1924*. London, S.P.C.K., 1926.

Smyth, Charles, *Cyril Forster Garbett, Archbishop of York*. London, Hodder and Stoughton, 1959.

—— 'Story of Lambeth: Bishops refused to make a martyr of Colenso' in *Church Times*, 27 June 1958, Supplement pp. ii and iii.

Smyth, Newman, *A Story of Church Unity, including The Lambeth Conference of Anglican Bishops and the Congregational–Episcopal Approaches*. New Haven, U.S.A., Yale University Press, 1923.

Spencer, Malcolm, *Impasse or Opportunity? The Situation after Lambeth*. London, S.C.M., 1922.

Spens, W., 'Lambeth Conference Reviews II (a) and (b). The Life and Witness of the Christian Community: Marriage and Sex' in *Theology*, vol. xxi, no. 126, December 1930.

Stacy, Paul, 'Lambeth Conference Reviews II (a)–(c) Sociological Issues' in *Theology*, vol. xxi, no. 124, October 1930.

Stephens, W. R. W., *A Memoir of Richard Durnford*. London, John Murray, 1899.

Stephenson, Alan M. G., *The First Lambeth Conference 1867*. Published for the Church Historical Society, London, S.P.C.K., 1967.

—— 'The First Lambeth Conference and *Punch*' in *Church Quarterly Review*, Jan. to March 1959.

—— '100 Years of Lambeth' in *Church Times*, Supplement 19 July 1968.

—— 'The Bible and the Lambeth Conferences' in *Theology*, July 1975.

—— (ed.), *Liberal Christianity in History*. Modern Churchmen's Union, Oxford, Holywell Press, 1969.

Stephenson, Gwendolen, *Edward Stuart Talbot, 1844–1930*. London, S.P.C.K., 1936.

Stevens, William Bacon, *The Lambeth Conference of 1878*. A Lecture delivered in the Church of the Holy Trinity, Philadelphia, Monday evening, December 9, 1878, by the Rt Rev. Wm. Bacon Stevens, Bishop of the Diocese of Pennsylvania. Philadelphia, McCalla and Stavely, 1879.

Stewart, Richard L., *Anglicans and Roman Catholics*. London, C.T.S., 1977.

Stone, Darwell, and Puller, F. W. *Who are Members of the Church? A Statement of evidence in criticism of a sentence in the Appeal to All Christian People made by the Lambeth Conference of 1920, which is fundamental to all the propositions of that Appeal.* Pusey House Occasional Papers No. 9. London, Longmans, Green and Co., 1921.

Storr, Vernon F., *God in the Modern Mind.* The Lambeth Series. London, James Nisbet & Co. Ltd., 1931.

—— and Harris, G. H., *The Call for Christian Unity.* The Challenge of a World Situation. A volume of Essays contributed at the request of the Anglican Evangelical Group Movement. London, Hodder and Stoughton, 1930.

Streeter, B. H., *Foundations. A Statement of Christian Belief in terms of Modern Thought* by Seven Oxford Men. London, Macmillan and Co. Ltd., 1912.

Subscription and Assent to the Thirty-Nine Articles. Report of the Archbishops' Commission on Christian Doctrine. London, S.P.C.K., 1968.

Sumner, George Henry, *Life of Charles Richard Sumner, Bishop of Winchester.* London, John Murray, 1876.

Sumner, John Bird, *Letter of the Most Reverend Father in God the Archbishop of Canterbury to the Bishops of the Reformed Church in America on the Third Jubilee of the S.P.G. With the answers that have been received from the American Bishops.* London, George Bell, 1851.

Sundkler, Bengt, *Church of South India. The Movement towards Union 1900–1947.* London, Lutterworth Press, 1965.

The Supply and Training of Candidates for Holy Orders. Report with Notes and Appendices. June 1908. Poole, W. H. Hunt, 1908.

Sweet, Charles F., *A Champion of the Cross, being the Life of John Henry Hopkins S.T.D., including Extracts and Selections from his writings.* New York, James Pott and Co., 1894.

Sykes, Colin, *Commentary on the Agreed Statement on Eucharistic Doctrine 1971.* London, C.L.A., 1977.

Symon, Dudley, *Lambeth Questions.* London, S.P.C.K., 1948.

Synodical Government in the Church of England Being the Report of a Commission appointed by the Archbishops of Canterbury and York. C.A. 1600. London, Church Information Office, 1966. (The 'Hodson Report').

Tavard, George H., *Two Centuries of Ecumenism. The Search for Unity.* Tr. Royce W. Hughes. A. Mentor-Omega Book, New York, 1962.

Taylor, John V., *Enough is Enough.* London, S.C.M., 1975.

Temple, F. S. (ed.), *William Temple. Some Lambeth Letters*. London, Oxford University Press, 1963.

Theological Colleges for Tomorrow. Being the Report of a Working Party appointed by the Archbishops of Canterbury and York, to consider the problems of the Theological Colleges of the Church of England. London, Church Information Office, 1968.

Thompson, J. M., *Miracles in the New Testament*. London, Edward Arnold, 1911.

Thomson, Ethel H., *The Life and Letters of William Thomson, Archbishop of York*. London, John Lane, 1919.

Thomson, George Malcolm, *The Lambeth Conference*. London, Faber and Faber, 1930.

Till, Barry, *Change and Exchange. Mutual Responsibility and the Church of England*. Church Information Office, Church House, Westminster, 1964.

—— *Changing Frontiers in the Mission of the Church*. London, S.P.C.K., 1965.

—— *The Churches Search for Unity*. London, Penguin, 1972.

Tomkins, Oliver, *A Time for Unity*. London, S.C.M., 1964.

Towards the Conversion of England. Being the Report of a Commission on Evangelism appointed by the Archbishops of Canterbury and York pursuant to a Resolution of the Church Assembly passed at the Summer Session 1943. London, Press and Publications Board of the Church Assembly, Westminster, 1945.

Towards Reconciliation. The Interim Statement of the Anglican–Methodist Unity Commission. London, S.P.C.K. and Epworth Press, 1967.

Tremenhere, George H., *Resolution 15 of the Lambeth Conference of 1930. An Address delivered to the Chapter of the Deanery of Wimborne on October 9th 1930*. Leighton Buzzard, Faith Press, 1931.

Trevor, Meriol, *Pope John*. London, Macmillan and New York, St Martin's Press, 1967.

Tucker, H. W., *Memoir of the Life and Episcopate of George Augustus Selwyn D.D., Bishop of New Zealand 1841–1869; Bishop of Lichfield 1867–1878*. London, William Wells Gardner, 1879.

Tulloch, A. P. S., *The Lambeth Proposals for Reunion not Absorption*. A Reply to the Rev. Dr Norman Maclean, St Cuthberts, by the Rev. A. P. S. Tulloch. 1920.

Underhill, Francis, 'Lambeth Conference Reports. Youth and its Vocation' in *Theology*, vol. xxi, no. 125, pp. 286–91, Nov. 1930.

Van Buren, Paul, *The Secular Meaning of the Gospel based on analysis of its Language*. London, S.C.M., 1963.

Vidler, A. R., *Soundings. Essays concerning Christian Understanding*. Cambridge University Press, 1966.

Visible Unity: Ten Propositions. The Churches' Unity Commission, Church House, London, 1975.

Visible Unity in Life and Mission. A Report for the Board for Mission and Unity on the Ten Propositions for the Churches' Unity Commission. G.S. 300. London, C.I.O., 1976.

Visible Unity in Life and Mission. Second Report by the Board for Mission and Unity. G.S. 300A. London, C.I.O., 1976.

Visible Unity in Life and Mission. Third Report by the Board for Mission and Unity on the Ten Propositions of the Churches' Unity Commission. G.S. 300B. London, C.I.O., 1977.

Visible Unity in Life and Mission. The Ten Propositions. A Discussion Paper for the Church of England. London, C.I.O., 1977.

Waddams, Herbert, 'The Next Lambeth Conference' in *Theology*, May 1965.

Wakefield, Gordon, and Perry, Michael, *Anglican–Methodist Unity. A Short Guide*. London, S.P.C.K. and Epworth Press, 1968.

Waller, E. H. M., *The Mission Field*. The Lambeth Series. London, James Nisbet and Co. Ltd., 1931.

Wand, J. W. C., *The Anglican Communion. A Survey*. London, Oxford University Press, 1948.

—— *Anglicanism in History and Today*. London, Weidenfeld and Nicolson, 1961.

—— *Changeful Page*. London, Hodder and Stoughton, 1965.

Warren, Max, *Crowded Canvas. Some Experiences of a Life-Time*. London, Hodder and Stoughton, 1974.

Weatherhead, Leslie, *The Christian Agnostic*. London, Hodder and Stoughton, 1965.

Webb, C. C. J., 'Lambeth Conference Reviews, I(b) The Christian Doctrine of God in relation to Non-Christian Religions and Ideals' in *Theology*, vol. xxi, no. 124, October 1930.

Webster, Douglas, *Mutual Irresponsibility. A Danger to be avoided*. London, S.P.C.K., 1963.

Welch, P. J., 'The Revival of an Active Convocation of Canterbury' in *Journal of Ecclesiastical History*, vol. viii, 1957, pp. 193–207.

Weston, Frank, *The Christ and His Critics*. An Open Letter to the European Missionaries of his Diocese. London, A. R. Mowbray and Co. Ltd.; Milwaukee, U.S.A., The Morehouse Publishing Co., 1919.

Weston, Frank, 'Lambeth Conference Reviews. I The Bishops and Reunion; and Interpretation' in *Theology*, vol. i, no. 4, pp. 238–43.

Wheaton, Nathaniel S., *A Journal of a Residence during Several Months in London in the years 1823 and 1824.* Hartford, U.S.A., 1830.

Whipple, Henry Benjamin, *Lights and Shadows of a Long Episcopate being reminiscences and recollections of the Right Reverend Henry Benjamin Whipple, D.D., LL.D., Bishop of Minnesota.* New York, The Macmillan Co., 1900.

Who's Who at Lambeth '68. Hartford, Connecticut, Church Missions Publishing Co., and Westminster, London, Church Information Office, 1968.

Wiles, Maurice, *The Remaking of Christian Doctrine.* London, S.C.M., 1974.

Wilkinson, John, *Mutual Responsibility. Questions and Answers.* London, S.P.C.K., 1965.

—— 'Lambeth in 1969' in *Church Quarterly Review*, vol. i, no. 3, Jan. 1969.

Williams, Cicily, *Diary of a Decade. More Memoirs of a Bishop's Wife.* London, George Allen and Unwin, 1970.

Williams, N. P., 'Lambeth Conference Reviews. II(a) and (b) The Life and Witness of the Christian Community. Marriage and Sex. Independent note.' in *Theology*, vol. xxi, no. 126, December 1930.

—— *Lausanne, Lambeth and South India. Notes on the present position of the Reunion Movement.* London, Longmans, Green and Co. Ltd., 1930.

Willis, J. J., *Recognition, Authorisation and Reunion.* Reprinted by permission from *The East and West* for April 1920. London, The Church Book Room.

—— Arthur, J. W., Neill, S. C., Broomfield, G. W., Orchard, R. K. and Noble, W. J., *Towards a United Church.* London, Edinburgh House Press, 1947.

Wilson, Harold (ed.), *Women Priests – Yes – now!* Surrey, Denholm House Press, 1975.

Wilson, H. A. (ed.), *The Anglican Communion. Past, Present and Future*, Being the Report of the Church Congress at Cheltenham, 1928. London, John Murray, 1929.

Wilson, Timothy (ed.), *All One Body.* London, Darton, Longman and Todd, 1969.

Winnington-Ingram, A. F., 'The Lambeth Conference of 1930' in *Theology*, vol. xxi, no. 123, September 1930.

Women and Holy Orders Being the Report of a Commision appointed by the Archbishops of Canterbury and York (C.A. 1617). London, Church Information Office, 1966.

Women in Ministry. Report of the Working Party set up jointly by the Ministry Committee of the Advisory Council for the Church's Ministry and the Council for Women's Ministry in the Church. Church House, Westminster, Church Information Office, 1968.

Wood, Michael H. M., *A Father in God. The Episcopate of William West Jones, D.D., Archbishop and Metropolitan of South Africa 1874–1908*. London, Macmillan and Co. Ltd., 1913.

Woods, Edward S., *Lausanne 1927. An Interpretation of the World Congress on Faith and Order held at Lausanne, August 3–21, 1927.* London, S.C.M., 1927.

Woods, Frank Theodore, *The Faith and Witness of the Church in this Generation.* The Lambeth Series. London, James Nisbet and Co. Ltd., 1931.

—— Weston, Frank, and Linton Smith, Martin, *Lambeth and Reunion. An Interpretation of the Mind of the Lambeth Conference of 1920.* London, S.P.C.K., 1921.

Wordsworth, Charles, *The Lambeth Conference and Church Reunion.* A Charge delivered at the Annual Synod of the United Diocese of St Andrews, Dunkeld, and Dunblane, at St Ninian's Cathedral, Perth, on Wednesday, August 29, 1888 with Preface and Appendix. Edinburgh, 1889.

Wordsworth, John, 'A Central Consultative Body' in *The Official Report of the Church Congress held at Nottingham on September 28th, 29th, 30th and October 1st 1897.* Edited by the Rev. C. Dunkley. London, Bemrose and Sons Ltd., 1897.

—— *The Episcopate of Charles Wordsworth, Bishop of St Andrews, Dunkeld, and Dunblane 1853–1892. A Memoir.* London, Longmans, Green and Co., 1899.

World Council of Churches. New Delhi Speaks. The Message of the Third Assembly, New Delhi, 18 November – 5 December 1961 and the Reports of the Assembly's Sections on Christian Witness, and Unity and An Appeal to All Governments and Peoples. London, S.C.M., 1962.

Yarnold, E. J., and Chadwick, Henry, *Truth and Authority.* A Commentary on the Agreed Statement of the Anglican–Roman

Catholic International Commission Venice 1976. London, Catholic Truth Society and S.P.C.K., 1977.

Yarnold, Edward, *Anglican Orders. A Way Forward*. London, Catholic Truth Society, 1977.

Z. 'The Life of Frank Weston, Bishop of Zanzibar' in *Church Quarterly Review*, vol. ciii, October 1926.

ADDENDA

Barber, Melanie, *Index to the Letters and Papers of Frederick Temple, Archbishop of Canterbury, 1896–1902*. London, Mansell, 1975.

Davies, J. Conway, 'Lambeth, Sex, and Romanticism' in *Church Quarterly Review*, vol. cxiv, 1932, pp. 60–79.

Fairweather, Eugene, 'Letter from an Anglican. Lambeth 1968' in *Clergy Review*, vol. 53, no. 8, August 1968, pp. 596ff.

Fremantle, W. H., *The Present Work of the Anglican Communion. Two Sermons preached in Canterbury Cathedral on the Sunday preceding the Episcopal Conference of 1888*. London, Rivingtons, 1888.

Gollock, Georgina, *Eugene Stock: A Biographical Study 1836–1928*. London, C.M.S., 1929.

Knight, Marcus, 'Anticipations of Lambeth' in *Church Quarterly Review*, vol. clviii, 1957, pp. 412–22.

Martin, Hugh, *Can we unite?* An examination of the Outline of a Reunion Scheme issued by the Lambeth Joint Conference. London, S.C.M., 1939.

Paton, Alan, *Apartheid and the Archbishop. The Life and Times of Geoffrey Clayton*. London, Jonathan Cape, 1974.

Ross, Alexander, J., *Memoir of Alexander Ewing, D.C.L., Bishop of Argyll and the Isles*. London, Daldy, Isbister, and Co., 1877.

St John, Henry, *Essays in Christian Unity*. London, Blackfriars Publications, 1955.

Strong, Thomas, 'Lambeth Conference 1930. Resolution No. 42' in *Church Quarterly Review*, vol. cxiv, 1932, pp. 80–91.

INDEX OF NAMES AND SUBJECTS